A Probus Guide to World Markets

•

THE PACIFIC RIM FUTURES AND OPTIONS MARKETS

A Comprehensive,
Country-by-Country
Reference to the World's
Fastest Growing
Financial Markets

•

KEITH K. H. PARK
STEVEN A. SCHOENFELD

Foreword by
Leo Melamed

PROBUS PUBLISHING COMPANY
Chicago, Illinois
Cambridge, England

ISBN   1-55738-207-7

Printed in the United States of America

BB

1   2   3   4   5   6   7   8   9   0

In memory of Professor Arnold P. Collery who was
a teacher, friend and scholar.

Keith K.H. Park

To my parents, for their love and encouragement.

Steven Schoenfeld

TABLE OF CONTENTS

FOREWORD

"The Mediterranean is the ocean of the past, the Atlantic the ocean of the present and the Pacific the ocean of the future," said John Hay, the U.S. Secretary of State at the turn of the century. While it can certainly be argued that the future took its good time in getting here, make no mistake, the future of the Pacific Rim has arrived.

Today, the countries of the Pacific Rim represent a combination of developed and developing nations that jointly embody an economic force equal to any region of the word. "Today," states John Naisbitt, in *Megatrends 2000*, "the Pacific Rim is undergoing the fastest period of economic expansion in history, growing at five times the growth rate during the industrial revolution."

The geographic area involved is as large as it is diverse. It accounts for two-fifths of the world's surface and nearly half of the world's population. By any standard, the nations that encompass the Pacific Rim are dissimilar in many fundamental respects, with differences in culture, political systems and economic orders. Their differences also run the gamut from those, in the words of the *Economist*, that are "as rich and stable as Japan and as poor and turbulent as China, as big and open as America and as small and closed as North Korea."

Japan is, of course, the financial colossus of the region, encompassing a vast and complex business infrastructure which includes some of the world's largest securities firms and banks. Australia and New Zealand provide the anchor on the South. Australia, almost as large as the continental U.S., is more British than Asian but its location makes it imperative for the continent to think Asian. The newly industrialized counties, or NICs as they are sometimes called, include Singapore, Hong Kong, South Korea and Taiwan. Hong Kong, of course, will revert back to China in 1997 and become an uncommon segment of this vast and underdeveloped giant. Then, there are the members of the Association of South East Asian Nations, (ASEAN), which in addition to Singapore, includes Indonesia, Malaysia, the Philippines and Thailand.

Although there are many ties other than geographical between these nations, for the purposes of this book there is a sufficient common denominator based on a similar economic evolution which brought some of these states to employ or consider employing the markets of futures and options. While their current experience with these markets is of recent vintage, as most learned observers are aware, futures markets are nothing new to the region. Indeed, it was in Japan, during the Edo period (1600-1867) that centralized futures markets were born. The place was Osaka, where feudal lords established warehouses to store and sell rice that was paid to them as land-tax by their villagers. In 1730, to protect themselves from wide price fluctuations between harvests, these merchants established the Dojima Rice Market, the first organized futures exchange.

Over the span of the next two hundred years there were from time to time some small agriculturally based futures markets in Japan. However, it was not until the birth of the Sydney Futures Exchange (SFE) in 1960 that futures again made their presence felt in the Pacific Rim. The SFE was also the first Asian-Pacific futures exchange to launch a financial contract in 1979. Then came the critical catalyst in the modern development of futures and options markets in the Pacific basin: it was the revolutionary link in 1984 between Singapore's SIMEX and the Chicago Mercantile Exchange (CME). This innovation served to spur the race for financial futures dominance in the region. A year later, Japan re-entered the futures markets arena in a meaningful fashion when the Tokyo Stock Exchange (TSE) launched its successful Japanese Government Bond contract. The New Zealand Futures Exchange opened in 1985, and in 1986, the Hong Kong Futures Exchange listed stock index futures. These important events were quickly followed by the inception of futures trading at the Osaka Securities Exchange (OSE) and the birth of the Tokyo International Financial Futures Exchange (TIFFE). There was no stopping the process now. The community of nations of the Pacific Rim had fully embraced the financial futures revolution.

Nor could it be otherwise. The vibrancy and native talent of Pacific based populations, the wealth achieved as a consequence of decades of successful manufacturing and export and the resulting potential of their financial centers combined to make the region a vast store of financial strength and a force equal to any in the world. This expanding capital market base could not continue very long or compete on a global scale without the development of futures markets. The advent of globalization, greater interdependence, modern telecommunication capabilities, instant informational flows, immediate recognition of financial risks and opportunities and intensified competition made the management of risk an essential prerequisite of success for every financial community. To address this new financial imperative, it was mandatory for the nations of the Pacific Rim to turn to the unique mechanisms provided by futures and options markets.

It was axiomatic. The financial futures revolution, launched in Chicago in 1972, blazed the trail for much of what has since followed in world capital centers. The CME was the first major exchange to recognize the significance of the demise of the Bretton Woods Agreement, the post World War II pact that instituted a fixed exchange-rate regime for the major world nations. To capture the potential of the free market epoch that was about to ensue, the CME created the International Monetary Market (IMM), the first futures exchange for the specific purpose of trading in financial instruments. The era of financial futures was thus born. While the new wave of futures began with currency contracts, it was quickly followed by futures contracts on U.S. government securities — Treasury bills at the Merc, and Ginnie Mae certificates and Treasury bonds at the Chicago Board of Trade (CBOT). Later, when in the early 80's the concept of cash settlement in lieu of physical delivery was instituted, the stage was set for the CME's introduced of Eurodollar futures. This led the way for stock index futures and initialed the era of index markets.

The financial futures revolution was destined to alter profoundly the history of markets. It established that there was a need for a new genre of risk management tools suitable for sophisticated strategies and responsive to professional and institutional money management. As a consequence, it proved the necessity of futures and options within the infrastructure of finance and alongside other traditional structures of capital markets. Most significantly, from their inception the markets of futures and options understood and embraced the common denominator of recent world upheavals: the spectacular advances in technology. Clearly, no other single factor was more instrumental in influencing political and economic change than was the technological revolution of recent years.

On the political front, modern telecommunications fostered instant mass and personal informational flows, in total disregard of national boundaries. It offered everyone a stark, uncompromising comparison of political and economic life, making it nearly impossible for governments to hide the truth from its people. On the economic front, modern telecommunications made instantaneous price information available to everyone around the globe and fostered massive capital flows in unencumbered fashion. It dramatically changed the nature of global capital markets forever. The markets of futures and options recognized this march of technology, understood its inexorable impact on commerce and trade, and willingly adapted to its demands. It is no accident that our markets thus represent one of the greatest growth arenas of the last two decades.

As logic would dictate, events in Eastern Europe and the Soviet Union during the last several years have dramatically confirmed the significance of the financial history of the last two decades. The bankruptcy of command economic order, the downfall of communist rule and the collapse of the Soviet empire serve as undeniable testimony to the value of capitalism and market driven economics. The markets of futures and options are integral to that victory. Indeed, what markets better epitomize price determination by virtue of the free forces of supply and demand than do the markets of futures and options?

During the past decade, beginning with the 1982 establishment of the London International Financial Futures Exchange (LIFFE), new financial futures exchanges have opened virtually every major world financial center, including the Marché à Terme International de France (MATIF) in Paris, the Swiss Options and Financial Futures Exchange (SOFFEX) in Zurich, the Deutsche TerminBorse (DTB) in Frankfurt, not to mention the exchanges in the Pacific Rim itself. The dramatic success of this history prompted Nobel Laureate Merton Miller, University of Chicago professor of finance, to nominate financial futures as "the most significant financial innovation of the last twenty years."

Indeed, if financial futures and options were not yet in place they would have to be invented:

- They are indispensable in a world that demands the ability to swiftly institute complex strategies or to adjust portfolio exposure between securities and cash in a cost effective manner.

- They are ideally suited for a world where tailored risk management strategies are on the increase and where opportunities rapidly appear and disappear on a constantly changing financial horizon.

- They are a vital option in a world in which it is often imperative to utilize a credit-worthy mechanism that preserves credit lines.

- They are without equal in providing a vast array of products combined with an envious measure of liquidity and an incomparably narrow bid/ask spread.

- They are the *avant garde* of market innovation and soon, as a consequence of GLOBEX, the after-hours electronic trading system being developed by the CME and the CBOT in conjunction with Reuters PLC, will achieve market coverage on a 24-hour basis.

- Finally and most significantly, they are well-positioned for a world where professional money management is the wave of the future.

Thus, what was imperative for the financial structures of other global regions became equally imperative for Pacific basin. Nor should we forget that the process is incomplete. Some of the Pacific Rim communities are just beginning to emerge from their formative development stage. More to the point, the vast financial potential of mainland China is yet to be unleashed. Is there any doubt that the same forces which brought about the downfall of command order economics in the Soviet Union will achieve a similar result in China? Is there any doubt that its highly competent people will someday in the coming decade join the market rebirths occasioned by the other Asian populations? I dare say, no. And, when it happens, it will exponentially effect the strength and vitality of the Pacific Rim.

Although there are some heavy macroeconomic clouds overhead, the long-term direction in the evolution of global markets is unmistakable. In a world where the distinctions between the major time zones has vanished, in a world where geographical borders that once could limit the flow of capital are but history, in a world where traditional internal protections that could insulate one's citizenry from external price and value influences are no longer valid, market driven economic order is quintessential and futures and options a critical component. For an expanding region such as the Pacific Rim, with its vast and diverse cultures and infrastructure, and with its still untapped and developing potential, there can be no other course.

Leo Melamed
Chairman Emeritus,
Chicago Mercantile Exchange
Chairman,
GLOBEX

PREFACE

In less than a decade, financial futures and options markets in the Pacific Rim have grown from infancy to global significance. Exchanges and contracts proliferated and activity boomed. In 1985, these markets comprised less than 0.5 percent of global listed derivative activity. In late 1990, they accounted for about 10 percent of a much larger pie. As the range of domestic and international participants in these dynamic markets has broadened, the interest and need for a comprehensive, analytical survey of the development, products, and activity in the Asian-Pacific financia futures and options markets has grown. This book attempts to supply the information that the market demands.

The book analyzes this spectacular market growth from two perspectives, that of general international financial market developments; and simultaneously, that of the practical informational needs of derivative market participants. Regarding the former, the book provides background on the evolution of the Far East futures markets from their infancy to the present and their role in the international financial system. In addition to looking back, we have attempted to look forward—fully aware of the risks of predicting trends in financial market development—and present our expectations for the future contours of the regional marketplace.

Regarding the second perspective, in order to serve the needs of current and potential market users, we have provided a relatively objective description of Asian-Pacific exchanges, products, and participants. For all major markets we have included contract specifications, volume figures, and open interest data. The appendices provid further information on exchanges, membership, regulations, and stock index composition. Furthermore, we provide a glossary of futures and options market terminology (including words specific to Asian markets) and frequently used abbreviations. We also analyze the current status and prospects of each contract and market, and the role that the products and exchange play in the region's and the world's derivative markets.

We must, however, add a caveat. When tackling a rapidly changing subject of such scope, a line must be drawn somewhere. We have limited our analysis to exchange-listed futures and options products whose underlying instrument is financial-related. Thus, despite the significance of both OTC derivative activity and commodity futures in the region, the book does not focus on either of these vital market areas. We have only briefly touched upon them when they have a significant impact on the exchanges and contracts that we do discuss.

The book is organized on a country-by-country basis, with the inevitable overlaps of coverage necessitated by a dynamic international financial market environment. Chapter One attempts to pull the strands together by presenting an overview of the region's exchanges and products, tracing the phases of their development and assessing how they fit into the global capital markets. The subsequent two chapters cover listed Japanese derivative products, first in their growing home market, and then in the United States. Chapter Four through Seven analyze the other major financial futures and options markets in the Pacific Rim. The final chapter, on emerging markets, is the most speculative. It explores the next wave of exchanges and new sources of derivative business as the region's financial futures industry continues to expand.

This continual expansion of the Asian-Pacific futures and options markets is what led us to embark on this book project. We began our association in Autumn 1988 through the introduction of Bob Tamarkin, then-editor of *Intermarket* magazine. At the time, Park was working in the Equity Portfolio Analysis Group of Salomon Brothers in New York and Schoenfeld was running his futures fund management and consulting firm, Intellicorp, form Singapore. Both of us shared a strong interest and involvement with the Far East, and we soon embarked on our first cooperative endeavor.

Park offered Schoenfeld the opportunity to contribute a chapter on Asian-Pacific financial futures markets to the books he was editing. Schoenfeld's research as a Fulbright Scholar at the National University of Singapore and the Institute of Southeast Asian Studies was the foundation for the chapter, which appeared in *The Global Equity Markets* and *The Global Bond Markets*. Little did we know that a two-year project that would span continents and stretch the limits of our friendship would emerge from this initial venture.

When Schoenfeld returned to New York in the summer of 1989, we had a number of stimulating conversation regarding the evolution of global derivative markets. One hot and hazy summer day, eating pizza in a Greenwich Village park, our discussion became surprisingly philosophical. Laughing together about "Other People's Money," then a popular Off-Broadway play, we agreed that despite the justified attack on the greed and immorality of Wall Street in the 1980s, the decade had brought some positive developments to the international financial markets.

As we argued and reminisced, we concluded that the 1980s bought us more than insider trading scandal and junk bonds. We agreed that the innovations in financial engineering which started in the mid-1980s would continue to have far-reaching impact on he global capital markets of the 1990s. The topic then shifted to Japan, which was just beginning to experience the full effect of derivative trading on its equity market. We recognized that many of the most dramatic changes in the Far East financial markets would occur in the coming decade. Before that humid afternoon was over, we had convinced each other of the need to write an analytical book on the Asian-Pacific financial futures and options revolution of the 1980s and its implications for the 1990s.

As would befit the globalization of markets, this book was written in three continents and at least six different time zones (not including work on airplanes while crossing other time zones). But given that one of the original rationales for the development of futures markets in the Far East was to serve as a time zone bridge, a little writer's jetlag and hefty telecommunications bills would seem a reasonable price to pay to produce this volume.

Our work reached a critical juncture in the summer of 1991, as both of us were heavily committed to consulting projects, Park for the American Stock Exchange in New York, and Schoenfeld for the Marché à Terme Internatinal de France (MATIF) in Paris. Both of us were urging each other on for that final push, and the cost was some tense moments and lost weekends. Park would like to apologize to Jane for having to come to Nantucket burdened with his laptop, and Schoenfeld regrets the invitations to Avignon and Bretagne that he had to turn down.

However, as the leaves began to turn, we finally finished the project. We are both relieved and please with the ultimate product. Above all, we are very happy that we can simply be friends again.

The task of writing this book was a great challenge because of the relentless growth of the Asian-Pacific financial markets in the past several years. At many points, as we struggled to integrate new information and update reams of data, it felt like we were aiming at a moving target. Although we attempted to make this volume as comprehensive as possible, it is likely that we overlooked certain issues and developments. Furthermore, despite our fact-checking efforts and many revisions, it is possible that factual errors have slipped into the text or tables. For these potential mistakes, we assume full responsibility and apologize in advance to our readers and sources of information.

Without our sources — of background information, statistical data, and graphic tables — this book would not have been possible. We also would like to express our gratitude to the scores of people who assisted us with this project in countless other ways. We have attempted to thank many of them by name in the Acknowledgements section whch follows the Preface. To all those who did not desire attribution, and to those who we might have inadvertently left out, thank you for your time and generosity.

We would also like to express our deep appreciation to the staff at Probus Publishing for their help and forbearance with two authors in different cities and sometimes on different wavelengths. We are particularly indebted to Pam van Giessen and Michael Ryder for keeping the project moving forward whenever it began to lose momentum. Our special thanks also go to Carol Bahr, Michelle Koenning, and Tina Moy.

Finally, we would like to thank our friends and family for their support, encouragement, patience, and tolerance of the author in their life.

Keith Park
Steven Schoenfeld

ACKNOWLEDGEMENTS

The authors would like to deeply thank the following friends who, despite their busy schedules, took the time to review various parts of the book and/or make valuable suggestions.

Mark Arimura -Salomon Brothers Asia Limited, Tokyo
Angelo Calvello -The Chicago Mercantile Exchange
Barbara Diamond-Diamond Asset Management, Chicago
James Foo-MMS International, Singapore
Gary Gastineau-Salomon Brothers, New York
William Grossman-The Chicago Board of Trade, Tokyo Office
John Kilgannon-Paine Webber, New York
Yoshikazu Kobashi-Goldman, Sachs (Japan) Corp.
Nicholas Ronalds-The Chicago Mercantile Exchange Tokyo Office
Maxwell Trautman-The Hong Kong Futures Exchange
Louis Tseng-Goldman, Sachs (Asia) Limited, Hong Kong
Mistutake Yoshimura-Japan Bond Research Institute, Tokyo

In addition, our thanks go out to the following friends who generously offered the authors their insights into the Asian-Pacific financial futures markets, helped the authors gather vast amounts of critical, hard to obtain statistics and data, or contributed in other important ways.

Mark Abing-The Singapore International Monetary Exchange
Alden Adkins-The Securities Exchange Commission of the U.S.
        Washington, D.C.
Kats Ashizawa-Daiwa Securities, New York
Ang Swee Tian-The Singapore International Monetary Exchange
Margi Badrov-The American Stock Exchange, New York
Michael Belkin-Salomon Brothers, New York
Greg Boland-The New Zealand Futures and Options Exchange
John Braddock-The American Stock Exchange, New York
Chris Bray-The Singapore International Monetary Exchange
Steve Brigham-The Johns Hopkins Foreign Policy Institute,
        Washington, D.C.

Richard Bullen, Jr.-Richard H. Bullen Inc., New York
S.T. Cha Don-Suh Securities, Seoul
Wynne Choi-The Hong Kong Futures Exchange
Robert Cox-Goldman, Sachs (Asia) Limited., Hong Kong
I-Lin Dieu-Prime Computer, Singapore
Kamal Eshan-Shearson Lehman Brothers, Singapore
Alain Farhi-Comhedge (Pte) Ltd., Singapore
Mark Farrington-Baring Securities (Japan) Ltd., Tokyo
Martin French-Asiamoney Magazine, Hong Kong
Thomas Gira-The Securities Exchange Commission of the U.S.,
        Washington, D.C.
Harold Hardman-The Commodity Futures Trading Commission of the
        U.S., Washington D.C.
Paul Hoff-James Capel Pacific, Tokyo
Frederick Holborn-The Johns Hopkins School of Advanced
        International Studies, Washington D.C.
Eric Holm-Morgan Stanley Japan Ltd., Tokyo
Heidi Jameel-The Chicago Mercantile Exchange
Jane Kang-The Commodity Futures Trading Commission of the U.S.,
        Washington, D.C.
David Kim-Daewoo Securities, New York
Debbie Kesler-The Tokyo Stock Exchange, New York Office
Michael Killian-Baring Securities (Japan) Ltd., Tokyo
Gary Knight-The Hong Kong Futures Exchange
Ben Krause-The American Stock Exchange, New York
X.L. Lee-Institute of Southeast Asian Studies, Singapore
Sarah de Leon-Goldman, Sachs & Co., New York
Liaw Hong Peng-The Singapore International Monetary Exchange
Susan Landgraf-The Chicago Board of Trade
Patricia Loh-Hotel Properties Limited, Singapore
Philipe Machuca-Lion Pacific Investment, Singapore
Norman Maines-Rodman & Renshaw, Chicago
Matthew Moran-The Chicago Mercantile Exchange
Minoru Nakamura-The Osaka Securities Exchange
Cynthia Neuwalder-The Commodity Futures Trading Commission of
        the U.S., Washington, D.C.
Ng Kok Song-Government of Singapore Investment Corporation
Ng Tee How-Goldman Sachs (Singapore) Pte. Ltd.
Quek Peck Lim-Morgan Grenfell Asia Securities, Singapore
Barbara Richards-The Chicago Mercantile Exchange

Debra Richman-National Book Network, Washington, D.C.
Andrew Robson-James Capel Pacific, Tokyo
Ann Rutledge-The Hong Kong Futures Exchange
Carol Sabia-Salomon Brothers, New York
Joe Stephaneli-The American Stock Exchange, New York
Ginger Szala-Futures Magazine, Chicago
Jane Takahashi-S.G. Warburg Securities (Japan) Inc., Tokyo
Masao Takamori-The Tokyo Stock Exchange
Barry Tan-Nomura Futures (Singapore) Pte. Ltd.
Tan Hup Thye-Refco (Singapore) Pte. Ltd.
Alan Tonelson-Economic Strategy Institute, Washington, D.C.
Ryoji Umeda-The Nagoya Stock Exchange
Ryuichi Ushiyama-Nihon Keizai Shimbun, Tokyo
Jack Walsh-The Chicago Mercantile Exchange
Clifford Weber-The American Stock Exchange, New York
Reddy Wong-Chase Manhattan Futures Corporation, Singapore
Adrian Wong-The Hong Kong Futures Exchange
Michael Wong-Credit Lyonnais Rouse (Pte) Ltd., Singapore
Hideaki Yamashita-The Tokyo Stock Exchange
Yeong Wai Cheong-Diamond Asset Management, Chicago
Charlotte Yew-Jardine Fleming Investment Management,
            Hong Kong
Robert Zielinski-Jardine Fleming Securities, Tokyo
Mark Zurack-Goldman, Sachs & Co., New York

Finally, the authors would like to express their sincere appreciation to those whom they failed to mention above, without whom this book could have never been completed.

OVERVIEW OF THE PACIFIC RIM FINANCIAL FUTURES AND OPTIONS MARKETS

Introduction

The world is becoming smaller. Political, economic, and social trends crisscross the globe with less and less regard for national borders and cultural frontiers. The Asian-Pacific region is becoming just another group of timezones in the non-stop march of history and economic progress.

A similar phenomenon has been taking place in the financial world. The impressive innovations in computer and telecommunication technologies in the 1980s have brought the world investment communities closer to each other than ever before, and this process of integration will only accelerate in the 1990s. Investors in New York, London, and Tokyo have instant and equal access to new market information via computer screens no matter where the information originates. As a result, investors around the globe are capable of adopting timely investment strategies in coping with rapidly changing market developments.

Because European and U.S. investors have the same access to information which Asian counterparts have, investment opportunities which appeal to Asian investors will be equally attractive to European and U.S. counterparts. As information flows have become more and more efficient, the world investment community has rapidly become integrated. We can no longer define an investment product which will only be subscribed by Asian investors. What appeals to Asian investors presents an equally interesting investment opportunity to international investors.

Chart 1: Total U.S. Dollar Returns from International Equity Markets (1985-1990)

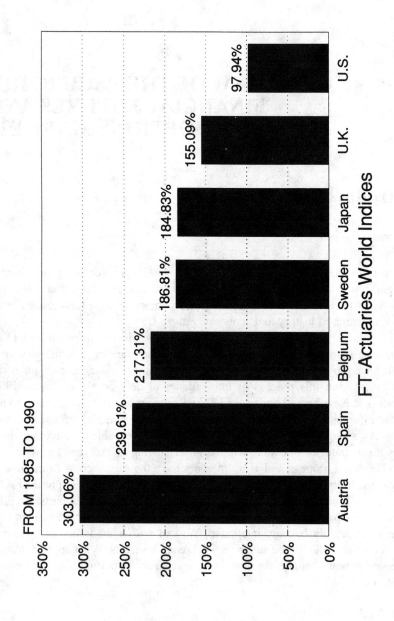

FROM 1985 TO 1990

Austria	Spain	Belgium	Sweden	Japan	U.K.	U.S.
303.06%	239.61%	217.31%	186.81%	184.83%	155.09%	97.94%

FT-Actuaries World Indices

Given the capabilities of computer and telecommunication technologies, global investors will trade anywhere in the world as long as the transaction enhances the return of their portfolio. As we can see in CHART 1, the total U.S. dollar returns from the equity markets of Austria, Belgium, Japan, Spain and Sweden from 1985 to 1990 far surpassed those from the U.S. and U.K., the traditionally popular markets of global institutional investors. These far superior investment opportunities abroad have been the major factor behind rising international equity flows. Worldwide investment in foreign shares increased from about $300bn in 1985 to $1,600bn in 1989 according to a Salomon Brothers estemate. Furthermore, more than one transaction in every seven in global equity markets has a foreign investor on the other side. Equity trading has truly become global. See TABLE 1 for a break-down of international equity flows in 1989.

However, with increased opportunity comes increased risk. High volatility in a foreign market can prevent prudent institutional investors from investing in that market despite the potentially superior investment opportunities it offers. This type of risk aversion consequently deters an efficient allocation of capital in the world economies. Although the first financial futures and options were introduced in the U.S. in the early 1970s, it was not until the mid-1980s that global institutional investors began to have access to exchange-traded international financial futures and options for the risk management of their international investment.

In finance, necessity has always been the primary inspiration for innovation. As the Bretton Woods system, which pegged various currencies to the U.S. dollar, collapsed in the early 1970s, unprecedented volatility emerged in the international foreign exchange markets. In order to enable better management of

TABLE 1: Gross Cross-Border Equity Flows, 1989 (US Dollars in Billions)

	US	Japan	UK	Continental Europe	Rest of World	Investor Total
			Market to			
Investor From:						
US	—	US$84.16	83.38	50.35	57.58	275.47
Japan	60.77	—	5.25	8.22	101.99	176.23
UK	7.22	76.50	—	109.59	40.82	324.13
Continental Europe	107.08	66.48	28.57	148.98	17.01	368.12
Rest of World	151.77	205.72	24.09	26.12	46.41	454.12
Market Total	416.84	432.86	141.30	343.26	263.81	1,598.05

Source: Salomon Brothers Inc.

the currency risk of international trade and investment, in 1972 the Chicago Mercantile Exchange introduced currency futures and options, the first success-ful financial futures contracts. Since then, there has been a tremendous prolifera-tion of financial futures and options on various financial instruments. (TABLES 2A, 2B and 2C list major international futures and options on equities, interest rates and currencies.)

Financial futures and options are basically contingent claims. The returns from holding financial futures and options are primarily contingent upon how the market will have moved from the current market position. The cost of estab-lishing a futures/options hedging program for an investment can be viewed as insurance premium paid in order to modify the risk/return profile of the eventual outcome of the investment. The extent of an investor's hedging program will depend on the level of his or her risk tolerance.

Table 2A: Major World Stock Index Futures and Options Contracts

NORTH AMERICA   **EXCHANGE**

Canadian Toronto 35 Index Futures	Toronto Stock Exchange
U.S. Standard & Poor 500 Index Futures	Chicago Mercantile Exchange
U.S. Standard & Poor 100 Index Options	Chicago Board Options Exchange
U.S. Major Market Index Futures	Chicago Board of Trade
U.S. Major Market Index Options	American Stock Exchange

EUROPE

Danish KFX Index Futures	Guarantee Fund for Danish Options & Futures
Dutch EOE Index Futures	Financiele Termijnmarkt Amsterdam
Finnish FOX Index Futures	Finish Options Market
French CAC-40 Index Futures	Marché à Terme International de France
German DAX Index Futures	Deutsche Terminboerse
Swedish OMX Index Futures	OM Stockholm & OM London
Swiss SMI Index Futures	Swiss Options & Financial Futures Exchange
U.K. FT-SE 100 Index Futures	London International Financial Future Exchange

ASIAN-PACIFIC

Australian All Ordinaries Index Futures	Sydney Futures Exchange
Hong Kong Hang Seng Index Futures	Hong Kong Futures Exchange
Japanese Nikkei Average Futures	Osaka Securities Exchange
Japanese Nikkei Average Options	Osaka Securities Exchange
Japanese TOPIX Index Futures	Tokyo Stock Exchange
Nikkei Average Futures	Singapore International Monetary Exchange
New Zealand Barclays Index Futures	New Zealand Futures and Options Exchange

Table 2B: Major World Currency Futures and Options Contracts

NORTH AMERICA	EXCHANGE
Australian Dollar Futures	Chicago Mercantile Exchange (CME)
British Pound Futures	CME
Canadian Dollar Futures	CME
Deutschemark Futures	CME
Japanese Yen Futures	CME
Swiss Franc Futures	CME
Options on Deutschemark Futures	CME
Options on Yen Futures	CME
Options on Swiss Franc Futures	CME
ECU Futures	Financial Instrument Exchange (FINEX)
Australian Dollar Options	Philadelphia Stock Exchange (PHLX)
British Pound Options	PHLX
Canadian Dollar Options	PHLX
Deutschemark Options	PHLX
French Franc Options	PHLX
Japanese Yen Options	PHLX
Swiss Franc Options	PHLX
ECU Options	PHLX
U.S. Dollar Index Futures	Financial Instrument Exchange

SOUTH AMERICA	
U.S. Dollar/Brazilian Cruzeiro Futures	Bolsa de Mercadorias and Futures

EUROPE	
British Pound/Dutch Guilder Futures	European Options Exchange
Irish Pound Futures	Irish Futures and Options Exchange
Spanish Peseta	Mercado Espanol de Futuros Financieros
U.S. Dollar/Deutschemark Futures	OM Stockholm
U.S. Dollar/Dutch Guilder Futures	European Options Exchange

ASIA	
Australian Dollar Futures	Sydney Futures Exchange
British Pound Futures	Singapore International Monetary Exchange (SIMEX)
Deutschemark Futures	SIMEX
Japanese Yen Futures	SIMEX
U.S. Dollar /Yen Futures	Tokyo International Financial Futures Exchange
New Zealand Dollar Futures	New Zealand Futures and Options Exchange
U.S. Dollar/NZ Dollar Futures	NZFOE

Table 2C: Major World Interest Rate Futures and Options Contract

NORTH AMERICA	EXCHANGE
Canadian Treasury Bond Futures	Montreal Exchange
U.S. Treasury Bond Futures	Chicago Board of Trade
U.S. Treasury Bond Futures Options	Chicago Board of Trade
U.S. 10-Year Treasury Note Futures	Chicago Board of Trade
Eurodollar Futures	Chicago Mercantile Exchange
Options on Eurodollar Futures	Chcago Mercantile Exchange

EUROPE	
Danish Treasury Bond Futures	Guarantee Fund for Danish Options & Futures
Dutch Treasury Bond Futures	Financiele Termijnmarkt Amsterdam
French 10-Year Treasury Bond Futures	Marché à Terme International de France (MATIF)
French 10-year Treasury Bond Futures Options	MATIF
French PIBOR Futures Options	MATIF
French Paris Interbank Offered Rate Futures	MATIF
French ECU Bond Futures	MATIF
French Euromark Futures	MATIF
German Government Bond Futures	Deutsche Terminboerse
Swedish Interest Rate Futures	OM Stockholm
U.K. Long Gilt Futures	London International Financial Futures Exchange (LIFFE)
U.K. Long Gilt Futures Options	LIFFE
U.K. German Government Bond Futures	LIFFE
U.K. ECU Bill Futures	LIFFE
U.K. Eurodollar Futures	LIFFE
U.K. Euromark Futures	LIFFE

ASIA	
Australian 90-Day Bank Bill Futures	Sydney Futures Exchange
Australian Treasury Bond Futures	Sydney Futures Exchange
Japanese 10-Year Government Bond Futures	Tokyo Stock Exchange
Japanese 20-Year Government Bond Futures	Tokyo Stock Exchange
Japanese Euroyen Futures	Tokyo International Financial Futures Exchange
New Zealand Bank Accepted Bill Futures	New Zealand Futures and Options Exchange
New Zealand 5-Year Government Stock Futures	New Zealand Futures and Options Exchange
Singapore Eurodollar Futures	Singapore International Monetary Exchange
Singapore Euroyen	SIMEX
Singapore Euroyen Futures Options	SIMEX

Some observers of the global financial markets claim that financial futures and options play no role in the formation of capital. Undoubtably, financial futures and options transactions are a zero-sum game, and a significant portion of activity is speculative. However, bona fide hedgers require the liquidity which speculators inject into markets by being the counterparty to hedging positions. Moreover, because financial futures and options can function as instruments to modify the risk/return profile of investments, they promote trading and investment in the underlying markets and as a result, enhance the liquidity of capital markets essential for corporate and government financing. Certainly, no investor wants to hold securities whose liquidity is less than adequate. Financial futures and options therefore enhance the efficiency of the capital formation process. Due in part to this vital role, trading of financial futures and options has been growing in quantum leaps.

The Asia-Pacific region has been a major contributor to this tremendous growth in global trading. In order to support its fast-growing equity and debt markets, and also, international trade of the region, financial futures and options on stock indices, interest rates and currencies emerged in the mid-1980s in Asia. Each financial center provides specific opportunities and has a unique structure of regulations, markets and players. As a whole, they have come a long way from the early 1980s, when financial futures and options were generally an alien concept in the region. As we enter the 1990s, the Far East financial futures and options markets will be refining their structure and products, and offering global institutional investors with a wide array of efficient risk management tools for both their investment in the region, and their exposure to risk during the Pacific time zone. In the 1990s, the Pacific Rim futures and options markets will gain a role equivalent to the prominence of their economies and financial markets. These markets have only just begun to realize their enormous potential, and their greatest growth lies in the future.

This chapter provides an overview of the Asian-Pacific financial futures and options markets, and consists of four parts. The first part discusses the Far East equity, bond and currency markets, and their financial futures and options contracts currently traded. The second part shows how Asian-Pacific financial futures and options can be applied to latest global investment strategies. The third part details how Pacific Rim financial futures and options markets have evolved from their infancy to their current state. In the final part, the rapid changes occurring in the Asian-Pacific financial futures markets and their impact on the future contours of the regional marketplace are discussed.

Underlying Markets of the Asian-Pacific Financial Futures and Options Contracts

Pacific Rim Equity Markets and their Futures and Options Contracts

As global equity investment expanded dramatically, the Asia-Pacific region has been a prime beneficiary. This has occured both because its equity markets showed stellar performances in the second half of the 1980s, and also because they offer an excellent means for the diversification of market risks due to their low correlations with U.S. and European equity markets.

As CHART 2A demonstrates, from 1985 to 1990, the Pacific Basin Index of the FT-Actuaries World Indices generated a total U.S. dollar return of 176.46% whereas the FT-Actuaries Europe and U.S. Indices, 169.00% and 97.94% respectively. CHART 2B shows the total return of each constituent country of the FT-Actuaries Pacific Basin Index between 1985 and 1990 vis-a-vis the FT-Actuaries U.S. Index. They all surpassed the performance of the U.S. market.

Also, as is visible in TABLE 3, the Asian equity markets have low correlations with the major European and U.S. markets. Therefore, investment in the Asian equity markets offers an excellent means for diversifying the market risks inherent in a global portfolio.

As demonstrated above, investment in Asian-Pacific equity markets has been unquestionably consistent with the essential goals of institutional global investing: the reduction of market risks and the enhancement of returns.[1] Furthermore, given the significant size of the Asian equity markets, global investors cannot ignore the investment opportunities offered by these markets. As Asian economies expanded dramatically in the past decade, their equity markets have grown significantly as well. Whereas the Asia-Pacific region accounted for 23% of the total market capitalization of the FT-Actuaries World Index at the end of 1980, it accounted for 35% at the end of 1990 − see CHART 3. At the end of 1990, Japan's market capitalization was the world's second largest after the U.S., comprising 33% of the FT-Actuaries World Index − the U.S. equity market accounted 35% of the FT-Actuaries World Index at the end of 1990. When American equities are excluded, Japan accounts for over 50% of international shares, as measured by the FT-Actuaries Europe and Pacific (EuroPac) Index as well as the other major indices.

Equity markets in Australia, Hong Kong, Singapore, Malaysia and New Zealand are much smaller than that of Japan, but they have been popular with global investors seeking the diversification of market risks and the enhancement

Chart 2A: Total U.S. Dollar Returns from Regional Equity Markets

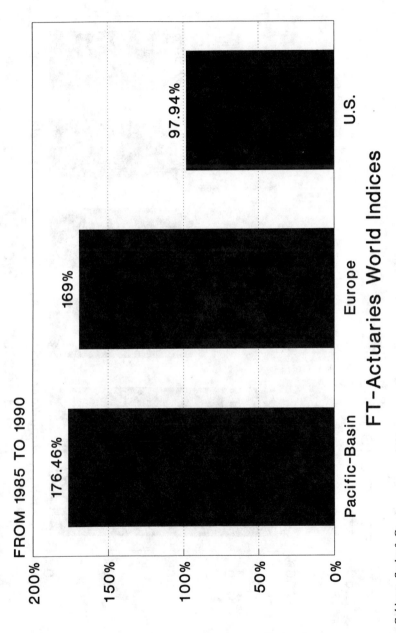

FROM 1985 TO 1990

176.46% Pacific-Basin

169% Europe

97.94% U.S.

200%
150%
100%
50%
0%

FT-Actuaries World Indices

Source: Goldman, Sachs & Co.

Chart 2B: Total U.S. Dollar Returns from Pacific-Basin Equity Markets

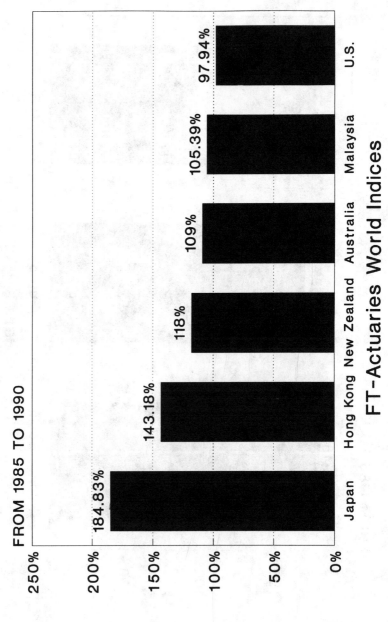

FROM 1985 TO 1990

Table 3:   Correlations of Asian Equity Markets with Major European and U.S. Markets*

	U.K.	France	Germany	U.S.
Japan	0.39	0.35	0.39	0.39
Australia	0.58	0.35	0.44	0.33
Hong Kong	0.36	0.27	0.36	0.22
Singapore	0.57	0.31	0.42	0.40
New Zealand	0.47	0.27	0.39	0.37

*Correlations of Local Currency Returns from Jan. 1986 to Dec. 1990
Source: FT-Actuaries World Indices Group of Goldman, Sachs & Co.

of returns. TABLE 4 shows the market capitalization weighting changes within the FT-Actuaries Pacific Basin Index between 1980 and 1990.

TABLE 5A and 5B detail the investment in the Asian equity markets by major global investors in 1988 and 1989. The global investment in the Asian-Pacific equity markets has increased from $385bn in 1988 to $545.71bn in 1989 — a 42% increase. This significant amount of investment in the Asian equity markets has been enhanced by the availability of risk management products.

As is visible in TABLE 6, the Asian equity markets are particularly volatile. Thus, as the Asia-Pacific region now comprises a significant portion of global institutional investors' portfolio, the risk management of investments in the region has become an essential part of global investment strategies.

For instance, when the price-earnings ratio of the Japanese equity market reached breathtaking heights in late 1988 and 1989, American, European and Asian investors were increasingly becoming defensive with regard to their investment in Japan. As fear of a collapse in Japanese stocks became a reality in the beginning of 1990, the risk management of investment in Japan was more indispensable than ever before, and the use of index futures and options soared. TABLE 7 lists the currently-traded Asian stock index futures and options contracts and their exchanges.

In the 1990s, the development of new equity index futures and options contracts is expected in Asia's emerging stock markets. The Asia-Pacific region has the largest emerging equity markets of the world. As is visible in CHART 4, in 1988 the Asian emerging equity markets accounted for 73% of the capitalization of the world's emerging markets.

Korea and Taiwan are the first and second largest emerging markets of the world. Their market capitalizations are larger than some well-established Euro-

Chart 3: Percentage Composition of World Equity Markets

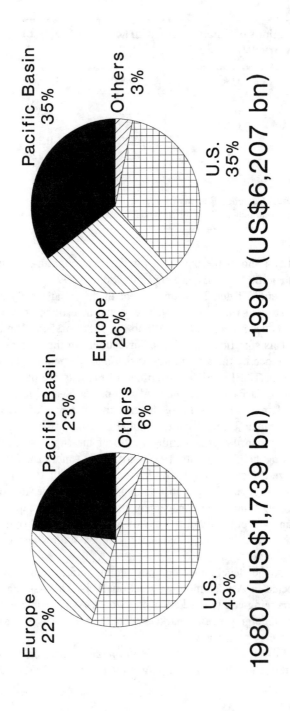

1980 (US$1,739 bn)   1990 (US$6,207 bn)

FT-Actuaries World Indices

Source: Goldman, Sachs & Co.

Table 4:   Percentage Composition of Pacific-Basin Equity Markets In 1980 and 1990

	1980	1990
Japan	73%	93.0%
Australia	14	4.0
Hong Kong	8	2.5
Singapore	2	1.0
Malaysia	2	0.3
New Zealand	1	0.2
Total Market Capitalization	US$403 bn	US$2,188 bn

Source: FT-Actuaries World Indices Group of Goldman, Sachs & Co.

Table 5A: Gross Cross-Border Equity Flows into Asia in 1988 (US Dollars in Billions)

Market to

	Japan	Australia	Hong Kong	Singapore	Investor Total
Investor From:					
US	US$66.96	4.87	5.34	1.36	78.53
Europe	120.49	13.58	7.83	0.95	142.85
Japan	–	3.32	4.50	1.00	8.82
Australia	3.50	–	2.50	0.25	6.25
Hong Kong	85.00	2.69	–	0.50	88.19
Singapore	2.00	0.00	1.00	–	3.00
Rest of World	49.12	6.82	0.96	0.15	57.0
Market Total	327.07	31.28	22.13	4.21	384.69

Source: Salomon Brothers Inc.

**Table 5A: Gross Cross-Border Equity Flows into Asia-Pacific in 1989
(US Dollars in Billions)**

Market to

	Japan	Australia	Hong Kong	Singapore	Investor Total
Investor From:					
US	US$84.16	5.47	7.26	3.23	100.12
Europe	142.98	14.86	17.48	6.98	182.30
Japan	—	2.90	17.44	5.16	25.50
Australia	4.07	—	3.30	1.25	8.62
Hong Kong	19.98	9.80	—	7.17	36.95
Singapore	8.31	2.25	2.25	—	12.81
Rest of World	173.36	1.62	3.71	0.72	179.41
Market Total	432.86	36.90	51.44	24.51	545.71

Source: Salomon Brothers Inc.

**Table 6:   Volatilities of Pacific-Basin and Major International
Equity Markets***

Japan	17.5%
Australia	15.9
Hong Kong	27.1
Singapore	18.8
New Zealand	22.4
U.S.	15.2
U.K.	13.2

*Measured by annualized standard deviations of local currency returns between Dec. 1987 and Sept. 1990

pean markets, such as Switzerland. In 1990, Taiwanese authorities partially opened their equity markets, to foreign investors, albeit with many restrictions. The Korean market is expected to follow with limited market liberalization in early 1992. Thailand, the Philippines, Indonesia, India, and Sri Lanka and Pakistan are also among the Asian emerging equity markets closely watched, and regularly entered, by global institutional investors. In the near future, infant markets in China, Vietnam, and Mongolia will also develop. They are becoming

Table 7: Currently Traded Asian Equity Index Futures And Options

	Exchange*	Listing Date
JAPAN		
Nikkei Stock Average Futures	OSE	9/88
Nikkei Stock Average Options	OSE	6/89
Topix Index Futures	TSE	9/88
Topix Index Options	TSE	10/89
Nagoya Options 25	NSE	10/89
AUSTRALIA		
All Ordinaries Index Futures	SFE	2/83
All Ordinaries Index Futures Options	SFE	6/85
Options on Australian equities	ASX	1976
SINGAPORE		
Nikkei Stock Average Futures	SIMEX	9/86
HONG KONG		
Hang Seng Index Futures	HKFE	6/86
NEW ZEALAND		
Barclays Share Price Index Futures	NZFOE	1/87
Barclays Share Price Index Options	NZFOE	2/89
Options on New Zealand equities	NZFOE	10/90

*OSE : The Osaka Securities Exchange
TSE : The Tokyo Stock Exchange
NSE : The Nagoya Stock Exchange
SFE : The Sydney Futures Exchange
SIMEX: The Singapore International Monetary Exchange
HKFE : The Hong Kong Futures Exchange
NZFOE: The New Zealand Futures and Options Exchange
ASX: The Australian Stock Exchange

much more attractive and accessible. In the 1990s, institutional investment in these markets is expected to rise dramatically. As in the case of more established Asian equity markets, emerging markets in Asia have low correlations with major world equity markets — see TABLE 8. Furthermore, they have recorded superb performances past five years as it is shown in CHART 5. As a result, the

Chart 4: Percentage Composition of World Emerging Equity Markets in 1990

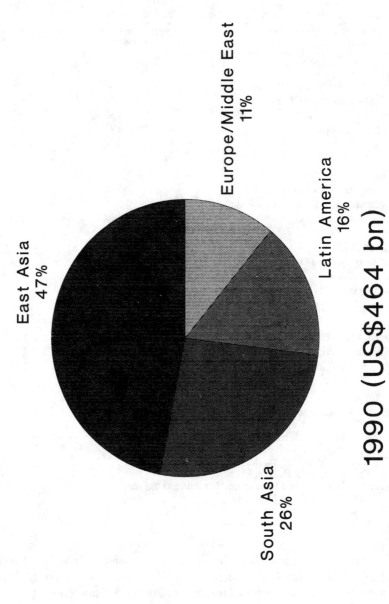

East Asia
47%

Europe/Middle East
11%

Latin America
16%

South Asia
26%

1990 (US$464 bn)

Source: International Finance Corp.

Table 8:   Correlations of Emerging Asian Equity Markets with Major European and U.S. Markets*

	U.K.	France	Germany	U.S.
Korea	0.1	0.1	0.1	0.1
Taiwan	0.0	0.0	0.2	-0.2
Thailand	0.0	0.2	0.2	-0.1
Malaysia	0.1	0.1	0.2	-0.2
Indonesia	0.0	-0.1	0.1	-0.1

*Correlations of bi-weekly US$ returns from Jan. 1988 to Sept. 1990

Source: Morgan Stanley Capital International

emerging equity markets of Asia offer excellent means for diversifying market risks and enhancing returns.

However, the Asian emerging equity markets are highly volatile, as can be seen in TABLE 9. In order to attract a significant amount of international investment, these markets need to develop adequate risk management tools. In ChapteR 8, the current efforts by these financial centers to establish financial futures and options markets are discussed.

Table 9:   Volatilities of Asian Emerging and Major International Equity Markets*

Korea	22.4%
Taiwan	44.2
Malaysia	20.0
Thailand	26.7
Indonesia	43.4
U.S.	15.2
U.K.	13.2

*Measured by annualized standard deviations of local currency returns between Dec. 1987 and Sept. 1990

Source: Morgan Stanley Capital International

Chart 5: Total U.S. Dollar Returns from Asian Emerging Equity Markets

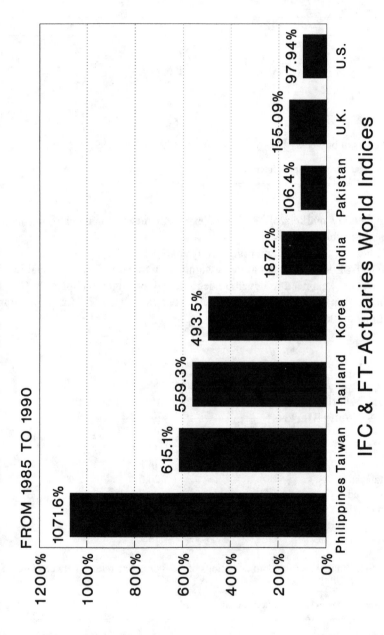

FROM 1985 TO 1990

1071.6%

615.1%

559.3%

493.5%

187.2%

106.4%

155.09%

97.94%

Philippines Taiwan Thailand Korea India Pakistan U.K. U.S.

IFC & FT-Actuaries World Indices

1200%
1000%
800%
600%
400%
200%
0%

Source: International Finance Corporation
Goldman, Sachs & Co.

Far Eastern Bond Markets and Their Futures and Options Contracts

With the exception of Japan, Australia, and New Zealand, the Asian-Pacific bond markets are still in their infancy, yet have potential for significant growth in the coming years. Japan, Australia and New Zealand offer opportunities for enhanced returns, diversification, and currency exposure. Deregulation, and the growth of international trading activity in offshore markets in Singapore, Hong Kong and Tokyo, have expanded heretofore inaccessible or nonexistent capital markets of the region. Korean and Taiwan have plans to develop more sophisticated corporate and government debt markets. Singapore, despite its budget surplus, is also hoping to develop a local bond market.

As is visible in CHART 6, according to the Salomon Brothers World Government Bond Indices, the government bond markets of Japan and Australia accounted for 21% and 0.97% respectively of the total market capitalization of the world government bond markets at the end of 1990. Due to its relatively small size, the New Zealand government bond market is not included in the Salomon Brothers World Government Bond Indices.

The Japanese government bond (JGB) market is the second largest in the world after the U.S. market, and global institutional investors have been holding a significant amount of JGBs in their portfolios. As a result of these international holdings, and around-the-clock market developments, JGBs are actively traded in London and New York as well as in Tokyo. According to an industry estimate, about $670 million and $870 million of JGBs are traded daily in New York and London respectively. Consequently, the risk management of investment in JGBs has been an important part of global bond portfolio management, and futures and options on JGBs have been actively traded. For instance, 10-year JGB futures are one of the most actively traded futures contracts in the world; its daily average volume in the first half of 1990 was 67,000 contracts. JGB Futures also trade in London and are listed in Chicago.[2]

Despite their relatively small sizes, the Australian and New Zealand government bond markets have been attracting global institutional investors seeking high-yielding, high-grade fixed income investments — see CHART 7. However, interest rates in Australia and New Zealand have been highly volatile, and the risk management products for these interest rates have been important to global institutional investors participating in these markets.

In addition, the large Asian cash markets in short-term deposits create numerous hedging needs. For example, the offshore Asiadollar market in Singapore had deposits valuing US$390 billion at the end of 1990. The major U.S. dollar, Yen, and Australian dollar short-term interest rate instruments now have

Chart 6: Percentage Composition of World Government Bond Markets in 1990 (Total Market Value: US$ 2,823.6 billion)

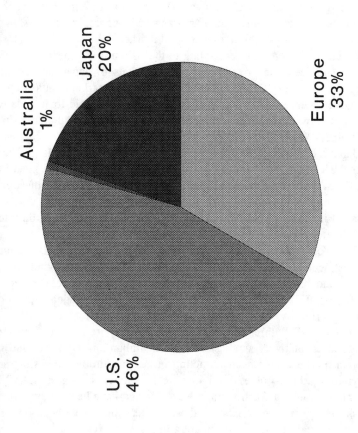

Japan
20%

Australia
1%

U.S.
46%

Europe
33%

Salomon Brothers World Govt. Bond Indices

Source: Salomon Brothers Inc.

Chart 7: Australian, Japanese & U.S. Ten-Year Government Bond Yields

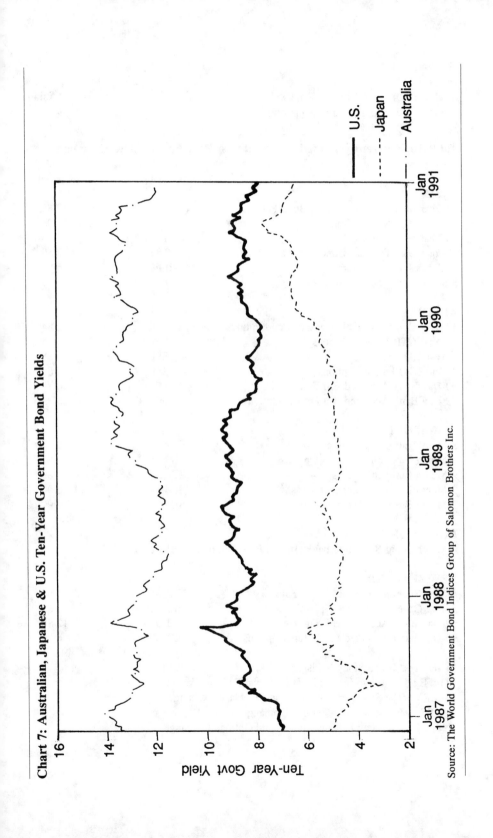

Source: The World Government Bond Indices Group of Salomon Brothers Inc.

related futures and options markets. TABLE 10 lists the currently-traded Asian interest rate futures and options contracts and their exchanges.

Table 10: Currently-Traded Asian Interest Rate Futures And Options

	*Exchange	Listing Date
JAPAN		
10-Year Japanese Government Bond Futures	TSE	10/85
10-Year JGB Futures Options	TSE	5/90
20-Year JGB Futures	TSE	7/88
10-Year U.S. Treasury Bond Futures	TSE	12/89
3-Month Euroyen Futures	TIFFE	6/89
3-Month Eurodollar Futures	TIFFE	6/89
AUSTRALIA		
10-Year Commonwealth Treasury Bond Futures	SFE	12/84
10-Year CTB Futures Options	SFE	11/85
3-Year CTB Futures	SFE	5/88
3-Year CTB Futures Options	SFE	6/88
90-Day Bank Accepted Bill Futures	SFE	10/79
90-Day Bank Accepted Bill Futures Options	SFE	5/85
SINGAPORE		
3-Month Eurodollar Futures	SIMEX	9/84
3-Month Eurodollar Futures Options	SIMEX	9/87
3-Month Euroyen Futures	SIMEX	10/89
3-Month Euroyen Futures Options	SIMEX	6/90
3-Month Euromark Futures	SIMEX	9/90
HONG KONG		
3-Month Hong Kong Interbank Offered Rate Futures	HKFE	2/90
NEW ZEALAND		
5-Year Government Stock No. 2 Futures	NZFOE	5/88
5-Year GS No. 2 Futures Options	NZFOE	12/88
90-Day Bank Accepted Bill Futures	NZFOE	12/86
90-Day Bank Accepted Bill Futures Options	NZFOE	6/89

*TSE : The Tokyo Stock Exchange
 TIFFE : The Tokyo International Financial Futures Exchange
 SIMEX : The Singapore International Monetary Exchange
 HKFE : The Hong Kong Futures Exchange
 NZFOE : The New Zealand Futures and Options Exchange

The Asian-Pacific Foreign Exchange Markets and Their Currency Futures and Options Contracts

Foreign exchange markets in the Far East have grown dramatically in the past decade. According to the survey of Bank for International Settlements (BIS) in April 1989, among the 21 major foreign exchange markets worldwide, Tokyo, Singapore, Hong Kong and Sydney were the largest foreign exchange centers — see TABLE 11.

Although the BIS survey recorded that the trading volume of New York surpassed that of Tokyo, many dealers consider Tokyo the equal of its American counterpart. Singapore, Hong Kong and Sydney also have very active international currency markets. The rivalry between Singapore and Hong Kong is heating up as 1997 apporaches when China will gain sovereignty of the British colony. In 1989, several international banks moved their foreign exchange trading desks or some of their currency dealers to Singapore from Hong Kong. Also, establishing a foreign exchange dealership in Singapore is considered 30% less costly than Hong Kong and 50% less than Tokyo, mainly because of lower salaries and rent.

In Tokyo, foreign exchange dealing is done largely by customer orders. Most of Japanese dealers are known to be afraid of taking major positions for their own account. In contrast, the Singapore market is dominated by about ten

Table 11: Average Daily Foreign Exchange Turnover in April 1989

Country	Forex Turnover	Market Share
U.K.	$187 bil.	25.3%
U.S.	129	17.4
Japan	115	15.5
Singapore	64	8.6
Switzerland	57	7.7
Hong Kong	49	6.6
Australia	30	4.1
France	26	3.5
Canada	15	2.0
12 Others	68	9.2
Total	$740 bil.	100.0

Source: Bank for International Settlements

major banks, and foreign exchange dealing in the city-state consists of a combination of customer orders and banks' proprietary trading. In Hong Kong, the participants in the market is numerous and the dealing is dominated by banks' proprietary trading.

Despite the differences, and some rivalry, the Asian-Pacific foreign exchange centers are closely intertwined, and each contributes to a unified, and highly liquid Pacific Rim market. For instance, according the dealers, when one Asian center closes for a holiday, trading volume in other Far East markets drops.

A significant amount of foreign exchange trading in the region is due to heavy local asset bases as well as 'hot' and mobile capital. The other main reason for the growth of the Asian-Pacific foreign exchange markets is the tremendous growth in the international trade of Asia with the other regions of the world — see TABLE 12. This has created increasing needs for managing currency risks. TABLE 13 lists the currently-traded Asian currency futures and options contracts and their exchanges.

Table 12: International Trade Among the Major Regions of the World in 1989 (in US$ Billion)

Export To

	European Community	North America	Asia	Others	Total
Export From					
Asia	120	210	300	70	700
European Community	660	95	80	255	1,090
North America	95	165	125	95	480
Others	265	115	70	400	850
Total	1,140	585	575	820	3,120

Source: The Economist

Table 13: Currently Traded Currency Futures and Options in the Far East

	*Exchange	Listing Date
JAPAN		
Japanese Yen/U.S. $ Futures	TIFFE	6/89
AUSTRALIA		
U.S. $/Australian $ Futures	SFE	2/88
U.S. $/Australian $ Futures Options	SFE	3/88
SINGAPORE		
U.S. $/Yen Futures	SIMEX	11/84
U.S. $/Yen Futures Options	SIMEX	11/87
U.S. $/Deutsche Mark Futures	SIMEX	9/84
U.S. $/Deutsche Mark Futures Options	SIMEX	11/87
U.S. $/British Pound Futures	SIMEX	
NEW ZEALAND		
New Zealand $/U.S. $ Futures	NZFOE	1/85
U.S. $/New Zealand $ Futures	NZFOE	11/88
U.S. $/New Zealand $ Futures Options	NZFOE	12/88

*TIFFE: The Tokyo International Financial Futures Exchange
SFE : The Sydney Futures Exchange
SIMEX: The Singapore International Monetary Exchange
NZFOE: The New Zealand Futures and Options Exchange

New Trends in Global Investing and Application of Asian-Pacific Financial Futures and Options

The expanding and maturing Asia-Pacific markets are now able to accommodate the same equity and bond derivative strategies that global institutional investors have been practicing in more developed markets such as the U.S. and U.K. Increased liquidity, closer integration, and more sophisticated local users have resulted in more efficient and liquid markets.

The growing trend toward the indexation of portfolios has increased the institutional need for equity index derivatives. Japan's predominant weighting in global equity indices — and the difficulty many fund managers have had in tracking broad index performance — have made Japanese index futures and options essential indexation tools. Australia, Hong Kong, and New Zealand have relatively small weightings in global institutional portfolios, but those who want to invest in these markets may opt to use derivatives instead of a cash position. Malaysia and Singapore will also likely have an equity index product in the near future, with Korea and Thailand also possibly following. By the mid-1990s, broadly-diversified equity positions in the Far East could be taken solely by using stock index futures.

In the following section, two of the most noticeable, new global investment trends are discussed. These two strategies extensively utilizes equity index derivatives and are expected to be more widely embraced by global institutional investors in the 1990s.

The enormous growth of managed futures assets in recent years is also beginning to impact the Pacific Rim derivative markets. This phenomenon, as well as the development of regionally-based funds is discussed below.

Global Equity Portfolio Indexation

Passive equity portfolio indexation has become a major strategy for domestic and international investing which has been increasingly adopted by institutional investors worldwide since the mid-1980s. According to Birinyi Associates, at the end of 1989, 25.2% of the total U.S. ERISA (Employee Retirement Income Security Act) pension assets was indexed to major international equity indices such as S&P 500, FT-SE 100, Nikkei 225, or MSCI EAFE (Europe, Australia, Far East) Indices. This contrasts to the levels in 1985 when only 1.03% of the total pension assets was indexed according to Salomon Brothers. In the U.K., according to Greenwich Associates, 8.8% of the total pension assets was indexed as of March 1990. The benchmark indices used for passive management tend to be market capitalization-weighted, and their constituent shares are highly-capitalized, international blue-chip equities. As a result, investments by international fund managers have been mostly concentrated on some 1,000 major international shares. As one seasoned market observer noted, ". . .it is not difficult to envisage a future characterized by a 'thundering thousand' superleague of global stocks, to rival the 'nifty fifty' of popular growth stocks that dominated the US market in the late 1960s."[3]

In addition to passive indexation, international investment managers have been preferring large capitalization equities because of their liquidity and the availability of index derivatives which can be used for managing the risk of holding these shares.

As a consequence of portfolio indexation, international fund managers have been aggressively utilizing basket trading and index derivatives for Pacific Rim equities such as Nikkei 225 (Japan/Singapore), All Ordinaries (Australia), Hang Seng (Hong Kong) and Barclays (New Zealand) index futures and options. Index derivatives complement basket trading by offering a cost-effective means to replicate stock indices without actually owning underlying shares or to manage the risk of holding actual shares. These instruments have a superior synergy with current and future global equity investment trends.

Global Tactical Asset Allocation

A new group of international fund managers which emerged in the mid-80s and continue to have a strong impact within the global investment community in the 1990s, is global tactical asset allocators. These global fund managers are not concerned with the prospect of individual shares but base their investment decision on the assessment of broad economic conditions and expected currency movements of specific markets. They switch in and out of markets by trading a basket of shares or utilizing index derivatives.

For example, by selling futures on All Ordinaries Share Price Index, a global tactical asset allocator could underweight his or her investment in the Australian equity market vis-a-vis other equity markets or the Australian bond market without selling actual shares. On the other hand, buying futures on Barclays Share Price Index will enable a fund manager to overweight the New Zealand equity market vis-a-vis other markets or the New Zealand bond market without an additional purchase of shares.

Growth of Institutional Investment in Managed Futures

Professionally-managed futures portfolios are gradually becoming accepted as an independent asset class by institutional investors. Institutions are attracted by the generally superior returns that managed futures provided, and the non-corrolation of returns with other institutional asset classes. Large investors have been actively seeking alternatives to bonds and equities since the 1987 stock market crash. The heightened interest of pension funds, corporate investment, and other institutions in speculative futures funds have helped boost the amount of money managed by professional futures traders by over 500% since the beginning of 1987, to an estimated $20 billion in early 1991, according to Managed Account Reports. Many industry officials expect this figure to reach at least $50 billion by mid-decade.

The bulk of these assets originate and are managed in the United States, although many funds are registered offshore. A high percentage of fund managers, known as CTA's (Commodity Trading Advisers) trade globally, and already provide substantial activity to Pacific-Rim exchanges. Furthermore, Asian-Pacific investors are showing rising interest in such investment vehicles. For example, as of mid-1991, approximately $2 billion was raised in Japan for various types of futures and commodities funds, predominantly managed offshore. This figure is expected to reach $10 billion by the middle of the decade. Australia has a small indigenous managed futures industry, with about $250 million of funds. Investors in Singapore, Hong Kong, New Zealand, Taiwan, and South Korea are also exhibiting growing interest in managed futures pools.

The phenomenal growth of professionally-traded futures assets will increase the necessity for managers to participate in markets around the world, both to diversify their trading positons and to gain a competitive edge. The Pacific Rim markets will undoubtedly benefit from this trend, especially since a growing proportion of investors—and eventually, managers—will come from within the region.

The Evolution of the Asian Financial Futures Markets

The advent of around-the-clock trading — in equity, bond and foreign exchange markets — has made 24-hour risk management essential. This has been one of the primary rationales for some of the futures and options products in the Asia-Pacific region, along with their serving domestic price discovery and hedging functions. These needs sparked the development of financial futures and options markets in the Far East in the 1980s.

These markets have enjoyed spectacular growth in the second half of the 1980s. Since their emergence in the mid-1980s, the region's futures exchanges have dramatically expanded their range of products and trading volumes. In 1985, these markets comprised less than one half percent of global futures activity. They now account for approximately 10% of a much larger pie. In this section, the historical evolution of Asian-Pacific financial futures and options markets is discussed, as well as the changing contours of the regional industry at the beginning of the 1990s

The First Phase

The first phase of Asia-Pacific financial futures market development was from 1979 to 1984. Exchanges at the periphery of the region's financial center-of-gravity were first to introduce new products and educate users on the concepts of exchange-traded financial futures and options contracts.

The Sydney Futures Exchange (SFE) was first, in 1979, with a do. In 1984, the Singapore International Monetary Exchange (SIMEX) was opened. It forged the first inter-exchange link, with the Chicago Mercantile Exchange (CME), and listed futures on international interest rates and currencies such as 3-month Eurodollar and the Japanese Yen.

Both regional exchanges faced an uphill battle to convince skeptical players on the merits of futures. The trading volume growth was impressive in percentage terms, but activity levels were minuscule compared to bigger exchanges in the U.S and London.

The Second Phase

From 1985 until early 1987, futures and options trading was proliferating around the world, and during this second phase of development, three new markets opened in Asia. Japan, Hong Kong and New Zealand recognized the benefits of developing futures trading. The Tokyo Stock Exchange (TSE) launched 10-year Japanese government bond futures in 1985; the New Zealand Futures Exchange (NZFE) was inaugurated the same year, and the Hong Kong Futures Exchange (HKFE) was restructured to accommodate financial futures in 1986. (The NZFE was renamed The New Zealand Futures and Options Exchange in 1990.)

In the beginning, domestic Japanese futures market development was restricted, and their residents were prohibited from trading in international futures markets. Other regional exchanges frantically scrambled to become the primary futures trading center in the Asian timezone before Japan was liberalized. Optimistic and grandiose expansion plans and linkage proposals were promulgated and implemented. Inter-exchange rivalry was heated, and the rhetoric was often bellicose, particularly between SIMEX and the SFE.

The Third Phase

The third phase began in May 1987, when the gradual liberalization of Japanese futures trading was initiated. Japanese financial firms were allowed to trade in overseas futures and options markets for their own accounts. Orders began to flow into the regional markets, and the Japanese built up their presence at various international futures exchanges. In June 1987, the Osaka Securities Exchange (OSE) listed a physically-settled stock index contract, the "Stock Futures 50." Meanwhile, the Japanese bureaucracy — under pressure from the domestic financial industry, and international governments, exchanges and firms — began to lay the groundwork for the substantial opening and expansion of domestic futures markets.

Regional futures exchanges, riding the crest of the worldwide stock market boom, enjoyed record trading volumes and a surge of confidence. Equity index futures in Hong Kong, Sydney and Singapore attracted institutional participation from around the globe as well as heavy domestic retail activity.

The euphoria ended in October 1987. The fallout from the international stock market crash of 1987 varied from exchange to exchange, but with one exception, the markets suffered significantly. Only in Japan, where the trading in the equity market was halted for the most of October 20th, did the market crash actually help futures trading activity. Japanese investors — accustomed to one-way bull markets — finally recognized the need for equity hedging mechanisms. The trading volume in the "Stock Futures 50" contract in Osaka grew substantially.

Elsewhere, the damage was severe. Australia and New Zealand suffered substantial drops in turnover and terrifying volatility. SIMEX, which managed to trade throughout the turmoil, lost much business, but had no defaults. The HKFE closed for four days, and the futures market collapsed. A government-arranged "lifeboat fund" was needed to save the exchange. Hong Kong futures turnover shrank by over 90%.

The regional futures markets entered a period of introspection and restructuring. The SFE and NZFE began to look inward for growth, assuming the role of "mother market" for their domestic cash markets. SIMEX continued to prospect for international business, since its domestic market and ability to list local contracts was limited. The HKFE underwent a drawn-out reorganization, which was designed to restore investor confidence.

In contrast, finally being aware of the need for risk management tools, the Japanese accelerated their futures market development plans. The contours of the Asia-Pacific derivative scene was changing. The Japanese, using their financial muscle, were moving to the vanguard. By late-1988, the new pattern was clear. Other regional markets would have to differentiate themselves and carve out unique niches if they were to prosper alongside the Japanese futures markets.

Nevertheless, 1988 was a remarkably successful year for most of the regional futures exchanges. The SFE, SIMEX, TSE, and OSE all set trading volume records. Investors and firms from Europe and the U.S. resumed their active trading, and increased their participation in the Asian futures markets. 1989 also witnessed a healthy trading volume growth and an expansion of markets and products, particularly in Japan, where a new financial futures exchange, the Tokyo International Financial Futures Exchange (TIFFE) was opened.

The Fourth Phase

As the 1990s begins, the Asia-Pacific futures and options markets have become more integrated with the rest of the world. They are poised for substantial growth, but will also have to compete with the new automated trading systems being developed by exchanges in Chicago, London, and elsewhere. While Japan may seem destined to capture the lion's share of turnover increase, global institutional investors will have the final choice of trading facility, based on such factors as market access, transaction costs, liquidity, regulatory environment, and sovereign risk. Japan's size thus becomes less relevant. The development of new contracts will likely remain in the hands of domestic exchanges in the region, whose innovation will determine their success.

The region's relative political stability has provided the foundation for financical growth, and the booming economies, the fuel. The financial futures and options markets in Japan, Australia, Singapore, Hong Kong, and New Zealand have become prominent players in the global derivative arena. The exchanges and industry have now moved into their fourth phase of development; one in which growth will be a greater challenge. The next section discusses in detail this fourth phase of the continuing evolution of the Asian-Pacific financial futures and options markets.

The Fourth Phase: The Shifting Contours of the Asian-Pacific Futures Industry and Markets

The headline-grabbing political and economic changes that swept through the region at the end of the 1980s will undoubtedly affect the young futures markets of the Far East. For example, the 1989 crackdown in China and the fallout in Hong Kong as 1997 approaches have greatly changed perceptions of the British colony's investment attractiveness. On the other hand, the end of the Cold War and the resulting political realignment is gradually opening the rigid societies of

North Korea and Vietnam, and rapidly opening Mongolia. Taiwanese investment is now welcomed throughout South-East Asia. Buoyant economic growth has spread beyond the "four dragons" (Hong Kong, Korea, Singapore and Taiwan) into the next generation of "NICs" (Newly Industrialized Countries), such as Thailand, Malaysia and Indonesia.

Furthermore, trade and investment in the region is breaking down political and cultural frontiers. Economic activity is moving beyond "NICs" and into "NETs." NETs, short for Natural Economic Territories, are sprouting up throughout East Asia. For example, Hong Kong and China's Guangzhou province are becoming economically integrated, and ties between Taiwan and Xiamen across the Formosa Strait are expanding dramatically. Similarly, Singapore and nearby areas of Malaysia and Indonesia are becoming economically linked in a "Growth Triangle."

Although these geoeconomic shifts will present numerous opportunities for the Asian-Pacific futures industry and exchanges, other less dramatic factors such as new trading technologies and new forms of competition have begun exerting greater impacts on the structure and future contours of the Asian financial futures and options markets.

Industry at a Crossroad

The explosive growth of derivative activity in Asia since the mid-1980s can be traced to the convergence of several favorable developments. Restrictions on financial futures and options were eased, and combined with other financial liberalizations, created a benevolent regulatory environment. As new exchanges and products were launched in the region, new users, recognizing their need for risk management tools, flocked to the markets. The additional instruments also attracted players from outside the region, who considered the Asian-Pacific markets as a key element of their global diversification strategies and sought to utilize the timezone bridge that these markets provide. These factors provided a windfall of trading volumes which propelled growth in the second half of the 1980s.

As the 1990s begins, it seems that the initial burst of pent-up demand has been satisfied. In most of the product areas, the "easy" gains in trading activity have been captured, and from now on, the exponential growth will be harder to achieve. Currently, the Pacific Rim financial futures and options exchanges confront the same phenomenon that the American futures industry has been observing — the passing of the "Golden Age of product development and proliferation." To some extent, system developments will take on a more important role in the future growth of Asian-Pacific futures exchanges.

Competition among exchanges and new technology development, such as electronic trading systems are forcing exchanges to redefine their niches and reorient their marketing strategies. Nonetheless, the potential for growth is still great. Although triple digit turnover increases will become less frequent, most regional industry leaders consider 20% annual growth in trading activities to be possible for much of the 1990s. The surge of professionally-managed futures assets worldwide will be one factor for continued growth. However, the expansion of the Asian-Pacific economies and the consequent growth of the regional capital markets will be the primary factors which create a "Second Golden Age" for the Pacific Rim financial futures and options markets, but this new era will have very different contours by the mid-1990s.

The Changing Nature of Competition

The nature of interexchange competition in the region, while still important, has changed markedly. The formerly heated — and often bitter — race for dominance within the timezone has been called off. Financial futures and options exchanges have finally realized that trading activities are not a zero-sum-game. As the competitive rush for international linkages ended, most exchanges — except for the Singapore International Monetary Exchange (SIMEX) — are now concentrating on domestic products, and all are stressing inter-exchange cooperation.

Within Japan, however, fierce interexchange competition broke out, with some surprising results. The Tokyo Stock Exchange (TSE), the world's second largest securities exchange, has lost two major battles to capture stock index activity. The TSE, which initiated financial futures trading in Japan with its extremely successful Japanese government bond (JGB) contract, has stumbled with its TOPIX index products. Within two years of trading, the Osaka Securities Exchange's (OSE) Nikkei Stock Average futures and options surpassed the TSE's contracts. Osaka is now the clearly dominant market, with all indicators showing its lead accelerating. Adding to the TSE's loss of face is the tiny Nagoya Stock Exchange's Option 25 contract, which has established itself as the number two index option in Japan, although it accounts for only a small fraction of the OSE's Nikkei option.

Competition in Japan also involves inter-industry rivalry. Major banks started and aggressively support the Tokyo International Financial Futures Exchange (TIFFE), which has been enviably successful with its Euroyen interest rate contract. But the TIFFE has fared much worse with its Eurodollar and Yen futures, the trading of which is essentially moribund. This has been a relief for the SIMEX, which trades similar contracts.

However, in the Euroyen arena, the SIMEX and TIFFE are competing head-to-head. Singapore's exchange launched Euroyen futures in October 1989, and it quickly become SIMEX's third most actively-traded contract with the second highest open interest. Although SIMEX's contract rarely achieves more than 10% of the TIFFE's trading volume — far from a threat to the TIFFE — SIMEX does highlight the higher transaction and margin costs in Tokyo. The Singapore exchange put further pressure on the TIFFE in June 1990, when it launched options on Euroyen futures — a full year before the TIFFE's Euroyen option introduction. The TIFFE, like other Japanese financial futures exchanges before it, clearly notices the pressure from the SIMEX, and it has extended its trading hours in the spring of 1991, when it has also switched to a fully automated trading system. The two exchanges have realized that they are not a threat to each other, and have begun limited cooperation. In July 1991 TIFFE and SIMEX signed an agreement providing for a common final settlement price for their Euroyen contracts.

The GLOBEX Factor

In 1987, recognizing that 24-hour trading had become the reality of global investing, the Chicago Mercantile Exchange and Reuters announced their joint venture plan for GLOBEX. This after-hour electronic trading system, through which futures and options contracts of the CME can be traded globally after the regular trading session of the CME ends. In 1988, the French futures exchange, the MATIF (Marché à Terme International de France), joined the GLOBEX project. In 1990, the Chicago Board of Trade, the world's largest futures exchange, which initially opposed any kind of electronic trading system, joined the CME/Reuters venture.

As 1991 began, the global financial community was still waiting for the launch of GLOBEX trading. The system is supposed to bring about the 24-hour electronic age of global dervative trading. However, no firm date for the launch of GLOBEX trading has been set. The industry consensus expects the initiation of GLOBEX trading in the first half of 1992, but its impact is uncertain. GLOBEX could turn out to be a major disappointment for global futures traders or a revolutionary leap for global financial trading. Nevertheless, GLOBEX at minimum indicates the evolutionary direction of derivatives trading.

According to preliminary GLOBEX plans, the after-hour electronic trading system will operate worldwide between 6:00 p.m. and 6:00 a.m. Chicago time. This means GLOBEX will occur between 9:00 a.m. and 9:00 p.m. in Tokyo time and between 12:00 a.m. and 12:00 p.m. in London Time — see CHART 8 for the trading hours of GLOBEX in the major world futures trading centers. Because GLOBEX will be operating throughout the regular trading hours of the Asian time zone, certain Pacific Rim futures exchanges perceive GLOBEX as an alternative, emerging futures exchange in the region and are concerned that the cross-exchange trading of Asian futures and options will occur on GLOBEX.

Cross-exchange futures trading can be defined as transactions in derivatives which are conducted either on investor's local exchange or on another exchange which is foreign to the national origins of the derivatives. For instance, American investors can now trade Nikkei Stock Average futures at the Chicago Mercantile Exchange, and also trade German government bond futures at LIFFE (the London International Financial Futures Exchange). Because of its superiority in providing a centralized, liquid medium for managing investment risk, the trading volume of futures on German government bonds listed on the LIFFE exceeds that of the same contract on the DTB (Deutsche Terminböerse) in Frankfurt by a 13-to-1 ratio. The presence of the underlying cash market does not necessarily guarantee the unchallenged monopoly of derivative instruments.

The cross-exchange trading of Asian-Pacific financial futures and options on GLOBEX presents Far East futures exchanges with significant challenges. Far East futures exchanges will no longer compete only against their domestic and other regional counterparts but also against GLOBEX. Initially, GLOBEX is planning to trade the futures and options contracts of the CME and CBOT such as the U.S. Treasury bond, S&P 500 index and Eurodollar futures which could attract traders around the globe. MATIF contracts will be added shortly after the launch. However, there is no reason why GLOBEX cannot list the proprietary contracts of Asian futures exchanges. No matter where the underlying cash market of a futures contract is located, investors will execute their trades of a futures contract on an exchange which offers low transaction costs, liquidity and efficiency in price discovery regardless of the exchange's domicile. The introduction of the GLOBEX trading network could affect the individual Asian-Pacific financial futures exchanges as well as the overall regional marketplace by providing an alternative trading place for transactions during the Asian timezone. If this happens, no exchange will feel the impact more than SIMEX, the CME's current Asian partner through a mutual-offset system established in 1984.

SIMEX's original purpose was to serve as the Asian link between the regular and off trading hours of Europe and the U.S. for around-the-clock trading. GLOBEX in many ways supplants that role, and particularly threatens SIMEX's vibrant international interest rate contract, Eurodollar futures. Singapore exchange officials stress the loyalty and goodwill that SIMEX has built up in the region over the past seven years. But the solid core of experienced SIMEX customers are also potential GLOBEX users. Ongoing CME/SIMEX negotiations about grafting the existing relationship onto GLOBEX have been inconclu-

Chart 8: Trading Around-the-Clock
Local time at various exchanges during Globex's proposed hours of operation
Contracts=Total 1990 Futures volume

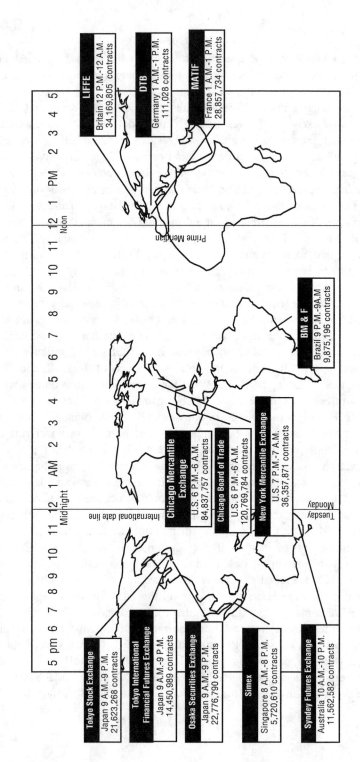

Source: International Herald Tribune

sive. SIMEX users and members hope for a quick and mutually beneficial agreement that removes the uncertainty and preserves the Singapore exchange's special relationship with the CME. If SIMEX has a vested interest in the system, its large open interest in Eurodollars could even help 'jump start' GLOBEX in Asia. However, there is little movement in that direction.

Capturing Japanese business is one of the main objectives of GLOBEX. The Japanese Finance Ministry announced in May 1990 that it would permit GLOBEX terminals in Japan, but has not set regulatory guidelines for their use. The key issue, according to a GLOBEX official, is whether Japanese financial firms — which have been able to have offshore futures accounts since 1987 — will be able to use these accounts to trade with GLOBEX in Japan. If not, and GLOBEX trades are then subject to domestic futures guidelines, such as the inability of brokers to return profits until positions are closed, the CME/CBOT/Reuters system will lose its competitive advantage in Japan.

Clearly, the Japanese Finance Ministry would like to protect its domestic futures markets — particularly TIFFE — against GLOBEX. The TSE adamantly opposes GLOBEX, and has upgraded its computer systems to give its trading screens 24-hour capability. In contrast, Osaka has expressed some interest in joining GLOBEX but its smaller member firms are balking. The OSE's Nikkei futures and options would enhance GLOBEX's popularity during European and American GLOBEX hours, which are 7:00 p.m. to 7:00 a.m. in New York time and 12:00 a.m. to 12:00 p.m. in London time. TIFFE has also expressed its interest in joining GLOBEX.

GLOBEX may be the most ambitious new trading technology in the global derivative scene, but much of Asia is upgrading and innovating to keep pace with such changes. The Sydney Futures Exchange (SFE), the region's second largest futures market, has negotiated to join GLOBEX, but has not made a commitment because of regulatory concerns in Australia and its desire to pursue its own computerized system. The Sydney Computerized Overnight Market (SYCOM) was launched in November 1989 with one contract (10-Year Commonwealth Treasury bond futures) and added three more in early 1990 (3-Year Commonwealth Treasury bond, 90-Day Bank Bill and All Ordinaries index futures). Although trading volume has been light, SYCOM has had a positive response from users. The New Zealand Futures and Options Exchange (NZFOE) has been screen-based from its inception, and its ATS II system is compatible with several markets in Europe, making future linkages possible, particularly if its merger with a larger exchange goes through.

Besides the TSE, Osaka trades its derivative products through fully computerized systems as well. The TIFFE upgraded its telephone dealing system in June 1991 and is now automated. Thus, by 1992 most Japanese financial futures and options exchange could theoretically join global networks or create their own. A combination of the two routes is one probable outcome.

Regulatory Liberalization and New Openings

The environment for new exchanges, GLOBEX, and other foreign-based screen systems will be determined by the evolving regulatory patterns in the region. Market liberalization will also open many new sources of business for the industry.

Just as the Japanese Finance Ministry has yet to set final procedures for GLOBEX, other regulatory bodies are evaluating screen-based trading within their jurisdictions. Hong Kong's Securities and Futures Commission, which succeeded in restructuring the Hong Kong Futures Exchange and reinforcing the colony's financial safeguards, has not yet decided whether to allow another market into its domain. The Monetary Authority of Singapore has indicated that it would consider GLOBEX terminals in the city-state as a separate exchange, and therefore require new authorization under the Futures Trading Act — unless, of course, GLOBEX brings the SIMEX into the system. Australian and New Zealand regulators may be amenable to foreign systems since both have indigenous computerized trading.

Despite hesitancy about new trading technology's impact on national control, the general Asian-Pacific regulatory trend has been toward further liberalization. For example, Taiwan has moved to legitimize brokerage activity and crack down on bucket shops. The island had a huge underground futures industry which sent abroad 30,000 to 50,000 trades per day. The Taiwanese Ministry of Economic Affairs submitted a bill to the Legislature which would set up a regulatory structure. The bill passed its first regulatory hudle in October 1990, and the second in early 1991. Asian industry leaders expect greatly increased Taiwanese business to flow to regional exchanges and those in Europe and the U.S.

Taiwan, a small and rich nation, has an extraordinarily high level of public speculation. About 20% of the population has a stock account and the Taipei Stock Exchange has the world's second highest turnover, even after its 64% drop between February and July of 1990. This volatility has sparked the recognition of the need for risk management tools. Taiwanese academics have already begun reasearch on a Taipei equity index future.

The Korean Stock Exchange, which also suffered a major drop of about 23% in 1990, has already identified the desirability of such instruments. In preparation for Seoul's scheduled market liberalization in early 1992, the exchange has established an automated equity trading systems and has entertained proposals for stock index futures. The opening of the Korean financial system will surely provide regional futures exchanges with a major new source of business.

Chinese entities — both People's Republic of China agencies operating abroad and domestic enterprises — are taking a higher profile in Asian and worldwide futures exchanges. The People's Republic has begun setting up their own commodity markets. The HKFE and CBOT have conducted many educational and advisory programs in China. In June 1990, China's Minister of Commerce approved the formation of a wheat cash market in Henan province. This appears to be a precursor to a futures market, and the Chinese are expected to be major futures players before they absorb Hong Kong in 1997.

The "emerging NICs" of Indonesia, Malaysia and Thailand have become larger and more sophisticated economies. Therefore their need for financial futures markets will arise. Both the Kuala Lumpur Commodities Exchange and a new exchange, the Kuala Lumpur Options and Financial Futures Exchange (KLOFFE), are hoping to lauch stock index futures. Malaysian equities have been very actively traded in Kuala Lumpur since their dual listing in Singapore was discouraged in early 1990. Significant financial liberalization and stock market expansion has also been occurring in Thailand and Indonesia. These rapidly growing countries will become another source of business for the region's derivative markets, particularly their closest neighbor, Singapore.

Innovation Still Critical

The entry of new participants from previously underdeveloped markets greatly expands potential financial futures market activities in Asia. But business will not flow automatically. To succeed in this new environment, the industry must adapt. The movement toward screen-based trading and computerized decision-making could be regarded as a paradigm shift — a whole new way of looking at the markets. Participants who do not recognize this qualitative change will be left behind even as economic and regulatory trends become more favorable.

Although the contours of the Asian Pacific derivative market are shifting, many of the paths to success remain the same. Innovation — by exchanges, brokers, traders, and customers — remains the key to survival in a dynamic environment. Although many of the new developments will be in trading systems, product innovation is equally essential for exchanges to thrive in the 1990s.

Exchanges will need to maintain rapid responsiveness to their users' needs. For example, a shortage of Australian government bonds developed in 1989, threatening the SFE's flagship contract. In response, the Sydney Futures Exchange created a hybrid futures contract. Futures on semi-government bonds, which are debt issued by Australian state governments, preserved Sydney's market niche and expanded its yield curve coverage.

SIMEX has been similarly refocusing its efforts to develop a strong franchise in its interest rate and energy complex and to gear its new contracts toward Singapore's strengths as a liability management and oil trading center. SIMEX's new Dubai and Fuel oil contracts, and its Euroyen futures options and Euromark futures are the indicators of this strategy.

The HKFE also attempted to focus on interest rates with its Hong Kong Interbank Offered Rate (HIBOR) futures contract. Launched in 1990, its first new product in four years was aimed at demonstrating to the international futures trading community that Hong Kong was still a progressive financial center. The new contract was designed to attract bank and other institutional activity. However, HIBOR was not an initial success, and the HKFE has now turned its attention to Hang Seng sub-index equity futures and index and stock options.

The power of innovation is most visible in Japan. In what was perceived as a David-versus-Goliath battle, the Osaka Securities Exchange took the pioneering steps to introduce equity derivatives in mid-1987. The TSE behemoth, with its huge resources and its natural geographical and institutional advantages, has been unable to catch up. It has now fallen far behind in both stock index futures and options, and may even have stumbled so badly as to have given the OSE an equal chance when options on individual equities are introduced in 1992.

The Asia-Pacific region, with a growing and increasingly affluent population base, indigenous companies moving into the top tier of global competitiveness, and increasing financial strength and sophistication, provides an ideal environment for derivative markets. The financial futures and options exchanges that continue to innovate − with new products, new technologies, and new sources of business − will undoubtedly thrive in the 1990s and beyond.

Endnotes

1.   For a detailed discussion of the risk/return benefits of global equity investing, see Keith K.H. Park, "Reduction of Risk and Enhancement of Return through Global Equity Diversification," The Global Equity Markets, (Probus Publishing 1991), p.3-15.

2.   For a detailed discussion of 10-Year JGB futures listed on the Chicago Board of Trade, see CHAPTER 3: JAPANESE DERIVATIVES LISTED IN THE U.S.

3.   Michael Howell, "International Equity Flows 1990 Edition: New Investors, New Risks and New Products," Salomon Brothers Inc, August 1990.

CHAPTER **2**

JAPAN –
THE ASIAN GIANT AWAKENS

Overview of the Japanese
Futures and Options Markets

Introduction

Within the Asia-Pacific region, the Japanese futures and options markets have come the furthest in the shortest amount of time. A new attitude of innovation, combined with enormous latent demand, has built the foundation for Asia's pre-eminent futures and options trading center. Japanese financial prowess is now expanding to derivative products as stock exchanges and financial institutions shift into high gear.

Until the second half of the 1980s, regulatory approval had not been granted for Japanese institutions to trade financial futures. Less than four years later, Japan emerged as a major player in the world futures industry. By the early 1990s, it has already become home to some of the most actively-traded financial futures and options contracts in the world. In addition, the increasing sophistication and capability of its budding futures industry is becoming a global force to be reckoned with.

The Japanese started gingerly in the early 1980s, studying foreign markets and domestic needs. Cautious Ministry of Finance bureaucrats and intraminister-ial consensus-building held back innovation. External pressure and the interna-tionalization of Japanese financial markets sped up the usual glacial pace of deregulation. Since then, the Japanese have moved with surprising speed and characteristic aggressiveness to develop new markets and products.

Japanese firms are now able to act as direct brokers for overseas business, and many anticipate an expanding flow of two-way activities. Japanese and for-eign exchanges, financial institutions, regulators, and investors are all scrambling to keep pace with the rapid changes. The 1990s promises to be the decade of Japan's emergence on the world futures and options scene.

Expanding Market Structure

Japan's first experiment with financial futures began in October 1985, when the Tokyo Stock Exchange listed 10-year Japanese government bond futures. After a shaky start, the market took off and became a vibrant component of the Tokyo debt market. Liberalization gained momentum in May 1987, when Japanese financial firms were allowed to deal for their own account in overseas futures markets. Since then, barriers have fallen rapidly, and firms and exchanges have steadily gained wider opportunities to dabble with new products.

In September 1988, the Tokyo Stock Exchange (TSE) and Osaka Securities Exchange (OSE) introduced cash-settled index futures — Tokyo Stock Price Index (Topix) and Nikkei Stock Average (Nikkei 225) futures. In mid-1989, nonfinancial corporations were allowed to use futures abroad. In June 1989, the OSE listed Nikkei 225 index options, and a new financial futures exchange, the Tokyo International Financial Futures Exchange (TIFFE), was inaugurated in Tokyo. Later the same year, the TSE and the Nagoya Stock Exchange (NSE) launched index options — Topix options and the Nagoya Option 25. Also, Japanese securities firms and banks were allowed to act as brokers for overseas futures business. This breathtaking expansion had quickly put Japan high up in the ranks of the world's derivative markets.

The Ministry of Finance's key decision, however, was to vertically integrate regulatory authority between cash and futures instruments. This followed exhaustive studies of America's 1987 stock market crash, and major "turf-battles" within the Ministry of Finance. The Ministry's Securities Bureau now reigns over stock index and bond futures and options, and the equity and long-term debt markets. Similarly, in addition to its traditional responsibility for short-term interest rates and interbank foreign exchange deals, the Ministry's Banking Bureau supervises the Tokyo International Financial Futures Exchange (TIFFE) which lists money market as well as currency futures.

This "gentlemen's agreement" has settled the basic issue of which exchanges can list which products, and which institutions can trade or broker new instruments. The general framework of a large and diverse futures industry is already visible. From one exchange trading one futures contract in late 1985, Japan has grown to four exchanges trading 12 different futures and options products by the early 1990s. (See Table 1 for currently-traded futures and options contracts in Japan.) Moreover, despite ambitious goals for their markets, most of the new products have become active and healthy.

Table 1: Currently-Traded Futures and Options Contracts in Japan and Their Exchanges

Contracts	Exchange
1. Nikkei 225 Index Futures	OSE
2. Nikkei 225 Index Options	OSE
3. Topix Index Futures	TSE
4. Topix Index Options	TSE
5. Nagoya Options 25	NSE
6. 10-year Japanese Government Bond Futures	TSE
7. Options on 10-year JGB Futures	TSE
8. 20-year JGB Futures	TSE
9. 10-year U.S. Treasury Bond Futures	TSE
10. 3-month Euroyen Futures	TIFFE
11. 3-month Eurodollar Futures	TIFFE
12. Japanese Yen-U.S. Dollar Currency Futures	TIFFE

Japanese Equity Futures and Options Contracts

Battle of the Index Futures

The Tokyo Stock Exchange is best known for its enormous equity market, and this is the arena for which it has the most potential for derivative products. However, despite its overwhelming advantage in the cash market, the TSE has not become the dominant index futures market. The TSE is attempting to build on its moderately successful Topix stock index futures with a cash Topix option, but is having numerous difficulties.

Topix is the acronym for the TSE's First Section index, the Tokyo Stock Price Index, which is a composite of all 1,108 larger, more established companies in the exchange's First Section. While less well-known than the Nikkei Stock Price Average, which consists of 225 top-rated Japanese companies listed in the First Section of the TSE, Topix was the performance benchmark used by most fund managers and institutions before the introduction of futures.

The cash-settled futures on Topix were launched in September 1988 and have been a success since their introduction. In their first year of trading, the daily average volume was close to 15,000 lots per day, with open interest at about 30,000 contracts. A significant deepening of the market occurred in mid-1989 as longer-term investors began participating. Growth slowed in 1990, and volume has leveled off to about 10,000 lots/day. Average month-end open interest for the April 1990-April 1991 period was below 10,000 contracts.

The TSE does not have this vibrant field to itself. A rival contract on the popular Nikkei 225 index was launched at the same time in 1988 by the Osaka Securities Exchange (OSE). The OSE was Japan's pioneer of equity derivatives, having introduced a physically-settled "Stock Futures 50" contract in June 1987. Although now obsolete and inactive, "Stock Futures 50" boosted the exchange's reputation and brought new domestic and foreign participants to the OSE.

The OSE's Nikkei contract thus started with a solid base of users, and has been extremely successful, challenging the Topix futures for the largest volume contract in Japan, and eventually, prevailing. Osaka led in both volume and open interest for the first three months, but its open interest fell behind in early 1989. But from mid-1989 and onwards, the Osaka Nikkei open interest has pulled steadily ahead — see Chart 1 for month-end open interests of the Nikkei 225 and Topix futures. Nikkei volume surpassed the Topix's in June 1989, and it has maintained its lead ever since, averaging over 20,000 lots per day after its first year of trading. In 1990 Osaka Nikkei's activity surged dramatically, and the contract was the most actively traded stock index future in the world. Daily average volume for the April 1990-April 1991 period was 75,000 lots, and by early 1991, open interest was approaching 200,000 contracts (see Chart 2 for the daily average trading values of the Nikkei and Topix index futures).

This competition, plus the existence of a small but well-established Nikkei futures market in Singapore, has broadened users choices and expanded trading opportunities. The interexchange rivalry — and even fiercer corporate market share competition — has given dealers much incentive to cross trade, so it is difficult to determine how much of the volume is real. While most observers agree that the percentage of customer business has increased since the first few months, it still remains relatively small.

In the first six months of trading, securities firms' proprietary deals accounted for about 90 percent of the Topix and Osaka Nikkei volumes, and never fell below 80 percent. Close to half of this activity is cross trading, particularly among the Japanese securities houses. Market share is the prime motivation, but there are also technical considerations. As in the Japanese government bond futures, traders often cross order to free up margin money.

Chart 1:   Month End Open Interest of Osaka Nikkei and Topix Futures

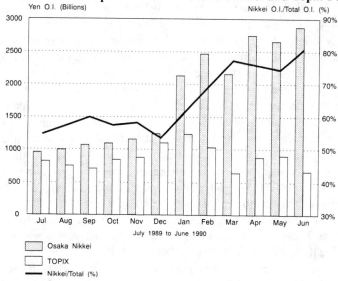

July 1989 to June 1990

Osaka Nikkei

TOPIX

Nikkei/Total (%)

Source: Goldman, Sachs (Japan) Corp.

Chart 2:   Average Daily Trading Value of Osaka Nikkei and Topix Futures

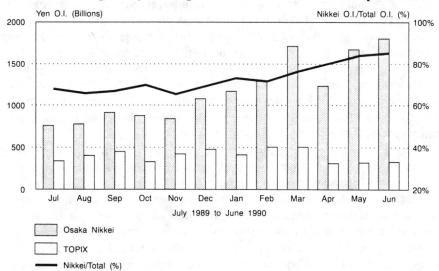

July 1989 to June 1990

Osaka Nikkei

TOPIX

Nikkei/Total (%)

Source: Goldman, Sachs (Japan) Corp.

Securities firms dealings also include index arbitrage activities. Foreign houses dominated this area early in the contracts' history. Until March 1989, Japanese firms were at a great disadvantage in cash/futures arbitrage, because of the formal and informal guidelines regarding the transactions in the shares undergoing financing—for example, Eurobond issues. Foreign securities firms took advantage of this wide open field and often found lucrative mispricings.

The playing field is now more level, and Japanese securities firms are free to trade any stocks for arbitrage purpose. The restrictions against short-selling have been eased, which has resulted in a more stable basis relationship. Also, the expiration procedures were modified so that settlement is based on the next day's opening price, as a means of eliminating expiration volatility. Although the Japanese houses still lag behind the three biggest American index arbitrageurs in Japan (Salomon Brothers, Morgan Stanley and Goldman Sachs), they have been steadily refining their trading techniques.

Even discounting arbitrage activities, which help check the one-sided nature of Japanese investors, around 40 percent of the first year's turnover in the stock index futures contracts was estimated to be artificial. An indicator of the depth of the market is the relative percentage of brokerage orders. By mid-1989, they had doubled over late 1988, to about 18 percent, much of this increase is the result of banks entering the market; and a good deal of their trading was wash deals.

This situation began to change toward late 1989, as institutional end users—trust funds, insurance companies, investment managers, and nonfinancial corporations, as well as banks began to participate more. The total non-member trading volume grew from less than 10 percent to as high as 60% in October 1990, and in early 1991 accounted for over 40% of activity of trading. Foreign customer orders have also grown and might rapidly expand if the Commodities Futures Trading Commission (CFTC) of the U.S. passes a "no action" ruling on the two contracts, which would allow U.S. institutional investors to trade them directly. (See Table 2A, 2B and 2C for the trading volumes of Nikkei index futures and options by types of investors.)

Since early December 1990, Japanese stock index futures have been consistently overpriced in comparison with the arbitrage-based futures valuation model which bases the fair value of stock index futures on stock index value, present value of expected dividend, and risk free interest rate. Given the substantial drop in Japanese equities in 1990, Japanese investors seem to be buying stock index futures based upon their future expectation that the Japanese equity market will significantly recover in 1991—the arbitrage-based theoretical futures price does not take into account future expectation directly into its valuation. Another theory holds that investors are holding positions in the futures instead of cash because of their lower costs, thus creating price inefficiencies. In any case, the currently richly-priced Japanese stock index futrues have presented U.S. investment banks such as Salomon Brothers and Morgan Stanley with a lucrative opportunity for stock index arbitrage. For example on January 25th 1991, such outstanding arbitrage totaled Yen846 billion ($6.5 billion) and involved the trading of 773 million shares.

Nikkei futures have not only grown relative to other index futures in Japan and around the world, but also when compared with the underlying Japanese stock market. In early 1990, the trading value of Nikkei futures first surpassed that of equities trading value on the TSE 1st section, and there has been no turning back. By late 1990, futures actively had a value two times greater than the cash market's, and in early 1991, it was often 3 or 4 times greater.

This rapid growth is even more impressive when one notes that it occured as Japanese regulatory authorities and exchanges burdened the futures contracts with more and more restrictions and higher costs in an attempt to limit the effect of futures activity on the underlying cash market. Beginning in August 1990, initial and maintenence margin rates were increased, and in a step likened to placing the market in wet concrete, the speed at which prices could move in a given 6 minute period was reduced, being in effect a time/price limit superimposed on existing limits. Two months later, trading hours were shortened, and in February 1991, margins were again raised.

It can be expected that the Ministry of Finance will continue to react to equity market volatility by slapping restrictions on derivative markets. But given recent experience it will neither affect cash market volatility nor stop the growth and maturation of Japan's vibrant stock index futures market.

New Options for Investors

Many Japanese finanial players remain wary of futures, both out of myths from the stock market crash of 1987 and cautious senior management attitudes. It is these investors as well as overseas fund managers and individuals who are attracted to options. The demand for Japanese index options could potentially dwarf that for the futures. The huge Japanese equity warrant market — particularly, the index warrants which have become popular in Tokyo and London since 1987 and the U.S. and Canada since 1990 — indicates a wide investor interest.

Japanese exchanges decided to list cash options instead of options on the existing futures contracts. Options are perceived as a safer way to hedge, and since the exchanges were trying to attract a new category of users, there was little reason to confuse the issue with options on futures. The Ministry of Finance also expressed a preference for cash options.

Table 2A: Nikkei Stock Average Futures Trading Volume by Type of Investors

1990	Jan.	Feb.	March	April	May	June	July	August	Sept.	Total
Member's Own Account	912,644 68.86%	894,527 62.61%	1,255,935 62.16%	1,096,284 63.83%	1,536,608 65.61%	1,507,138 65.77%	1,463,207 63.05%	1,493,650 49.84%	1,074,989 41.06%	11,234,982 58.94%
Insurance Companies	28,047 2.12%	20,035 1.40%	51,800 2.56%	53,873 3.14%	83,266 3.56%	89,824 3.92%	92,818 4.00%	118,541 3.96%	132,804 5.07%	671,008 3.52%
Banks	213,461 16.10%	299,812 20.98%	407,966 20.19%	264,172 15.38%	330,812 14.13%	399,151 17.42%	445,292 19.19%	730,149 24.36%	875,200 33.43%	3,966,015 20.81%
Other Financial Institutions	8,749 0.66%	9,226 0.65%	14,136 0.70%	11,046 0.64%	18,043 0.77%	11,552 0.50%	8,566 0.37%	21,605 0.72%	20,497 0.78%	123,420 0.65%
Investment Trust Co.	38,395 2.90%	43,644 3.05%	55,510 2.75%	52,571 3.06%	51,168 2.18%	48,718 2.13%	45,632 1.97%	143,469 4.79%	124,087 4.74%	603,194 3.16%
Business Corporations	36,255 2.74%	44,791 3.14%	77,524 3.84%	80,797 4.70%	125,649 5.37%	92,178 4.02%	96,511 4.16%	164,110 5.48%	148,826 5.69%	866,641 4.55%
Other Corporations	7,706 0.58%	7,263 0.51%	16,051 0.79%	22,678 1.32%	24,251 1.04%	16,276 0.71%	9,933 0.43%	20,428 0.68%	13,618 0.52%	138,204 0.73%
Securities Companies	5,419 0.41%	5,322 0.37%	10,580 0.52%	9,691 0.56%	14,119 0.60%	9,311 0.41%	17,516 0.75%	34,324 1.15%	39,283 1.50%	145,565 0.76%
Individuals	4,590 0.35%	5,014 0.35%	10,317 0.51%	13,297 0.77%	16,869 0.72%	11,379 0.50%	8,475 0.37%	13,574 0.45%	13,103 0.50%	96,618 0.51%
Foreigner	70,187 5.30%	99,086 6.94%	120,586 5.97%	113,124 6.59%	141,123 6.03%	105,858 4.62%	132,809 5.72%	257,218 8.58%	175,423 6.70%	1,215,414 6.38%
Total	1,325,453 100.0%	1,428,720 100.0%	2,020,405 100.0%	1,717,533 100.0%	2,341,908 100.0%	2,291,385 100.0%	2,320,759 100.0%	2,997,068 100.0%	2,617,830 100.0%	19,061,061 100.0%

*The amount of agency transactions by non-integrated securities companies excluded.
*This table is compiled from figures reported on the basis of weekly total (purchase and sales).
*The total volume of a week which ranges over two months is reckoned in date for the month which includes a majority of the trading days of the week.
Source: The Osaka Securities Exchange.

Table 2B: Nikkei Stock Average Put Options Trading Volume by Type of Investors

1990	Jan.	Feb.	March	April	May	June	July	August	Sept.	Total
Member's Own Account	530,162 75.16%	519,409 74.43%	357,460 74.09%	343,052 79.61%	502,205 82.20%	587,994 81.97%	736,884 80.86%	543,732 66.08%	391,011 57.67%	4,511,869 74.49%
Insurance Companies	5,360 0.76%	6,286 0.90%	3,474 0.72%	3,550 0.82%	2,733 0.45%	3,642 0.51%	4,130 0.45%	6,693 0.81%	8,003 1.18%	43,871 0.72%
Banks	53,357 7.56%	50,453 7.23%	29,172 6.05%	20,684 4.80%	26,386 4.32%	28,578 3.98%	35,888 3.94%	64,138 7.80%	87,771 12.95%	396,427 6.54%
Other Financial Institutions	834 0.12%	1,275 0.18%	596 0.12%	928 0.22%	1,314 0.22%	766 0.11%	929 0.10%	1,910 0.23%	1,515 0.22%	10,067 0.17%
Investment Trust Co.	7,787 1.10%	8,581 1.23%	2,824 0.59%	1,390 0.32%	1,762 0.29%	2,813 0.39%	2,295 0.25%	8,179 0.99%	5,418 0.80%	41,049 0.68%
Business Corporations	33,384 4.73%	34,353 4.92%	33,550 6.95%	18,953 4.40%	36,676 6.00%	42,703 5.95%	69,026 7.57%	78,662 9.56%	70,189 10.35%	417,496 6.89%
Other Corporations	1,625 0.23%	2,790 0.40%	1,698 0.35%	758 0.18%	1,429 0.23%	2,005 0.28%	1,941 0.21%	5,527 0.67%	5,423 0.80%	23,196 0.38%
Securities Companies	3,294 0.47%	3,053 0.44%	5,870 1.22%	3,503 0.81%	3,367 0.55%	4,007 0.56%	7,071 0.78%	9,497 1.15%	5,481 0.81%	45,143 0.75%
Individuals	25,785 3.66%	19,139 2.74%	12,564 2.60%	11,911 2.76%	15,891 2.60%	19,850 2.77%	18,638 2.05%	32,175 3.91%	32,403 4.78%	188,356 3.11%
Foreigner	43,761 6.20%	52,483 7.52%	35,253 7.31%	26,201 6.08%	19,227 3.15%	25,002 3.49%	34,508 3.79%	72,281 8.78%	70,806 10.44%	379,522 6.27%
Total	705,349 100.0%	697,822 100.0%	482,461 100.0%	430,930 100.0%	610,990 100.0%	717,360 100.0%	911,270 100.0%	822,794 100.0%	678,020 100.0%	6,056,996 100.0%

*The amount of agency transactions by non-integrated securities companies excluded.
*This table is compiled from figures reported on the basis of weekly total (purchase and sales).
*The total volume of a week which ranges over two months is reckoned in date for the month which includes a majority of the trading days of the week.
Source: The Osaka Securities Exhange.

Table 2C: Nikkei Stock Average Call Options Trading Volume by Type of Investors

1990	Jan.	Feb.	March	April	May	June	July	August	Sept.	Total
Member's Own Account	560,059 77.70%	618,942 73.13%	655,864 82.31%	794,556 84.70%	729,020 81.85%	531,742 79.35%	600,313 78.20%	867,590 74.14%	515,765 63.82%	5,873,851 77.20%
Insurance Companies	2,192 0.30%	4,597 0.54%	5,514 0.69%	6,145 0.66%	1,906 0.21%	6,599 0.98%	7,316 0.95%	8,022 0.69%	6,010 0.74%	48,301 0.63%
Banks	48,830 6.77%	62,874 7.43%	30,659 3.85%	30,955 3.30%	30,691 3.45%	24,091 3.58%	23,871 3.11%	62,828 5.37%	83,345 10.31%	398,072 5.23%
Other Financial Instititions	890 0.12%	1,323 0.16%	1,193 0.15%	1,851 0.20%	1,181 0.13%	1,866 0.28%	2,228 0.29%	2,778 0.24%	2,899 0.36%	16,209 0.21%
Investment Trust Co.	15,224 2.11%	22,120 2.61%	9,678 1.21%	4,523 0.48%	4,182 0.47%	2,689 0.40%	4,862 0.63%	8,096 0.69%	5,934 0.73%	77,308 1.02%
Business Corporations	36,777 5.10%	57,692 6.82%	35,391 4.44%	43,455 4.63%	63,611 7.14%	53,986 8.06%	69,592 9.06%	101,266 8.65%	85,472 10.58%	547,242 7.19%
Other Corporations	2,286 0.32%	4,076 0.48%	3,457 0.43%	4,566 0.49%	2,554 0.29%	2,043 0.30%	2,271 0.30%	6,052 0.52%	11,175 1.38%	38,480 0.51%
Securities Companies	779 0.11%	4,182 0.49%	4,844 0.61%	5,211 0.56%	5,166 0.58%	3,365 0.50%	5,814 0.76%	8,089 0.69%	6,472 0.80%	43,922 0.58%
Individuals	34,423 4.78%	40,840 4.83%	26,288 3.30%	25,868 2.76%	30,047 3.37%	23,903 3.57%	25,382 3.31%	45,467 3.89%	48,000 5.94%	300,218 3.95%
Foreigner	19,311 2.68%	29,728 3.51%	23,911 3.00%	20,981 2.24%	22,330 2.51%	19,908 2.97%	26,055 3.39%	60,042 5.13%	43,106 5.33%	265,372 3.49%
Total	720,771 100.0%	846,374 100.0%	796,799 100.0%	938,111 100.0%	890,688 100.0%	670,120 100.0%	767,704 100.0%	1,170,230 100.0%	808,178 100.0%	7,608,975 100.0%

*The amount of agency transactions by non-integrated securities companies excluded.
*This table is compiled from figures reported on the basis of weekly total (purchase and sales).
*The total volume of a week which ranges over two months is reckoned in date for the month which includes a majority of the trading days of the week.
Source: The Osaka Securities Exchange.

As with its Stock Futures 50, the Osaka Securities Exchange was again at the vanguard of equity derivatives in Japan. It launched Nikkei 225 index options in June 1989, four months ahead of the Tokyo Stock Exchange. The value of the cash options is calculated in the same way as the Nikkei futures—1,000 yen times the Nikkei 225 index. Four consecutive months are listed with strike prices at intervals of 500 Nikkei points. The options are a unique modified American style: they can be exercised before expiration, but only on a designated day, (Thursday), each week. The minimum margin for sellers is also the same as the Nikkei futures, at 25 percent of the contract value or six million yen, whichever is greater. Trading was initially on the OSE floor, but a computerized dealing system was brought on-line during the first year of trading.

Many users have questioned the near-term bias created by the four-monthly-options series, and the initial trading has born out of these fears. On most days, only the nearby expiration month trades consistently. Yet, this has not dampened institutional enthusiasm for the options, especially since brokers are able to provide quotes for back months upon request. Others have complained about unusual exercise procedures and the inherent uncertainties of a contract where the trading stops prior to expiration. The steep margin requirement for writers was also questioned, particularly since customer cross-margining with futures positions is banned.

Despite the various shortcomings of the options market structure in Japan, activity has been buoyant from the inception. Most foreigners have accepted the quirks as more of the idiosyncrasies of doing business in Japan. A number of "gaijin" (foreign) firms joined as Special Members of the OSE for futures and options trading. Such firms as Baring Securities and Salomon Brothers who made an early commitment have benefited immensely.

Osaka's Nikkei options have developed into a healthy market with a broad mix of institutional users and retail customers. It has also served as a training ground for trust and other investment funds to explore new strategies. By the end of 1989, two more index options were launched in Japan: the Topix option on the TSE, and the Option 25 at the Nagoya Stock Exchange. Whereas the TSE's Topix options—listed on October 20, 1989—were expected to eventually capture half of the index options market, the NSE's new institutional options were thought to have a slim chance to carve out even a narrow market niche. To the surprise of market analysts, however, the Topix options faltered badly. The Option 25, which initially established only a small niche, has since surpassed Topix options activity. (See Chart 3).

The Topix options—like Osaka's Nikkei—have the same value as the futures contracts, but are based on the cash index. They are also of a modified American style, and have a 25 percent margin for writers. Four consecutive

Chart 3:   Nikkei, Topix, and Nagoya Options

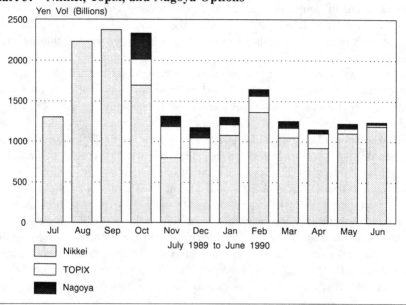

months are listed at any one time, and commissions are fixed on the same sched-ule as Osaka's options.

Japanese market participants expected huge interest for the Topix options, since Topix was the primary benchmark index for the majority of portfolio man-agers. However, Osaka's four month headstart had given it an important lead in depth and liquidity. Moreover, institutions' greater familiarity with the Nikkei index futures has enabled the Nikkei options to upstage the Topix contract. The TSE's huge equity turnover did not insure Tokyo the majority of Japan's index options activity. By late 1990, Topix option daily average volume and month-end open interest sunk below 1,000 contracts. The products' lackluster perfor-mance has been a great disappointment to the TSE.

The Nagoya Stock Exchange, Japan's third largest stock exchange, has had a similarly difficult time, but eventually eked out a minor victory. The NSE, which lags far behind Osaka in equity turnover, made a desperate bid for some of the new derivative activities. It spent about four billion yen to develop a new index of widely-traded, large market-capitalization shares. Dubbed "Option 25," it is modeled roughly on the American Stock Exchange's Major Market Index options, and is designed to be useful to institutional investors. It was launched on October 17, 1989.

Nagoya exchange officials hope to differentiate their product and carve out a market share for large hedgers. The option is therefore European-style in the hope that the lower premium will attract buyers. The other contract specifications are similar to the Topix options. In fact, the NSE bases its index calculations on TSE stock quotes.

Nagoya options activity has disproved the exchange's skeptics, and has kept alive hopes for long-term survival. A number of institutions have found the contracts useful hedging and trading tools, and by early 1991, volume and open interest doubled that of Topix options. (See Chart 3 for the average daily trading values of the Nikkei, Topix and Nagoya index options.)

One caveat for trading the Nikkei and Topix futures and options is that because they are traded through computerized trading systems, traders should be aware that the frequent pauses in trading — and occasional lock-ups — occur in the stock index futures and options contracts. Electronic trading tends to function smoothly in normal market environments, but exhibits serious structural weaknesses at times of market stress. The presence of the on-screen market makers with their bids and offers cannot be guaranteed in an extremely volatile market.

Nikkei Stock Average Futures

Exchange: The Osaka Securities Exchange.

Contract Unit: 1,000 yen times the Nikkei Stock Average (Nikkei 225).

The Nikkei Stock Average: Like the Dow Jones Industrial Average, the Nikkei index is a price-weighted index. It consists of 225 top-rated Japanese companies listed in the First Section of the the Tokyo Stock Exchange.[1]

While the 225 component shares represent some 19 percent of the TSE First Section issues, they account for some 57 percent of the TSE First Section's total trading volume and 51 percent of its total market capitalization.

The calculation of Nikkei 225 began on May 16, 1949, when the TSE was reopened after the second world war. Currently, the Nikkei 225 index is calculated by Nihon Keizai Shimbun, Inc. (NKS), a Japanese financial information services firm. The value of Nikkei 225 is disseminated at 60-second intervals during the trading hours. Any change in the Nikkei 225 is

Contract Months: A cycle of March, June, September, and December. Five contract months are listed at all times.

Minimum Fluctuation: Ten (10) points per the Nikkei Stock Average.

Value of Minimum Fluctuation: 10,000 yen

Daily Price Limit: +/– 900 points if the futures price is between 20,000 and 30,000. 1,2000 points if it is between 30,000 and 40,000.

Last Day of Trading: The business day immediately prior to the second Friday (or, the preceding Thursday if the second Friday is a holiday) of the contract month. The trading in a new contract month begins on the business day following the last trading day of the just-expired contract month.

Settlement Date: The fourth business day following the last trading day of the just-expired contract month.

Margin Requirement for Customers: The margin has to be deposited by the customer to the regular member or special participant of the OSE by 12:00 P.M. of the third business day from the day of sale or purchase of the contract. The amount of the margin shall be 25 percent or more of the contract value. The minimum amount of the margin shall be six million yen.

Margin Requirement for Members: The amount of the margin shall be 20 percent or more of the contract value calculated on the basis of the first settlement price of each contract month. For each opening sale or purchase, the margin shall be deposited with the OSE by 12:00 P.M. of the fourth business day from the day of the said opening sale or purchase.

Trading Hours: 9:00 A.M. to 11:00 A.M.; 12:30 P.M. to 3:10 P.M. (On half-trading days, trading hours are 9:00 A.M. to 11:15 A.M. only.)

Method of Trading: A computerized trading system.

Table 3: Brokerage Commission Rates for Nikkei 225 Futures

Contract Value	Commission Rate
Up to 100 million yen	0.04%
Over 100 million yen and up to 300 million yen	0.03% + 10,000 yen
Over 300 million yen and up to 500 million yen	0.02% + 40,000 yen
Over 500 million yen and up to 1 billion yen	0.01% + 90,000 yen
Over 1 billion yen	0.005% + 140,000,000 yen

Table 4A: Trading Volume of Nikkei Stock Average Futures

	1985	1986	1987	1988	1989	1990
January	n/l*	n/l	n/l	n/l	390,142	607,484
February	n/l	n/l	n/l	n/l	310,142	680,491
March	n/l	n/l	n/l	n/l	419,890	1,118,468
April	n/l	n/l	n/l	n/l	358,619	864,548
May	n/l	n/l	n/l	n/l	414,545	1,119,396
June	n/l	n/l	n/l	n/l	460,323	1,207,803
July	n/l	n/l	n/l	n/l	472,476	1,295,198
August	n/l	n/l	n/l	n/l	517,530	1,386,897
September	n/l	n/l	n/l	560,319	537,598	1,319,125
October	n/l	n/l	n/l	401,368	518,882	
November	n/l	n/l	n/l	441,803	453,313	
December	n/l	n/l	n/l	488,904	579,187	
Average	n/l	n/l	n/l	473,099	453,554	
Total	n/l	n/l	n/l	1,892,394	5,442,647	

Table 4B: Open Interest of Nikkei 225 Index Futures

	1985	1986	1987	1988	1989	1990
January	n/l	n/l	n/l	n/l	15,043	57,003
February	n/l	n/l	n/l	n/l	17,072	72,841
March	n/l	n/l	n/l	n/l	17,177	77,382
April	n/l	n/l	n/l	n/l	18,250	91,770
May	n/l	n/l	n/l	n/l	22,647	80,482
June	n/l	n/l	n/l	n/l	28,507	88,821
July	n/l	n/l	n/l	n/l	27,761	92,766
August	n/l	n/l	n/l	n/l	29,056	144,567
September	n/l	n/l	n/l	13,506	30,186	161,045
October	n/l	n/l	n/l	15,756	30,786	
November	n/l	n/l	n/l	14,826	31,757	
December	n/l	n/l	n/l	14,837	33,063	
Average	n/l	n/l	n/l	14,731	25,106	

*Not Listed
(1) Trading of Topix futures began on September 3, 1988.
(2) Open Interest is as of the end of each month.
(3) Open Interest of an expiring contract month is included up to the day preceding the settlement date of that contract month.
(4) Open Interest is calculated by counting the net number of futures contracts which remain liquidated by additional offsetting transactions or by physical deliver after taking account of matched but as yet unsettled bought and sold contracts.

Source: The Osaka Securities Exchange

Nikkei Stock Average Options

Exchange: The Osaka Securities Exchange.

Contract: Call and put options based on the Nikkei Stock Average (Nikkei 225).

Contract Unit: 1,000 yen times Nikkei 225.

Expiration Cycles: Four consecutive near-term expiration month trading system.

Expiration Dates: The business day prior to the second Friday of the contract month. If the Exchange decides necessary, it may change: (1) the number of option months, (2) the first day of trading in a new option month, and (3) the last day of trading in expiring options.

Value of Minimum Fluctuation: Up to 1000 level of Nikkei 225 — 5 points; Over 1000 level of Nikkei 225 — 10 points.

Daily Price Limit: +/– 900 points if index is between 20,000 and 30,000.

Exercise and Settlement: Exercise of index option is settled by the payment of cash and not delivery of securities. The amount of cash settlement is calculated by multiplying 1,000 yen and the difference between the exercise price of the option and the closing value of the index on the day of exercise (or the Special Settlement Price of Nikkei 225 in case of March, June, September, and December options.

Margin Requirement for Customers: (Contract value + exercise price x 25 percent) x 1,000 yen x number of opening sales contracts. The minimum required amount of margin is six million yen. Additional margin is necessary when a shortage of the deposited margin exceeds 3 percent of (exercise price x 1,000 yen x number of sales contracts).

Margin Requirement for Members: (Closing option price + 6 percent of Nikkei 225) x 1,000 yen x number of opening sales contracts.

Trading Hours: 9:00 A.M. to 11:00 A.M.; 12:30 P.M. to 3:10 P.M. (3:00 P.M. on the last day of trading for all option months except March, June, September, and December options).

Trading System: Individual auction through a computer-assisted trading system.

Table 5:   Brokerage Commission Rates for Nikkei 225 Options

Contract Value	Commission Rate
Up to 1 million yen	2.00%
Over 1 million yen and up to 3 million yen	1.50% + 5,000.00 yen
Over 3 million yen and up to 5 million yen	1.00% + 20,000.00 yen
Over 5 million yen and up to 10 million yen	0.75% + 32,500.00 yen
Over 10 million yen and up to 30 million yen	0.60% + 47,500.00 yen
Over 30 million yen and up to 50 million yen	0.45% + 92,500.00 yen
Over 50 million yen	0.30% + 167,500.00 yen

Table 6A: Trading Volume of Nikkei Stock Average Options

	1985	1986	1987	1988	1989	1990
January	n/l*	n/l	n/l	n/l	n/l	645,976
February	n/l	n/l	n/l	n/l	n/l	777,700
March	n/l	n/l	n/l	n/l	n/l	727,087
April	n/l	n/l	n/l	n/l	n/l	691,565
May	n/l	n/l	n/l	n/l	n/l	726,859
June	n/l	n/l	n/l	n/l	984,710	729,633
July	n/l	n/l	n/l	n/l	798,181	931,033
August	n/l	n/l	n/l	n/l	1,484,905	932,592
September	n/l	n/l	n/l	n/l	1,384,070	760,551
October	n/l	n/l	n/l	n/l	1,005,798	
November	n/l	n/l	n/l	n/l	457,524	
December	n/l	n/l	n/l	n/l	495,247	
Average	n/l	n/l	n/l	n/l	944,348	
Total	n/l	n/l	n/l	n/l	6,610,435	

Tokyo Stock Price Index (Topix) Futures

Exchange: The Tokyo Stock Exchange.

Contract Unit: 10,000 yen times the Tokyo Stock Price Index (Topix). The decimal fractions of Topix are discarded in calculating the contract value.

Table 6B: Open Interest of Nikkei Stock Average Options

	1985	1986	1987	1988	1989	1990
January	n/l	n/l	n/l	n/l	n/l	32,491
February	n/l	n/l	n/l	n/l	n/l	47,127
March	n/l	n/l	n/l	n/l	n/l	30,254
April	n/l	n/l	n/l	n/l	n/l	25,713
May	n/l	n/l	n/l	n/l	n/l	28,835
June	n/l	n/l	n/l	n/l	12,962	38,735
July	n/l	n/l	n/l	n/l	18,818	42,765
August	n/l	n/l	n/l	n/l	19,466	65,272
September	n/l	n/l	n/l	n/l	23,696	54,978
October	n/l	n/l	n/l	n/l	25,506	
November	n/l	n/l	n/l	n/l	22,723	
December	n/l	n/l	n/l	n/l	29,432	
Average	n/l	n/ll	n/l	n/l	21,800	

*Not Listed
(1) Trading of Nikkei stock average options began on June 12, 1989.
(2) Open Interest is as of the end of each month.
(3) Open Interest of an expiring contract month is included up to the day preceding the settlement date of that contract month.
(4) Open Interest is calculated by counting the net number of futures contracts which remain liquidated by additional offsetting transactions or by physical deliver after taking account of matched but as yet unsettled bought and sold contracts.

Source: The Osaka Securities Exchange

Tokyo Stock Price Index: Topix is a composite index of all common stocks listed on the First Section of the Tokyo Stock Exchange. The base date of Topix is January 4, 1968. The index is weighted by the market-capitalization of each component share. In other words, a price change in a constituent share exerts influence on the index in proportion to its relative market capitalization. Topix is computed and published via the exchange's Market Information System every 60 seconds. (See Appendix III for the list of the Tokyo Stock Price Index's component stocks and their relative weightings in the index.)

Contract Months: A cycle of March, June, September, and December. Five contract months are traded at all times.

Minimum Fluctuation: One (1) full point (10,000 yen).

Value of Minimum Fluctuation: 10,000 yen.

Daily Price Limit: +/– 60 points when index is between 2,000. +/– 90 points when index is between 2,000 and 3,000.

Last Day of Trading: The business day immediately prior to the second Friday (or, the preceding Thursday if the second Friday is a holiday) of the contract month. The trading in a new contract month begins on the business day following the last trading day of the just-expired contract month.

Settlement Date: The third business day following the second Friday (or, the preceding Thursday if the second Friday is a holiday) of the contract month.

Margin Requirement for Customers: Greater of 25 percent of transaction value or six million yen.

Margin Requirement for Members: 20 percent or more of the first trading day's closing price of each contract month.

Trading Hours: 9:00 A.M. to 11:00 A.M.; 12:30 P.M. to 3:10 P.M. (On half-day holidays, trading hours are 9:00 A.M. to 11:15 A.M. only.)

Trading System: Pure auction through the Computer-assisted Order Routing and Execution System for Futures (CORES-F) .

Tokyo Stock Price Index (Topix) Options

Exchange: The Tokyo Stock Exchange.

Contract: Call and put options based on the Tokyo Stock Price Index (Topix).

Contract Unit: 10,000 yen times Topix.

Expiration Cycles: Monthly (four near-term months). The longest option period is four months.

Expiration Dates: The business day prior to the second Friday of the contract month. In case of the March, June, September, and December contracts, the options expire on the second Friday of the contract month. Last day of

Exhibit 1: Trading by CORES-F

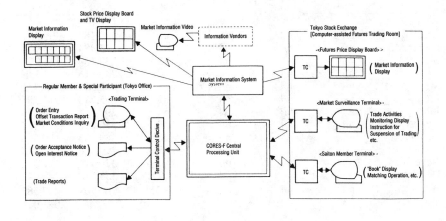

Note TC : Terminal Control Device

Table 7: Brokerage Commission Rates for Topix Futures

Contract Value	Commission Rate
Up to 100 million yen	0.04%
Over 100 million yen and up to 300 million yen	0.03% + 10,000.00 yen
Over 300 million yen and up to 500 million yen	0.02% + 40,000.00 yen
Over 500 million yen and up to 1 billion yen	0.01% + 90,000.00 yen
Over 1 billion yen	0.005% + 140,000.00 yen

Table 8A: Trading Volume of Topix Futures

	1985	1986	1987	1988	1989	1990
January	n/l*	n/l	n/l	n/l	345,180	309,383
February	n/l	n/l	n/l	n/l	275,484	353,966
March	n/l	n/l	n/l	n/l	357,184	436,954
April	n/l	n/l	n/l	n/l	240,916	273,328
May	n/l	n/l	n/l	n/l	252,285	275,072
June	n/l	n/l	n/l	n/l	295,213	286,285
July	n/l	n/l	n/l	n/l	292,844	307,870
August	n/l	n/l	n/l	n/l	350,290	278,522
September	n/l	n/l	n/l	392,671	349,356	179,566
October	n/l	n/l	n/l	401,564	290,966	115,445
November	n/l	n/l	n/l	508,034	324,776	127,378
December	n/l	n/l	n/l	584,871	353,018	147,245
Average	n/l	n/l	n/l	471,785	310,626	257,585
Total	n/l	n/l	n/l	1,887,140	3,727,512	3,091,014

Table 8B: Open Interest on Topix Futures

	1985	1986	1987	1988	1989	1990
January	n/l	n/l	n/l	n/l	22,693	46,209
February	n/l	n/l	n/l	n/l	28,519	40,660
March	n/l	n/l	n/l	n/l	28,707	31,406
April	n/l	n/l	n/l	n/l	26,854	39,153
May	n/l	n/l	n/l	n/l	25,891	37,159
June	n/l	n/l	n/l	n/l	25,741	29,144
July	n/l	n/l	n/l	n/l	30,709	30,376
August	n/l	n/l	n/l	n/l	28,821	30,112
September	n/l	n/l	n/l	13,199	26,454	21,537
October	n/l	n/l	n/l	15,093	30,908	25,200
November	n/l	n/l	n/l	16,449	30,714	25,477
December	n/l	n/l	n/l	14,616	38,353	28,638
Average	n/l	n/l	n/l	14,839	28,697	32,089

*Not Listed
(1) Trading of Topix futures began on September 3, 1988.
(2) Open Interest is as of the end of each month.
(3) Open Interest of an expiring contract month is included up to the day preceding the settlement date of that contract month.
(4) Open Interest is calculated by counting the net number of futures contracts which remain liquidated by additional offsetting transactions or by physicaldelivery after taking account of matched but as yet unsettled bought ansd sold contracts.

Source: The Tokyo Stock Exchange

trading in all Topix option months is the day prior to the second Friday of the expiration month. Trading in a new option month begins on the next day of the last trading day of the nearest option month.

If the Exchange deems necessary, it may adjust: (1) the number of option months, (2) the first day of trading in a new option month, and (3) the last day of trading in expiring options.

Value of Minimum Fluctuation: 0.5 point or 5,000 yen in value.

Daily Price Limit: +/– 60 points when index is below 2,000.

Exercise and Settlement: Exercise of index option is settled by the payment of cash and not delivery of securities. The amount of cash settlement is calculated by multiplying 10,000 yen and the difference between the exercise price of the option and the closing value of the index on the day of exercise (or the Special Settlement Price of Topix in case of March, June, September, and December options if the exercise notice is tendered on the expiration day).

Margin Requirement for Customers: Greater of six million yen or the amount computed by the following formula:
(The transaction value of the option contract + 25 percent of the exercise price) x 10,000 yen x number of option contracts sold.

Margin Requirement for Members: Equal to or greater than the amount computed by the following formula:
(The closing option premium + 20 percent of the closing value of Topix) x 10,000.00 yen x number of option contracts sold.

Trading Hours: 9:00 A.M. to 11:00 A.M.; 12:30 P.M. to 3:10 P.M. (3:00 P.M. on the last day of trading for all option months except March, June, September, and December options).

Trading System: Individual auction through the Computer-assisted Order Routing and Execution System for Options (CORES-O).

Exhibit 2: Trading by CORES-O

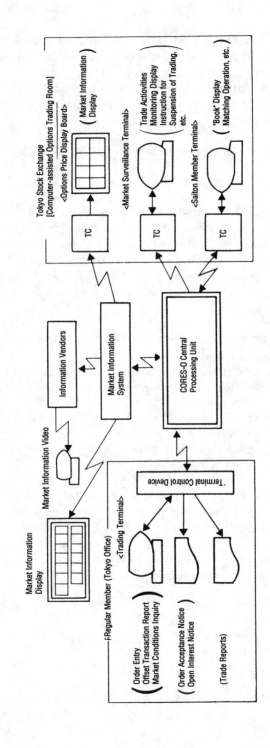

Note TC : Terminal Control Device

Table 9:   Brokerage Commission Rates for Topix Options

Contract Value	Commission Rate
Up to 1 million yen	2.00%
Over 1 million yen and up to 3 million yen	1.50% + 5,000.00 yen
Over 3 million yen and up to 5 million yen	1.00% + 20,000.00 yen
Over 5 million yen and up to 10 million yen	0.75% + 32,500.00 yen
Over 10 million yen and up to 30 million yen	0.60% + 47,500.00 yen
Over 30 million yen and up to 50 million yen	0.45% + 92,500.00 yen
Over 50 million yen	0.30% + 167,500.00 yen

Table 10A: Trading Volume of Topix Options

	1985	1986	1987	1988	1989	1990
January	n/l*	n/l	n/l	n/l	n/l	77,295
February	n/l	n/l	n/l	n/l	n/l	118,300
March	n/l	n/l	n/l	n/l	n/l	91,065
April	n/l	n/l	n/l	n/l	n/l	80,996
May	n/l	n/l	n/l	n/l	n/l	22,277
June	n/l	n/l	n/l	n/l	n/l	16,623
July	n/l	n/l	n/l	n/l	n/l	13,108
August	n/l	n/l	n/l	n/l	n/l	10,484
September	n/l	n/l	n/l	n/l	n/l	9,883
October	n/l	n/l	n/l	n/l	4,642,957	6,325
November	n/l	n/l	n/l	n/l	85,465	6,397
December	m/l	n/l	n/l	n/l	77,146	10,874
Average	n/l	n/l	n/l	n/l	1,601,856	38,552
Total	n/l	n/l	n/l	n/l	4,805,568	462,627

Table 10B: Open Interest of Topix Options

	1985	1986	1987	1988	1989	1990
January	n/l	n/l	n/l	n/l	n/l	2,668
February	n/l	n/l	n/l	n/l	n/l	2,639
March	n/l	n/l	n/l	n/l	n/l	855
April	n/l	n/l	n/l	n/l	n/l	344
May	n/l	n/l	n/l	n/l	n/l	365
June	n/l	n/l	n/l	n/l	n/l	751
July	n/l	n/l	n/l	n/l	n/l	99
August	n/l	n/l	n/l	n/l	n/l	38
September	n/l	n/l	n/l	n/l	n/l	990
October	n/l	n/l	n/l	n/l	9,246	145
November	n/l	n/l	n/l	n/l	6,159	90
December	n/l	n/l	n/l	n/l	3,737	644
Average	n/l	n/l	n/l	n/l	6,381	827

*Not Listed
(1) Trading of Topix futures began on October 20, 1989.
(2) Open Interest is as of the end of each month.
(3) Open Interest of an expiring contract month is included up to the day preceding the settlement date of that contract month.
(4) Open Interest is calculated by counting the net number of futures contracts which remain liquidated by additional offsetting transactions or by physicaldelivery after taking account of matched but as yet unsettled bought ansd sold contracts.

Source: The Tokyo Stock Exchange

Nagoya Option 25

Exchange: The Nagoya Stock Exchange.

Contract: Call and put options based on the the Option 25 Index (Option 25).

Option 25 Index: The Option 25 index is a price-weighted average of the leading 25 common stocks listed in the first sections of the TSE, OSE, and NSE. The index is broad-based in the sense that the component issues are selected from 20 industries, and that a maximum of three issues per industry is selected. Also, the component stocks have to meet the following criteria:

1. Market Value	200 billion yen or more
2. Number of listed shares	300,000 shares or more
3. Trading Volume in 1987	300,000 shares or more
or between 1985 and 1987	1,000,000 shares or more

According to the NSE, the above criteria assure that the index will reflect a normal market trend, maintain liquidity, and exclude an intentional price manipulation. (See Appendix III for the list of Option 25's component stocks and their relative weightings in the index.)

Contract Unit: 10,000 yen times Option 25.

Expiration Cycles: Monthly (four near-term months). The longest option period is four months.

Expiration Dates: The business day prior to the second Friday of the contract month.

Value of Minimum Fluctuation: 0.5 point or 5,000 yen in case of price 100 points or less; 1.0 point or 10,000 yen in case of price above 100.

Daily Price Limit: Around 3 percent of the previous day's value of Option 25.

Exercise Price: At 25-point intervals.

Exercise Type: European (exercizable on last trading day only).

Exercise and Settlement: Settlements are made in cash. The cash settlement is equal to the difference between the exercise price and the closing value of Option 25.

Margin Requirement for Customers: Greater of six million yen or the amount computed by the following formula:
(The transaction value of the option contract + 25 percent of the exercise price) x 10,000.00 yen x number of option contracts sold.

Margin Requirement for Members: Equal to or greater than the amount computed by the following formula:
(The closing option premium + 20 percent of the closing value of Topix) x 10,000.00 yen x number of option contracts sold.

Trading Hours: 9:00 A.M. to 11:00 A.M.; 12:30 P.M. to 3:10 P.M.
(3:00 P.M. on the last trading day of the contract month).

Trading System: Individual floor auction system.

Table 11: Brokerage Commission Rates for Option 25

Contract Value	Commission Rate
Up to 1 million yen	2.00%
Over 1 million yen and up to 3 million yen	1.50% + 5,000.00 yen
Over 3 million yen and up to 5 million yen	1.00% + 20,000.00 yen
Over 5 million yen and up to 10 million yen	0.75% + 32,500.00 yen
Over 10 million yen and up to 30 million yen	0.60% + 47,500.00 yen
Over 30 million yen and up to 50 million yen	0.45% + 92,500.00 yen
Over 50 million yen	0.30% + 167,500.00 yen

Table 12A: Trading Volume of Nagoya Option 25

	1985	1986	1987	1988	1989	1990
January	n/1*	n/1	n/1	n/1	n/1	110,837
February	n/1	n/1	n/1	n/1	n/1	113,525
March	n/1	n/1	n/1	n/1	n/1	116,623
April	n/1	n/1	n/1	n/1	n/1	60,258
May	n/1	n/1	n/1	n/1	n/1	57,756
June	n/1	n/1	n/1	n/1	n/1	49,034
July	n/1	n/1	n/1	n/1	n/1	38,301
August	n/1	n/1	n/1	n/1	n/1	31,412
September	n/1	n/1	n/1	n/1	n/1	25,200
October	n/1	n/1	n/1	n/1	1,198,599	31,848
November	n/1	n/1	n/1	n/1	101,882	22,335
December	n/1	n/1	n/1	n/1	103,550	36,367
Average	n/1	n/1	n/1	n/1	468,010	57,791
Total	n/1	n/1	n/1	n/1	1,404,031	693,496

Table 12B: Open Interest of Nagoya Option 25

	1985	1986	1987	1988	1989	1990
January	n/l	n/l	n/l	n/l	n/l	2,756
February	n/l	n/l	n/l	n/l	n/l	5,281
March	n/l	n/l	n/l	n/l	n/l	5,807
April	n/l	n/l	n/l	n/l	n/l	2,786
May	n/l	n/l	n/l	n/l	n/l	5,687
June	n/l	n/l	n/l	n/l	n/l	9,580
July	n/l	n/l	n/l	n/l	n/l	7,392
August	n/l	n/l	n/l	n/l	n/l	5,082
September	n/l	n/l	n/l	n/l	n/l	4,542
October	n/l	n/l	n/l	n/l	72,757	1,464
November	n/l	n/l	n/l	n/l	8,546	1,683
December	n/l	n/l	n/l	n/l	6,986	2,387
Average	n/l	n/l	n/l	n/l	29,430	4,537

*Not Listed
(1) Trading of Nagoya Option 25 began on Oct. 17, 1989.
(2) Open Interest is as of the end of each month.
(3) Open Interest of an expiring contract month is included up to the day preceding the settlement date of that contract month.
(4) Open Interest is calculated by counting the net number of futures contracts which remain to be liquidated by additional offsetting transactions or by physical delivery after taking account of matched but as yet unsettled bought and sold contracts.

Source: The Nagoya Stock Exchange

Table 13: Summary of Contract Specifications

FUTURES

Contract Specifications	NIKKEI(OSE)	NIKKEI(SIMEX)	NIKKEI(CME)	TOPIX(TSE)
Contract Size (Multiple of Index)	1000	500	5	10000
Minimum Price Fluctuation	10 points (¥10000)	5 points (¥2500)	5 points (25.00 US$)	1 point (¥10000)
Daily Price Limit	+/- 900 if index 20000-30000	10%	+/- 900	+/- 60 points
Contract Months	Mar, Jun, Sep, Dec	Mar, Jun, Sep, Dec	Mar, Jun, Sep, Dec	Mar, Jun, Sep, Dec
Trading Hours	9:00 - 11:00 am 12:30 - 3:10 pm	8:00 am - 2:15 pm	8:00 am - 3:15 pm	9:00 - 11:00 am 12:30 - 3:10 pm
Last Day of Trading	Thursday before 2nd Friday	3rd Wed. of contract month	Thursday before 2nd Friday	Thursday before 2nd Friday
Initial Margin	25% of contract value, ¥6m min. (8% cash)	¥1,250,000	US$18,000	25% of contract value, ¥6m min. (8% cash)
Variation Margin	Called if loss is > or = to 3%	Called if loss is 20%	Called if loss is US$6000	Called if loss is > or = to 3%
Currency Denomination	Yen	Yen	US$	Yen
Settlement Method	Cash settled	Cash settled	Cash settled	Cash settled
Final Settlement Price	Based on Special Quotation	Based on closing value of NSA on 3rd Wed. of contract month	Based on Special Quotation	Based on Special Quotation

* Most active contracts listed

OPTIONS

Contract Specifications	NIKKEI(OSE)	NIKKEI(CME) (on futures)	TOPIX(TSE)	OPTION25(NSE)
Contract Size (Multiple of Index)	1000	5	10000	10000
Minimum Price Fluctuation	5 points if < ¥1000 10 points if > ¥1000	5 points (US$ 25.00)	0.5 points (¥5000)	0.5 points if < ¥100 1.0 point if > ¥100
Daily Price Limit	+/- 900 if spot 20000-30000	If/when futures are suspended, then simultaneously suspended.	+/- 60	+/- 3% from close of index day before
Contract Months	4 nearest months	12 calander months	4 nearest months	4 nearest months
Trading Hours	9:00 - 11:00 am 12:30 - 3:10 pm	8:00 am - 3:15 pm	9:00 - 11:00 am 12:30 - 3:10 pm	9:00 - 11:00 am 12:30 - 3:10 pm
Last Day of Trading	Thursday before 2nd Friday each month	Thursday before 2nd Friday of Mar, Jun, Sep, Dec Others = Fri. before 3rd Sat.	Thursday before 2nd Friday each month	Thursday before 2nd Friday each month
Initial Margin	Premium received + (25% x exercise price x 1000) ¥6m min.	Calculated using risk-based off-setting system called SPAN	Premium received + (25% x exercise price x10000) ¥6m min.	Premium received + (25% x exercise price x 10000) ¥6m min.
Variation Margin	Called if loss is > or = to (exer. price x 3% x 1000)	Calculated using risk-based off-setting system called SPAN	Called if loss is > or = to (exer. price x 3% x10000)	Called if loss is > or = to (exer. price x 3% x 10000)
Currency Denomination	Yen	US$	Yen	Yen
Settlement Method	Cash settled	Cash settled for Mar, Jun, Sep, Dec converted to future	Cash settled	Cash settled
Final Settlement Price	Same as futures for Mar, Jun, Sep, Dec Otherwise based on NSA at expiry	Based on SQ for Mar, Jun, Sep, Dec receive future	Same as futures for Mar, Jun, Sep, Dec Otherwise based on Topix at expiry	Based on the close of actual Opt. 25 Ind. on last trading day
Strike	¥500 interval	¥500 interval	¥50 interval	¥25 interval
Exercise	On Thursdays only	Everyday	Everyday	European Style

Source: S.G. Warburg Securities (Japan) Inc.

Table 14: Comparison of Trading Costs

The table below provides cost comparisons for trading in and out of each investment. We provide an average price and trading size for each, with the equivalent equity exposure given in yen beneath. The average trade size provides an indication of general liquidity without incurring a market impact. Total costs as a percentage are calculated. In addition, costs relative to the equivalent equity exposure are given.

Cost Comparisons	Equity	USD Wts	Yen CBs	N225 Futures OSE	N225 Futures SIMEX	N225 Futures CME	N225 Options OSE	Topix Futures TSE
Denomination	¥	US$	¥	¥	¥	US$	¥	¥
Average Trade								
Average Price	1,000	10	100	25,000	25,000	25,000	500	1,800
Average Amount	50,000	100	100,000,000	50	20	3	20	5
Equity Equivalent Value (¥)	50,000,000	28,000,000	100,000,000	1,250,000,000	250,000,000	51,750,000	25,000,000	90,000,000
Percentage Costs (round trip)	(%)	(%)	(%)	(%)	(%)	(%)	(%)	(%)
Commission	2.4	0	0.8	0.04	0.02	0.007	1.6	0.08
Spread Costs	1	10	1	0.04	0.04	0.04	1	0.05
Sales tax	0.3	0	0.3	0.0001	0.0	0	0.05	0.0002
Clearing Fee	0	0	0	0	0.0008	0.00112	0	0
NFA Fee	0	0	0	0	0	0.00008	0	0
Total Costs	3.7	10	1.7	0.0821	0.0608 ¥ 0.090	0.0482	2.625	0.1322

Note: There is a transfer tax of 0.3%, and a capital gains tax of 1% when selling warrants

Source: S.G. Warburg Securities (Japan) Inc.

Japanese Bond Futures and Options Market

The Japanese Government Bond Market

The Japanese government bond market is the second largest sovereign debt market in total market capitalization after the U.S. Treasury bond market. At the end of 1989, the total amount of the outstanding Japanese government bonds reached some 90 trillion yen, or $599.7 billion.[2]

The Japanese government bond market comprises: (1) 2- to 4-year medium-term coupon bonds, (2) 5-year (zero-coupon) bonds, (3) 10-year long-term bonds, and (4) 20-year super-long coupon bonds. 10-year JGBs is the largest segment of the JGB market. The total amount of the outstanding 10-year issues totaled some 75 trillion yen as of the end of 1989, which is approximately 80 percent of all yen-denominated government debt issues. Consequently, 10-year JGBs are the most actively traded. According to an early 1990 estimate, the average daily turnover of the 10-year JGBs in Tokyo is between 7-10 trillion yen, or $47-67 billion. Also, significant amounts are traded daily in London and New York as well: 130 billion yen ($867 million) in London and 100 billion yen ($667 million) in New York. It should also be noted that the majority of the cash JGB issues are traded over-the-counter.

The JGBs are issued monthly in the primary market through the Ministry of Finance. Sixty percent of all 10-year JGB primary-market issuance is done through Government Bond Underwriting Syndicate consisting of some 750 registered Japanese and foreign representative institutional firms. The other 40 percent of the new JGB issues is sold by an auction-type system in which investors submit bids for a particular issue without a specification of price.

The Tokyo Stock Exchange: Holding the High Ground

The Tokyo Stock Exchange, the world's second largest equity market, also offers Japan's broadest slate of debt derivative products. As of the end of the first half of 1990, the TSE trades four distinct products, with more on the horizon. (See Table 15 for the list of the currently-traded bond derivatives at the TSE.)

Japan's first and most actively-traded debt contract is the TSE's 10-year JGB futures, which was launched on October 19, 1985. In mid-1990, it was trading over 70,000 lots per day, with an open interest of more than 170,000 positions. Because of its large contract size of 100 yen million, the 10-Year JGB

Table 15: Bond Futures and Options at the TSE

1. 10-year Japanese Government Bond (JGB) Futures
2. Options on 10-year JGB Futures
3. 20-year JGB Futures
4. 10-year U.S. Treasury Bond Futures

futures have now become the contract with the largest daily trading value in the world.

There have always been some doubts about the level of genuine activity, since much trading is for member firms' proprietary accounts. The red-hot market share competition between Japanese banks and securities firms has artificially boosted volume, and cross-trading has been rampant as in the case of the stock index futures.

Some cross-trading is also executed for accounting purposes, since Japan's margin rules lock up access to excess equity. Members' own trading consistently accounts for close to 90 percent of volume, with insurance companies and on financial firms taking up the bulk of remaining activity. By mid-1989, the banks took the lead in the market share as they geared up for the new financial futures exchange, the Tokyo International Financial Futures Exchange. In the first half of that year, they generated 59 percent of the TSE bond futures' turnover.

Observers estimate that less than five percent of the trading activity is bonafide hedging. Furthermore, commissioned trades rarely account for more than 15 percent of the turnover. Thus, over 80 percent of activity is dealing between members, of which probably half is cross-trading. Nevertheless, the wash trades do not negate the price discovery function of the Japanese government bond futures market, since futures market activity is more than three times that of the cash market.

Japanese government bond futures also trade on the London International Financial Futures Exchange (LIFFE) and the Chicago Board of Trade (CBOT). Whereas the LIFFE contract is fairly active and attracts a broad array of Japanese and other international institutions, the trading of the CBOT contract has been moribund.[3]

U.S. Treasury Bond Futures

The Japanese, who have been active users of the U.S. Treasury bond (T-bond) futures in Chicago since 1987, now have a nearly identical product in their own backyard. The TSE launched 20-year U.S. T-bond futures in December 1989. Although the Singapore International Monetary Exchange (SIMEX) and the Sydney Futures Exchange (SFE) failed to successfully build U.S. T-bond futures markets in the Asian timezone, Tokyo, a home to the largest foreign investors in U.S. government debt, should have better luck. In mid-1990, the U.S. T-bond contract was trading over 3,600 lots per day. The institutional investors in Japan now have a futures pricing mechanism for the U.S. Treasury bonds during all major cash trading hours.

The TSE U.S. bond futures is similar—but not fungible—to the Chicago Board of Trade contract. The contract size is the same, at $100,000; but the underlying instrument is the 20-year bond, which is more widely held by Japanese investors. Margin requirement and settlement procedures are also different.

The TSE has also experienced its first failure. In July 1988, the TSE launched a 20-year JGB contract, hoping to capture business in longer maturities. By mid- 1989, turnover—never impressive—dried up, and the TSE admitted to being "premature." In mid-1990, the 20-yen JGB contract was trading little over 100 lots per day. The exchange officials blamed a thin cash market as the Ministry of Finance slowed issues at the extreme end of the yield curve. The TSE has no plans for delisting, since it is hoping that government debt structure might still shift to longer maturities in the near future.

Options on JGB Futures

Following the launch of the U.S. Treasury Bond futures, the TSE is expanding its range of debt products into options. Options on 10-yen Japanese government bond futures were launched in May 1990. The initial activity levels have been encouraging. During the first three months of 1991, the 10-yen JGB options contract was trading 8,000 lots per day. However, the TSE does not have a monopoly in this area as it does with the JGB futures. The over-the-counter bond options, which are approved and administered by the Ministry of Finance, began trading in April 1989 with banks, securities firms, and Japanese institutional investors as active participants. The TSE, which views its fixed commission rates as sacrosanct, may find it difficult to compete in this area.

Possible New Contracts

The OSE announced in mid-1989 that it was considering plans for the world's first convertible bond (CB) futures contract. The current market capitalization of the Japanese CB market is around 16 trillion yen, with over 1000 issues listed. CBs are popular among institutional investors, and an OSE executive claimed that a CB futures market would encourage new issues as well as offering a hedging instrument. Osaka has also considered listing derivatives other Japanese and Asian stock market indices, and options on individual stocks.

The TSE is also considering new products, particularly as it faces new competition in the interest rate complex. A shorter-term bond contract is one possible new offering.

Ten-Year Japanese Government Bond Futures

Exchange: The Tokyo Stock Exchange.

Contract: Standardized 6 percent, 10-year Japanese government bond.

Contract Month: Cycle of March, June, September, and December. Five contract months are traded at all times.

Trading Unit: Japanese government bonds 100 million yen face value.

Delivery Date: 20th of each contract month.

Deliverable Grade: Exchange listed Japanese government bonds having maturity of seven years or more but less than eleven years.

Minimum Fluctuation: 1/100 point per 100 points 10,000 yen per contract.

Daily Price Limit: Two points upward or downward two million yen per contract.

Table 16: Brokerage Commission Rates for 10-year JGB Futures

Contract Value	Commission Rate
Over 0.5 billion yen and up to 1 billion yen	0.01% + 25,000 yen
Over 1 billion yen and up to 5 billion yen	0.005% + 75,000 yen
Over 5 billion	0.0025% + 200,000 yen
Up to 0.5 billion yen	0.015%

Table 17A: Trading Volume of 10-Year JGB Futures

	1985	1986	1987	1988	1989	1990
January	n/l*	162,128	1,481,490	1,271,943	1,355,101	1,347,507
February	n/l	321,908	1,617,766	1,390,013	1,383,969	1,347,700
March	n/l	641,400	2,293,630	1,516,950	1,893,418	1,500,223
April	n/l	595,722	1,955,120	1,159,209	1,107,786	1,108,155
May	n/l	598,985	1,532,583	1,359,263	1,221,089	1,404,447
June	n/l	719,434	1,711,381	1,911,502	1,634,556	1,405,652
July	n/l	820,526	1,546,427	1,787,845	1,741,548	1,414,608
August	n/l	1,145,682	1,593,506	1,865,585	1,835,039	1,547,662
September	n/l	941,893	1,339,127	1,727,552	2,042,593	1,179,211
October	204,897	1,106,888	983,008	1,671,672	1,622,235	1,397,912
November	124,227	984,960	1,062,130	1,624,462	1,600,855	1,396,108
December	123,429	1,356,303	1,145,466	1,433,776	1,503,701	1,257,386
Average	150,851	782,986	1,521,803	1,559,981	1,578,491	1,358,881
Total	452,553	9,395,829	18,261,634	18,719,772	18,941,890	16,306,571

Table 17B: Open Interest of 10-Year JGB Futures

	1985	1986	1987	1988	1989	1990
January	n/l	24,932	132,716	137,382	169,845	198,971
February	n/l	38,522	155,719	131,442	189,916	208,265
March	n/l	46,063	133,004	120,792	138,678	144,081
April	n/l	57,773	123,676	118,192	184,439	143,384
May	n/l	84,134	116,866	129,081	150,868	172,055
June	n/l	77,385	142,888	141,762	166,841	144,393
July	n/l	102,901	149,011	167,612	218,315	169,840
August	n/l	119,841	190,068	183,900	261,822	162,416
September	n/l	115,290	129,747	144,203	172,097	137,808
October	27,630	117,559	133,503	155,488	201,827	151,662
November	23,325	98,529	132,865	162,649	210,788	175,829
December	17,837	101,055	129,407	124,766	182,517	150,910
Average	22,931	81,999	139,123	143,106	187,329	163,301

*Not Listed
(1) Trading of 10-year JGB futures began on Oct. 19, 1985.
(2) Open Interest is as of the end of each month.
(3) Open Interest of an expiring contract month is included up to the day preceding the settlement date of that contract month.
(4) Open Interest is calculated by counting the net number of futures contracts which remain to be liquidated by additional offsetting transactions or by physical delivery after taking account of matched but as yet unsettled bought and sold contracts.

Source: The Tokyo Stock Exchange

Last Day of Trading: The 9th business day prior to each delivery date. The trading day in a new contract month begins on the next business day following the the last trading day.

Margin Requirement for Customers: Greater of 3 percent nominal transaction value or six million yen.

Margin Requirement for Members: Not less than 2 percent of nominal value of his net total long or short positions of the same contract month.

Trading Hours: 9:00 A.M. to 11:00 A.M.; 1:00 P.M. to 3:00 P.M.

Trading System: Computer-assisted Order Routing and Execution System for Futures (CORES-F).

Options on 10-year Japanese Government Bond Futures

Exchange: The Tokyo Stock Exchange.

Contract: Call and put options based on the 10-year Japanese government bond futures.

Contract Months: The two closest following months chosen from the March–June–September–December cycle.

Exercise Price: Seven exercise prices are set at 1–yen intervals to bracket the current Japanese Government bond futures prices. Additional exercise prices will be established as the underlying JGB futures price rises or fall.

Exercise: A buyer of a Japanese government bond futures and option may exercise the option on any business day prior to expiration.

Expiration Date: The last business day of the month prior to the delivery month of the underlying JGB futures.

Last Day of Trading: Expiration Date.

Minimum Fluctuation: 1/100 point per 100 points 10,000 yen per contract.

Daily Price Limit: Two points upward or downward two million yen per contract.

Margin Requirements for Customers: Greater of six million yen or the amount computed by the following formula:

(The price at which an option is sold x 100 million yen/100 yen + 100 million yen x 3 percent) x number of options contracts sold.

Margin Requirements for Members: Equal to or greater than the amount computed by the following formula:
(Each day's closing price of an option x 100 million yen/100 yen + 100 million yen x 2 percent) x number of options contracts sold.

Trading Hours: 9:00 A.M. to 11:00 A.M.; 1:00 P.M. to 3:00 P.M.

Trading System: Computer-assisted Order Routing and Execution System for Options (CORES-O).

Table 18: Brokerage Commission Rates for Options on 10-Year JGB Futures

Contract Value	Commission Rate
Up to 5 million yen	1.30%
Over 5 million yen and up to 10 million yen	0.85% + 22,500.00 yen
Over 10 million yen and up to 50 million	0.45% + 62,500.00 yen
Over 50 million	0.25% + 162,000.00 yen

Table 19A: Trading Volume of Options on 10-Year JGB Futures

	1986	1987	1988	1989	1990	1991
January	n/l*	n/l	n/l	n/l	n/l	155,770
February	n/l	n/l	n/l	n/l	n/l	159,528
March	n/l	n/l	n/l	n/l	n/l	169,128
April	n/l	n/l	n/l	n/l	n/l	
May	n/l	n/l	n/l	n/l	446,091	
June	n/l	n/l	n/l	n/l	307,384	
July	n/l	n/l	n/l	n/l	311,316	
August	n/l	n/l	n/l	n/l	278,965	
September	n/l	n/l	n/l	n/l	251,133	
October	n/l	n/l	n/l	n/l	267,676	
November	n/l	n/l	n/l	n/l	231,874	
December	n/l	n/l	n/l	n/l	193,369	
Average	n/l	n/l	n/l	n/l	285,976	
Total	n/l	n/l	n/l	n/l	2,287,808	

Table 19B: Open Interest of Options on 10-Year JGB Futures

	1986	1987	1988	1989	1990	1991
January	n/l	n/l	n/l	n/l	n/l	56,914
February	n/l	n/l	n/l	n/l	n/l	20,197
March	n/l	n/l	n/l	n/l	n/l	44,257
April	n/l	n/l	n/l	n/l	n/l	
May	n/l	n/l	n/l	n/l	23,720	
June	n/l	n/l	n/l	n/l	38,408	
July	n/l	n/l	n/l	n/l	41,974	
August	n/l	n/l	n/l	n/l	17,447	
September	n/l	n/l	n/l	n/l	34,038	
October	n/l	n/l	n/l	n/l	50,230	
November	n/l	n/l	n/l	n/l	20,324	
December	n/l	n/l	n/l	n/l	41,683	
Average	n/l	n/l	n/l	n/l	33,478	

*Not Listed
(1) Trading of Options on 10-year JGB futures began on May 11, 1990.
(2) Open Interest is as of the end of each month.
(3) Open Interest of an expiring contract month is included up to the day preceding the settlement date of that contract month.
(4) Open Interest is calculated by counting the net number of futures contracts which remain to be liquidated by additional offsetting transactions or by physical delivery after taking account of matched but as yet unsettled bought and sold contracts.

Source: The Tokyo Stock Exchange

Twenty-Year Japanese Government Bond Futures

Exchange: The Tokyo Stock Exchange.

Contract: Standardized 6 percent, 20-year Japanese government bond.

Contract Month: Cycle of March, June, September, and December. Five contract months are traded at all times.

Trading Unit: Japanese government bonds 100 million yen face value.

Delivery Date: 20th of each contract month.

Deliverable Grade: Exchange listed Japanese government bonds having maturity of 15 years or more but less than 21 years.

Minimum Fluctuation: 1/100 point per 100 points 10,000.00 yen per contract.

Daily Price Limit: Three points upward or downward three million yen per contract.

Last Day of Trading: The 9th business day prior to each delivery date. The trading day in a new contract month begins on the next business day following the last trading day.

Margin Requirement for Customers: Greater of 4.5 percent nominal transaction value or six million yen.

Table 20: Brokerage Commission Rates for 20-Year JGB Futures

Contract Value	Commission Rate
Up to 0.5 billion yen	0.015%
Over 0.5 billion yen and up to 1 billion yen	0.01% + 25,000.00 yen
Over 1 billion yen and up to 5 billion yen	0.005% + 75,000.00 yen
Over 5 billion	0.0025% + 200,000.00 yen

Table 21A: Trading Volume of 20-Year JGB Futures

	1985	1986	1987	1988	1989	1990
January	n/l*	n/l	n/l	n/l	4,484	1,553
February	n/l	n/l	n/l	n/l	3,445	2,132
March	n/l	n/l	n/l	n/l	3,529	1,468
April	n/l	n/l	n/l	n/l	2,233	769
May	n/l	n/l	n/l	n/l	1,227	2,231
June	n/l	n/l	n/l	n/l	1,520	873
July	n/l	n/l	n/l	24,636	1,716	504
August	n/l	n/l	n/l	2,407	2,207	1,257
September	n/l	n/l	n/l	1,762	2,131	438
October	n/l	n/l	n/l	4,491	1,817	485
November	n/l	n/l	n/l	2,980	2,241	761
December	n/l	n/l	n/l	3,183	2,184	453
Average	n/l	n/l	n/l	6,577	2,395	1,077
Total	n/l	n/l	n/l	39,459	28,734	12,924

Table 21B: Open Interest of 20-Year JGB Futures

	1985	1986	1987	1988	1989	1990
January	n/l	n/l	n/l	n/l	1,848	518
February	n/l	n/l	n/l	n/l	908	576
March	n/l	n/l	n/l	n/l	792	610
April	n/l	n/l	n/l	n/l	320	511
May	n/l	n/l	n/l	n/l	237	493
June	n/l	n/l	n/l	n/l	376	492
July	n/l	n/l	n/l	1,256	530	432
August	n/l	n/l	n/l	311	232	298
September	n/l	n/l	n/l	247	291	248
October	n/l	n/l	n/l	1,266	288	221
November	n/l	n/l	n/l	1,247	391	370
December	n/l	n/l	n/l	1,449	551	291
Average	n/l	n/l	n/l	963	564	422

*Not Listed
(1) Trading of 20-year JGB futures began on July 8, 1988.
(2) Open Interest is as of the end of each month.
(3) Open Interest of an expiring contract month is included up to the day preceding the settlement date of that contract month.
(4) Open Interest is calculated by counting the net number of futures contracts which remain to be liquidated by additional offsetting transactions or by physical delivery after taking account of matched but as yet unsettled bought and sold contracts.

Source: The Tokyo Stock Exchange

Margin Requirement for Members: Not less than 3 percent of nominal value of his net total long or short positions of the same contract month.

Trading Hours: 9:00 A.M. to 11:00 A.M.; 1:00 P.M. to 3:00 P.M.

Trading System: Computer-assisted Order Routing and Execution System for Futures (CORES-F).

U.S. Treasury Bond Futures

Exchange: The Tokyo Stock Exchange.

Contract: Standardized 8 percent, 20-year U.S. Treasury bond.

Contract Month: Cycle of March, June, September, and December. Five contract months are traded at all times.

Trading Unit: $100,000 face-valued U.S. Treasury bonds.

Delivery Date: Last business day of each contract month.

Deliverable Grade: U.S. Treasury bonds maturing at least 15 years if not callable, and if callable, are not callable at least 15 years from the first day of the delivery month.

Minimum Fluctuation: 1/32 point per 100 points $31.25 per contract.

Daily Price Limit: Three points above or below from the previous day's settlement price at the Chicago Board of Trade.

Last Day of Trading: The same day as the last trading day at the Chicago Board of Trade for each contract month. That is, the 7th CBOT business day prior to CBOT's last business day of the month.

Margin Requirement for Customers: Greater of 4.5 percent nominal transaction value or $45,000.00.

Margin Requirement for Members: 3 percent of nominal transaction value.

Trading Hours: 9:00 A.M. to 11:00 A.M.; 1:00 P.M. to 3:00 P.M.

Trading System: Computer-assisted Order Routing and Execution System for Futures (CORES-F).

Table 22: Brokerage Commission Rates for U.S. T-Bond Futures

Contract Value	Commission Rate
Up to 1 million yen	0.03%
Over 1 million yen and up to 3 million yen	0.02% + $100
Over 3 million yen and up to 5 million yen	0.015% + $250
Over 5 million yen and up to 10 million yen	0.008% + $600
Over 10 million	0.004% + $1,000.

Table 23A: Trading Volume of U.S. Treasury Bond Futures

	1985	1986	1987	1988	1989	1990
January	n/l*	n/l	n/l	n/l	n/l	53,009
February	n/l	n/l	n/l	n/l	n/l	54,005
March	n/l	n/l	n/l	n/l	n/l	70,341
April	n/l	n/l	n/l	n/l	n/l	74,942
May	n/l	n/l	n/l	n/l	n/l	72,888
June	n/l	n/l	n/l	n/l	n/l	55,101
July	n/l	n/l	n/l	n/l	n/l	45,482
August	n/l	n/l	n/l	n/l	n/l	23,067
September	n/l	n/l	n/l	n/l	n/l	21,364
October	n/l	n/l	n/l	n/l	n/l	20,528
November	n/l	n/l	n/l	n/l	n/l	16,032
December	n/l	n/l	n/l	n/l	140,804	11,649
Total	n/l	n/l	n/l	n/l	140,804	43,201
Average	n/l	n/l	n/l	n/l	140,804	518,408

Table 23B: Open Interest of U.S. Treasury Bond Futures

	1985	1986	1987	1988	1989	1990
January	n/l	n/l	n/l	n/l	n/l	12,595
February	n/l	n/l	n/l	n/l	n/l	9,330
March	n/l	n/l	n/l	n/l	n/l	7,680
April	n/l	n/l	n/l	n/l	n/l	11,460
May	n/l	n/l	n/l	n/l	n/l	2,244
June	n/l	n/l	n/l	n/l	n/l	7,465
July	n/l	n/l	n/l	n/l	n/l	5,420
August	n/l	n/l	n/l	n/l	n/l	2,719
September	n/l	n/l	n/l	n/l	n/l	2,603
October	n/l	n/l	n/l	n/l	n/l	2,115
November	n/l	n/l	n/l	n/l	n/l	1,305
December	n/l	n/l	n/l	n/l	13,874	1,112
Average	n/l	n/l	n/l	n/l	13,874	5,504

*Not Listed
(1) Trading of U.S. T-bond futures began on December 1, 1989.
(2) Open Interest is as of the end of each month.
(3) Open Interest of an expiring contract month is included up to the day preceding the settlement date of that contract month.
(4) Open Interest is calculated by counting the net number of futures contracts which remain to be liquidated by additional offsetting transactions or by physical delivery after taking offsetting transactions or by physical delivery after taking account of matched but as yet unsettled bought and sold contracts.

Source: The Tokyo Stock Exchange

Japanese Short-Term Interest Rate and Currency Futures and Options Contracts

Banker's New Futures Market

The most significant new addition to the development of the Japanese futures and options markets is the Tokyo International Financial Futures Exchange (TIFFE). The TIFFE has changed not only Japan's financial landscape, but also has affected derivative markets in the Pacific Rim region and the world. Futures trading at the TIFFE began on June 30, 1989, with contracts on 3-month Euroyen and Eurodollar interest rates, and the yen/dollar exchange rate. By virtue of the huge assets controlled by its institutional membership, the exchange has become active despite its many inefficiencies.

The Ministry of Finance stressed the need for Japan to develop domestic futures exchanges, partly to enable it to maintain tight control of trading activity, and thus, gave Japanese banks the sovereignty over short-term interest rate and currency futures as a part of 1988's turf division process described earlier in this chapter. The TIFFE was set up by Japan's Federation of Bankers' Associations. Initially, the total membership was limited to 350 firms, with a maximum of 100 as clearing members. Net capital requirements for Japanese clearing firms was set at 50 billion yen ($350 million), but lowered to five billion yen for experienced foreign futures companies. The TIFFE hoped to attract skilled overseas brokers and traders to give the market an initial boost. However, less than 20 foreign firms joined. At the end of 1990, there were a total of 264 member firms. (See Appendix II for list of TIFFE's members.)

The Federation has been striving to overcome the market perception that the TIFFE would be a "city-banks only" exchange, by drawing in membership from securities firms, long-term credit and trust banks, insurance companies, and foreign institutions.

Enthusiasm for the exchange was initially lukewarm among foreign institutional players for several reasons. Aside from the high cost of entry, many foreign firms fear the market will develop as an isolated Japanese dealers' playground. The TIFFE is not linked with any other exchanges and has no intention to do so. Differing settlement procedures make the TIFFE contracts less compatible with existing markets in Chicago, London, and Singapore.

A number of brokers also questioned the viability of the TIFFE's yen/dollar futures. They cite the huge and efficient foreign exchange spot, forward, and swap markets in Tokyo—where volume often reaches $100 billion a day—as formidable competition. There is little incentive to use futures when the cash market is highly developed, as the Singapore International Monetary Exchange

(SIMEX) discovered in the past few years. Singapore's liquid and accessible foreign exchange market has inhibited the growth of currency futures at SIMEX. These initial fears were created in the contract's first year trading as daily volume fell to embarrassing low single digits on occasion.

In early 1991, TIFFE acknowledged its failure and announced that the contract specification would be modified. According to the announced revision, the contract will be priced on a one U.S. dollar basis as in case of the foreign exchange cash markets. The exchange hopes that the more familiar format will attract more traders from the cash market.

The first year-and-a-half of trading at the TIFFE indicated a very strong interest in the Euroyen futures and steadily declining activity in the Eurodollar contract. The Euroyen is considered by market participants as a phenomenal success. In 1990, 29 million Euroyen contracts were traded at the TIFFE, making it the second most active, short-term interest rate futures in the world. The exchange and its members hope that this volume will serve as a foundation for the growth in the other contracts and those still on the drawing board.

The exchange also hopes that its new "Fully Automated Computer Trading System" (FACTS) will provide a strong base for a further increase in turnover. FACTS replaced the TIFFE's previous telephone-based system in February 1991 and has brought about a major improvement in the exchange's order-processing capability.

Inter-Market Dynamics

Of the three futures contracts which the TIFFE offers, only the Euroyen contract was unique, at least until SIMEX quickly listed a similar contract in October 1989. Bank dealers see a great need only for this particular TIFFE contract and claim that it has boosted liquidity in Tokyo's short-term money markets through its risk management mechanism.

The TIFFE Eurodollar contract had bright prospects, but has not met expectations. While there is unquestionably latent demand for the product in Japan, potential users have a variety of other markets to trade. In the Asian timezone, SIMEX has developed a liquid Eurodollar futures market which now regularly doubles the Eurodollar volume at the London International Financial Futures Exchange (LIFFE). Tight quotes are made by SIMEX locals up to eighteen months out, and the open interest is almost 10 percent of the leading Eurodollar contract at the Chicago Mercantile Exchange. Japanese banks have remained the heavy users of the SIMEX contract. To the surprise of many, they have not shifted much of their business to the TIFFE, but some expect SIMEX to suffer. If anything, SIMEX has benefited from the TIFFE contract.

The deciding factor in the Euroyen and Eurodollar competition in the Asian timezone might be GLOBEX. The electronic trading joint venture between the Chicago Mercantile Exchange (CME), Chicago Board of Trade (CBOT), and Reuters might include SIMEX, but has not received approval from Japan's Ministry of Finance. If GLOBEX is integrated with SIMEX, it will pose a formidable challenge to the TIFFE. If SIMEX and GLOBEX stand alone, the TIFFE will have a better chance to emerge as a viable contender for dominating short term interest rate futures trading in the Asia–Pacific region.

Industry in the Making

The rivalry with SIMEX may have briefly injected some uncertainty about the success of the TIFFE, but such competition is beneficial to the developing futures markets in the region. Institutional users benefit from the expanding menu of trading vehicles.

For example, SIMEX differentiated itself in 1990 by launching Options on Euroyen futures, which attracted institutional users from Japan and elsewhere. By mid 1991, TIFFE was expected to respond to this proven demand and launch its own Euroyen options.

The outcome of the market share battle is difficult to predict, but the growth of the financial futures market in Tokyo is assured. The combination of a huge, internationalizing asset base and increasingly-sophisticated financial technology, is creating a growing institutional demand for new products in Japan.

Three-Month Euroyen Interest-Rate Futures

Exchange: The Tokyo International Financial Futures Exchange.

Contract Unit: 100 million yen.

Contract Months: March, June, September, and December.

Price Quotation: 100.00 minus annual interest rate which is 90/360 day base. For instance, 95.25 represents 4.75 percent.

Minimum Fluctuation: 0.01

Value of One Point: 2,500 yen.

Last Day of Trading: Two business days prior to the third Wednesday of the contract month.

Table 24A: Trading Volume of Euroyen Futures

	1985	1986	1987	1988	1989	1990
January	n/l*	n/l	n/l	n/l	n/l	1,821,196
February	n/l	n/l	n/l	n/l	n/l	1,202,388
March	n/l	n/l	n/l	n/l	n/l	2,207,178
April	n/l	n/l	n/l	n/l	n/l	2,204,678
May	n/l	n/l	n/l	n/l	n/l	2,865,820
June	n/l	n/l	n/l	n/l	368,518	2,010,128
July	n/l	n/l	n/l	n/l	783,282	2,637,998
August	n/l	n/l	n/l	n/l	814,212	3,281,578
September	n/l	n/l	n/l	n/l	1,415,994	2,251,962
October	n/l	n/l	n/l	n/l	1,756,882	4,066,408
November	n/l	n/l	n/l	n/l	1,822,518	1,779,504
December	n/l	n/l	n/l	n/l	2,028,746	2,498,548
Average	n/l	n/l	n/l	n/l	1,284,307	2,402,282
Total	n/l	n/l	n/l	n/l	8,990,152	28,827,386

Table 24B: Open Interest of Euroyen Futures

	1985	1986	1987	1988	1989	1990
January	n/l	n/l	n/l	n/l	n/l	163,070
February	n/l	n/l	n/l	n/l	n/l	193,259
March	n/l	n/l	n/l	n/l	n/l	163,242
April	n/l	n/l	n/l	n/l	n/l	183,582
May	n/l	n/l	n/l	n/l	n/l	263,733
June	n/l	n/l	n/l	n/l	16,806	230,243
July	n/l	n/l	n/l	n/l	81,269	276,054
August	n/l	n/l	n/l	n/l	99,474	398,933
September	n/l	n/l	n/l	n/l	128,032	370,057
October	n/l	n/l	n/l	n/l	150,915	464,273
November	n/l	n/l	n/l	n/l	173,195	492,159
December	n/l	n/l	n/l	n/l	149,961	309,489
Average	n/l	n/l	n/l	n/l	66,638	292,341

*Not Listed
(1) Trading of Euroyen futures started in June 1989.
(2) Open Interest is as of the end of each month.
(3) Open Interest of an expiring contract month is included up to the day preceding the settlement date of that contract month.
(4) Open Interest is calculated by counting the net number of futures contracts which remain to be liquidated by additional offsetting transactions or by physical delivery after taking account of matched but as yet unsettled bought and sold contracts.

Source: The Tokyo International Financial Futures Exchange

Settlement Date: The business day following the last day of trading.

Settlement: Cash Settlement.

Three-Month Eurodollar Interest-Rate Futures

Exchange: The Tokyo International Financial Futures Exchange.

Contract Unit: $1 million.

Contract Months: March, June, September, and December.

Price Quotation: 100.00 minus annual interest rate which is 90/360 day base. For instance, 91.50 represents 8.50 percent.

Minimum Fluctuation: 0.01

Value of One Point: $25

Last Day of Trading: Two business days prior to the third Wednesday of the contract month.

Settlement Date: The business day following the last day of trading.

Settlement: Cash Settlement.

Table 25A: Trading Volume of Eurodollar Futures

	1985	1986	1987	1988	1989	1990
January	n/l*	n/l	n/l	n/l	n/l	5,404
February	n/l	n/l	n/l	n/l	n/l	2,914
March	n/l	n/l	n/l	n/l	n/l	1,708
April	n/l	n/l	n/l	n/l	n/l	652
May	n/l	n/l	n/l	n/l	n/l	390
June	n/l	n/l	n/l	n/l	62,880	488
July	n/l	n/l	n/l	n/l	66,538	530
August	n/l	n/l	n/l	n/l	28,094	390
September	n/l	n/l	n/l	n/l	15,812	290
October	n/l	n/l	n/l	n/l	15,380	1,940
November	n/l	n/l	n/l	n/l	9,446	1,400
December	n/l	n/l	n/l	n/l	7,238	720
Average	n/l	n/l	n/l	n/l	29,341	1,402
Total	n/l	n/l	n/l	n/l	205,388	16,826

Table 25B: Open Interest of TIFFE Eurodollar Futures

	1985	1986	1987	1988	1989	1990
January	n/l	n/l	n/l	n/l	n/l	754
February	n/l	n/l	n/l	n/l	n/l	563
March	n/l	n/l	n/l	n/l	n/l	418
April	n/l	n/l	n/l	n/l	n/l	429
May	n/l	n/l	n/l	n/l	n/l	466
June	n/l	n/l	n/l	n/l	2,218	65
July	n/l	n/l	n/l	n/l	3,417	20
August	n/l	n/l	n/l	n/l	3,054	10
September	n/l	n/l	n/l	n/l	2,061	5
October	n/l	n/l	n/l	n/l	1,670	40
November	n/l	n/l	n/l	n/l	1,983	100
December	n/l	n/l	n/l	n/l	1,305	40
Average	n/l	n/l	n/l	n/l	1,309	243

*Not Listed
(1) Trading of Eurodollar futures started in June 1989.
(2) Open Interest is as of the end of each month.
(3) Open Interest of an expiring contract month is included up to the day preceding the settlement date of that
(4) Open Interest is calculated by counting the net number of futures contracts which remain to be liquidated by additional offsetting transactions or by physical delivery after taking account of matched but as yet unsettled bought and sold

Source: The Tokyo International Financial Futures Exchange

Japanese Yen/U.S. Dollar Currency Futures

Exchange: The Tokyo International Financial Futures Exchanges.

Exchange Contract Unit: 12.5 million yen.

Contract Months: March, June, September, and December.

Price Quotation: The U.S. dollar value equal to 1 yen in units of 0.000001. For instance, 0.008000 represents $1.00 = 125 yen.

Minimum Fluctuation: 0.000001

Value of One Point: $12.50

*Daily Price Limit:*None.

Last Day of Trading: Two business days prior to the third Wednesday of the contract month.

Settlement Date: The third Wednesday of the contract month.

Settlement: Physical delivery of Japanese yen in Tokyo and U.S. dollars in New York.

U.S. Dollar/Japanese Yen Currency Futures

*Exhange:*The Tokyo International Financial Futures Exchange

*Contract Unit:*U.S. $50,000

*Contract Months:*March, June, September and December on a 5 month cycle.

*Minimum Price Fluctuation:*U.S. $0.05

*Value of One Point:*Yen2,500 per tick.

*Daily Price Limit:*None.

*Last Day of Trading:*Two business days prior to the third Wednesday of the contract months.

*Settlement Date:*The third Wednesday of the contract month.

*Settlement:*Physical delivery of Yen in Tokyo and dollars in New York.

*Trading Hours:*9:00 A.M.-12:00 P.M.*
    1:30 P.M.-3:30 P.M.*
    * on last trading day: 9:00 A.M.-10:45 A.M.

Table 26A: Trading Volume of Japanese Yen Futures

	1985	1986	1987	1988	1989	1990
January	n/l*	n/l	n/l	n/l	n/l	472
February	n/l	n/l	n/l	n/l	n/l	484
March	n/l	n/l	n/l	n/l	n/l	1,020
April	n/l	n/l	n/l	n/l	n/l	740
May	n/l	n/l	n/l	n/l	n/l	660
June	n/l	n/l	n/l	n/l	8,330	760
July	n/l	n/l	n/l	n/l	4,342	640
August	n/l	n/l	n/l	n/l	13,480	670
September	n/l	n/l	n/l	n/l	4,062	8,608
October	n/l	n/l	n/l	n/l	2,084	18,684
November	n/l	n/l	n/l	n/l	1,230	15,160
December	n/l	n/l	n/l	n/l	1,060	9,868
Average	n/l	n/l	n/l	n/l	4,941	4,814
Total	n/l	n/l	n/l	n/l	34,588	57,766

Table 26B: Open Interest of Japanese Yen Futures

	1985	1986	1987	1988	1989	1990
January	n/l	n/l	n/l	n/l	n/l	31
February	n/l	n/l	n/l	n/l	n/l	30
March	n/l	n/l	n/l	n/l	n/l	30
April	n/l	n/l	n/l	n/l	n/l	50
May	n/l	n/l	n/l	n/l	n/l	10
June	n/l	n/l	n/l	n/l	565	10
July	n/l	n/l	n/l	n/l	344	34
August	n/l	n/l	n/l	n/l	579	14
September	n/l	n/l	n/l	n/l	442	10
October	n/l	n/l	n/l	n/l	387	200
November	n/l	n/l	n/l	n/l	237	333
December	n/l	n/l	n/l	n/l	31	110
Average	n/l	n/l	n/l	n/l	215	72

*Not Listed
(1) Trading of Eurodollar futures started in June 1989.
(2) Open Interest is as of the end of each month.
(3) Open Interest of an expiring contract month is included up to the day preceding the settlement date of that contract month.
(4) Open Interest is calculated by counting the net number of futures contracts which remain to be liquidated by additional offsetting transactions or by physical delivery after taking account of matched but as yet unsettled bought and sold contracts.

Source: The Tokyo International Financial Futures Exchange

Looking to the Future

Booming Domestic Activity

The proliferation of the Japanese futures and options markets and a new readiness to participate is most apparent in large Japanese firms' activities. Securities Houses, City Banks, Insurance Companies, Trust Banks, Regional Banks, Investment Trusts, and even the Postal Savings system behemoth are deploying resources into the futures and options markets.

Japanese life and nonlife insurance firms are beginning to unleash their huge assets. These companies have been doing their homework and picking the brains of their brokers, foreign, and domestic. They have greatly increased their trading in the JGB derivatives and are becoming more noticeable in the index futures and options markets.

Other Japanese institutions are also becoming increasingly active, both at home and abroad. Most noticable are the Trust Banks and Investment Trust Companies, whose share of index futures and options activity has grown dramatically in recent years. These two types of institutions have also become much more active in overseas derivative markets.

Japanese banks have also expanded their futures and options activity dramatically, and notably in TIFFE. Their use of equity index products grew rapidly in 1990, and most city banks have set up derivative units, often based in London or New York.

Japanese buisness corporations have also become active users of futures and options markets, particularly currency and index products. Even with the demise of their "zaitech" speculative activity, they can be expected to be increasingly significant and sophisticated derivative users.

The Ministry of Posts and Telecommunications (MoPT) has also begun to become a significant market force. This Ministry is by far Japan's largest recipient of savings. In addition to overseeing the country's enormous postal savings system, the MoPT has under its management life insurance and annuity funds valued at about 4.5 trillion yen ($320 billion) at the end of fiscal 1988. Beginning in April 1989, the MoPT was authorized to use futures and options trading in the management of its insurance and annuity funds. The Ministry hopes to increase the return on funds currently invested in equities, bonds, and cash. Although proceeding gingerly, because of its size, the MoPT is expected to become a major player — and will give a major boost to volume in the domestic markets.

Japan's Integration

Though many in Japan hope to make Tokyo the center of the global capital markets, few see it as a near-term possibility. Japan's trading systems, structure and markets are too different from the mainstream of the world markets. Nevertheless, the differences are expected to narrow. There are more foreign firms active in the Japanese markets than ever before, and vice-versa. The net result is the integration of a growing Japanese market and industry into the world's futures and options community.

Japan will inevitably become the predominant futures and options center for the Asia-Pacific timezone and may one day become the world's biggest trading arena in terms of trading volume. The contour of a huge industry in Japan is already visible. With the Ministry of Finance's division of activities resolved, firms and exchanges are focusing on building up business, and Japan's financial strength may enable it to pump a huge amount of money into its new markets. Many predict that the new markets gearing up in Japan will rival the U.S. in turnover and trading value by the turn of the century.

However, it will not be easy to develop true acumen and sophistication. Understanding this, Japanese institutions have been aligning themselves with the U.S. derivative trading specialists. In June 1989, ORIX Corp., a major Japanese leasing firm, paid $80 million for 33 percent of Commodities Corp. which is one of the world's largest futures money managers. Since then, three funds managed by Commodities Corp. have been offered by ORIX, with a total value of 26 billion yen. In February 1991, Nomura Securities linked with a futures trading powerhouse, Tudor Investment Corp., by forming Tudor/Nomura Global Trading Partners. Putting up the bulk of the initial $60 million capitalization for this 50-50 joint venture, Nomura has gained access to the trading techniques needed to flourish in the coming years.

The Japanese derivative market has become far too significant for global institutional investors to bypass. For instance, the Japanese equity market still accounts for more than 50 percent of the MSCI Europe, Australia, and Far East (EAFE) index even after its breath-taking dive in 1990. Furthermore, at the end of 1989, U.S. pension fund managers held 34.5 percent of their international assets in Japan, and the U.K. pension fund managers, 25 percent of their foreign equity portfolio. Thus, for many international fund managers, the Japanese futures and options contracts have already become an essential component of risk management of global institutional investment.

Endnotes

1. The listed shares at the Tokyo Stock Exchange are divided into two sections: the First Section and the Second Section. Usually, a newly listed share is assigned to the Second Section. The Exchange reviews each share traded in the Second Section at the end of its business year in order to determine whether it satisfies the reassignment rules of the First Section. If it does, it will be traded in the First Section. In contrast, if a share traded at the First Section does not meet the requirement of the First Section assignment, the share will be conversely moved to the Second Section. In general, the First Section is the marketplace for the shares of larger companies, and the Second Section for those of smaller and newly-listed companies. Currently, some 1,150 companies are listed in the First Section, and some 450 companies in the Second Section.

2. In the section on bond futures, the yen values are converted into U.S. dollars using the exchange rate of 150 yen/$1.00 prevailing at the end of 1989.

3. For a further discussion of JGB futures contract traded at the CBOT, see **Chapter 3: JAPANESE DERVATIVES LISTED IN THE U.S.**

JAPANESE DERIVATIVES
LISTED IN THE U.S. —

New Era for Global Risk Management

U.S. Investment in Japan

Investment in international stocks and bonds by America. ERISA (Employee Retirement Income Security Act) funds reached $109 billion—about 3.5 percent of total assets—in 1990, and will grow to $180 billion by 1994 according to an industry estimation. California Public Employee Retirement System (CALPERS), which has some $55 billion under management, invested $9 billion in international stocks and bonds in 1990. Small-sized U.S. institutional funds are also aggressively venturing into international markets. For instance, Firefighters Retirement System in Charlotte, North Carolina, set aside $9 million (or almost 11 percent) out of its $84 million for international investment in 1990.

Currently, nearly 35 percent of international assets held by U.S. pension funds is estimated to be in Japan. As the Japanese equity market began to show signs of stress in 1990 after a long-bull market which defied the logic of Western equity analysts, there was a flurry of offerings of the Japanese derivatives in the U.S. capital markets in 1990. This was a natural reaction to the need for risk management of the substantial U.S. investment in Japan.

Warrants on the Nikkei 225 Index

The biggest success for Japanese derivative offerings in the U.S., so far, has been put warrants on the Nikkei Stock Average listed on the American Stock Exchange (AMEX) during the first quarter of 1990. Following the success of the put warrants, the AMEX launched two series of call warrants on the Nikkei index in April 1990. The put Nikkei warrants seemed too good to be true: a new financial product in which the issuers, underwriters, and initial purchasers are all making money. Even more surprising was that profits came from an occurrence that foreigners had been consistently mispredicting—a crack in the Japanese equity market.

For once, foreigners were right about the Japanese equity market. After mispredicting Tokyo's downfall for the bulk of its relentless bull run in the 1980s, U.S.-based traders finally got a chance to be right as the 1990s began. Furthermore, warrants on the Nikkei index signal the changing role of exchanges in innovation of financial products, and a new era for global risk management products.

A Coup for the American Stock Exchange

Listing Nikkei put warrants helped save the AMEX from its dwindling fortunes. Even though it is the third largest stock exchange in the U.S., its market share has been falling, to a dismal 4 percent behind the 48 percent of the New York Stock Exchange and 41 percent of NASDAQ—NASDAQ is a nationwide electronic network of securities dealers established by the National Association of Securities Dealers.

The traditional exchanges such as the NYSE and the AMEX have been losing their trading volumes to the growing U.S. institutional adaptation of cost-effective, anonymous, 24-hour, off-the-exchange trading activities. These include: Instinet, which is an electronic order-matching network operated by Reuters; and Instinet's Crossing Network and Jefferies & Co.'s POSIT (Portfolio System for Institutional Trading System), which are after-hours portfolio trading systems.

Without the trading volume from the Nikkei warrants and other warrants on international equity indices—such as the FT-SE 100 of the U.K. and CAC-40 of France—turnover at the AMEX could have been down by 6 percent in 1990. After the impressive success of the Nikkei warrants, the AMEX listed two series of the FT-SE 100 put warrants in March and May of 1990 and two series of the CAC-40 put warrants in November 1990. According to the AMEX, the turnover of equity index warrants accounted for 13.10 percent of the Exchange's aggregate equity trading volume in 1990.

As the recession on Wall Street continued into its fourth year, American exchanges have seen their turnover continue to suffer. Consequently, the U.S. exchanges have been aggressively adapting to the changing market realities by taking advantage of the globalization of U.S. institutional and retail investment. Exchanges are no longer playing a passive role by merely providing a physical location where financial instruments can be traded. For instance, the AMEX initiated the introductory development of warrants on international equity indices, and provided active assistance to issuers and underwriters in overcoming a maze of regulatory hurdles for international derivatives. As the inter-exchange competition for a shrinking pie intensifies, exchanges are metamorphosing themselves into initiators and innovators. This will be an increasingly visible trend in the 1990s.

U.S. Exchange's Index Battle

It is not only among the Tokyo Stock Exchange (Topix futures and options), the Osaka Securities Exchange (Nikkei futures and options), the Nagoya Stock Exchange (Options 25), and the Singapore International Monetary Exchange (Nikkei futures) where an intense competition for dominance of index futures and options on the Japanese equity market continues. Seeing the success of the Nikkei warrants at the AMEX, in September 1990, three U.S. exchanges including the AMEX rushed to list index futures and options on the Japanese equity market.

The Chicago Mercantile Exchange (CME) listed Nikkei index futures and options; the Chicago Board of Trade (CBOT) listed Topix index futures and options; and the AMEX listed options on the Japan Index—the AMEX's proprietary Japanese equity market index, which is a modified, price-weighted index that measures the aggregate performance of 210 common stocks actively traded on the Tokyo Stock Exchange. So far, the CME and AMEX contracts have been moderately successful whereas the trading of the CBOT contract is currently moribund.

Japanese Government Bond Futures and Options

In September 1990, the CBOT listed Japanese government bond (JGB) futures and options. However, the globality of risk management tools does not necessarily guarantee the success of new listings. Despite the relatively liquid cash market in New York—almost $700 million of JGBs is traded daily in New York—the turnovers for JGB futures and options have been disappointing. In the first two months of 1991, trading volume for the JGB futures and options have been nil.

Exchange-traded Warrants on the Nikkei Stock Average

Warrants are very much like options, except usually longer dated. Stock index warrants behave much like options: put warrants on an equity index will reward holders if the index declines; call warrants, if the index rises. However, differing from options, warrants cannot be created by sellers or writers, but only by corporate issuance.

So far, five different issuers—A/S Eksportfinans, Bankers Trust, The Kingdom of Denmark, Paine Webber Group Inc., and Salomon Inc.—have sold six series of put warrants on the Nikkei Stock Average. Salomon has issued two series: one expiring on January 19, 1993, with a strike level of 36,821.14; another issue expiring on February 16, 1993, with a strike level of 37,471.99. The six series expire at different dates in the same year, 1993, and have different strike levels, but are all listed on the American Stock Exchange.

After the enormous success of the put warrants, two issuers—Salomon Inc. and Paine Webber Group Inc.—sold two series of call warrants on the Nikkei index. Both call series are also listed on the AMEX and expire in April, 1993. Salomon's call warrants have a strike price level of 28,442.94, and Paine Webber's, 29,249.06. Table 1A and 1B list the Nikkei put and call warrants currently traded on the AMEX.

All Nikkei warrants have a three year life, and will be settled based on the difference between the index values on the dates of settlement and issuance. That figure will then be divided by a specified divisor (2, 5, 10, or 15) and converted to the cash settlement value at the yen/dollar exchange rates specified at the time of issuance. The currency conversion is done by dividing the Nikkei index value by the yen/dollar rates. As a result, the divisors and yen/dollar conversion rates reduce the contract size of the Nikkei warrants substantially. For instance, at the Nikkei index value of 23,000.00, the contract size of the CME Nikkei futures will be $115,000.00—the multiplier of $5.00. In case of the Kingdom of Denmark Nikkei put warrants, the contract size will be $31.61—the division of the Nikkei index value (23,000.00) by the divisor of 5 and the yen/dollar conversion rate of 145.52. This small contract size of the Nikkei warrants significantly reduces their utility to institutional hedgers.

The Nikkei warrants are targeted mostly to retail investors as well as to some institutional investors, since U.S. retail investors are increasingly aware of investment opportunities abroad. For instance, the Nikkei put and call warrants can be traded in odd lots (i.e., less than 100 warrants) as well as in a round lot of 100 warrants. Moreover, the issuing prices of most of the Nikkei warrants

Table 1A: Nikkei Put Warrants at the AMEX

Issuer (Symbol)	Strike Level	Expiration	Public Distribution (in millions)
Paine Webber Group Inc.			
(PXB)	29,249.06	4/08/93	7.00
A/S Eksportfinans			
(EXW)	29,424.58	4/22/93	8.625
Salomon Inc.			
(SXA)	36,821.14	1/19/93	13.80
Bankers Trust of New York			
(BTB)	37,206.42	1/16/93	6.00
Salomon Inc.			
(SXO)	37,471.99	2/16/93	10.00
Kingdom of Denmark			
(DXA)	37,516.77	1/03/93	10.35

Source: The American Stock Exchange.

Table 1B: Nikkei Call Warrants at the AMEX

Issuer (Symbol)	Strike Level	Expiration	Public Distribution (in millions)
Salomon Inc.			
(SXZ)	28,442.94	4/06/93	6.50
Paine Webber Group Inc.			
(PXA)	29,249.06	4/08/93	5.00

Source: The American Stock Exchange.

were less than $5 apiece. Retail volume has been substantial—greater than institutional volume by most analysts' estimates. The warrants were the first U.S.-listed vehicle for individuals to bet on the Japanese equity market as a whole, and they became available at just the right time. The first Nikkei put warrants were introduced in January 1990. Since then, the Japanese equity market plunged 32.5 percent as of November, 1990, and an investor who purchased the Nikkei put warrants in January 1990 saw his investment soar by some 360 percent.

Also, the Nikkei warrants are popular among some institutional investors who face restrictions on using overseas Nikkei futures and options and who do not have have futures and options hedging facilities in Japan and/or Singapore.

Trading has been extremely active, with the average daily volumes of the eight issues exceeding 1.6 million units. Domestic money managers and hedge funds bought many of the warrants, to speculate, and for some, to protect their portfolios from the impact of a big Nikkei decline.

Arbitraguers also found lucrative opportunities from Nikkei warrant trading. The implied volatility of the AMEX warrants was low in relation to the index, and particularly low when compared to the OTC Nikkei warrants traded in London and Toronto, and the index options listed in Osaka and Tokyo.

Arbitrageurs were not the only ones making risk-free money. The issuers raised low-cost capital by selling the warrants priced for retail distribution, and fully hedging their liabilities at a wholesale cost by using the OTC warrants and listed index options and futures. For example, in the prospectus of its Nikkei warrants, Salomon states that it will look for options and futures hedges on the Osaka Stock Exchange (OSE) and the Singapore International Monetary Exchange (SIMEX) where Nikkei index futures and options are traded. Hedgers for the issuers—usually, investment banks who underwrite the warrants—maintain a delta-neutral exposure, and the nimble ones are reaping additional profits by rolling their hedges from rich to cheap instruments. Salomon Brothers is considered particularly adept at these maneuvers. However, if anyone has lost through participation in Nikkei warrant deals, it must be the Japanese institutional investors who took the other side of position in U.S. investment banks' over-the-counter hedging program and sold put options on the Nikkei too cheaply.

A less happy side to the Nikkei warrant saga is that the U.S. issuers' active hedging in the Japanese futures and options markets was blamed for aggravating the downfall of the Japanese equity market, and irritated Japanese regulators. Japanese regulators since then have imposed a moratorium on any new issuance of the Nikkei warrants—ending a source of innovative financial engineering. Unsurprisingly the Japanese Ministry of Finance had mush less to say about the tremendous number of the Nikkei put warrants issued by Japanese corporations in conjunction with bonds in the Eurobond market in the 1980s, which substantially lowered their financing costs and helped them undertake cross-border acquisitions of large corporations and landmark real estate. More surprisingly, this type of hedging activities has also elicited the concerns of the American Securities and Exchange Commission (SEC). Currently, the American SEC is not approving any issuance of warrants on the U.S. equity indices such as S&P 500 and Major Market Indices.

Since the warrants trade in the U.S. timezone, Tokyo's previous night's performance affects price movements at the opening, and accounts for the bulk of price changes. As the day progresses, the warrants react to a variety of other factors. These include London and U.S. trading of Japanese equities, the American equity and bond markets, and the yen/dollar exchange rate. It is not uncommon for a change in sentiment to cause the puts to rise even after a gain in Japanese equities or vice versa.

"Caveat emptor" must be the watchword for market participants. Not only are the warrants subject to many pricing variables, but clauses in the prospectuses protect issuers from a variety of "extraordinary events" that would otherwise benefit warrant-holders. Denmark can cancel its warrants, and Bankers Trust and Salomon can suspend the exercise for ten days.

All have seemingly liberal definitions of "extraordinary events" such as the suspension of trading of a specified number of index component shares, which happens frequently in Tokyo during order imbalances. "Natural calamities" and "international crises" — such as Tokyo earthquake or an oil crisis — can also trigger the issuers' defensiv clauses.

Therefore, while warrants supposedly give buyers limitless upside with limited risk, these warrants appear to have great, but definitely limited profit potential. However, for most investors who were on board for the first year's wild ride, the limited profit was good enough.

Nikkei Put and Call Warrants

Exchange: The American Stock Exchange.

Trading Unit: A Round Lot of 100 Warrants or Odd Lots (i.e., less than 100 Warrants).

Underlying Index: The Nikkei Stock Average.

Trading Hours: 9:30 A.M. to 4:00 P.M. (New York time).

Price Quotations: Quotations in U.S. dollars per Warrant. A fraction of a U.S. dollar in one eighth. A quote of 6 3/8 represents a price of $637.50 for a round lot.

Minimum Exercise Amount: Varies depending on each series of Warrant. For DXA, PXB, EXW, SXZ and PXA, 500 Warrants. For SXA and SXO, 250 Warrants. For DXA, 100 Warrants.

Exercise Limits: Varies depending on each series of Warrant. For DXA and EXW, 2,000,000 Warrants on any exercise date and 500,0000 Warrants per person on any exercise date. For PXB and PXA, 1,000,000 Warrants on any exercise date and 250,000 Warrants per person on any exercise date. For SXA, SXO, BTB and SXZ, no limits.

Exercise Date: Before any Warrants can be exercised, the trade must have settled (generally five business days). The exercise date is the New York business day on which an exercise notice is received by 3:00 P...M...

Valuation Date: The closing price of the Nikkei Stock Average for the next Tokyo business day following the exercise date is used to determine the cash settlement value of the exercised warrants.

Settlement Date: For trades, five business days. For the exercise before the expiration date: DXA and EXW are settled in five business days from the exercise date; SXA, SXO, and SXZ, in two business days from the valuation date; PXB and PXA, five business days from the valuation date; BTB, eight business days from the valuation date.

Settlement Value: U.S. dollar cash settlement value is greater of zero and the amount calculated by the formula:

- *Put Warrants:*

$$\frac{(\text{The Srike Level} - \text{The Closing of the Nikkei})}{\text{Yen/Dollar Exchange Rate}} \times \frac{1}{\text{Divisor}}$$

- *Call Warrants:*

$$\frac{(\text{The Closing of the Nikkei} - \text{The Strike Level})}{\text{Yen/Dollar Exchange Rate}} \times \frac{1}{\text{Divisor}}$$

Warrant Divisor: For BTB, the divisor is 2; for DXA, SXA, SXO, PXB and EXW, 5; for PXA, 10; and for SXZ, 15.

Table 2: Monthly Trading Volume of Nikkei Warrants

Issuer	Denmark	Salomon Inc.	Bankers Trust	Salomon Inc.	Salomon Inc.	Paine Webber	Paine Webber	Eksportfinans	
Symbol Put or Call Expiration	DXA.WS Put 1/3/93	SXA.WS Put 1/19/93	BTB.WS Put 1/16/93	SXO.WS Put 2/16/93	PXB.WS Put 4/8/93	EXW.WS Put 4/22/93	SXZ.WS Call 4/6/93	PXA.WS Call 4/8/93	TOTAL VOLUME
1/90	15,275,000	13,491,000	not listed	n/l	n/l	n/l	n/l	n/l	28,766,000
2/90	7,781,000	10,517,000	9,132,000	11,866,000	n/l	n/l	n/l	n/l	39,296,000
3/90	10,989,000	19,636,000	9,836,000	11,755,000	n/l	n/l	n/l	n/l	52,216,000
4/90	8,561,000	12,503,000	4,589,000	8,855,000	3,461,000	889,000	13,626,000	3,161,000	55,645,000
5/90	2,699,000	4,671,000	1,637,000	2,393,000	1,856,000	1,463,000	4,837,000	5,153,000	24,709,000
6/90	3,342,000	4,192,000	1,957,000	3,295,000	1,490,000	1,809,000	1,792,000	1,216,000	19,093,000
7/90	2,539,000	4,068,000	1,829,000	1,990,000	1,609,000	984,000	1,693,000	734,000	15,446,000
8/90	13,427,000	17,136,000	6,102,000	8,642,000	15,230,000	9,156,000	3,704,000	1,537,000	74,934,000
9/90	7,146,000	8,673,000	2,452,000	4,365,000	9,215,000	5,170,000	2,049,000	1,722,000	40,792,000
10/90	6,810,000	7,429,000	1,940,000	3,034,000	7,935,000	5,345,000	2,485,000	2,437,000	37,415,000
11/90	3,500,000	4,459,000	623,000	1,404,000	3,927,000	2,859,000	987,000	814,000	18,573,000
12/90	2,200,000	2,826,000	432,000	642,000	2,524,000	2,540,000	917,000	829,000	12,910,000
1/91	3,273,000	5,619,000	489,000	1,230,000	4,244,000	4,788,000	915,000	1,067,000	21,625,000
2/91	1,623,000	4,375,000	261,000	1,052,000	3,507,000	3,867,000	6,227,000	4,231,000	25,143,000
3/91	1,375,000	1,210,000	1,333,000	313,000	1,396,000	2,213,000	1,855,000	1,049,000	10,744,000

Source: The American Stock Exchange.

Yen/Dollar Exchange Rate: For BTB and PXA, fluctuating rates; for DXA, a fixed rate of 145.325 yen/dollar; for SXA, 145.520 yen/dollar; for SXO, 144.554 yen/dollar; for PXB, 159.800 yen/dollar; for EXW, 158.840 yen/dollar; and SXZ, 158.800 yen/dollar.

Japanese Index Futures and Options

Seizing the momentum of the successful launching of exchange-traded Nikkei warrants, Amercan. exchanges launched futures and options on Japanese equity market indices in September 1990. The Japanese Ministry of Finance was known to be opposed to U.S. trading of futures and options on its equity market indices, but CFTC approval had already been given to the CME and CBOT. The CME listed futures and options on the Nikkei priced in U.S. dollars, and the CBOT, futures on the Topix priced in the Japanese yen.

Not being able to acquire the licensing agreement for the Nikkei Stock Average, the AMEX listed options on its internally-created Japan Index. The Japan Index (JPN) is designed in such a way that it closely tracks the Nikkei. Like the Nikkei index, the JPN is price-weighted, and constructed to reflect the movement of the large capitalization stocks listed in the First Section of the TSE. The number of the constituent shares for the JPN is 210, while the number for the Nikkei is 225. The Japan Index is calculated once a day, based on the closing prices of the constituent shares on the Tokyo Stock Exchange; the index value is disseminated by the AMEX before the opening of trading.

Within six months of trading, the CME emerged as the primary survivor of the U.S. battle of Japanese index products. The dominance of Nikkei futures and options over Topix in Japan obviously helped the CME. Moreover, the U.S. dollar settlement term has made the trading of the CME contracts more user-friendly. In contrast, CBOT Topix traders have to tally their position in yen. Less than a month after listing, trading on the CBOT's contract became moribund. Consequently, options on the Topix futures, which had been listed by the CBOT, were never traded. In contrast, turnover for the CME futures averaged about 600 contracts a day in their first six months, and has continued to grow. Furthermore, the open interest has grown steadily since the inception — and some observers believe it may soon rival the SIMEX Nikkei contract.

Options on the Nikkei Stock Average might have consolidated the AMEX leadership on the Japanese derivatives. However, despite the high correlation with the Nikkei index (greater than 0.99 according to the AMEX), the Japan

Index is obviously not the Nikkei itself, and still needs to establish its recognition among traders as an index substitutable for the benchmark Nikkei index. Moreover, its contract size is almost five times smaller than that of the CME Nikkei futures and as a result, incurs higher transaction costs for institutional hedgers. Also, the lack of flexibility, due to its "European-styling," is an additional disadvantage of the AMEX contract. Nevertheless, options on the JPN have been steadily gaining ground in the global derivative markets, given that they are only listed cash options on the Japanese equity market index outside Japan. As of January 1991, the average daily volume for the previous four months has been close to 2,000 contracts.

Nikkei Stock Average Futures

Exchange: The Chicago Mercantile Exchange.

Contract Unit: $5 times the Nikkei Stock Average.

Minimum Price Fluctuation: Five index points ($25.00 per contract).

Trading Hours: 8:00 A.M. to 3:15 P.M. (Chicago time).

Contract Months: Cycle of March, June, September, and December.

Table 3:   Monthly Trading Volume and Month-End Open Interest of Nikkei Futures

Month	Volume	Open Interest
9/90	2,000	966
10/90	17,566	3,818
11/90	14,174	3,892
12/90	18,308	3,924
1/91	12,247	4,096
2/91	26,118	7,349

Source: The Chicago Mercantile Exchange.

Last Day of Trading: First business day preceding the determination of the final settlement price; usually, the business day preceding the second Friday of the contract month.

Settlement: Cash settlement.

Options on Nikkei Futures

Exchange: The Chicago Mercantile Exchange.

Contract Unit: One Nikkei futures contract.

Strike Price: Five-hundred point intervals.

Minimum Price Fluctuation: Five index points ($25.00 per contract). A trade may occur at a price of 2.5 index points ($12.50) if such trades result in the liquidation of position for both parties to the trade.

Trading Hours: 8:00 A.M. to 3:15 P.M. (Chicago time).

Contract Months: All twelve calendar months. The underlying instrument for the three monthly option expirations within a quarter is the quarter-end futures contract.

Table 4:   Monthly Trading Volume and Month-End Open
Interest of Options on Nikkei Futures

Month	Volume	Open Interest
9/90	735	658
10/90	4,124	2,152
11/90	2,426	3,307
12/90	1,508	1,093
1/91	1,406	1,338
2/91	989	1,495

Source: The Chicago Mercantile Exchange.

Last Day of Trading: (1) March, June, September, December — same date and time as the underlying futures contract, and (2) the other eight months — Friday preceding the third Saturday of the contract month.

Settlement: Cash settlement.

Tokyo Stock Price Index (TOPIX) Futures

Exchange: The Chicago Board of Trade.

Contract Unit: 5,000 yen times the Tokyo Stock Price Index (Topix)

Minimum Price Fluctuation: One-half index point or 2,500 yen (about $16).

Daily Price Limit: Seventy (70) index points (350,000 yen).

Trading Hours: 8:15 A.M. to 3:15 P.M. (Chicago time); 6:00 P.M. to 8:15 P.M. (Sunday through Thursday).

Contract Months: Cycle of March, June, September, December.

Last Trading Day: Same as the Topix futures traded at the Tokyo Stock Exchange. The last trading day for the TSE Topix futures is the first business day prior to the second Friday of the contract month. If this day is not a CBOT business day, the last day of trading is the first CBOT business day prior to the last trading day of the TSE Topix futures.

Settlement: Cash settlement.

Table 5: Monthly Trading Volume and Month-End Open Interest of Topix Futures

Month	Volume	Open Interest
9/90	167	112
10/90	63	88
11/90	0	88
12/90	0	0
1/91	0	0
2/91	0	0

Source: The Chicago Board of Trade

Position Limit: 8,000 contracts net long or net short in all months combined.

Reportable Position: 500 contracts in any one month.

Options on the Japan Index

Exchange: The American Stock Exchange.

The Japan Index: The Japan Index is a modified price-weighted index which consists of 210 common stocks actively traded on the Tokyo Stock Exchange. The Index is designed to represent the broad cross section of Japanese industries. Based upon the closing prices on the TSE, the Index is calculated once a day and disseminated before the opening of trading. The Index is denominated in U.S. dollars, using the fixed exchange rate of 100 yen per one U.S. dollar. For instance, if the yen price of the index is 30,500, the Index value will be 305. The base date of the index was April 2, 1990, and its value was 280.00.

According the American Stock Exchange, it has made an agreement with the TSE that the TSE may request changes in the Japan Index or the options contract under certain circumstances, and that the Exchange will make the relevant implementation if it determines the request are justified. See Appendix VI for the list of the JPN constituent shares and their relative weightings in the index.

Contract Unit: $100 times the Japan Index.

Trading Hours: 9:30 A.M. to 4:15 P.M. (New York time).

Expiration Months: Three consecutive near-term months plus five additional expiration months of a June-December cycle. For instance, in June 1991 the following expiration months will be listed: July 1991, Aug. 1991, Sept. 1991, Dec. 1991, June 1992, Dec. 1992, June 1993, and Dec. 1993.

Expiration Day: The Saturday following the third Friday of the expiration months.

Last Trading Day: The second business day prior to the last business prior to the expiration day (normally Thursday).

Table 6:   Monthly Trading Volume and Month-End Open Interest of Japan Index Options

Month	Volume	Open Interest
9/90	7,352	4,484
10/90	53,341	14,987
11/90	38,766	18,109
12/90	31,423	11,034
1/91	31,683	11,537
2/91	32,275	16,121
3/91	19,401	12,521

Source: The American Stock Exchange.

Exercise Limit: The options can be exercised only on the last business day prior to the expiration day.

Settlement: Cash settlement.

Position Limit: 25,000 contracts on the same side of the market if no more than 15,000 of such contracts are in the nearest expiration months series.

Futures and Options on Japanese Government Bonds

Approximately $700 million Japanese government bonds (JGBs) are traded in New York daily. Given this size of the secondary market trading, a solid demand for the JGB futures and options seems natural. However, trading on the CBOT contracts have been as dismal as the CBOT's equity index counterparts. Call options on the JGB futures were listed but never traded. One explanation for this unimpressive reception by the U.S. institutional investment community might be due to the yen settlement terms. Also, the unwillingness of the CBOT floor traders to make a liquid market has been pointed out as another obstacle against the success of the JGB contracts.

Futures on Long-Term Japanese Government Bonds

Exchange: The Chicago Board of Trade.

Contract Unit: One JGB with a face value at maturity of 20,000,000 yen or multiple thereof.

Trading Hours: Monday through Friday, 7:20 A.M. to 2:00 P.M. (Chicago time); Evening trading hours (Sunday through Friday), 5:40 P.M. to 8:15 P.M. (central standard time) and 6:40 to 9:15 P.M. (central daylight saving time).

Deliverable Grade: JGBs with an initial maturity of less than eleven years, and a remaining maturity of at least seven years. The bonds must be in registered or book-entry form, and be registered in the name of one entity exempt from Japanese withholding tax on JGB coupon interest.

Price Quotation: Points (200,000 yen) and 1/100 of a point (2,000 yen)

Minimum Price Fluctuation: 1/100 of a point (2,000 yen).

Daily Price Limit: Two (2) points or 400,000 yen per contract.

Contract Months: Cycle of March, June, September, and December.

Last Trading Day: The CBOT business day preceding the ninth Tokyo Stock Exchange business day prior to delivery day.

Delivery Day: The 20th day of the contract month, or the next TSE business day if the 20th day is not a business day.

Delivery Method: By buyer's and seller's Japanese custodian through the Bank of Japan and a delivery firm designated by the Board of Trade Clearing Corporation (BOTCC). The invoice price is the final settlement price multiplied by the appropriate conversion factor, plus 100 percent of accrued interest.

Table 7: Monthly Trading Volume and Month-End Open Interest of JGB Futures

Month	Volume	Open Interest
9/90	1,411	575
10/90	1,367	161
11/90	261	193
12/90	23	0
1/91	0	0
2/91	0	0

Source: The Chicago Board of Trade.

Options on Long-Term Japanese Government Bond Futures

Exchange: The Chicago Board of Trade.

Contract Unit: One CBOT long-term Japanese government bond futures contract with 20,000,000 yen face value.

Trading Hours: Monday through Friday, 7:20 A.M. to 2:00 P.M. (Chicago time); Evening trading hours (Sunday through Friday) 5:40 P.M. to 8:15 P.M. (central standard time) and 6:40 P.M. to 9:15 P.M. (central daylight saving time).

Minimum Price Fluctuation: 1/100 of a point (2,000 yen).

Strike Prices: Listed in one-point (200,000) strike intervals per JGB futures contract month to bracket the near-by CBOT JGB futures price.

Daily Price Limit: Two points above or below the previous day's settlement premium (expandable to three points). No limits on the last day of trading.

Contract Months: Cycle of March, June, September, and December.

Table 8:   Monthly Trading Volume and Month-End Open
            Interest of Put Options on JGB Futures

Month	Volume	Open Interest
9/90	0	0
10/90	475	475
11/90	0	0
12/90	0	0
1/91	0	0
2/91	0	0

Source: The Chicago Board of Trade.

Last Trading Day: 12:00 P.M. on the last Friday preceding by at least five business days the last business day of the month preceding the option contract month. For example, the last trading day for the December 1990 JGB options in November 23, 1990.

Expiration: At 10:00 A.M. (Chicago time) on the first Saturday following the last day of trading.

Exercise: Option buyers may exercise the option by 6:00 P.M. (Chicago time) on any day prior to expiration. Options at least two points in-the-money on the last day of trading are automatically exercised.

A New Era for Global Risk Management Products

In the 1990s, risk management tools for foreign investment will not to be limited only to local derivative products. Exchanges, in conjunction with the global investment community, are aggressively pioneering risk management tools for international investment. U.S.-based investors no longer need to trade the Japanese equity index futures and options listed in Japan or Singapore. Now, they can lay off the risk of their Japanese investment in their own backyard. We have also seen this occurring in Europe as well. The futures on the German government bonds listed on the Deutsche Terminböerse (DTB) in Frankfurt are also traded on the London International Financial Futures Exchange (LIFFE). Furthermore, the daily turnover of the London contract exceeds that of its counterpart in Frankfurt by a ratio 13-to-1.

However, the modest success of the Nikkei futures and the Japan Index options confirms the importance of the linkage between cash and derivative markets in driving derivative trading. Despite substantial U.S. investment in the Japanese equity market, the insufficient existence of the Japanese equity trading during the U.S. trading hours makes the efficient pricing of the Nikkei futures and Japan Index options extremely difficult. Consequently, no arbitrage between the derivatives and their underlying cash market can be done. Nevertheless, constant innovations in the global capital markets will lead us in the near future to the age when European and U.S. investors can actively trade Japanese equities among themselves through an electronic trading system such as SEAQ International of the London Stock Exchange during their overlapping trading hours and establish a liquid cash market for Japanese equities outside of Japan. This would subsequently bring about actively traded Japanese futures and options markets in the European and U.S. times zones.

C H A P T E R
4

AUSTRALIA –
ESSENTIAL RISK MANAGEMENT FOR INVESTING DOWN UNDER

Overview of the Australian Futures and Options Markets

Introduction

The Sydney Futures Exchange (SFE) is the second largest futures exchange in the Pacific Rim region after the Tokyo Stock Exchange and in 1989 was the ninth largest in the world (Table 1 lists the ten largest futures exchanges in the world). Founded in 1960, it was Asia-Pacific's first futures exchange, and also the first – on October 17, 1979 – to list a financial futures contract, 90-day Bank Accepted Bill futures. Along with New Zealand, Australia is the first to open the trading day in the Pacific Rim time zone, hours before Japan, Hong Kong, or Singapore. The exchange has expanded rapidly in recent years, as the restrictions which had prevented overseas residents from trading in Australian markets were lifted in December 1983. In 1989, the SFE traded close to 12 million futures and options contracts (Chart 1 shows the trading volume growth of the SFE from 1979 to 1989).

The Sydney Futures Exchange lists a unique range of Australian financial derivatives essential to the management of investments in the Australian capital markets (Table 2 lists the currently-traded contracts at the SFE). The SFE has made a few notable attempts to launch international products, but they have ended in failure. The exchange now emphasizes the domestic nature of its product range, while actively nurturing international participation both during and after the Australian market hours via its automated trading system, the Sydney Computerized Overnight Market (SYCOM). For instance, in order to enhance

Table 1:   Top Ten Futures Exchanges of the World

Exchange	Jan.–Dec. 1989 Total Futures and Options Trading Volume (Number of Contracts Traded)
1. Chicago Board of Trade (CBOT)	138,351,317
2. Chicago Mercantile Exchange (CME)	104,654,457
3. New York Mercantile Exchange (NYMEX)	38,490,463
4. Marche a Terme International de France (MATIF)	26,002,003
5. London International Financial Futures Exchange (LIFFE)	23,859,316
6. Tokyo Stock Exchange (TSE)	22,698,136
7. New York Commodity Exchange Inc. (COMEX)	19,052,955
8. Tokyo Commodity Exchange for Industry	12,017,889
9. Sydney Futures Exchange (SFE)	11,826,439
10. New York Coffee, Sugar & Cocoa Exchange (NYCSCE)	11,217,844

Source: The Sydney Futures Exchange.

Chart 1:   Sydney Futures Exchange Limited Annual Volume (1979-1989)

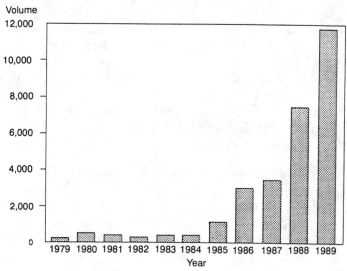

Source: The Sydney Futures Exchange.

Table 2: Currently-Traded Futures and Options Contracts at the SFE

1. 90-Day Bank Accepted Bill Futures
2. Options on 90-Day Bank Accepted Bill Futures
3. 10-Year Commonwealth Treasury Bond Futures
4. Options on 10-Year Commonwealth Treasury Bond Futures
5. 3-Year Commonwealth Treasury Bond Futures
6. Options on 3-Year Commonwealth Treasury Bond Futures
7. Australian Semi-Government Bond Futures*
8. Options on Australian Semi-Government Bond Futures*
9. All Ordinaries Share Price Index Futures
10. Options on All Ordinaries Share Price Index Futures
11. Australian Dollar Futures
12. Options on Australian Dollar Futures
13. Wool Futures
14. Live Cattle Futures

* These two contracts were delisted in December 1990.

international participation, the SFE established links with the London International Financial Futures Exchange (LIFFE) in October 1986, and the New York Commodity Exchange (COMEX) in November 1986 — the linkage between the LIFFE and SFE was the first one between two non-U.S. exchanges.[1] The SFE lists eight futures contracts and six options on futures. All but two are in financial-related items.[2] The vast bulk of institutional, local and retail activities is in the short and long term Australian interest rate contracts. Smaller, but still significant business is done in stock index futures and options.

The demand for Australian risk management tools has supported the tremendous growth of the SFE. By mid-1988, the exchange was bursting at its seams. The trading volume for its ten most popular financial futures and options was up by 40 percent in 1988 over 1987, despite a severe drop in the turnover of All Ordinaries Share Price Index futures and options after the international stock market crash of 1987.

In February 1989, the SFE moved to a new, customized trading floor which has incorporated latest technologies in computers, telecommunications, acoustics, and space efficiency. This new premises will assist the exchange to reach its full potential. The turnovers for 1989 was about 75 percent higher than the year-earlier period. The Sydney Futures Exchange has literally and figuratively built a strong foundation for the 1990s (Chart 2 and Chart 3 show the

Chart 2: Sydney Futures Exchange, Futures Contract Volumes, 1985-1989

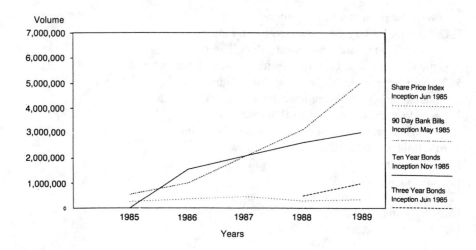

Source: The Sydney Futures Exchange.

Chart 3: Sydney Futures Exchange, Option Contract Volumes, 1985-1989

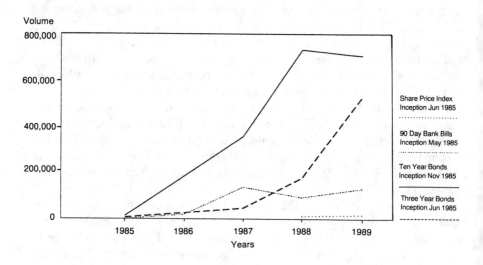

Source: The Sydney Futures Exchange

trading volume growth of selected futures and options contracts of the SFE from 1985 to 1989).

Although Australia has an excellent geographical position, the exchange has had little success with international products like the Eurodollar interest rate and U.S. Treasury bond futures. Nevertheless, the Australian futures market is still important for foreign institutional investors.

Because of the relatively high yields available on the country's debt, Australian dollar bonds and bills have become a significant component of many international fixed income portfolios. (Chart 4 shows the historical yield movement of 10-year Australian Treasury Bonds vis-a-vis 10-year U.S. Treasury Bonds). Australian interest and exchange rates are notoriously volatile, thus necessitating efficient hedging vehicles. This is where the SFE finds its widening niche in the international futures markets.

Market Structure

At the end of 1989, there were over 380 members of the SFE, divided into three categories: Floor Membership, Associate Membership and Local Membership. Floor membership is the highest class of membership and provides the right to trade on behalf of clients and for proprietary accounts. This category was limited to 29 members because of space constraints on the old premises (Table 3 lists the Floor Members of the SFE) — for more detailed information on Floor Members of the SFE, refer to Appendix II. A restructuring of membership — which will allow more firms to have a presence in the pits — is now under consideration. In December 1991 the exchange will switch to a member-owned clearing house.

Floor membership has become the preserve of the largest Australian and foreign banks and brokers. Their presence has displaced commission houses and commodity firms. This has introduced much treasury and institutional participation into the marketplace.

There are three forms of Associate Membership: (1) Full Associate Members, (2) Introducing Broker Associate Members, and (3) Market Associate Members. Full Associate members trade on their own behalf or on behalf of clients, but their orders are executed by Floor Members. Introducing Broker Associate Members can advise clients on futures and options trading, but have orders executed and accounts maintained by Floor Members. Market Associate Members trade for their own accounts and have no floor presence.

The SFE actively nurtures its Local Members, since they provide much-needed liquidity to the markets. There are about 80 locals on the SFE floor, with an occasional supplement of Chicago and London traders on the exchange's spe-

Chart 4: Australian & U.S. Ten-Year Government Bond Yields
Weekly Data: January 1987 to January 1991

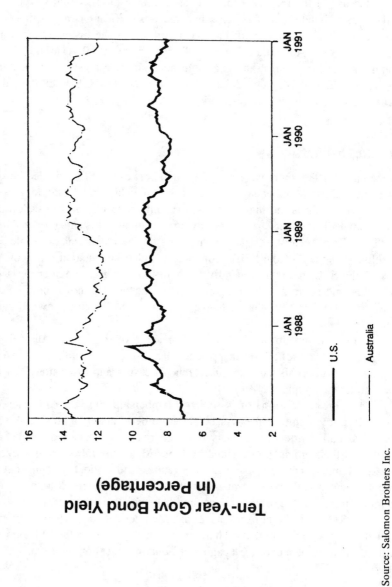

Source: Salomon Brothers Inc.

Table 3:   FLOOR MEMBERS

All-States Futures Pty Limited
ANZ McCaughan Futures Limited
Australian Gilt Futures Limited
Australian Interdealer Brokers Pty Limited
Bain Refco Commodities Limited
Barclays deZoete Wedd Australia Futures Pty Limited
Bisley Commodity Brokers Limited
BNY Australia Limited
BT Australia Limited
C., A. & L. Bell Commodities Corp. Pty Limited
Capel Court Corporation Limited
CitiFutures Limited
Commonwealth Bank of Australia
Credit Lyonnais Rouse Australia Pty Limited
CS First Boston Australia Futures Pty Limited
HKBA Futures Limited
Fay Richwhite Futures Australia Limited
LCF Limited
Macquarie Bank Limited
McIntosh Risk Management Limited
Merrill Lynch, Pierce, Fenner, Smith & Co. Limited
J. P. Morgan Australia Limited
National Australia Bank Limited
Ord Westpac Futures Limited
SBC Dominquez Barry Futures Limited
SBV Futures Pty Limited
Schroders Australia Limited
State Bank of New South Wales
Tullett & Tokyo (Australia) Pty Ltd
J. B. Were Futures Pty Limited

Source: The Sydney Futures Exchange.

cial local permit plan. Locals often account for up to 50 percent of the trading volume in some contracts.

Sydney's futures community is regulated by federal legislation and a self-regulatory system administered by the SFE. In practice, the legislation, known as the Futures Industry Code, delegates much of the regulatory responsibility to Australian futures exchanges — the SFE is presently the only active exchange; Melbourne's Australian Financial Futures Market is dormant. Since the end of 1987, the Code has been effective in all Australian states and territories.

The Australian regulatory environment received the approval of the Commodity Futures Trading Commission (CFTC) of the U.S. in November 1988, and the SFE became the first foreign exchange to gain an exemption from Part 30 of the U.S. Commodity Exchange Act. As a result of this and subsequent rulings, SFE members can promote exchange products, except All Ordinaries index options in the U.S without the CFTC registration. The CFTC decision was based in part on its satisfaction that the SFE regulations and the federal industry code provide client protections similar to those which apply in the U.S. — on CFTC approval, refer to Appendix V. The new Sydney Futures Exchange Clearing House will adopt the increasingly standardized American method of clearing, and thus further improve the SFE's attractiveness to international users.

Sydney Overnight Computerized Market (SYCOM)

On November 30, 1989, the SFE doubled its trading hours by offering an after-hours screen dealing system, Sydney Overnight Computerized Market (SYCOM), and became the world's first futures exchange to extend its trading hours in this way. The extended trading hours are from 4:40 P.M. to 2:00 A.M., Sydney time.

Although SYCOM is a very sophisticated system, it is user-friendly through the utilization of off-the-shelf personal computers linked by a telephone. The SYCOM system does not replicate the function of the trading pit, but allocates orders on a price and time priority. The SFE claims that it takes one-hundredth of a second for an order to be received by the host processor. Furthermore, orders may be lodged into SYCOM during the preopening period of the trading session. This capability of SYCOM enables it to achieve an equilibrium price at the beginning of the SYCOM session.

Currently, only Floor Members of the SFE are eligible to have terminals, and all terminals are located in Sydney. However, as futures trading is becoming more and more globalized, the SFE plans to provide international communication links between Floor Members in Sydney and overseas offices and also, to make an order entry system for SYCOM trades available through a major financial services network. Initially, only 10-Year Commonwealth Treasury bond futures were traded on SYCOM, but since then, All Ordinaries Share Price Index, 90-Day Bank Accepted Bill, and 3-Year Commonwealth Treasury Bond futures, have been added. By late 1991, all active SFE options contracts are expected to be listed on SYCOM.

All trades executed on SYCOM are cleared with the contracts traded on the exchange floor in the following day's session. Also, the cost to a Floor Member for a trade executed on SYCOM is the same as that for a contract executed on the trading floor.

SYCOM has enabled the SFE to project itself as a technological leader in the international futures industry. Also, if SYCOM becomes a more mature and complete system as planned by the SFE, the SFE will be able to attract the overseas business and maintain its place as a leading futures market in the Pacific Rim time zone.

Australian Equity Futures And Options Contracts

The Australian equity market has attracted a significant amount of domestic and international institutional funds since late 1983 when the Australian capital markets were liberalized to foreign investment. In order to enhance the internationalization of its capital markets, the Australian government further eased the restrictions on inward foreign investment in October 1985, and raised the minimum level at which investment by foreigners needs official approval. As of December 1990, Australia accounted for 2.2 percent of the Europe, Australia, Far East (EAFE) Index of Morgan Stanley Capital International, although it had been higher before the international market crash of October 1987.

The most popular domestic indicator of the share market is the Australian Stock Exchange's All Ordinaries Share Price Index. The index is a capitalization-weighted group of over 250 companies listed on the Sydney and Melbourne Stock Exchanges.[3] The market value of these firms accounts for nearly 90 percent of the total market capitalization of the Australian equity market. The share futures contract at the SFE is based on this index, and trades in three month cycles on units of A$100.00 times the index.

Before the 1987 crash, All Ordinaries Share Price Index futures were heavily traded with broad institutional and retail participation. However, the trading volume in 1988 dropped 51 percent to 307,000 down from 625,000 in 1987, and since then, recovered somewhat, up about 1 percent in 1990 from the 1988 level. Institutional investors have become the primary users of the index futures. While less liquid than before the 1987 crash, the futures contract still tracks the Australian equity market quite accurately, and are suitable for portfolio hedging and passive equity indexation strategies.

Options on All Ordinaries Share Price Index futures lost much business since the crash of 1987, but remain popular with institutional investors, and have regained the precrash turnover levels. Although only 82,000 options were traded in 1990, down from 137,000 in 1987, over 185,000 were traded in 1990. The options trade two consecutive futures cycles, with strike prices 25 index points apart.

The Sydney Stock Exchange launched call options on Australian equities in 1976, and introduced put options in 1982. Currently, options on 27 companies are traded on the exchange and cleared through the Options Clearing House Pty. Ltd.

All Ordinaries Share Price Index Futures

Contract Unit: A sum of money equal to one hundred times the Australian Stock Exchange's All Ordinaries Share Price Index expressed in Australian dollar terms.

The All Ordinaries Share Price Index: The Australian Stock Exchange's All Ordinaries Share Price Index is calculated by using the market prices of over 250 Australian companies listed on the Sydney and Melbourne Stock Exchanges. The market capitalization of these companies represents nearly 90 percent of the market value of all shares listed on Australian stock exchanges.

The Index is market capitalization-weighted. Each component share is weighted by multiplying the number of shares outstanding in the company by the price per share to give a total market value known as the company's market capitalization.

Because the Index is market capitalization weighted, a company with a large market capitalization exerts more influence on the movement of the Index than a company whose market value is smaller.

See Appendix IV for a list of the All Ordinaries Share Price Index's constituent shares and their relative weighings in the Index.

Contract Months: March, June, September and December — out to 18 months.

Trading Hours: 9:30 A.M. to 12:30 P.M.; 2:00 P.M. to 4:10 P.M.

Quotations: Prices are quoted in the same form as the All Ordinaries Share Price Index expressed to one decimal place.

Minimum Price Fluctuation: 0.1 index point which is equal to A$10.00.

Mandatory Cash Settlement: All bought and sold contracts in existence at the close of the last trading day of the contract month must be settled in cash by the Clearing House.

Price for Cash Settlement: The closing quotation for the All Ordinaries Share Price Index on the last trading day of the contract month is the price for cash settlement, and is declared by the Clearing House. The closing price is calculated to one decimal place. The Australian Stock Exchange (Sydney) Limited provides the settlement price to the Clearing House at 12:00 P.M. on the business day following the last trading day of the contract month.

Margin Requirement: Minimum margin deposits are determined by the Clearing House, and subject to change from time to time. a$5500 in March 1991.

Commission: Commissions are negotiable as from June 1, 1984.

Table 4A: Open Outcry Trading Volume of All Ordinaries Index Futures

	1986	1987	1988	1989	1990	1991
January	24,508	43,308	11,258	24,331	19,238	39,103
February	31,281	66,000	20,566	25,550	18,364	31,926
March	36,745	68,547	35,720	24,174	27,679	
April	33,186	61,249	18,160	27,354	22,056	
May	43,865	63,507	23,344	35,476	24,148	
June	30,756	62,835	26,276	24,013	22,923	
July	37,863	50,631	20,887	23,738	27,935	
August	29,454	46,906	25,231	28,786	29,601	
September	49,266	46,594	49,569	34,351	23,301	
October	61,048	61,127	29,444	44,677	41,133	
November	52,823	30,493	24,190	18,853	28,574	
December	55,344	23,502	22,828	14,543	25,049	
Average	40,512	52,058	25,623	27,154	25,833	
Total	486,139	624,699	307,473	325,846	310,001	

Table 4B: SYCOM Trading Volume of All Ordinaries Index Futures

	1986	1987	1988	1989	1990	1991
January	n/l*	n/l	n/l	n/l	n/l	1,342
February	n/l	n/l	n/l	n/l	35	572
March	n/l	n/l	n/l	n/l	206	
April	n/l	n/l	n/l	n/l	192	
May	n/l	n/l	n/l	n/l	182	
June	n/l	n/l	n/l	n/l	208	
July	n/l	n/l	n/l	n/l	177	
August	n/l	n/l	n/l	n/l	976	
September	n/l	n/l	n/l	n/l	430	
October	n/l	n/l	n/l	n/l	666	
November	n/l	n/l	n/l	n/l	319	
December	n/l	n/l	n/l	n/l	369	
Average	n/l	n/l	n/l	n/l	313	
Total	n/l	n/l	n/l	n/l	3,760	

Table 4C: Open Interest of All Ordinaries Index Futures

	1986	1987	1988	1989	1990	1991
January	n/a**	n/a	4,563	3,492	4,816	12,124
February	n/a	n/a	5,139	4,712	5,536	14,446
March	n/a	n/a	6,262	4,762	8,131	
April	n/a	n/a	3,780	4,717	5,396	
May	n/a	n/a	4,902	5,368	7,053	
June	n/a	n/a	5,963	5,776	7,633	
July	n/a	n/a	4,080	5,060	6,622	
August	n/a	n/a	5,029	7,089	8,026	
September	n/a	n/a	5,268	6,620	9,230	
October	n/a	n/a	3,830	6,328	6,999	
November	n/a	n/a	5,676	6,154	9,836	
December	n/a	n/a	6,353	5,224	7,980	
Average	n/a	n/a	5,070	5,442	7,272	

*Not Listed
**Not Available
(1) The open outcry trading of All Ordinaries Index futures began on Feb. 16, 1983, and the SYCOM trading, on Feb. 23, 1990.
(2) Open Interest is as of the end of each month and includes SYCOM trades as well since SYCOM trades are cleared with next day's open outcry trades.
(3) Open Interest of an expiring contract month is included up to the day preceding the settlement date of that contract month.
(4) Open Interest is calculated by counting the net number of futures contracts which remain to be liquidated by additional offsetting transactions or by physical delivery after taking account of matched but as yet unsettled bought and sold contracts.

Source: The Sydney Futures Exchange

Clearing House Fee and Exchange Levy: A$2.50 a round turn, subject to change from time to time.

Settlement Day: The second business day following the last permitted day for trading.

Options on All Ordinaries Share Price Index Futures

Contract Unit: One All Ordinaries Share Price Index futures.

Contract Month: Two nearby months of the major calendar cycle which is March, June, September and December.

Trading Hours: 9:30 A.M. to 12:30 P.M.; 2:00 P.M. to 4:10 P.M.

Exercise Declaration Day: The last day of trading in the corresponding future contract. (European-Style Options)

Exercise Prices: Exercise prices are in multiples of 25.0 on an index basis. When trading in a new option contract begins, the corresponding futures contract will have already been trading for some time.

Initially, the exercise price is the closing futures price — rounded to the nearest 25.0 — on the day immediately preceding the first day of trading in the new option contract.

In addition to this exercise price, the next exercise price above that and the next exercise price below that will be added. New exercise prices are added automatically as the market moves over time. There always exist least one in-the-money option, and at least one out-of-the-money option.

Premium: The premium is quoted in minimum fluctuations of 0.1. For instance, the dollar value of an option premium of 63.0 is A$6,300.00.

Although the full premium may not be posted to a selling Clearing Member's account until the option position is closed out or until it expires unexercised, the seller receives a credit for any move in the market which results in a reduction of the premium on the option.

Margin Requirement: All options contracts are marked to market on a daily basis. Consequently, the profits on option positions can be withdrawn as they accrue. For the public dealing through an SFE member, the option deposit is no less than that set by the Clearing House, and the SFE member is not prevented by SFE rules from releasing unrealized profits to clients.

Table 5A: Trading Volume of Options on All Ordinaries Index Futures

	1986	1987	1988	1989	1990	1991
January	994	5,675	3,672	6,537	10,603	36,018
February	604	4,723	3,525	6,535	6,059	20,572
March	1,270	8,743	6,650	7,327	20,296	
April	344	5,898	2,790	7,734	5,787	
May	1,980	14,053	10,230	18,322	30,209	
June	1,527	14,311	9,277	13,055	16,591	
July	2,799	15,849	5,434	12,235	12,325	
August	2,230	23,358	5,563	20,339	19,215	
September	2,840	21,953	12,210	15,069	12,676	
October	3,795	13,850	6,824	14,739	18,584	
November	4,155	6,624	7,100	10,875	19,282	
December	4,553	2,041	8,959	7,067	14,369	
Average	2,258	11,423	6,853	11,653	15,500	
Total	27,091	137,078	82,234	139,834	185,996	

Table 5B: Open Interest of Options on All Ordinaries Index Futures

	1986	1987	1988	1989	1990	1991
January	n/a*	n/a	4,084	5,390	16,221	27,279
February	n/a	n/a	5,304	7,574	16,645	32,469
March	n/a	n/a	7,053	8,969	22,142	
April	n/a	n/a	3,229	6,064	16,252	
May	n/a	n/a	8,634	10,130	25,800	
June	n/a	n/a	8,975	12,970	21,738	
July	n/a	n/a	5,837	10,808	19,233	
August	n/a	n/a	6,907	18,673	25,427	
September	n/a	n/a	9,122	19,249	26,076	
October	n/a	n/a	7,176	12,134	23,075	
November	n/a	n/a	10,150	15,209	33,261	
December	n/a	n/a	11,224	16,746	31,419	
Average	n/a	n/a	7,308	11,993	23,107	

*Not Available
(1) Trading of Options on All Ordinaries Index futures began on June 18, 1985.
(2) Open Interest is as of the end of each month.
(3) Open Interest of an expiring contract month is included up to the day preceding the settlement date of that contract month.
(4) Open Interest is calculated by counting the net number of futures contracts which remain to be liquidated by additional offsetting transactions or by physical delivery after taking account of matched but as yet unsettled bought and sold contracts.

Source: The Sydney Futures Exchange

Options on Australian Equities

Exchange: The Australian Stock Exchange (Sydney) Ltd.

Contract Unit: 1000 shares in any of the following Australian companies:

Amcor
Australian and New Zealand Banking Group Ltd.
Broken Hill Proprietary Ltd.
Broken Hill Gold Mines Ltd.
Bougainville Copper Ltd.
Boral Ltd.
B.T.R. Nylex Ltd.
Coles Myer Ltd.
C.R.A. Ltd.
C.S.R. Ltd.
Elders IXL Ltd.
Fletcher Challenge Ltd.
Industrial Equity Ltd.
Lend Lease Corporation Ltd.
M.I.M. Holdings Ltd.
National Australia Bank Ltd.
North Broken Hill Peko Ltd.
News Corporation Ltd.
Pacific Dunlop Ltd.
Pioneer International Ltd.
QCT Resources Ltd.
Santos Ltd.
TNT Holdings Ltd.
Westpac Banking Corporation
Western Mining Holdings Ltd.

Minimum Price Fluctuation: The minimum fluctuation of A$0.01 represents a change in contract value of A$10.

Strike Prices: Increments of A$0.10, A$0.25, and A$0.50.

Exercise: Options may be exercised on any business day up to and including the day of expiration.

*Last Day of Trading:*Last business day of the month.

*Position Limit:*500 contracts per series for cash-coveraged writers only.

Australian Bond Futures and Options Contracts

Australian Bond Futures

The attraction of institutional investors to high-yielding Australian dollar bonds has made interest rate futures the core business of the Sydney Futures Exchange. Much of the surge in the exchange's trading volume in the past four years is attributable to the increasing popularity of its 90-day Bank Accepted Bill and 10-year Commonwealth Treasury bond futures and options. Commonwealth Treasury bonds (CTBs) are issued by the Federal Government of Australia.

In the last three years of the 1980s, these four instruments accounted for over 85 percent of total exchange turnover, the bulk of which was in the futures contracts. In mid-1988, the SFE filled the gap in its yield curve coverage by listing 3-year CTB futures and options. Futures on 10-year CTBs were introduced in 1984, and have grown to become the SFE's second most traded contract after 90-day Bank Accepted Bill futures. The daily trading volume has averaged to be some 10,000 contracts in 1988—the total annual turnover was 2.9 million contracts. In 1989, despite some initial liquidity problems in the cash market, 10-year CTB futures recorded 3.2 million trades. In the beginning, the bond contract was cash-settled, based on a poll of dealers. Since then, the restrictions on physical settlement have been lifted.

In the spring of 1988, the 10-year CTB contract has faced a serious problem—a shortage of actual bonds due to the budget surpluses of the Australian Federal Government. Furthermore, the Australian Treasury decided to restructure its borrowing toward short-term debt, and the previously thin cash market has become thinner. The futures trading volume was estimated at 20 times physical turnover. The expirations became subject to manipulation, and the exchange needed a dramatic solution.

The innovative answer was the listing of the Australian Semi-Government Treasury bond futures and options contracts at the SFE in December 1989. Due to the scarcity of CTBs, institutional investors were using Australian Semi-Government Treasury bonds (SGTBs) more and more as the vehicles for their fixed-income investment.

Australian SGTBs are issued by: (1) the central borrowing authorities of the various Australian state governments; (2) by State-owned power, water and other utilities with a state government guarantee behind their debt; and (3) by the federally-owned telephone company, Telecom, whose debt carries an implied federal government guarantee.

The growing interest in Australian SGTBs in turn created the need for hedging the risk of holding these fixed-income papers. As a result, the futures contract on Australian SGTBs began its trading in October 1989, and further filled out SFE's yield curve coverage. The SGTB futures contract was based on an index of bonds floated by the above three main issuers.

The initial trading activity was disappointing because by the time of the listing, liquidity returned to the Australian government bond market. This resulted in the reduced need for the SGTB futures contract. Nonetheless, because of the price correlation with the cash market, the SFE still hoped the contract would become one of its major futures contracts. However, as the dismal turnover continued, the SFE delisted SGTB futures in December 1990.

Three-year CTB futures have been successful since their launch in May 1988. As the supply of long-term bonds gets tighter, many investors have been forced toward the short end of the yield curve. Many market participants expect the contracts to rival those of 10-year CTBs and 90-day Bank Accepted Bill in the near future.

Australian Bond Options

Due to the institutional demand for longer term hedging mechanisms, options on 10-year Commonwealth Treasury bond futures has been quite successful. These are the SFE's second most popular option, trading 512,000 contracts in 1990. The options have been an effective tool for fixed-income investors to lock in or protect the yields on Australian debt. Options on Australian Semi-Government Treasury bond futures was launched in December 1989, and was delisted concurrently with the futures contract in December 1990.

Options on 3-year CTB futures has not been as successful as the futures contract. However, its turnover has been growing rapidly. In 1990, the trading volume grew over 200% from the 1989 level. However, the 1990 average daily turnover of some 300 contracts indicates that the liquidity of this options contract still needs further improvement.

10-Year Commonwealth Treasury Bond Futures

Contract Unit: Commonwealth Treasury bonds with: (1) a face value of A$100,000; (2) a nominal coupon rate of twelve percent per annum; (3) a maturity of 10-years. No tax rebate is allowed.

Contract Months: March, June, September and December — up to twelve months ahead.

Trading Hours: 8:30 A.M. to 12:30 P.M.; 2:00 P.M. to 4:30 P.M.

Price Quotations: Prices are quoted in yield percent per annum per A$100.00 face value in multiples of 0.005 percent. For quotation purposes, the yield is deducted from 100.000.

Minimum Price Fluctuation: The minimum price fluctuation of 0.005 percent equals approximately A$25.00 per contract, depending on the level of interest rates.

Mandatory Cash Settlement: All bought and sold contracts in existence at the close of the last trading day of the contract month are settled by the Clearing House at cash settlement price.

Table 6A: Open Outcry Trading Volume of 10-Year Commonwealth Treasury Bond Futures

	1986	1987	1988	1989	1990	1991
January	52,947	101,061	142,836	201,120	190,005	177,509
February	114,601	132,116	167,538	301,217	236,580	258,063
March	112,417	167,478	320,975	310,392	361,000	
April	130,021	143,564	215,646	242,506	191,244	
May	110,671	167,292	394,181	348,422	315,964	
June	111,775	185,710	245,742	313,574	224,406	
July	199,676	185,672	175,190	201,304	190,815	
August	218,368	174,031	281,691	266,246	351,219	
September	158,689	224,480	362,431	320,243	291,309	
October	144,283	275,257	168,164	231,752	200,199	
November	66,148	184,846	219,859	224,474	303,677	
December	94,240	122,396	221,425	258,201	236,063	
Average	126,153	171,992	242,973	268,288	257,707	
Total	1,513,836	2,063,903	2,915,678	3,219,451	3,092,481	

TABLE 6B: SYCOM Trading Volume of 10-Year Commonwealth Treasury Bond Futures

	1986	1987	1988	1989	1990	1991
January	n/l*	n/l	n/l	n/l	4,051	5,595
February	n/l	n/l	n/l	n/l	5,355	8,845
March	n/l	n/l	n/l	n/l	5,654	
April	n/l	n/l	n/l	n/l	4,833	
May	n/l	n/l	n/l	n/l	7,197	
June	n/l	n/l	n/l	n/l	6,527	
July	n/l	n/l	n/l	n/l	7,013	
August	n/l	n/l	n/l	n/l	9,755	
September	n/l	n/l	n/l	n/l	6,866	
October	n/l	n/l	n/l	n/l	9,923	
November	n/l	n/l	n/l	n/l	8,638	
December	n/l	n/l	n/l	2,344	5,528	
Average	n/l	n/l	n/l	2,344	6,778	
Total	n/l	n/l	n/l	2,344	81,340	

TABLE 6C: Open Interest of 10-Year Commonwealth Treasury Bond Futures

	1986	1987	1988	1989	1990	1991
January	n/a**	n/a	31,380	54,278	51,454	37,523
February	n/a	n/a	41,132	64,986	70,078	66,188
March	n/a	n/a	38,026	31,815	46,880	
April	n/a	n/a	52,531	46,380	56,179	
May	n/a	n/a	76,381	60,974	69,271	
June	n/a	n/a	30,988	36,452	42,174	
July	n/a	n/a	38,143	42,129	47,129	
August	n/a	n/a	60,379	66,429	57,613	
September	n/a	n/a	32,208	45,081	35,967	
October	n/a	n/a	38,145	50,157	40,822	
November	n/a	n/a	50,017	30,469	59,038	
December	n/a	n/a	25,578	37,650	20,826	
Average	n/a	n/a	42,909	47,233	49,786	

*Not Listed
**Not Available
(1) The open outcry trading of 10-year Commonwealth Treasury bond futures began on Dec. 5, 1984, and the SYCOM trading, on Nov. 30, 1989.
(2) Open Interest is as of the end of each month and includes SYCOM trades as well since SYCOM trades are cleared with next day's open outcry trades.
(3) Open Interest of an expiring contract month is included up to the day preceding the settlement date of that contract month.
(4) Open Interest is calculated by counting the net number of futures contracts which remain to be liquidated by additional offsetting transactions or by physical delivery after taking account of matched but as yet unsettled bought and sold contracts.

Source: The Sydney Futures Exchange

Cash Settlement Price: On the last trading day of the contract month, twelve dealers, brokers and banks provide yields to two decimal places at which they would buy and sell 10-year Commonwealth Treasury bonds. After excluding the two highest buying and the two lowest selling quotations, the arithmetic mean of the remaining yields provided is used as cash settlement price.

Last Trading Day: The fifteenth day of the cash settlement month—or the next succeeding business day where the fifteenth day is not a business day. Trading ceases at 12:00 P.M.

Options on 10-Year Commonwealth Treasury Bond Futures

Contract Unit: One A$100,000 face value, 12 percent coupon, 10-year Commonwealth Treasury bond futures contract for a specified contract month.

Contract Months: Two nearby months of the major calendar cycle which is March, June, September and December.

Trading Hours: 8:30 A.M. to 12:30 P.M.; 2:00 P.M. to 4:30 P.M.

Declaration Day: The last trading day of the futures contract month, that is, the fifteenth day of the month or the next succeeding business day. (European-Style Options)

Exercise Price: Exercise prices are quoted in yield percent per annum in multiples of 0.25 percent. When trading in a new option contract begins, the corresponding futures contract will have already been trading for some time. Initially, the exercise price is the closing futures price—rounded to the nearest 0.25 percent—on the day immediately preceding the first day of trading in the new option contract.

In addition to this exercise price, the next two strike prices above that and the next two exercise prices below that are added. New exercise prices are added automatically as the market moves over time. It should be noted that there is always available at least one in-the-money option and at least one out-of-the-money option.

Table 7A: Trading Volume of Options on 10-Year Commonwealth T-Bond Futures

	1986	1987	1988	1989	1990	1991
January	7,451	13,619	31,786	56,032	31,324	41,719
February	12,498	15,835	47,498	74,587	47,265	52,052
March	9,588	12,142	79,295	44,478	49,516	
April	12,304	16,671	58,306	67,366	36,815	
May	13,546	36,755	97,719	82,479	52,218	
June	8,785	34,382	54,785	40,818	25,359	
July	25,923	32,208	54,916	60,590	38,724	
August	29,410	29,843	91,699	75,239	65,021	
September	15,959	36,594	55,185	61,804	37,029	
October	24,950	76,385	42,925	57,178	34,497	
November	11,149	46,228	71,993	51,481	72,822	
December	11,634	22,754	35,858	36,911	20,965	
Average	15,266	31,118	60,164	59,080	42,630	
Total	183,197	373,416	721,965	708,963	511,555	

Table 7B: Open Interest of Options on 10-Year Commonwealth T-Bond Futures

	1986	1987	1988	1989	1990	1991
January	n/a*	n/a	22,179	38,808	21,669	30,513
February	n/a	n/a	33,323	64,206	37,251	55,856
March	n/a	n/a	34,210	23,951	23,440	
April	n/a	n/a	47,231	43,560	36,746	
May	n/a	n/a	63,150	57,104	48,600	
June	n/a	n/a	14,958	17,889	21,655	
July	n/a	n/a	18,274	35,369	34,313	
August	n/a	n/a	62,703	51,949	49,327	
September	n/a	n/a	21,277	29,363	21,179	
October	n/a	n/a	32,124	37,327	34,730	
November	n/a	n/a	8,063	47,105	66,774	
December	n/a	n/a	20,627	13,414	14,499	
Average	n/a	n/a	31,510	38,337	34,182	

*Not Available
(1) Trading of Options on 10-Year Commonwealth T-Bond futures began on Nov. 6, 1985.
(2) Open Interest is as of the end of each month.
(3) Open Interest of an expiring contract month is included up to the day preceding the settlement date of that contract month.
(4) Open Interest is calculated by counting the net futures contracts which remain to be liquidated by additional offsetting transactions or by physical delivery after taking account of matched but as yet unsettled bought and sold contracts.

Source: The Sydney Futures Exchange

Premium: The premium is quoted in minimum fluctuations of half point, 0.005 percent—each point representing 0.01 percent—with dollar value of each point calculated as the change in the contract value as the futures price moves from the exercise price to the exercise price minus 0.01. As a result, a move in the option price of one point has a different dollar value for each exercise price.

3-Year Commonwealth Treasury Bond Futures

Contract Unit: Commonwealth Treasury Bonds with: (1) a face value of A$100,000; (2) a coupon rate of 12 percent per annum; (3) a maturity of three years. No tax rebate is allowed.

Contract Months: March, June, September and December—as designated by the Board of the Exchange.

Trading Hours: 8:30 A.M. to 12:30 P.M.; 2:00 P.M. to 4:30 P.M.

Quotations: Prices are quoted yield percent per annum in multiples of 0.01 percent per annum. For quotation purposes, the price are deduced from 100.00.

Minimum Price Fluctuation: The minimum fluctuation of 0.01 represents a change in contract value of around A$20 to A$25, varying with the level of interest rates.

Mandatory Cash Settlement: All bought and sold contracts in existence at the close of the last trading day of the contract month are settled by the Clearing House at cash settlement price.

Cash Settlement Price: At 11:30 A.M. of the last trading day of the contract month, the yields at which twelve randomly-selected bond dealers would buy and sell each of the series of Commonwealth Treasury bonds designated by the Board of the exchange for that contract month are collected. After discarding the two highest buying and the two lowest selling quotations for each designated bond, the arithmetic mean of the remaining yields are calculated for cash settlement price.

Designated Bonds: For the initial trading months of June 1988 and September 1988, the bonds designated by the Board of the exchange for the purpose of calculating the cash settlement price were the following:

13%   January 1991
12%   April 1991
12%   December 1991
13%   February 1992

For the subsequent trading months, the bonds designated by the Board of exchange are announced prior to the beginning of trading in each contract month.

Margin Requirement: The minimum deposit on a contract is the deposit level determined by the Clearing House from time to time.

Last Day of Trading: Trading terminates on the fifteenth day of the contract month, or the next succeeding business day if the fifteenth day is not a business day. Trading ceases at 12:00 P.M.

Settlement Day: Contracts still in existence at the close of trading in the contract month are settled in cash on the business day following the last day of trading.

Table 8A: Open Outcry Trading Volume of 3-Year Commonwealth Treasury Bond Futures

	1986	1987	1988	1989	1990	1991
January	n/l*	n/l	n/l	62,122	74,907	82,422
February	n/l	n/l	n/l	85,419	119,413	139,621
March	n/l	n/l	n/l	91,329	189,837	
April	n/l	n/l	n/l	69,794	82,545	
May	n/l	n/l	49,363	90,189	131,177	
June	n/l	n/l	57,249	94,722	122,513	
July	n/l	n/l	38,478	68,745	89,951	
August	n/l	n/l	67,830	72,704	138,975	
September	n/l	n/l	75,982	80,870	172,653	
October	n/l	n/l	63,530	75,246	126,064	
November	n/l	n/l	108,858	86,807	178,549	
December	n/l	n/l	66,371	88,719	147,371	
Average	n/l	n/l	65,958	80,556	131,163	
Total	n/l	n/l	527,661	966,666	1,573,955	

Table 8B: SYCOM Trading Volume of 3-Year Commonwealth Treasury Bond Futures

	1986	1987	1988	1989	1990	1991
January	n/l	n/l	n/l	n/l	n/l	2,310
February	n/l	n/l	n/l	n/l	236	4,431
March	n/l	n/l	n/l	n/l	2,831	
April	n/l	n/l	n/l	n/l	1,975	
May	n/l	n/l	n/l	n/l	3,746	
June	n/l	n/l	n/l	n/l	2,253	
July	n/l	n/l	n/l	n/l	3,312	
August	n/l	n/l	n/l	n/l	2,656	
September	n/l	n/l	n/l	n/l	6,230	
October	n/l	n/l	n/l	n/l	3,751	
November	n/l	n/l	n/l	n/l	3,697	
December	n/l	n/l	n/l	n/l	3,066	
Average	n/l	n/l	n/l	n/l	2,813	
Total	n/l	n/l	n/l	n/l	33,753	

Table 8C: Open Interest of 3-Year Commonwealth Treasury Bond Futures

	1986	1987	1988	1989	1990	1991
January	n/l	n/l	n/l	35,523	26,041	34,178
February	n/l	n/l	n/l	31,960	34,107	37,523
March	n/l	n/l	n/l	22,702	28,478	
April	n/l	n/l	n/l	39,034	29,326	
May	n/l	n/l	11,498	53,328	46,477	
June	n/l	n/l	10,433	23,458	21,304	
July	n/l	n/l	15,784	24,482	25,502	
August	n/l	n/l	15,700	28,527	40,012	
September	n/l	n/l	18,672	18,180	32,358	
October	n/l	n/l	19,511	26,532	37,768	
November	n/l	n/l	32,845	30,469	44,226	
December	n/l	n/l	19,788	15,614	25,297	
Average	n/l	n/l	18,029	29,151	32,575	

*Not Listed
(1) The open outcry trading of 3-year Commonwealth Treasury bond futures began on May 17, 1988, and the SYCOM trading, on Feb. 23, 1990.
(2) Open Interest is as of the end of each month and includes SYCOM trades as well since SYCOM trades are cleared with next day's open outcry trades.
(3) Open Interest of an expiring contract month is included up to the day preceding the settlement date of that contract month.
(4) Open Interest is calculated by counting the net number of futures contracts which remain to be liquidated by additional offsetting transactions or by physical delivery after taking account of matched but as yet unsettled bought and sold contracts.

Source: The Sydney Futures Exchange

Options on 3-Year Commonwealth Treasury Bond Futures

Contract Unit: One 3-year Commonwealth Treasury bond futures contract with a face value of A$100,000.

Contract Months: The initial contract months were September 1988 and December 1988. Currently, a cycle of March, June, September and December.

Trading Hours: 8:30 A.M. to 12:30 P.M.; 2:00 P.M. to 4:30 P.M.

Exercise Prices: Set at intervals of 0.25 percent per annum. New exercise prices are created automatically as the underlying futures contract price moves.

Premiums: Quoted in multiples of 0.005 percent per annum. The minimum fluctuation in the premium represents a change in the option value of approximately $10.00 to $13.00, varying with the exercise price.

Expiration: The last day of trading in the underlying 3-year Commonwealth Treasury bond futures contract. Trading ceases at 12:00 P.M.

Exercise: Options may be exercised on any business day up to and including the day of expiration. In-the-money options are automatically exercised at expiration unless abandoned.

Table 9A: Trading Volume of Options on 3-Year Commonwealth T-Bond Futures

	1986	1987	1988	1989	1990	1991
January	n/l*	n/l	n/l	2,225	3,137	6,146
February	n/l	n/l	n/l	2,940	4,173	5,001
March	n/l	n/l	n/l	3,572	7,861	
April	n/l	n/l	n/l	854	2,213	
May	n/l	n/l	n/l	3,518	8,086	
June	n/l	n/l	511	1,224	7,399	
July	n/l	n/l	271	1,399	4,252	
August	n/l	n/l	1,474	1,709	8,781	
September	n/l	n/l	2,516	1,608	7,999	
October	n/l	n/l	5,364	3,442	9,398	
November	n/l	n/l	6,260	751	6,402	
December	n/l	n/l	2,040	1,871	5,681	
Average	n/l	n/l	2,634	2,093	6,282	
Total	n/l	n/l	18,436	25,113	75,382	

Table 9B: Open Interest of Options on 3-Year Commonwealth T-Bond Futures

	1986	1987	1988	1989	1990	1991
January	n/l	n/l	n/l	3,081	1,940	7,549
February	n/l	n/l	n/l	3,826	4,724	9,711
March	n/l	n/l	n/l	1,939	5,129	
April	n/l	n/l	n/l	2,558	5,914	
May	n/l	n/l	n/l	5,387	9,019	
June	n/l	n/l	584	1,030	3,750	
July	n/l	n/l	270	2,117	6,574	
August	n/l	n/l	2,120	3,195	9,573	
September	n/l	n/l	2,037	1,526	5,340	
October	n/l	n/l	6,331	4,122	9,386	
November	n/l	n/l	180	3,562	12,466	
December	n/l	n/l	1,931	730	4,568	
Average	n/l	n/l	1,922	2,756	6,532	

*Not Listed
(1) Trading of Options on 3-Year Commonwealth T-Bond futures began on June 16, 1988.
(2) Open Interest is as of the end of each month.
(3) Open Interest of an expiring contract month is included up to the day preceding the settlement date of that contract month.
(4) Open Interest is calculated by counting the net number of futures contracts which remain to be liquidated by additional offsetting transactions or by physical delivery after taking account of matched but as yet unsettled bought and sold contracts.

Source: The Sydney Futures Exchange

Australian Money Market and Currency Futures and Options Contracts

The 90-day Bank Accepted Bill (BAB) futures were the SFE's first financial future, and are its biggest and most successful contract. Launched in October 1979, the contract sustained a steady growth in the mid-1980s, and since then, has had a remarkable growth. It had the trading volume of almost three million contracts in 1988. This was up 44 percent from the 1987 turnover, which was up 94 percent from the 1986 level. In 1990, the activity surged to over 5 million contracts.

One reason for such growth is the high volatility of Australian short-term interest rates. Liquidity is high, and the dollar value of 90-day BAB futures trading is often bigger than the cash market. The futures market is deep enough to accommodate trades in distant months, up to two years out. This facilitates the creation of synthetic longer-term securities, using the distant futures to by-pass the quarterly rollovers on 90-day BABs.

Options on 90-day BAB futures are available for the first four consecutive trading months. Although their underlying future is the SFE's most active contract, the options contract traded only as much as 27 percent of the turnover of options on 10-year Commonwealth Treasury bond futures in February 1988. However, liquidity has improved markedly with the 1989 turnover up some 170 percent, and surpassed that of options on 10-year CTB futures in 1990.

One of the key elements of volatility with Australian investments is the wide movements of the country's currency. This volatility helps make the Australian dollar the world's sixth most actively traded currency. The SFE launched revised Australian dollar futures and options in February 1988. The new contract, priced and margined in U.S. dollars, is similar, but not fungible, to the contract at the Chicago Mercantile Exchange. The SFE hopes to draw activity into the "mother market," but has not even had a modest success. Trading in both the futures and options has been moribund.

90-Day Bank Accepted Bill Futures

Contract Unit: A$500,000 face value of 90-day Bank Accepted Bills of exchange.

Delivery Months: March, June, September, and December — up to three years ahead.

Table 10A: Open Outcry Trading Volume of 90-Day Bank Accepted Bill Futures

	1986	1987	1988	1989	1990	1991
January	65,077	175,390	125,370	299,122	681,291	277,382
February	83,869	161,503	200,645	497,733	584,584	403,627
March	71,904	147,954	236,065	386,359	614,530	
April	100,249	124,628	234,993	641,531	289,401	
May	94,697	162,126	390,815	621,114	365,165	
June	63,868	155,949	285,337	545,159	262,354	
July	127,478	196,515	186,222	467,561	329,550	
August	112,956	170,775	331,134	438,734	401,858	
September	108,819	221,804	267,418	572,000	341,336	
October	101,077	245,117	259,488	529,352	356,529	
November	66,253	180,330	327,164	492,366	521,929	
December	82,457	152,605	165,255	419,406	266,392	
Average	89,892	174,558	250,826	492,536	417,910	
Total	1,078,704	2,094,696	3,009,906	5,910,437	5,014,919	

Table 10B: SYCOM Trading Volume of 90-Day Bank Accepted Bill Futures

	1986	1987	1988	1989	1990	1991
January	n/l*	n/l	n/l	n/l	4,402	4,133
February	n/l	n/l	n/l	n/l	9,333	8,386
March	n/l	n/l	n/l	n/l	6,439	
April	n/l	n/l	n/l	n/l	3,337	
May	n/l	n/l	n/l	n/l	3,792	
June	n/l	n/l	n/l	n/l	2,505	
July	n/l	n/l	n/l	n/l	5,924	
August	n/l	n/l	n/l	n/l	5,798	
September	n/l	n/l	n/l	n/l	3,939	
October	n/l	n/l	n/l	n/l	5,324	
November	n/l	n/l	n/l	n/l	8,090	
December	n/l	n/l	n/l	n/l	6,622	
Average	n/l	n/l	n/l	n/l	5,459	
Total	n/l	n/l	n/l	n/l	65,505	

Table 10C: Open Interest of 90-Day Bank Accepted Bill Futures

	1986	1987	1988	1989	1990	1991
January	n/a**	n/a	39,085	118,077	155,548	277,382
February	n/a	n/a	53,279	166,213	116,837	403,627
March	n/a	n/a	40,649	123,112	113,060	
April	n/a	n/a	58,560	156,920	112,648	
May	n/a	n/a	65,045	152,183	125,109	
June	n/a	n/a	55,752	140,693	123,595	
July	n/a	n/a	67,842	130,212	117,139	
August	n/a	n/a	87,844	148,052	139,379	
September	n/a	n/a	67,363	114,590	122,962	
October	n/a	n/a	81,788	137,155	161,766	
November	n/a	n/a	108,757	155,880	190,032	
December	n/a	n/a	69,954	101,544	133,277	
Average	n/a	n/a	66,327	137,053	134,279	

*Not Listed
**Not Available
(1) The open outcry trading of 90-day Bank Accepted Bill futures began on Oct. 17, 1979, and the SYCOM trading, on Jan. 11, 1990.
(2) Open Interest is as of the end of each month and includes SYCOM trades as well since SYCOM trades are cleared with next day's open outcry trades.
(3) Open Interest of an expiring contract month is included up to the day preceding the settlement date of that contract month.
(4) Open Interest is calculated by counting the net number of futures contracts which remain to be liquidated by additional offsetting transactions or by physical delivery after taking account of matched but as yet unsettled bought and sold contracts.

Trading Hours: 8:30 A.M. to 12:30 P.M.; 2:00 P.M. to 4:30 P.M.

Standard Delivery: Five A$100,000 face-valued bank accepted bills or bank negotiable certificates of deposit. Or, one A$500,000 face-valued bank accepted bill or bank negotiable certificate of deposit (NCD) which matures mature 85~95 days from settlement day.

Quotations: One hundred minus annual percentage yield to two decimal places. The minimum fluctuation of 0.01 percent equals approximately $11.00 per contract, varying with the level of interest rates.

Last Day of Trading: 12:00 P.M. on the business day immediately prior to settlement day.

Settlement Day: The second Friday of the delivery month.

Options on 90-Day Bank Accepted Bill Futures

Contract Unit: One A$500,000 face-valued 90-day Bank Accepted Bill futures contract for a specified contract month on the Sydney Futures Exchange.

Contract Months: Put and call options available on the four nearest months in the futures delivery cycle, which are March, June, September and December.

Exercise Prices: Set at interval of 0.50 percent per annum yield. New option strike prices are created automatically as the underlying futures contract moves.

Premiums: Quoted in yield percent per annum. The minimum fluctuation of 0.01 percent represents approximately $11 per option, varying with the exercise price.

Expiration: At the close of trading on Friday one week prior to the settlement day for the corresponding futures contract. Options may be exercised on any business day up to and including the day of expiration. In-the-money options are automatically exercised at expiration unless abandoned.

Table 11A: Trading Volume of Options on 90-Day Bank Accepted Bill Futures

	1986	1987	1988	1989	1990	1991
January	2,057	1,880	4,926	28,373	93,422	43,984
February	2,680	2,401	8,516	34,362	62,411	53,468
March	2,553	3,319	10,726	25,671	50,421	
April	3,083	2,191	12,665	42,393	33,841	
May	3,664	4,027	34,514	51,411	61,291	
June	2,627	2,483	13,324	33,463	31,558	
July	4,079	6,826	13,550	49,672	43,960	
August	4,603	6,570	22,692	55,426	46,384	
September	1,310	9,639	16,586	54,752	41,523	
October	1,774	8,500	21,465	68,518	47,763	
November	2,439	7,490	20,795	45,144	59,610	
December	764	2,707	12,040	25,934	33,457	
Average	2,636	4,836	15,983	42,927	50,470	
Total	31,633	58,033	191,799	515,119	605,641	

Table 11B: Open Interest of Options on 90-Day Bank Accepted Bill Futures

	1986	1987	1988	1989	1990	1991
January	n/a*	n/a	6,800	28,801	69,120	76,966
February	n/a	n/a	11,030	34,680	76,959	99,537
March	n/a	n/a	8,411	22,927	42,929	
April	n/a	n/a	10,526	37,856	52,422	
May	n/a	n/a	16,585	45,104	70,094	
June	n/a	n/a	8,055	30,496	40,700	
July	n/a	n/a	5,131	45,354	52,611	
August	n/a	n/a	16,119	57,352	70,252	
September	n/a	n/a	9,393	40,924	53,721	
October	n/a	n/a	17,014	70,025	74,883	
November	n/a	n/a	21,625	73,909	93,459	
December	n/a	n/a	14,481	35,315	56,277	
Average	n/a	n/a	13,117	43,562	62,786	

*Not Available
(1) Trading of Options on 90-Day Bank Accepted Bill futures began on May 10, 1985.
(2) Open Interest is as of the end of each month.
(3) Open Interest of an expiring contract month is included up to the day preceding the settlement date of that contract month.
(4) Open Interest is calculated by counting the net number of offsetting transactions or by physical delivery after taking account of matched but as yet unsettled bought and sold contracts.

Source: The Sydney Futures Exchange

Australian Dollar Futures

Contract Unit: One hundred thousand Australian dollars (A$100,000.00).

Contract Months: March, June, September, and December — up to six months ahead.

Trading Hours: 8:30 A.M. to 4:30 P.M.

Quotations: Prices is quoted in U.S. dollars per Australian dollar in multiples of 0.0001 U.S. dollars. The minimum fluctuation of 0.0001 U.S. dollars is equal to US$10 per contract.

Last Day of Trading: Two business days prior to the third Wednesday of the contract month. Trading ceases at 3:00 P.M.

Settlement Day: The third Wednesday of the contract month.

Options on Australian Dollar Futures

Contract Unit: One A$100,000 Australian dollar futures contract for a specified contract month on the Sydney Futures Exchange.

Table 12A: Trading Volume of Australian Dollar Futures

	1986	1987	1988	1989	1990	1991
January	n/l*	n/l	n/l	477	0	5
February	n/l	n/l	927	759	0	0
March	n/l	n/l	2,205	308	11	
April	n/l	n/l	1,190	230	0	
May	n/l	n/l	4,389	299	0	
June	n/l	n/l	4,443	1,550	4	
July	n/l	n/l	1,728	225	0	
August	n/l	n/l	1,528	646	0	
September	n/l	n/l	3,801	155	9	
October	n/l	n/l	1,174	26	0	
November	n/l	n/l	938	31	0	
December	n/l	n/l	949	25	14	
Average	n/l	n/l	2,116	394	3	
Total	n/l	n/l	23,272	4,731	38	

Table 12B: Open Interest of Australian Dollar Futures

	1986	1987	1988	1989	1990	1991
January	n/l	n/l	n/l	248	3	12
February	n/l	n/l	221	480	3	12
March	n/l	n/l	249	32	2	
April	n/l	n/l	22	48	2	
May	n/l	n/l	874	59	2	
June	n/l	n/l	870	145	2	
July	n/l	n/l	795	27	2	
August	n/l	n/l	662	25	2	
September	n/l	n/l	577	6	7	
October	n/l	n/l	322	8	7	
November	n/l	n/l	242	7	7	
December	n/l	n/l	24	3	7	
Average	n/l	n/l	442	91	4	

*Not Listed
(1) Trading of Australian Dollar futures began on Feb. 24, 1988
(2) Open Interest is as of the end of each month.
(3) Open Interest of an expiring contract month is included up to the day preceding the settlement date of that contract month.
(4) Open Interest is calculated by counting the net number of futures contracts which remain to be liquidated by addition offsetting transactions or by physical delivery after taking account of matched but as yet unsettled bought and sold contracts.

Source: The Sydney Futures Exchange

Contract Months: Put and call options available on the two nearest futures contract months (March, June, September, and December).

Exercise Prices: Set at intervals of US$0.0100 per Australian dollar.

Expiration: At the close of trading on the second Friday immediately prior to the third Wednesday of the underlying contract month.

Exercise of Options: Options may be exercised on any business day up to and including the day of expiration. In-the-money options are automatically exercised at expiration unless abandoned.

Table 13A: Trading Volume of Options on Australian Dollar Futures

	1986	1987	1988	1989	1990	1991
January	n/l*	n/l	n/l	0	0	0
February	n/l	n/l	n/l	0	0	0
March	n/l	n/l	21	1	0	
April	n/l	n/l	773	1	0	
May	n/l	n/l	1,469	1	0	
June	n/l	n/l	67	1	0	
July	n/l	n/l	22	0	0	
August	n/l	n/l	4	0	0	
September	n/l	n/l	150	1	0	
October	n/l	n/l	35	0	0	
November	n/l	n/l	55	0	0	
December	n/l	n/l	9	1	0	
Average	n/l	n/l	261	1	0	
Total	n/l	n/l	2,605	6	0	

Table 13B: Open Interest of Options on Australian Dollar Futures

	1986	1987	1988	1989	1990	1991
January	n/l	n/l	n/l	0	0	0
February	n/l	n/l	n/l	0	0	0
March	n/l	n/l	21	1	0	
April	n/l	n/l	0	0	0	
May	n/l	n/l	1,001	0	0	
June	n/l	n/l	31	0	0	
July	n/l	n/l	48	0	0	
August	n/l	n/l	50	0	0	
September	n/l	n/l	150	1	0	
October	n/l	n/l	185	1	0	
November	n/l	n/l	185	1	0	
December	n/l	n/l	24	0	0	
Average	n/l	n/l	170	0	0	

*Not Listed
(1) Trading of Options on Australian Dollar futures began on Mar. 15, 1988.
(2) Open Interest is as of the end of each month.
(3) Open Interest of an expiring contract month is included up to the day preceding the contract month. settlement date of that
(4) Open Interest is calculated by counting the net number of futures contracts which remain to be liquidated by additional offsetting transactions or by physical delivery after taking account of matched but as yet unsettled bought and sold contracts.

Source: The Sydney Futures Exchange

Looking to the Future

The SFE's earlier attempts to develop internationally-oriented products resulted in failure. In 1986, Sydney forged a much-publicized link with the London International Financial Futures Exchange (LIFFE) to trade 3-month Eurodollar interest rate and 10-year U.S. Treasury bond futures. There was a flurry of activity in the initial months, but few international players were interested—preferring the existing the Eurodollar futures market in Singapore and the liquid Asian cash U.S. Treasury bond markets.

In early 1987, following years of preparation, the SFE inaugurated its second international link with the New York Commodity Exchange (COMEX). The COMEX 100 ounce gold contract fared only slightly better than the LIFFE interest rate futures. Although trading volume was often nil, the contract still remained listed and enabled the SFE members to have an access to the COMEX market at a low cost.

Since then, both of these ventures have been completely abandoned. The trading of 10-year U.S. T-Bond and 3-month Eurodollar interest rate futures was suspended in the beginning of January 1989; the trading of the COMEX gold futures was suspended at the end of September 1989. The SFE, however, is secure in its role in the global and regional marketplace. The exchange has acknowledged that its strength is derived from the support of the Australian banking, institutional, and brokerage community. The focus is on the "home base" of activity in Australian financial derivatives, and broadening the range of users. The SFE's agreement-in-principle to join the GLOBEX automated trading network was a major part of this strategy, but the exchange has now moved ahead with its own after-hours system, Sydney Computerized Overnight Market (SYCOM).

Although the SFE has continued discussions with Reuters and the Chicago Mercantile Exchange regarding its participation in GLOBEX, it is clearly pursuing an independent course with SYCOM. As of January 1991, this strategy has been successful. SYCOM has attracted a core group of users and has ironed out technical problems. The SFE has added more products to the system, and SYCOM has proven its effectiveness during numerous highly volatile trading sessions. Meanwhile, the launch of GLOBEX has already been postponed twice. Thus, the SFE has gotten an earlier start in overnight trading than if it had waited to link up with the CME/CBOT/Reuters venture. Nonetheless, the SFE still reserves its option to join GLOBEX in the future.

Australia's prime attraction for institutional investors is its currency and debt markets. The country's equity market also offers opportunities, particularly in the natural resource sector. The SFE aims to provide derivative products which will be essential to comprehensive Australian investment strategies. The exchange's impressive growth and innovation in the late 1980s, despite a generally difficult environment for the international futures industry, signal the SFE's competitive position for the 1990s. With thirty years in operation and over a decade worth of experience with financial futures, its aim is true.

Endnotes

1. The links with the LIFFE and COMEX, however, were not effective and produced inconsistent trading volumes. Consequently, the significant cost of maintaining such arrangements forced the three exchanges to discontinue their links.

2. The two commodity contracts currently-traded at the SFE are Live Cattle and Wool futures. Wool futures began its trading in May 1960. In April 1978, the first gold futures contract outside of North America was listed at the SFE, but is presently not traded any more.

3. Australia has six stock exchanges and trading floors, located in Sydney, Melbourne, Perth, Hobart, Adelaide, and Brisbane. These exchanges were amalgamated on April 1, 1987, to form The Australian Stock Exchange Limited (ASX). It was incorporated by an act of the Commonwealth Parliament called the Australian Stock Exchange and National Guarantee Fund Act, 1987.

SINGAPORE –
STRIVING TO MAINTAIN INNOVATION

Overview of the Singapore Futures and Options Markets

Introduction

The Singapore International Monetary Exchange (SIMEX) – Asia's pioneering financial futures market – has provided institutional investors with a reliable locus for risk management since 1984. Through its innovative mutual-offset link with the Chicago Mercantile Exchange, SIMEX has carved out a significant slice of international futures trading, particularly in interest rate contracts.

The Singaporean exchange successfully emerged from its infancy and has built a global reputation. However, the shifting contours of regional and global futures markets is forcing SIMEX to forge a new identity and find a path to continued growth. Heavy competition, from within and outside the region, threatens SIMEX's unique niche in the Asian time zone. Furthermore, new trading technologies threaten to reduce the relevance of the exchange.

The development of the GLOBEX electronic trading system puts one of SIMEX's primary reasons for existence – its role as a timezone bridge – in jeopordy. SIMEX has yet to decide whether to join the Chicago Mercantile Exchange/Chicago Board of Trade/Reuters screen trading system. The Singapore exchange, whose innovation greatly boosted regional derivative trading, must now choose how it wishes to participate in the next stage of the futures revolution.

Although SIMEX has forfeited the leading edge in technological innovation, it still boasts a number of major strengths. Singapore's strategic geographical location in the heart of the most dynamic economic region in the world, combined with the strength and sophistication of the city-state's financial sector, provides a solid base for the support and development of futures and options trading. The financial industry was the largest contributor to Singapore's economic growth in 1990.

The international outlook of Singapore also supports the exchange. Of the 199 operating Asian Currency Units in the city-state, all but 13 are managed by foreign banks. Twenty Japanese Merchant Banks and Securities firms now have offices in Singapore. In fact, the sources of SIMEX customer activity has been steadily broadening since its inception, and is now about evenly split among three groups: Japan, the U.S. and the U.K., and Singapore and Hong Kong. (See CHART 1.)

In addition, SIMEX's open outcry system, with a large number of local traders providing constant bids and offers, provides users with liquidity, rapid execution, and low transaction costs. Finally, the exchange and its members, through their proven reliability and efficiency, have built up a reservoir of good will among customers throughout the region. With these positive factors as a foundation, SIMEX has adopted a three-pronged strategy for increased trading activity which capitalizes on Singapore's regional importance and advanced financial system.

Chart 1:   Analysis of SIMEX Customers' Trades 1990

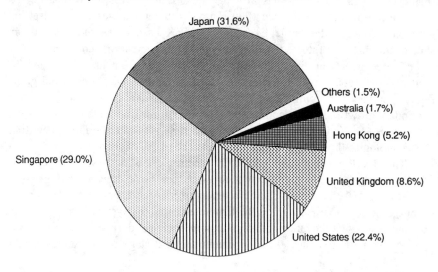

Source: The Singapore International Monetary Exchange

First, SIMEX is fostering growth in its existing range of financial futures products by positioning itself to capture primary, spillover, and arbitrage activity from bigger markets, particularly Japan. Secondly, it hopes to gain from the increased familiarity and experience with futures and options among its immediate neighbors in Southeast Asia. The third prong of its strategy is continued diversification — both vertically (within existing product areas) and laterally (to new areas). The expansion of financial products has continued to be perused when demand is perceived, as with its Euroyen and Euromark contracts. SIMEX has also moved to aggressively diversify into commodity trading, particularly with its expanding energy complex. (See TABLE 1 for the currently traded futures and options contracts at SIMEX.)

Thus, the Singapore exchange is well-positioned to capitalize on its natural strengths and regional economic developments. It provides a secure and efficient risk management facility for institutional investors, corporate treasurers and traders worldwide. Yet to truly secure its continuing significance in the 1990s, it must return to its roots at the cutting edge of financial innovation.

Table 1:   Currently-Traded SIMEX Futures and Options Contracts

Equity
Nikkei Stock Average Futures

Interest Rates
3-Month Eurodollar Futures
3-Month Eurodollar Futures Options
3-Month Euroyen Futures
3-Month Euroyen Futures Options
3-Month Eurodeutschmark Futures

Currency
Japanese Yen Futures
Japanese Yen Futures Options
Deutschemark Futures
Deutschemark Futures Options
British Pound Futures

Commodity
Gold Futures
High Sulphur Fuel Oil Futures
Dubai Crude Oil Futures
Gasoil Futures

Asia's Futures Pioneer

SIMEX's history is an intriguing mixture of government initiatives, international financial market developments, and private sector reactions. When the Singaporean authorities moved to reorganize the chaotic Gold Exchange of Singapore in 1983, they asked the Chicago Mercantile Exchange (CME) for assistance. Officials from East and West both recognized the potential of financial futures in Asia and the accelerating globalization of the industry. The exchange was revamped along CME lines and renamed the Singapore International Monetary Exchange (SIMEX), and a unique mutual-offset system was created to link it with Chicago. Gold trading was reinstated in July 1984, and futures contracts on Eurodollars, Deutschemarks, and Yen that were fungible with the CME's were launched in Autumn 1984. A new era in global futures trading thus began.

This quiet "financial revolution" was slow to catch on. SIMEX did much groundwork to educate Asian investors and recruit locals to fill the pits. But its first full year of trading in 1985 registered a turnover of just 538,000, a daily average of 2150 contracts. 1986 saw the launching of contracts on Japan's Nikkei Stock Average and the British Pound. Turnover increased 38%, but was still averaging only 3500 lots per day.

The exchange broke out of its doldrums in early 1987. Even before the Japanese Finance Ministry permitted financial institutions to trade in overseas markets, new participants were entering the market. In May of that year, the orders from Japan flooded in, and turnover in the Eurodollar and Nikkei contracts surged. Unprecedented volatility, even before that year's global equity market crash, gave further impetus to trading activity. Daily average volume reached a healthy 8,600 contracts in 1987, with a peak of over 16,000 in October. Total trading volume was up 145% from 1986, to 2,142,900. Turnover continued to grow in 1988 to 2,872,600, and exploded in 1989 to 6,270,900 futures and options contracts. 1990 saw the exchange register its first-ever annual decline in activity, down 8.78% to 5,720,600 contracts. (See CHART 2.) SIMEX volume resumed its growth in the first half of 1991, with a 6% increase over the year-earlier period.

While these levels of activity remain small when compared to Chicago's, SIMEX has played a meaningful and innovative trailblazing role in the region, where financial futures and options were, and to some extent still remain, relatively mysterious. As in the West, many new contracts are disappointments, but in Asia, each product introduced serves an educational role even if it eventually fades away — as was the case with SIMEX's U.S. Treasury bond contract, which also had the first night-trading session of any exchange.

SIMEX has been much more successful with its Nikkei Stock Average contract. Its listing in Singapore is considered one of the major catalysts for Japan's

Chart 2: SIMEX Annual Volume and Month-End Open Interest

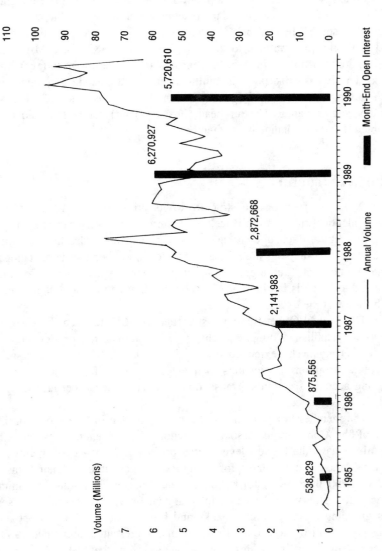

Source: The Singapore International Monetary Exchange

recalcitrant bureaucrats' decision to legalize stock index futures in Japan. Furthermore, SIMEX served as a vital training ground for Japanese securities houses and their institutional customers.

Among the exchange's less publicized achievements is the development of its locals, a difficult task in Asian societies which tend to value consensus over individualism. SIMEX is the only market in Asia with locals, and their numbers and sophistication continue to grow. In September 1987, the SIMEX listed the first options on futures in Asia (on Eurodollars and currency futures), and since 1986, has been well-versed in multi-currency settlements, beginning with the Yen and expanding to the Deutschemark in 1990. The addition of other currency futures, such as an ECU (European Currency Unit) contract, would pose little problem for the exchange or its members.

Market Structure

SIMEX is patterned on the structure of its original mentor, the CME. It has nearly identical rules, compliance, audit, surveillance, membership, and clearing house structure. Exchange committees and management also have a similar format. Market participants are protected by a common bond system, segregation of customer accounts, and a gross margining system. Overseas users find the structure and safeguards familiar, and are comfortable with doing a significant amout of business at the exchange.

The Mutual-Offset trading system between SIMEX and the CME enables positions established on one exchange to be transferred or liquidated on the other exchange. The extended trading hours derived from the linkage enable futures and options participants to manage risk in different time zones within existing account structures. Transaction costs are reduced because margin must only be posted once.

The membership structure is also similar to that in Chicago, with the addition of the Commercial Associate category for the energy market. **Clearing Members** have the highest level of responsibility. They are all members of the clearing house and are liable for all trades that pass through their firms. At the end of 1990 there were forty clearing members, each holding a minimum of three seats. Almost all the major international futures players are represented in this grouping, with American banks and brokers having the greatest numbers. Singapore, British and French firms are also represented, and since 1988, all of Japan's "Big Four" securities houses, plus one city bank, have taken clearing membership.

Corporate Non-Clearing Members can have booths on the floor and order-fillers in the pits, but must have their trades processed by clearing members. Japanese banks are the largest contingent in this category which accounted for 37 members in early 1991. American and British investment banks, Japanese securities firms and Southeast Asian companies are also well represented in this membership category. A list of corporate members is provided in the appendices.

A new type of non-clearing membership was added in early 1989, originally for fuel oil futures. **Commercial Associate** members need to hold only one seat, valid only for the energy complex. They may have employees on the floor but not in the pits, and must process their trades through clearing members. Regional and international oil trading companies are the main users of this membership facility, and a total of 12 have joined the exchange. They accounted for some 16% of all energy trades in 1990.

There are over 400 **Individual Non-Clearing Members,** or locals, at SIMEX. As in Chicago, they trade for their own account or execute orders in the pit for member firms. The majority of locals are Singapore citizens and ethnically Chinese, but a polyglot collection of "foreign locals" can also be found in the pits. Aside from Malaysians, Indonesians, Thais, and Burmese from within the region, there are members from the United States, Great Britain, France, Canada, Italy, and Belgium. The locals as a group have built up their capital and experience, and are able to support liquid markets wherever there is adequate order flow. Locals in the SIMEX Eurodollar and Euroyen pits have become particularly sophisticated, quoting complex spreads and deferred contracts up to three years out.

Regulatory Structure

Futures market activity in Singapore is regulated under the Futures Trading Act. The Act, which was made law in 1987, confers upon the Monetary Authority of Singapore (MAS) power over the futures industry. Under this statute, it has powers similar to those held by the Commodity Futures Trading Commission (CFTC) in the United States. However, the MAS is also the city-state's central bank and overseer of all financial markets. Thus, it also combines the roles held by the U.S. Securities and Exchange Commission (SEC) and some functions (shared with the Finance Ministry) of the U.S. Federal Reserve Bank.

The MAS has a reputation as a tough enforcer of statutes and a zealous protector of the stability of the large banking sector in Singapore. For example, the MAS stood firm in its decision deny the Bank of Credit and Commerce International (BCCI) a license, despite repeated lobbying attempts, in order to protect Singapore's financial integrity. It also sets the tone for financial policy, particularly the city-state's reluctance to internationalize the Singapore dollar. While some participants in Singapore's financial markets complain about the occasional heavy-handedness of the supervisory authorities, in times of market stress, most users admit to feeling very secure about their funds in Singapore while being worried about other financial centers.

Consolidation and Growth

After record-shattering turnover in October 1987, SIMEX, as was the case of other futures exchanges worldwide, suffered a large drop in trading activity in the months that ensued. Price limits on the Nikkei contract were established in order to boost user confidence, and the launch of options on Eurodollar and currency futures brought in some new players. By April 1988, trading volume returned to 1987 levels and open interest had increased 65%. Activity surpassed record marks in June, and achieved new records for 1988. Activity in 1989 greatly surpassed year-earlier levels, almost by a factor of three, and the exchange thus ended the decade on an impressive growth track. In September 1989, the SIMEX further integrated itself into Singapore's financial community by moving to ultra-modern new premises in the heart of the city-state's business district.

In 1990, SIMEX added three new contracts (options on Euroyen futures, Euromark futures and Crude Oil futures), revised its moribund gold contract, and introduced a strip trading facility for Eurodollar trading. Despite this frenetic development, total volume in 1990 fell for the first time in the exchange's history. Even though futures activity worldwide was also down sharply, and SIMEX's share of global Eurodollar activity continued to grow, its performance in 1990 indicates that the exchange cannot count on the listing of new products to ensure future growth.

Threats from East and West

Although SIMEX's overall statistics are impressive, it still has a dangerously narrow base of activity. 76% of 1990 volume was in Eurodollar and Nikkei futures, with the former taking the lion's share. Beginning in early 1991, Euroyen futures has also begun to account for a major segment of exchange volume. The potential problems of the Singapore futures market are compounded by the accelerating competition emerging from within and outside the region. Particularly troubling is that the above three "bread and butter" contracts have the most to lose or gain, depending on activity patterns in the newly developing markets.

One threat comes from Japan, which has expanded its domestic financial futures activity at a blistering pace. SIMEX prefers to view Japanese market growth as an opportunity for parallel growth, citing the interactive nature of financial markets. Whether such a synergy develops depends on SIMEX maintaining its role as a regional innovator. A second, and larger threat comes from electronic trading systems, particularly the GLOBEX network which will trade a number of directly-competing products during SIMEX trading hours. SIMEX is confident that it can maintain its cost and efficiency edge when compared to electronic networks, but eventually the exchange might need to decide whether — and in what format — to join such a network, at least for some of its products. It might also set up its own screen-trading system.

SIMEX may even soon face light competition from two of its ASEAN neighbors, Malaysia and the Philippines, which are both developing financial futures markets. In these two cases, however, SIMEX can be expected to be a net gainer from increased derivative activity in its hinterland.

Equity Futures and Options Contracts in Singapore

Japanese Stock Index Futures

SIMEX affirmed its role as Asia's futures market pioneer when, in September 1986, it launched Nikkei Stock Average futures. It was thus the world's first exchange to list Japanese stock index futures. At that time, such contracts were prohibited in Japan, and thus SIMEX, along with two powerful partners, the Nihon Keizai Shimbun (the owner and compiler of the Nikkei Stock Average) and the CME, which had the license for futures trading on the index outside Japan and Europe, decided not to wait for the Japanese Finance Ministry to liberalize. In fact, the initiation of Japanese index trading outside of Japan was a form of "gaiatsu," or foreign pressure, that was used by those Japanese parties interested in stimulating political and bureaucratic movement at home.

Meanwhile, the revolutionary contract got off to a very slow start in Singapore. Since most Japanese users could not participate (and most were also unfamiliar with the general concept of stock index futures), the SIMEX Nikkei contract had to rely on institutional orders from the U.S., Singapore, and Europe for order flows, and undercapitalized locals for liquidity. There was also almost no cash-futures arbitrage to keep the futures contract in line with the underlying market, and discounts not only to fair value, but even to the cash, were frequent occurances.

Nevertheless, the critical need for a hedging mechanism for Japanese stocks eventually brought in bigger players, and SIMEX's Nikkei locals grew accustomed to the high volatility of the contract. By early 1987, activity was growing steadily, and when Japanese users were permitted to use overseas futures that May, volume surged. By June 1987, when the physically-settled Stock Futures 50 began trading in Osaka, SIMEX's Nikkei had carved out an important niche for itself. It was the preferred vehicle for international fund managers, U.S.-based traders, and Japanese short-term traders, who valued the Singapore exchange's low transaction costs and their ability to trade away from the scrutiny of Japanese regulators.

The international stock market crash of 1987 had a dramatic impact on both the SIMEX Nikkei futures market and Japanese willingness to use stock index futures. In the morning of October 20th, as Asian investors absorbed the shock of Wall Street's 508-point plummet, the Japanese equity market and its futures market were unable to open because of order imbalances and individual share price limits. Thus, SIMEX became the only market in which to transact Japanese equity exposure in the world. Not surprisingly, the forces of supply and demand created major mispricings. As desperate sell orders flowed into the Nikkei pit, the December contract at one point lost almost 80% of its value. While some criticized the small SIMEX market for its wild movements, others noted that at least, the market was actively providing firm price quotes, unlike its Japanese counterparts, and at least, it was open and had no defaults, unlike the Hong Kong stock and futures exchanges.

While some Japanese users were disturbed by the volatility, their investors, realizing that the laws of gravity apply even to the Japanese stock market, recognized the utility of hedging tools. Activity in Osaka's Stock Futures 50 contract increased substantially in the first part of 1988, and Japanese institutions also increased their use of the Nikkei contract at SIMEX. Japan's "Big Four" securities houses began to prepare themselves for the launching of cash-settled index futures in Japan, and gained much needed experience in the SIMEX market. The frequent mispricings in the months after the market crash also attracted major U.S. firms such as Morgan Stanley, Salomon Brothers, and Goldman, Sachs to conduct active Osaka-SIMEX and cash-futures arbitrage.

When cash-setteled Japanese stock index futures were launched in Japan in September 1988, with TOPIX futures on the Tokyo Stock Exchange and Nikkei 225 futures on the Osaka Securities Exchange, many observers expected the SIMEX Nikkei market to disappear, or at least fade into obscurity. However, trading activity in Singapore expanded due to several factors: arbitrage activity from Japan; the efficiency of open outcry trading in times of market stress; lower transaction and margin costs; and the U.S. CFTC approval of SIMEX Nikkei futures contract for American investors(and lack of approval for the Japanese contracts).

In the first full year of Japanese stock index futures trading, the Singapore market unambiguously benefited. SIMEX Nikkei volume was about 40% higher than in the previous period. Open interest, however, was well below record levels and its value was about 80% less than Osaka's. The increased volume came from institutions, particularly American ones, drawn to the greater liquidity that Osaka-SIMEX arbitrage has created. Arbitrage and spread trading of the two Nikkei contracts against TOPIX also boosted volume.

In 1990, SIMEX Nikkei futures again proved their value, by actively trading during the most volatile days of Japan's ten-month long market meltdown, while the contracts in Tokyo and Osaka were jammed because of order imbalances and increasingly difficult and expensive to trade because of the Ministry of Finance's ever-tightening price limits and ever-rising margin requirements. Although SIMEX's absolute level of Nikkei trading volume grew slightly in 1990, its relative share of Japanese index activity declined sharply despite the SIMEX contracts structural assets. The contract is currently healthy, liquid, and boasts much lower margin requirements and transaction costs than its rivals in Japan. The daily average volume in early 1991 was over 3,000 lots a day, with an open interest of about 7,000 positions. Yet, the primary market is now undeniably in Osaka, and despite its cost and efficiency advantages, the SIMEX Nikkei contract will remain a satellite contract, — albeit a very valuable one in times of market stress.

Since late 1990, the SIMEX Nikkei contract has faced an unexpected threat from the U.S. futures market. Many U.S. investors who boosted their activity in the Nikkei might shift their trading to the Chicago Mercantile Exchange's new U.S. dollar-priced Nikkei futures and futures options (both of which were launched in September 1990) even though it trades when the underlying market is closed.[1] For certain long-term investors, this is not a deterrent, as is clear from the quick rise in Chicago's open interest toward the SIMEX levels. Chicago Nikkei volume, however, remains less than one-third of SIMEX's.

SIMEX officials do not seem overly concerned, claiming that such a development may not impair the exchange's customer base, for the more that American users trade their domestic Nikkei contracts, the more they will need the Singapore market to adjust their positions during the trading hours of the underlying market. Furthermore, any expansion of U.S. interest in Japanese derivatives can only help the SIMEX contract, even if it is incremental gains.

SIMEX had hoped to attract players with options on Nikkei futures in early 1989, but its plans were postponed because of negotiations with the CME about

GLOBEX. Osaka listed options in June 1989, and thus, was one step ahead of SIMEX in establishing this new and vibrant niche. Exchanges in Tokyo and Nagoya followed in September 1989 with their own options contracts, which have been less successful than Osaka's. But the existence of three options markets in Japan makes an uphill battle inevitable if the smaller Singapore exchange decides to list futures options on the Nikkei as it still claims to be planning. Furthermore, the CME's options on Nikkei futures has taken away another segment of SIMEX's potential market.

All-in-all, the SIMEX Nikkei contract can be considered an important market for the risk transferral and price discovery function it performs when the primary markets experience structural problems, and for the continuing educational exposure to equity derivatives it is providing to users in Southeast Asia. This latter service will become more recognized as regional index futures develop toward the middle of the decade.[2]

Forthcoming Singapore Equity Derivatives

Although SIMEX Nikkei futures are used by a broad cross-section of Singapore investors, they are not the product with the most potential in either the city-state or its region. Singapore has one of the most developed equity markets in Southeast Asia, and a broadening range of local and international investors. A stock index future on Singapore equities would have great potential, both to strengthen SIMEX's foundations and to attract new users. Since Singapore is also becoming an important fund management center and lists numerous regional equities, SIMEX has also begun assessing the feasibility of listing a Pan-Asian stock index future. Impetus for both these possible new equity derivatives is coming from both internal and external factors. These developments are discussed in the section of this chapter entitled *New Product Areas and New Directions.*

Another Singapore equity derivative innovation is already well on its way toward fruition. The Stock Exchange of Singapore (SES) is in the final stages of planning for options on individual shares. Options trading on a few major, highly liquid, local stocks is expected to begin by early 1992. Once Singapore equity market participants grow familiar with options on individual shares, the likelihood for launching local stock index futures and options will increase.

Nikkei Stock Average Futures

Contract Size: Nikkei Stock Average futures price multiplied by 500 Japanese Yen

Contract Month: March, June, September, December and the Spot Month

Trading Hours: Monday to Friday
    8:00 a.m. - 2:15 p.m. (Singapore Time)
    9:00 a.m. - 3:15 p.m. (Tokyo Time)
    12:00 a.m. - 6:15 a.m. (London Time)
    6:00 p.m. - 12:15 a.m. (Chicago Time)

Note: The SIMEX Nikkei market closes for all Tokyo Stock Exchange holidays, even if it is a Singapore business day.

Minimum Price Fluctuation: 5 points Value of 1 tick =Yen2,500

Daily Price Limit: Whenever the price moves by 5% in either direction from the previous day's settlement price, trading within the price limit of 5% is allowed for the next 30 minutes. Thereafter, an expanded price limit of 10% (above and below the previous day's settlement price) will apply for the remainder of the day.

If, for two consecutive Business Days, the settlement price reaches the expanded price limit of 10% (in either direction), there will be no price limits on the third day. On the fourth day, the price limits are reinstated.

There will be no price limits on the Last Trading Day for the expiring Contract Month.

Last Trading Day: Third Wednesday of the contract month.

Delivery Day: Last Trading Day.

Table 2A: Trading Volume of Nikkei Stock Average Futures

	1985	1986	1987	1988	1989	1990
January	n/l*	n/l	3,837	19,901	65,017	56,156
February	n/l	n/l	7,842	20,177	89,485	53,180
March	n/l	n/l	20,233	36,551	99,724	82,438
April	n/l	n/l	17,090	27,176	73,900	66,977
May	n/l	n/l	21,409	29,511	66,117	56,519
June	n/l	n/l	48,406	65,972	82,410	65,606
July	n/l	n/l	47,755	43,214	65,143	62,106
August	n/l	n/l	39,729	45,707	63,459	114,049
September	n/l	15,764	54,561	78,643	69,867	114,485
October	n/l	7,353	51,662	41,188	55,828	117,295
November	n/l	4,217	23,603	86,588	61,186	46,563
December	n/l	6,259	27,312	92,293	66,829	45,139
Average	n/l	8,398	30,287	48,910	71,580	73,376
Total	n/l	33,593	363,439	586,921	858,965	880,513

Table 2B: Open Interest of Nikkei Stock Average Futures

	1985	1986	1987	1988	1989	1990
January	n/l	n/l	1,704	5,496	4,337	3,522
February	n/l	n/l	2,648	6,301	4,739	3,958
March	n/l	n/l	3,747	5,547	4,057	2,886
April	n/l	n/l	4,758	5,869	3,276	2,759
May	n/l	n/l	5,789	6,893	3,799	2,857
June	n/l	n/l	6,583	7,309	3,889	2,880
July	n/l	n/l	9,157	9,016	3,892	3,762
August	n/l	n/l	8,792	11,010	3,532	5,740
September	n/l	1,392	7,131	9,721	2,995	7,041
October	n/l	1,391	8,971	9,652	2,904	6,791
November	n/l	1,644	8,171	6,175	3,482	6,451
December	n/l	1,375	5,233	5,022	3,045	4,502
Average	n/l	1,451	6,057	7,334	3,662	4,429

*Not Listed
(1) Trading of Nikkei Stock Average futures began on Sept. 3, 1986.
(2) Open Interest is as of the end of each month.
(3) Open Interest of an expiring contract month is included up to the day preceding the settlement date of that contract month.
(4) Open Interest is calculated by counting the net number of futures contracts which remain to be liquidated by additional offsetting transactions or by physical delivery after taking account of matched but as yet unsettled bought and sold contracts.

Source: The Singapore International Monetary Exchange

The Singapore Money Market and Currency Futures and Options Contracts

The core of SIMEX turnover is in the interest rate complex, and much of its roots lies in its relatively quiet currency futures. These two groups of contracts have helped propel the exchange into international prominence, and will continue to serve the important timezone bridging (between regular and non-business hours of the U.S. and Europe) role for which they were initially designed. While currency futures have never attracted significant activity because of competition from Singapore's enormous cash foreign exchange market, SIMEX's interest rate complex is used by a broad base of American, Asian, and European institutions, and has maintained a respectable proportion of global activities in some of its contracts.

Interest Rate Futures and Options

SIMEX now offers a total of three futures and two futures options contracts on global interest rates. (See TABLE 3.) This expanding complex is designed to serve as a "one-stop risk management center" for international users. While this is an ambitious goal, the exchange has undoubtedly succeeded with three of these five products, and may eventually prevail with others.

SIMEX's Eurodollar futures have been its "bread and butter" contract almost since the exchange's inception. At points in SIMEX's history, it accounted for over 80% of activity. In 1990, it still contributed close to 60% of total trading volume, but that ratio is dropping as the exchange broadens its contract base. In 1989, daily average Eurodollar volume was over 15,000 lots. Although annual Eurodollar volume fell for the first time in 1990, in line with a worldwide trading slowdown which affected many markets in the region, its share of global Eurodollar activity rose for the sixth consecutive year, to an impressive 8.8%. (See CHART 3.)

The SIMEX Eurodollar market is sophisticated and very liquid, rarely trading less than 10,000 contracts per day, and with a deep open interest of 40,000 to 50,000 positions. This is due both to broad and active institutional participation, and to locals who are willing to actively quote spreads, strips, and distant contract months, often as far out as 3 years.

A formal one-year Eurodollar Strip facility was added in June 1990 to meet the growing demands of the interest rate swap market. Market users can now obtain a strip of four consecutive Eurodollar contract months in a single transac-

---

Table 3: Currently-Traded Interest Rate Futures and Options at SIMEX

3-Month Eurodollar Futures
3-Month Eurodollar Futures Options

3-Month Euroyen Futures
3-Month Euroyen Futures Options

3-Month Eurodeutschmark Futures

Chart 3: SIMEX Share of World Eurodollar Volume

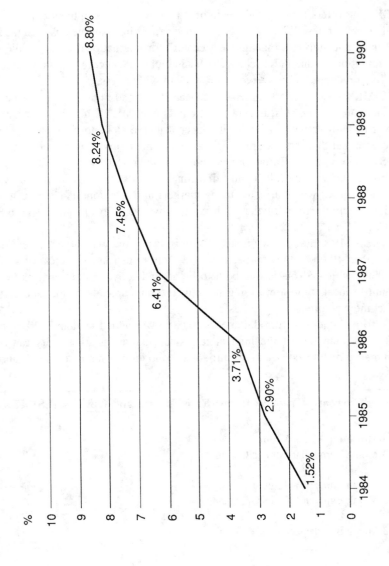

%

10	
9	8.80%
8	8.24%
7	7.45%
6	6.41%
5	
4	3.71%
3	2.90%
2	1.52%
1	
0	1984 1985 1986 1987 1988 1989 1990

Source: The Singapore International Monetary Exchange

tion at a single price. This enables swap participants to hedge their exposure or replicate swaps with greater efficiency and cost advantages.

SIMEX has been much less successful with its options on Eurodollar futures, the first options on futures in Asia. Introduced in September 1987, the product never attracted a broad user base, partly because, despite its fungibility with CME Eurodollar options, they are not a part of the mutual offset system. The average daily volume rarely surpasses 100 puts and calls despite the deep liquidity in the underlying futures.

In addition to the challenge from Japanese stock index futures, its was also feared that new interest rate futures in Japan might drain business from the SIMEX Eurodollar contract. The Tokyo Stock Exchange listed U.S. Treasury Bond futures in December 1989. Around-the-clock trading of bond futures would then have been an alternative to Eurodollars for some users. This threat, however, did not materialize. More serious concerns were raised earlier that year when the SIMEX's Eurodollar futures became exposed to direct competition on another flank.

In June 1989, the Tokyo International Financial Futures Exchange (TIFFE) began trading futures on short-term Yen deposit (Euroyen) and Eurodollar futures as well as the Yen/Dollar exchange rate. Before the start of TIFFE, direct orders from Japan accounted for over 10% of SIMEX Eurodollar volume, with another 15% coming indirectly. This direct threat also did not materialize, and in fact, rather than taking business from the exchange, TIFFE has generated more business for SIMEX by stimulating overall futures trading by Japanese institutions, especially banks.

At the time, SIMEX did not take its Eurodollar activity for granted, and decided to protect its market share. It responded in October 1989 by launching its own Euroyen deposit futures. The contract has similar specifications as the TIFFE product, and is aimed at the current users of the Japanese contract and participants in Singapore's rapidly expanding offshore Yen market. The exchange set low margin requirements for Eurodollar and Euroyen spreads, facilitating interest rate differential trading.

To many observers' surprise, SIMEX succeeded with the Euroyen, benefiting from the above mentioned factors as well as arbitrage activity between the two markets. The Euroyen has become the exchange's third most active contract in 1990, and second highest in open interest. (See TABLE 4.) By early 1991, became the second most active, with daily average volume of over 4000 lots. On days with volatile movements in Japanese interest rates, the Euroyen sometimes surpasses the Eurodollar in volume.

To piggyback on this success, in June 1990, SIMEX introduced the world's first options on Euroyen futures, almost a full year before they were

Table 4: Annual Turnover of Most Active SIMEX Futures Contracts

	1984	1985	1986	1987	1988	1989	1990
Eurodollar	33,589	294,760	459,847	1,159,630	1,881,132	3,862,413	3,469,009
Euroyen	n/l*	n/l	n/l	n/l	n/l	168,788	816,513
Nikkei	n/l*	n/l	33,593	363,439	586,921	858,965	880,513

Source: The Singapore International Monetary Exchange

launched at the TIFFE. These have also been very successful, attracting substantial Japanese institutional activity. Daily average volume is around 400 puts and calls, with total open interest usually above 10,000 lots. The exchange officials hope that the strong performance of Euroyen options will eventually rub off on the less buoyant Eurodollar options.

As if to acknowledge the importance of the SIMEX Euroyen market, in July 1991, TIFFE and the Singapore exchange concluded a formal agreement whereby TIFFE agreed to provide SIMEX with its Euroyen futures settlement price. This agreement makes the two contracts completely fungible, and will facilitate intermarket arbitrage.

In a bid to further expand its interest rate complex, SIMEX introduced 3-month Euromark interest rate futures in September 1990. It has been less successful in this endeavor, although the contract is far from dead. Euromark futures trade between 100 and 200 lots per day, with a thin open interest of around 500 contracts. To augment this contract, SIMEX has agreed with the London International Financial Futures Exchange (LIFFE), which has a very active Euromark contract, on a common settlement price on contract expiration.

3-Month Eurodollar Futures

Contract Size: US$1,000,000 per contract.

Contract Months: March, June, September, December, listed on a 4-year cycle.

Trading Hours: 7:45 a.m. - 5:20 p.m. (Singapore Time)
8:45 a.m. - 6:20 p.m. (Tokyo Time)
11:45 p.m. - 9:20 a.m. (London Time)
5:45 p.m. - 3:20 a.m. (Chicago Time)
Trading Hours on Last Trading Day:
7:45 a.m. - 11:05 a.m. (Singapore Time)

8:45 a.m. - 12:05 p.m. (Tokyo Time)
11:45 p.m. - 3:05 a.m. (London Time)
5:45 p.m. - 9:05 a.m. (Chicago Time)

Minimum Price Fluctuation: 0.01% (Value of 1 tick = US$25).

Daily Price Limit: None

Last Trading Day: Second London business day immediately preceding the third Wednesday of the contract month.

Delivery Day: Third Wednesday of the contract month.

Final Settlement Price: The SIMEX Eurodollar futures contract is traded on a Mutual Offset System with that of the Chicago Mercantile Exchange (CME) in which Eurodollar futures traded at one exchange can be transferred to or liquidated at the other.

In the above arrangement, the SIMEX Eurodollar futures contract has the same final settlement price as that of the CME counterpart contract. On the last trading day, the CME Clearing House will determine the LIBOR (London Interbank Offered Rate) 3-month Eurodollar time deposit funds both at the time of termination of trading and at a randomly selected time within the last 90 minutes of trading.

Table 5A: Trading Volume of Eurodollar Futures

	1985	1986	1987	1988	1989	1990
January	n/a*	36,906	3,837	118,153	194,491	335,861
February	n/a	21,937	7,842	118,215	260,895	328,475
March	n/a	21,054	20,233	104,316	353,293	232,707
April	n/a	35,199	17,090	106,582	410,624	211,128
May	n/a	33,408	21,409	139,426	435,690	217,117
June	n/a	32,698	48,406	221,629	422,948	220,578
July	n/a	37,594	47,755	149,615	284,009	244,374
August	n/a	47,546	39,729	172,814	347,753	459,485
September	n/a	70,306	54,561	149,908	260,492	284,345
October	n/a	53,700	51,662	137,620	435,786	385,113
November	n/a	38,615	23,603	267,470	258,877	294,952
December	n/a	30,884	27,312	195,384	197,555	254,874
Average	24,563	38,321	30,287	156,761	321,868	289,084
Total	294,760	459,847	1,519,630	1,881,132	3,862,413	3,469,009

Table 5B: Open Interest of Eurodollar Futures

	1985	1986	1987	1988	1989	1990
January	1,236	3,154	16,012	25,907	35,420	32,467
February	1,774	3,835	14,046	27,112	48,573	34,835
March	1,297	2,980	14,148	20,110	51,192	31,629
April	1,220	5,311	11,679	28,285	49,578	39,659
May	1,800	7,138	11,158	32,246	49,361	36,855
June	1,979	7,121	13,109	32,030	36,129	28,004
July	2,086	9,722	16,739	33,299	42,088	37,156
August	2,430	11,997	19,977	44,678	38,123	42,198
September	2,282	15,114	20,986	27,591	32,219	33,355
October	2,593	16,317	25,653	34,558	29,659	33,024
November	3,488	17,271	25,297	36,180	37,334	46,428
December	2,554	15,095	15,461	24,588	30,650	31,738
Average	2,062	9,588	17,022	30,549	40,027	35,612

*Not Available
(1) Trading of Eurodollar futures began on Sept. 4, 1984.
(2) Open Interest is as of the end of each month.
(3) Open Interest of an expiring contract month is included up to the day preceding the settlement date of that contract month.
(4) Open Interest is calculated by counting the net number of futures contracts which remain to be liquidated by additional offsetting transactions or by physical delivery after taking account of matched but as yet unsettled bought and sold contracts.

Source: The Singapore International Monetary Exchange

The final settlement price will be 100 minus the arithmetic mean, rounded to the nearest 1/100th of a percentage point, of the LIBOR at these two times.

Position Limit: 3,000 contracts, net long or net short in all contract months combined. Higher position limits may be granted for bona fide hedging transactions upon written application to SIMEX.

Options on Eurodollar Futures

Contract Size: One Eurodollar Futures Contract covering a 3-month deposit on US$1,000,000.00.

Contract Months: March, June, September and December contracts on a one-year cycle.

Trading Hours:
8:30 a.m. - 5:20 p.m. (Singapore Time)
8:45 a.m. - 6:20 p.m. (Tokyo Time)
12:30 a.m. - 9:20 a.m. (London Time)
6:30 p.m. - 3:20 a.m. (Chicago Time)

Minimum Price Fluctuation: 0.01 Eurodollar point (US$25) except that trades may occur at a price of US$1.00 or less if such trades result in the liquidations of positions for both parties to the trade.

Strike Price: 50-point intervals for Eurodollar level below 91.00 and 25-point intervals for Eurodollar levels above 91.00.

When a new contract month is listed for trading, the SIMEX will list put and call options at the strike price that is nearest the previous day's settlement price of the underlying futures contract.

In addition, all eligible strike prices in a range of 1.50 SIMEX Index points above and below the strike price that is nearest that futures price will be listed for trading. If at the beginning of trading, the previous day's settlement price of the underlying futures' is exactly between two strike prices, all eligible strike prices in a range of 1.50 SIMEX index points above and below that futures price will be listed for trading.

Thereafter, the SIMEX will add for trading all eligible Strike Prices in a range of 1.50 SIMEX Index points above and below the strike price nearest the previous day's settlement price. For instance, strike prices of 90.50, 91.00, 91.25, 91.50, 91.75, 92.00, 92.25, 92.50, 92.75, 93.00, 93.25 and 93.50 are listed on Day 1. The futures settlement price on Day 1 is 92.26. On Day 2, a new strike price 93.75 will be added to the list of available strike prices for trading.

No new Options will be listed if less than 10 calendar days remain to the termination of trading.

Daily Price Limit: None.

Last Trading Day: Second London business day immediately preceding the third Wednesday of the contract month.

Margin Requirement: No margin is required for put or call option buyers, but the full premium must be paid in cash. Margins on short options positions and combinations of options/futures positions should be checked with brokers.

Table 6A: Trading Volume of Options on Eurodollar Futures

	1985	1986	1987	1988	1989	1990
January	n/l*	n/l	n/l	601	1,922	777
February	n/l	n/l	n/l	466	641	1,111
March	n/l	n/l	n/l	1,405	457	969
April	n/l	n/l	n/l	662	1,455	858
May	n/l	n/l	n/l	676	546	939
June	n/l	n/l	n/l	253	944	1,257
July	n/l	n/l	n/l	106	1,213	2,159
August	n/l	n/l	n/l	3,354	927	958
September	n/l	n/l	1,018	1,322	618	628
October	n/l	n/l	2,273	376	777	2,063
November	n/l	n/l	4,029	1,188	697	615
December	n/l	n/l	1,087	453	296	755
Average	n/l	n/l	2,102	905	874	1,091
Total	n/l	n/l	8,407	10,862	10,493	13,089

Table 6B: Open Interest of Options on Eurodollar Futures

	1985	1986	1987	1988	1989	1990
January	n/l	n/l	n/l	385	1,037	822
February	n/l	n/l	n/l	626	1,361	1,444
March	n/l	n/l	n/l	1,209	326	1,069
April	n/l	n/l	n/l	1,565	821	1,781
May	n/l	n/l	n/l	2,084	793	2,286
June	n/l	n/l	n/l	208	557	2,171
July	n/l	n/l	n/l	285	988	2,293
August	n/l	n/l	n/l	2,215	1,625	2,813
September	n/l	n/l	116	668	588	1,409
October	n/l	n/l	645	944	1,228	2,550
November	n/l	n/l	1,901	1,532	1,364	3,101
December	n/l	n/l	244	213	637	1,725
Average	n/l	n/l	727	995	944	1,955

*Not Listed
(1) Trading of options on Eurodollar futures began on Sept. 25, 1987.
(2) Open Interest is as of the end of each month.
(3) Open Interest of an expiring contract month is included up to the day preceding the settlement date of that contract month.
(4) Open Interest is calculated by counting the net number of futures contracts which remain to be liquidated by additional offsetting transactions or by physical delivery after taking account of matched but as yet unsettled bought and sold contracts.

Source: The Singapore International Monetary Exchange

Exercise Procedure: Option buyers may exercise on any trading day. Exercise results in a long futures position for a call buyer or a put seller, and a short futures position for a put buyer or a call seller. The futures position is effective on the trading day immediately following exercise, and is marked-to-market to the settlement that day.

Expiration: Options expire at 7:30 p.m. on the business day following the last trading day. However, a considerably earlier cut-off-time for exercising expiring Options can be set by broker. Exercise deadlines should always be checked with broker.

    A Eurodollar option that is in-the-money and has not been liquidated or exercised prior to the termination of trading shall be exercised automatically unless a specific, contrary instruction is delivered to SIMEX Clearing House by 7:30 p.m. on the expiration day.

3-Month Euroyen Futures

Contract Size: Yen100,000,000 per contract

Contract Months: March, June, September, December, listed on a 2-year cycle

Trading Hours: 8:00 a.m. - 5:00 p.m. (Singapore Time)
9:00 a.m. - 6:00 p.m. (Tokyo Time)
12:00 a.m. - 9:00 a.m. (London Time)
6:00 p.m. - 3:00 a.m. (Chicago Time)
Trading Hours on Last Trading Day:
8:00 a.m. - 10:00 a.m. (Singapore Time)
9:00 a.m. - 11:00 a.m. (Tokyo Time)
12:00 a.m. - 2:00 a.m. (London Time)
6:00 p.m. - 8:00 p.m. (Chicago Time)

Minimum Price Fluctuation: 0.01% (Value of 1 tick = Yen2500).

Daily Price Limit: None

Last Trading Day: Second business day immediately preceding the third Wednesday of the contract month.

Delivery Day: On third Wednesday of the contract month by cash settlement.

Table 7A: Trading Volume of Euroyen Futures

	1985	1986	1987	1988	1989	1990
January	n/l*	n/l	n/l	n/l	n/l	33,332
February	n/l	n/l	n/l	n/l	n/l	27,212
March	n/l	n/l	n/l	n/l	n/l	47,887
April	n/l	n/l	n/l	n/l	n/l	40,781
May	n/l	n/l	n/l	n/l	n/l	81,392
June	n/l	n/l	n/l	n/l	n/l	75,041
July	n/l	n/l	n/l	n/l	n/l	75,535
August	n/l	n/l	n/l	n/l	n/l	100,855
September	n/l	n/l	n/l	n/l	n/l	75,986
October	n/l	n/l	n/l	n/l	58,006	132,034
November	n/l	n/l	n/l	n/l	58,773	71,548
December	n/l	n/l	n/l	n/l	52,009	54,440
Average	n/l	n/l	n/l	n/l	56,263	68,004
Total	n/l	n/l	n/l	n/l	168,788	816,043

Table 7B: Open Interest of Euroyen Futures

	1985	1986	1987	1988	1989	1990
January	n/l	n/l	n/l	n/l	n/l	10,614
February	n/l	n/l	n/l	n/l	n/l	12,618
March	n/l	n/l	n/l	n/l	n/l	12,449
April	n/l	n/l	n/l	n/l	n/l	18,963
May	n/l	n/l	n/l	n/l	n/l	27,782
June	n/l	n/l	n/l	n/l	n/l	26,042
July	n/l	n/l	n/l	n/l	n/l	26,545
August	n/l	n/l	n/l	n/l	n/l	35,890
September	n/l	n/l	n/l	n/l	n/l	35,394
October	n/l	n/l	n/l	n/l	2,806	27,897
November	n/l	n/l	n/l	n/l	8,169	24,690
December	n/l	n/l	n/l	n/l	7,136	17,767
Average	n/l	n/l	n/l	n/l	6,037	23,054

*Not Listed
(1) Trading of Euroyen futures began on Oct. 27, 1989.
(2) Open Interest is as of the end of each month.
(3) Open Interest of an expiring contract month is included up to the day preceding the settlement date of that contract month.
(4) Open Interest is calculated by counting the net number of futures contracts which remain to be liquidated by additionaloffsetting transactions or by physical delivery after taking account of matched but as yet unsettled bought and sold contracts.

Source: The Singapore International Monetary Exchange

Final Settlement Price: On the last trading day, the SIMEX Clearing House will determine the SIBOR (Singapore London Interbank Offered Rate) for 3-month Euroyen time deposit funds quoted by major banks both at the time of termination of trading and at a randomly selected time within the last 90 minutes of trading.

The final settlement price will be 100 minus the arithmetic mean, rounded to the nearest 1/100th of a percentage point, of the SIBOR at these two times.

Position Limit: 3,000 contracts, net long or net short in all contract months combined. Higher position limits may be granted for bona fide hedging transactions upon written application to SIMEX.

Options on Euroyen Futures

Contract Size: One SIMEX Euroyen Futures Contract covering a 3-month deposit on Yen100,000,000.

Contract Months: March, June, September and December contracts listed on a one-year cycle.

Trading Hours: 8:00 a.m. - 5:00 p.m. (Singapore Time)
9:00 a.m. - 6:00 p.m. (Tokyo Time)
12:00 a.m. - 9:00 a.m. (London Time)
6:00 p.m. - 3:00 a.m. (Chicago Time)

Minimum Price Fluctuation: 0.01 Euroyen point (Yen2500) except that trades may occur at a price of Yen$100 or less if such trades result in the liquidations of positions for both parties to the trade.

Strike Price: Stated in terms of the SIMEX Index for the Euroyen futures contract at intervals of 0.25.

When a new contract month is listed for trading, the SIMEX will list put and call options at the strike price that is nearest the previous day's settlement price of the underlying futures contract.

In addition, all eligible strike prices in a range of 0.75 SIMEX Index points above and below the strike price that is nearest that futures price will be listed for trading.

Table 8A: Trading Volume of Options on Euroyen Futures

	1985	1986	1987	1988	1989	1990
January	n/l*	n/l	n/l	n/l	n/l	n/l
February	n/l	n/l	n/l	n/l	n/l	n/l
March	n/l	n/l	n/l	n/l	n/l	n/l
April	n/l	n/l	n/l	n/l	n/l	n/l
May	n/l	n/l	n/l	n/l	n/l	n/l
June	n/l	n/l	n/l	n/l	n/l	8,268
July	n/l	n/l	n/l	n/l	n/l	10,173
August	n/l	n/l	n/l	n/l	n/l	10,765
September	n/l	n/l	n/l	n/l	n/l	9,500
October	n/l	n/l	n/l	n/l	n/l	8,240
November	n/l	n/l	n/l	n/l	n/l	8,586
December	n/l	n/l	n/l	n/l	n/l	6,544
Average	n/l	n/l	n/l	n/l	n/l	8,868
Total	n/l	n/l	n/l	n/l	n/l	62,076

Table 8B: Open Interest of Options on Euroyen Futures

	1985	1986	1987	1988	1989	1990
January	n/l	n/l	n/l	n/l	n/l	n/l
February	n/l	n/l	n/l	n/l	n/l	n/l
March	n/l	n/l	n/l	n/l	n/l	n/l
April	n/l	n/l	n/l	n/l	n/l	n/l
May	n/l	n/l	n/l	n/l	n/l	n/l
June	n/l	n/l	n/l	n/l	n/l	3,330
July	n/l	n/l	n/l	n/l	n/l	5,034
August	n/l	n/l	n/l	n/l	n/l	7,874
September	n/l	n/l	n/l	n/l	n/l	6,354
October	n/l	n/l	n/l	n/l	n/l	8,352
November	n/l	n/l	n/l	n/l	n/l	10,955
December	n/l	n/l	n/l	n/l	n/l	7,186
Average	n/l	n/l	n/l	n/l	n/l	7,012

*Not Listed
(1) Trading of options on Euroyen futures began on June 19, 1990.
(2) Open Interest is as of the end of each month.
(3) Open Interest of an expiring contract month is included up to the day preceding the settlement date of that contract month.
(4) Open Interest is calculated by counting the net number of futures contracts which remain to be liquidated by additional offsetting transactions or by physical delivery after taking account of matched but as yet unsettled bought and sold contracts.

Source: The Singapore International Monetary Exchange

Thereafter, the SIMEX will add for trading all eligible Strike Prices in a range of 0.75 SIMEX Index points above and below the strike price nearest the previous day's Settlement Price. No new Options will be listed if less than 10 calendar days remain to the termination of trading.

Daily Price Limit: None.

Last Trading Day: Second business day immediately preceding the third Wednesday of the contract month.

Exercise Procedure: Option buyers may exercise on any trading day. A Euroyen option that is in-the-money and has not been liquidated or exercised prior to the termination of trading shall be exercised automatically unless a specific, contrary instruction is delivered to the SIMEX Clearing House by 7:30 p.m. on the expiration day.

3-Month Euromark Futures

Contract Size: DM1,000,000 per contract

Contract Months: March, June, September, and December, listed on a 1-year cycle

Trading Hours: 8:15 a.m. - 5:30 p.m. (Singapore Time)
9:15 a.m. - 6:30 p.m. (Tokyo Time)
12:15 a.m. - 9:30 a.m. (London Time)
6:15 p.m. - 3:30 a.m. (Chicago Time)

Minimum Price Fluctuation: 0.01% Value of 1 tick = DM25

Daily Price Limit: None.

Last Trading Day: Second business day immediately preceding the third Wednesday of the contract month.

Position Limit: 3,000 contracts, net long or net short in all contract months combined.

Delivery Day: On third Wednesday of the contract month by cash settlement.

Table 9A: Trading Volume of Euromark Futures

	1986	1987	1988	1989	1990
January	n/l*	n/l	n/l	n/l	n/l
February	n/l	n/l	n/l	n/l	n/l
March	n/l	n/l	n/l	n/l	n/l
April	n/l	n/l	n/l	n/l	n/l
May	n/l	n/l	n/l	n/l	n/l
June	n/l	n/l	n/l	n/l	n/l
July	n/l	n/l	n/l	n/l	n/l
August	n/l	n/l	n/l	n/l	n/l
September	n/l	n/l	n/l	n/l	22,019
October	n/l	n/l	n/l	n/l	24,414
November	n/l	n/l	n/l	n/l	8,667
December	n/l	n/l	n/l	n/l	2,088
Average	n/l	n/l	n/l	n/l	14,297
Total	n/l	n/l	n/l	n/l	57,188

Table 9B: Open Interest of Euromark Futures

	1986	1987	1988	1989	1990
January	n/l	n/l	n/l	n/l	n/l
February	n/l	n/l	n/l	n/l	n/l
March	n/l	n/l	n/l	n/l	n/l
April	n/l	n/l	n/l	n/l	n/l
May	n/l	n/l	n/l	n/l	n/l
June	n/l	n/l	n/l	n/l	n/l
July	n/l	n/l	n/l	n/l	n/l
August	n/l	n/l	n/l	n/l	n/l
September	n/l	n/l	n/l	n/l	1,333
October	n/l	n/l	n/l	n/l	1,998
November	n/l	n/l	n/l	n/l	1,744
December	n/l	n/l	n/l	n/l	760
Average	n/l	n/l	n/l	n/l	1,459

*Not Listed
(1) Trading of Euromark futures began on Sept 20, 1990.
(2) Open Interest is as of the end of each month.
(3) Open Interest of an expiring contract month is included up to the day preceding the settlement date of that contract month.
(4) Open Interest is calculated by counting the net number of futures contracts which remain to be liquidated by additional offsetting transactions or by physical delivery after taking account of matched but as yet unsettled bought and sold contracts.

Source: The Singapore International Monetary Exchange

Currency Futures and Options

Along with Eurodollar futures, currency futures were SIMEX's pioneering contracts on the mutual-offset system with the CME in 1984. Unlike Eurodollars, however, they have never attracted a broad-based user group. Activity is mostly small lot orders from individuals and trading organizations, such as futures funds which are taking advantage of the mutual-offset facility. The daily average volume for the three contracts hovers at 600 lots, with a combined open interest of 1,000 to 1,500 positions. The Yen contract is the most active, followed closely by the Deutschemark, with the British Pound far behind.

Options on currency futures were never popular at SIMEX, despite — or perhaps because of — an active OTC currency option market in Singapore. Options on Yen and Mark futures were listed in November 1987, and traded lightly for about six months. They have been essentially extinct since late 1988.

The SIMEX currency market can best be described as a convenient facility for international futures traders to adjust their positions in the Asian timezone. Firm quotes can be obtained for nearby months, and the mutual offset system makes the market useful and efficient for certain spread and arbitrage traders.

Japanese Yen Futures

Contract size: Yen12,500,000 per contract.

Contract months: March, June, September, and December.

Trading Hours: 8:15 a.m. - 5:05 p.m. (Singapore Time)
9:15 a.m. - 6:05 p.m. (Tokyo Time)
12:15 a.m. - 9:05 a.m. (London Time)
6:15 p.m. - 3:05 a.m. (Chicago Time)

Minimum Price Fluctuation: US$0.000001 per Yen (Value of 1 tick = US$12.50)

Daily Price Limit: None.

Last Trading Day: Second business day immediately preceding the third Wednesday of the contract month.

Delivery Day: Third Wednesday of the contract month.

Table 10A: Trading Volume of Japanese Yen Futures

	1985	1986	1987	1988	1989	1990
January	n/a*	11,944	6,398	12,192	47,477	8,000
February	n/a	15,233	4,219	10,813	36,486	10,701
March	n/a	9,051	5,451	15,476	41,940	17,701
April	n/a	9,724	10,497	12,271	24,503	10,462
May	n/a	12,781	5,332	5,250	19,324	14,445
June	n/a	8,280	8,062	20,168	21,407	8,770
July	n/a	13,220	9,456	13,394	20,356	11,434
August	n/a	8,455	8,822	14,760	23,030	7,955
September	n/a	7,351	8,816	21,218	18,511	6,550
October	n/a	7,110	9,556	32,824	21,711	8,518
November	n/a	5,662	9,363	31,328	6,967	8,320
December	n/a	2,528	7,601	31,352	5,070	3,565
Average	2,628	9,278	7,798	18,421	23,899	9,702
Total	31,537	111,339	93,573	221,046	286,782	116,421

Table 10B: Open Interest of Japanese Yen Futures

	1985	1986	1987	1988	1989	1990
January	79	1,335	892	963	1,450	1,163
February	273	1,064	928	1,094	2,444	938
March	492	691	980	846	854	1,483
April	347	991	909	1,749	2,230	1,202
May	168	1,762	596	1,995	2,577	1,593
June	65	1,291	803	1,774	1,060	736
July	405	1,433	1,285	4,195	1,981	865
August	511	2,677	727	5,346	2,259	1,018
September	720	1,351	520	2,228	541	572
October	916	1,454	666	1,247	651	480
November	832	1,667	437	1,645	492	526
December	235	696	675	731	671	170
Average	420	1,368	785	1,984	1,434	896

*Not Available
(1) Trading of Japanese yen futures began on Nov. 7, 1984.
(2) Open Interest is as of the end of each month.
(3) Open Interest of an expiring contract month is included up to the day preceding the settlement date of that contract month.
(4) Open Interest is calculated by counting the net number of futures contracts which remain to be liquidated by additional offsetting transactions or by physical delivery after taking account of matched but as yet unsettled bought and sold

Source: The Singapore International Monetary Exchange

Options on Japanese Yen Futures

Contract Size: One Japanese Yen futures contract covering Yen12,500,000.

Contract Months: March, June, September, December, and serial months. Listing for the serial month cycle includes the spot month, the first deferred, and the second deferred contract months. This is in addition to the contract month options currently listed in the March quarterly cycle — for instance, February, March, April, June and September options are listed; when February options expire, March, April, May, June and September Options will be listed.

Trading Hours: 8:15 a.m. - 5:05 p.m. (Singapore Time)
9:15 a.m. - 5:15 p.m. (Tokyo Time)
12:15 a.m. - 9:05 a.m. (London Time)
6:15 p.m. - 3:05 a.m. (Chicago Time)

Minimum Price Fluctuation: 0.0001 ($0.000001)=US$12.50 (Same as Japanese Yen Futures).

Strike Price: Intervals of 0.01 — for instance, US$0.0062, US$0.0063, US$0.0064 and etc. For options in the March quarterly cycle, when a new contract month is listed for trading, there will be nine put and call strike prices: the nearest strike to the underlying futures price, the next four higher and the next four lower. For instance, if the March Japanese Yen futures price closes at US$0.6651 on the   previous day, the strike prices listed for March puts and calls will be: 63, 64, 65, 66, 67, 68, 69, 70, and 71.

A new strike price will be listed for both puts and calls when the underlying futures price touches within half a strike price interval of either the fourth highest or fourth lowest strike prices. For instance, if the March Japanese Yen futures price touched 0.6751 after the options are listed as in the above example, then a new strike price at 72 will be listed for puts and calls the next day. No new options will be listed, however, with less than 10 calendar days until expiration.

For options not included in the March quarterly cycle, SIMEX will list put and call options at any exercise price listed for trading in the next March quarterly cycle futures options that is nearest the expiration of the option. Options may be listed for trading up to and including the termination of trading.

Table 11A: Trading Volume of Options on Japanese Yen Futures

	1985	1986	1987	1988	1989	1990
January	n/l*	n/l	n/l	5,661	1,363	0
February	n/l	n/l	n/l	7,885	187	15
March	n/l	n/l	n/l	7,390	553	0
April	n/l	n/l	n/l	7,594	183	0
May	n/l	n/l	n/l	4,995	6	0
June	n/l	n/l	n/l	11,439	0	0
July	n/l	n/l	n/l	3,093	0	0
August	n/l	n/l	n/l	3,874	35	0
September	n/l	n/l	n/l	2,913	0	0
October	n/l	n/l	n/l	3,020	0	0
November	n/l	n/l	1012	1,929	0	0
December	n/l	n/l	1,427	1,260	0	0
Average	n/l	n/l	1,220	5,088	194	1
Total	n/l	n/l	2,439	61,053	2,327	15

Table 11B: Open Interest of Options on Japanese Yen Futures

	1985	1986	1987	1988	1989	1990
January	n/l	n/l	n/l	4,427	2,402	0
February	n/l	n/l	n/l	5,970	1,940	11
March	n/l	n/l	n/l	8,023	696	0
April	n/l	n/l	n/l	10,249	743	0
May	n/l	n/l	n/l	10,142	695	0
June	n/l	n/l	n/l	8,209	5	0
July	n/l	n/l	n/l	8,825	5	0
August	n/l	n/l	n/l	9,119	9	0
September	n/l	n/l	n/l	7,018	0	0
October	n/l	n/l	n/l	6,299	0	0
November	n/l	n/l	527	5,835	0	0
December	n/l	n/l	1,193	3,071	0	0
Average	n/l	n/l	860	7,266	541	1

*Not Listed
(1) Trading of options on Japanese yen futures began in Nov. 27, 1987.
(2) Open Interest is as of the end of each month.
(3) Open Interest of an expiring contract month is included up to the day preceding the settlement date of that contract month.
(4) Open Interest is calculated by counting the net number of futures contracts which remain to be liquidated by additional offsetting transactions or by physical delivery after taking account of matched but as yet unsettled bought and sold contracts.

Source: The Singapore International Monetary Exchange

Premium Quotations: Quotations are US cents per Japanese Yen. A quote of 0.0050 represents an Option price of $625.00 (=US$0.0000050 x Yen12,500,000).

Daily Price Limit: None.

Last Trading Day: Two Fridays before the third Wednesday of the contract month. If that Friday is an exchange holiday, the last trading day will be the immediatelty preceding business day.

Margin Requirement: No margin required for put and call options buyers, but the full premium must be paid in cash. Margins on short option positions and combinations of options/futures positions should be checked with broker.

Exercise Procedure: Option buyers may exercise on any trading day. Exercise results in a long futures position for a call buyer or a put seller, and a short futures position for a put buyer or a call seller. The futures position is effective on the trading day immediately following exercise, and is marked-to-market to the settlement that day. If the futures position is not offset prior to the expiration of trading in the futures contract, delivery of physical currency will result or be required.

Expiration: Options expire at 7:30 p.m. on the last trading day. However, a considerably earlier cut-off time for exercising expiring options can be set by broker. Exercise deadlines should always be checked with broker. There is no automatic exercise of the expiring in-the-money currency options by the SIMEX Clearing House.

Deutschemark Futures

Contract size: DM125,000 per contract.

Contract Month: March, June, September, December and the spot month.

Trading Hours: 8:20 a.m. - 5:10 p.m. (Singapore Time)
9:20 a.m. - 6:10 p.m. (Tokyo Time)
12:20 a.m. - 9:10 a.m. (London Time)
6:20 p.m. - 3:10 a.m. (Chicago Time)

Table 12A: Trading Volume of Deutschemark Futures

	1985	1986	1987	1988	1989	1990
January	n/a*	22,548	23,682	6,740	11,460	11,069
February	n/a	16,799	28,410	6,212	6,192	12,351
March	n/a	20,819	13,912	6,633	5,190	8,448
April	n/a	24,159	12,097	4,892	4,797	3,450
May	n/a	16,399	5,776	2,766	7,776	7,040
June	n/a	15,205	9,643	10,517	7,403	3,346
July	n/a	16,009	6,286	8,886	5,329	3,706
August	n/a	15,980	5,603	15,783	5,371	4,349
September	n/a	20,058	5,491	6,296	7,878	3,779
October	n/a	18,397	5,644	10,591	9,141	2,928
November	n/a	18,640	7,746	11,916	7,600	2,486
December	n/a	8,749	6,517	6,461	5,516	1,317
Average	14,196	17,814	10,901	8,141	6,971	5,356
Total	170,346	213,762	130,807	97,693	83,653	64,269

Table 12B: Open Interest of Deutschemark Futures

	1985	1986	1987	1988	1989	1990
January	512	647	958	506	1,357	653
February	454	614	1,488	993	1,033	536
March	598	868	775	181	549	441
April	610	1,109	714	626	640	463
May	576	1,813	496	964	1,730	1,051
June	424	1,078	598	1,516	333	251
July	625	1,086	308	1,384	362	565
August	1,009	1,525	442	1,638	966	547
September	591	862	186	728	346	126
October	1,893	1,831	575	1,583	528	382
November	2,795	2,744	856	1,884	399	394
December	305	619	333	679	381	161
Average	866	1,233	644	1,057	719	464

*Not Available
(1) Trading of Deutschmark futures began in Sept. 7, 1984.
(2) Open Interest is as of the end of each month.
(3) Open Interest of an expiring contract month is included up to the day preceding the settlement date of that contract month.
(4) Open Interest is calculated by counting the net number of futures contracts which remain to be liquidated by additionaloffsetting transactions or by physical delivery after taking account of matched but as yet unsettled bought and sold contracts.

Source: The Singapore International Monetary Exchange

Minimum Price Fluctuation: US$0.0001 per DM (Value of 1 tick = US$12.50).

Daily Price Limit: None.

Last Trading Day: Second business day immediately preceding the third Wednesday of the contract month.

Delivery Day: Third Wednesday of the contract month.

Options on Deutschemark Futures

Contract Size: One Deutschemark Futures contract covering DM125,000.

Contract Months: March, June, September, December and Serial Months. Listing for the serial month cycle includes the spot month, the first deferred, and the second deferred contract months. This is in addition to the contract month options currently listed in the March quarterly cycle — for instance, February, March, April, June and September Options are listed; when February Options expire, March, April, May, June and September options will be listed.

Trading Hours: 8:20 a.m. - 5:10 p.m. (Singapore Time)
9:20 a.m. - 6:10 p.m. (Tokyo Time)
12:20 a.m. - 9:10 a.m. (London Time)
6:20 p.m. - 3:10 a.m. (Chicago Time)
Minimum Price Fluctuation:
0.01 (US$0.0001) = US$12.50 (same as DM futures)

Strike Price: Intervals of one cent — for instance, US$0.0052, US$0.0053, US$0.0054 and etc.

For Options in the March quarterly cycle, when a new contract month is listed for trading, there will be nine put and call strike prices: the nearest strike to the underlying futures price, the next four higher and the next four lower. For instance, if the March Deutschemark futures price closes at US$0.5651 on the previous day, the strike prices listed for March Puts and Calls will be: 53, 54, 55, 56, 57, 58, 59, 60, and 61.

A new strike price will be listed for both puts and calls when the underlying futures price touches within half a strike price interval of either the fourth highest or fourth lowest Strike Prices. For instance, if the March Deutschemark futures price touched 0.5751 after the options are listed as in the above example, then a new strike price at 62 will be listed for puts and calls the next day. No new options will be listed, however, with less than 10 calendar days until expiration.

For Options not included in the March quarterly cycle, SIMEX will list put and call options at any exercise price listed for trading in the next March quarterly cycle futures options that is nearest the expiration of the option. Options may be listed for trading up to and including the termination of trading.

Premium Quotations: Quotations are cents per Deutschemark. A quote of 0.50 represents an Option price of US$625.00 (US$0.0050 x DM125,000).

Daily Price Limit: None .

Last Trading Day: Two Fridays before the third Wednesday of the contract month. If that Friday is an exchange holiday, the last trading day will be the business day immediately preceding.

Margin Requirement: No margin required for put and call options buyers, but the full premium must be paid in cash. Margins on short option positions and combinations of options/futures positions should be checked with broker.

Exercise Procedure: Option buyers may exercise on any trading day. Exercise results in a long futures position for a call buyer or a put seller, and a short futures position for a put buyer or a call seller. The futures position is effective on the trading day immediately following exercise, and is marked-to-market to the settlement that day. If the futures position is not offset prior to the expiration of trading in the futures contract, delivery of physical currency will result or be required.

Expiration: Options expire at 7:30 p.m. on the last trading day. However, a considerably earlier cut-off time for exercising expiring options can be set by broker. Exercise deadlines should always be checked with broker. There is no automatic exercise of the expiring in-the-money currency options by the SIMEX Clearing House.

Table 13A: Trading Volume of Options on Deutschemark Futures

	1985	1986	1987	1988	1989	1990
January	n/l*	n/l	n/l	1,241	348	0
February	n/l	n/l	n/l	671	371	0
March	n/l	n/l	n/l	1,019	291	0
April	n/l	n/l	n/l	2,933	276	0
May	n/l	n/l	n/l	873	31	0
June	n/l	n/l	n/l	1,868	0	0
July	n/l	n/l	n/l	442	0	0
August	n/l	n/l	n/l	507	20	0
September	n/l	n/l	n/l	517	0	0
October	n/l	n/l	n/l	855	0	0
November	n/l	n/l	221	198	0	0
December	n/l	n/l	896	296	0	0
Average	n/l	n/l	559	952	111	0
Total	n/l	n/l	1,117	11,420	1,337	0

Table 13B: Open Interest of Options on Deutschmark Futures

	1985	1986	1987	1988	1989	1990
January	n/l	n/l	n/l	878	203	0
February	n/l	n/l	n/l	966	272	0
March	n/l	n/l	n/l	863	385	0
April	n/l	n/l	n/l	3,073	151	0
May	n/l	n/l	n/l	3,110	113	0
June	n/l	n/l	n/l	2,791	45	0
July	n/l	n/l	n/l	2,613	45	0
August	n/l	n/l	n/l	2,401	45	0
September	n/l	n/l	n/l	2,028	0	0
October	n/l	n/l	n/l	2,592	0	0
November	n/l	n/l	117	2,458	0	0
December	n/l	n/l	663	641	0	0
Average	n/l	n/l	390	2,035	105	0

*Not Listed
(1) Trading of options on Deutschmark futures began on Nov. 27, 1987.
(2) Open Interest is as of the end of each month.
(3) Open Interest of an expiring contract month is included up to the day preceding the settlement date of that contract month.
(4) Open Interest is calculated by counting the net number of futures contracts which remain to be liquidated by additional offsetting transactions or by physical delivery after taking account of matched but as yet unsettled bought and sold contracts.

Source: The Singapore International Monetary Exchange

British Pound Futures

Contract Size: 62,500.00 per contract.

Contract Months: March, June, September, December and the spot month.

Trading Hours: 8:25 a.m. - 5:15 p.m. (Singapore Time)
9:25 a.m. - 6:15 p.m. (Tokyo Time)
12:25 a.m. - 9:15 a.m. (London Time)
6:25 p.m. - 3:15 a.m. (Chicago Time)

Minimum Price Fluctuation: US$0.0002 per (Value of 1 tick = US$12.50).

Daily Price Limit: None.

Last Trading Day: Second business day immediatly preceding the third Wednesday of the contract month.

Delivery Day: Third Wednesday of the contract month.

Table 14A: Trading Volume of British Pound Futures

	1985	1986	1987	1988	1989	1990
January	n/l*	n/l	815	89	95	115
February	n/l	n/l	504	32	137	64
March	n/l	n/l	1,592	331	221	279
April	n/l	n/l	931	404	104	388
May	n/l	n/l	1,127	228	150	366
June	n/l	n/l	1,323	550	218	267
July	n/l	6,373	488	340	53	299
August	n/l	2,642	276	164	98	129
September	n/l	3,186	525	112	669	170
October	n/l	2,219	481	154	745	201
November	n/l	2,468	250	6	227	239
December	n/l	1,090	12	131	157	106
Average	n/l	2,996	694	212	240	219
Total	n/l	17,978	8,324	2,541	2,874	2,623

Table 14B: Open Interest of British Pound Futures

	1985	1986	1987	1988	1989	1990
January	n/l	n/l	307	122	97	99
February	n/l	n/l	384	67	249	125
March	n/l	n/l	206	161	185	119
April	n/l	n/l	446	296	162	168
May	n/l	n/l	399	163	243	113
June	n/l	n/l	530	272	132	128
July	n/l	377	554	189	100	140
August	n/l	377	686	234	112	69
September	n/l	1,552	117	234	159	72
October	n/l	1,405	146	136	135	73
November	n/l	1,436	142	142	123	134
December	n/l	222	30	80	122	42
Average	n/l	895	329	175	152	107

*Not Listed
(1) Trading of British pound futures began on July 1, 1986.
(2) Open Interest is as of the end of each month.
(3) Open Interest of an expiring contract month is included up to the day preceding the settlement date of that contract month.
(4) Open Interest is calculated by counting the net number of futures contracts which remain to be liquidated by additionaloffsetting transactions or by physical delivery after taking account of matched but as yet unsettled bought and sold contracts.

Source: The Singapore International Monetary Exchange

New Product Areas and New Directions

Facing the Challenges of the 1990s

The nature of SIMEX's timezone bridging role is likely to change dramatically in the coming years. Ironically, the prime impetus for change is the Singapore exchange's original mentor in Chicago. Ever since the CME's September 1987 announcement of its GLOBEX electronic trading venture with Reuters, the forward momentum of the SIMEX-Merc relationship has waned. Although exchange officials on both sides of the Pacific Ocean have maintained genuine cordiality, difficult negotiations have strained their rapport.

The relationship is still extremely important for SIMEX, as about 25% of its volume came via the mutual-offset system in 1990, although this figure is down from over 35% in the 1980s. Furthermore, the link with the CME provides an intangible but crucial aura of security and technical sophistication. However, by all assessments from Chicago, mutual-offset volume has been somewhat disappointing.

The GLOBEX joint venture among the CME, CBOT and Reuters, which will introduce electronic trading outside of normal Chicago hours, will greatly affect SIMEX. The Singapore exchange has probably lost its opportunity to join the system on preferential terms, and still has not articulated a clear strategy to address major technological changes flowing through the futures industry. While it correctly stresses the efficiency and cost advantages of its open outcry system, particularly when compared to the cumbersome screen systems in Japan, SIMEX must still address the challenge faced by its international products – whether the Eurodollar on GLOBEX or Euromark on APT (Automated Pit Trading) of the LIFFE – being launched on their "mother market's" screen system.

The exchange is clearly at an important crossroads in its short existence. SIMEX is hoping to improve activity in current products and expand with related financial contracts when the timing is right. For example, longer term interest rate contracts are being explored. SIMEX is also increasing its cooperation with other international exchanges, such as the TIFFE and LIFFE. But it is also hedging its future by moving into commodity products, particularly the energy complex. Singapore officials have begun to realize that some promising development trails lie close to home.

Rapidly Expanding Energy Complex

In February 1989, SIMEX launched its first energy contract, on High Sulphur Fuel Oil, along with inducements to attract new members. Simultaneously, the Singapore government introduced a broad range of tax concessions for international oil trading activities conducted in the republic.

Activity has grown steadily, although major spot market users are still reluctant to participate in large amounts. Daily average Fuel Oil volume is in the 700 lot range, with open interest a healthy 3000-5000 contracts. The exchange has since moved rapidly into other energy contracts. A crude oil future was launched in June 1990, based on Dubai Fateh, which is actively traded in Asia. It has not been a success, with volume dwindling to double digits.

SIMEX has persisted, however, in developing this complex, and in June 1991, launched Gasoil futures, with an agreement for joint settlement with London's International Petroleum Exchange (IPE). Research and discussions are underway with the IPE on listing its successful Brent Crude contract at SIMEX.

The move into energy futures contracts also prompted the exchange to revive its moribund gold contract in mid-1990. SIMEX's original product, 100 ounce gold futures began trading in July 1984, but were inactive since late 1986. Like foreign currencies, gold trading in the Asian cash market is cheap and accessible, giving little natural demand for futures. The new contract is cash-settled, and has managed to stay alive, with daily volume of 40-100 lots and open interest of just over 100. SIMEX is also exploring other commodities for listing. Singapore's resource-rich neighbors still depend on the city-state's vital entrepot role for their agricultural and mineral products, and thus SIMEX is well-positioned to gain from this synergy.

New Equity Derivative Possibilities

SIMEX has done very well by becoming a locus for international financial risk management, but in a round-the-clock trading environment, the exchange will be more secure with a foundation of domestic activity. With the fate of many of its international contracts somewhat out of its hands, it is logical for SIMEX to focus on domestic and regional products.

The most natural extension of its financial futures complex is an index product for the Singapore stock market. The exchange had actually completed the difficult groundwork by September 1987, having secured regulatory approval and completed negotiations with the Stock Exchange of Singapore. A third quarter 1988 launch of a stock index future was targeted. However, the following month's global stock market crash naturally shelved the plans, and the Monetary Authority of Singapore (MAS) waited for the dust to settle before giving a green light to SIMEX.

The green light has yet to come, mostly out of concerns that a Singapore dollar-denominated contract will be the first wedge toward internationalizing the city-state's currency, a move that the Ministry of Finance and Singapore's leaders still vehemently oppose. This is one of the biggest hurdles that SIMEX must overcome, but an essential one if it is to reach its potential as a risk management center for regional as well as international products.

A listing is probably only a matter of time — and timing — since both the market and regulatory environment must be right. Foreign investors have greatly increased their involvement in Singapore equities since 1988, and greater amounts of overseas Chinese funds have also found their way to Singapore. There is little doubt that a broad range of investors would flock to index futures on Singapore shares. The movement toward listing equity derivatives in Malaysia, whose financial markets are significantly less developed than Singapore's, is an indication of the pent-up demand that exists in Singapore. In fact, just as SIMEX's listing of Nikkei futures served as a catalyst for equity derivative activity in Japan, the launch of Malaysian index futures by the new KLOFFE (Kuala Lumpur Options and Financial Futures Exchange) or the existing stock or commodity exchange might serve as an impetus for Singapore.

So far, SIMEX officials have reacted cautiously to developments in Kuala Lumpur, and have focused on the spillover benefits for the exchange that would come with increased activity in Malaysia. According to SIMEX, any new instruments which develop hedging and trading facilities in the region would be positive. But exchange members are already hoping that the KLOFFE brings more than simply a slice of new business from its northern neighbor. Perhaps, they hope, SIMEX and MAS officials will finally realize the time is ripe for a Singapore stock index.

Much depends on the reaction of the MAS and the Ministry of Finance. The MAS must balance its development objectives for Singapore's markets with its regulatory objectives as the city-state's financial watchdog. An element of "face" will also be involved. Singapore prides itself on being at the cutting edge of financial techniques, and seeing Malaysia list stock index futures might be enough to dissipate conservatism at the exchange and the MAS. Innovation often comes from necessity. When the Malaysian government forced companies to delist their shares in the city-state, the Stock Exchange of Singapore created CLOB International to trade Malaysian equities over-the-counter. Similarly, a shock from its northern neighbor may move SIMEX toward further innovation.

Even if SIMEX cannot secure approval for a Singapore stock index, it has begun the groundwork for a pan-regional stock index future which would be priced in U.S. dollars. This would clearly be a second-best alternative since a new index would have to be created and promoted, but it still has long-term potential, particularly for quantitative investment strategies.

New Directions for the 1990s

In its first seven years SIMEX strived to make its mark as an international exchange with innovative financial futures and options products. It has succeeded with some of its contracts, and undoubtedly helped develop regional awareness and activity in futures. It continues to provide institutions and international traders with a valuable risk transferral facility in the Asian time zone. And it has proven its reliability in times of stress, particularly during the October 1987 international stock market crash, when markets in Hong Kong, Tokyo, and Osaka were closed or could not establish prices.

As new trading technology and competition place its role as the Asian link in 24-hour trading in jeopardy, the exchange is seeking new momentum and a stronger identity closer to home. SIMEX, like the Singapore economy as a whole, has done extremely well in identifying niches where it can play a meaningful role. It may do so again with energy futures and local and regional stock indices. If the exchange aggressively implements its three-pronged strategy (discussed at the beginning of this chapter), it will achieve a healthy balance of products, activity, and participants that will carry it successfully through the 1990s.

Endnotes

1. For a detailed discussion of the CME Nikkei contracts, see **Chapter 3: JAPANESE DERIVATIVES LISTED IN THE U.S.**

2. For a detailed discussion of current developments in the regional emerging futures markets, see **Chapter 8: EMERGING ASIAN FUTURES MARKETS.**

C H A P T E R

6

HONG KONG –
STRUGGLING AGAINST POLITICAL
AND FINANCIAL TURBULENCE

Overview of the Hong Kong
Futures Market

Introduction

International institutional investors have frequently made Hong Kong a key component of their Asian portfolios. It has the third largest weighting in the region after Japan and Australia in the major global equity indices – the Hong Kong equity market had approximately a 1.4 percent weighting in the MSCI EAFE index at the end of 1990 – is more accessible than the less internationalized regional markets such as Korea and Taiwan.

For much of the 1980s, investment in the Hong Kong market has been rewarding. Yet, in contrast to some other Asian markets, a buy and hold approach can be dangerous. As events in the 1980s have demonstrated, Hong Kong can be a treacherously volatile market, stemming from political factors and the high level of participation by Hong Kong individual investors. Three times in the decade, stock prices have had rapid drops of over 50 percent in less than six months – in 1983, 1987, and 1989. As a result, risk management tools for Hong Kong assets should play an important role in international institutional investment.

The territory's entrepreneurial and speculative environment would ideally provide substantial liquidity to derivative markets on local and China-related instruments. In 1986 and 1987, these factors seemed well on their way to providing a solid base of activity. Index futures on the colony's popular Hang Seng index – which was Hong Kong's only financial futures contract until 3-month

HIBOR futures were listed in February 1990 — were at one time the most active stock index futures outside of the U.S. The market attracted a diverse group of users, and served various international institutional needs. However, the stock market crash of 1987 devastated the contract, and the Hong Kong Futures Exchange (HKFE) has since then had great difficulty in building a reliable, active, and secure market to serve international institutional investment needs.

In the 1990s, Hong Kong, the Pacific Basin's second largest financial center; and bastion of free enterprise, faces great political and economic uncertainties. The imminent return to Chinese sovereignty in 1997 has made investment in the British colony riskier than ever despite the boost to confidence of the new airport project. Furthermore, while most Asian financial centers have put the world stock market crash of 1987 well behind them, Hong Kong was still feeling the aftereffects in 1990. Only in 1991 did Hong Kong equities surpass their pre-crash highs, and the HKFE regain institutional interest.

The Stock Market Crash of 1987

The territory's reputation was greatly damaged by a 4-day exchange closure during the market crash of 1987, lax regulatory control, and subsequent revelations of serious corruption. The exodus of overseas funds from the colony's capital markets in 1988 and 1989, despite booming double-digit real GDP growth rates, was a natural reaction to the magnitude of blunders and wrongdoings by the exchange officials in October 1987.

Ronald Li, then-Chairman of the Stock Exchange of Hong Kong, unilaterally decided to close the market after New York's 508 point plunge on October 19. Local and foreign investors were infuriated, and the wave of selling that hit the exchange when it reopened after the weekend on October 26 was much greater than if the exchange had stayed open. In just over a week, Hong Kong equities lost half of their value.

The 4-day suspension was also imposed on the futures market, exacerbating already critical margin difficulties. The largest default in the history of futures exchanges ensued, necessitating a government-backed HK$2 billion (US$257 million) "lifeboat fund" to save the market from collapse.

Once the dust settled, but before the financial wounds had healed, investigations began. Aside from finding that Ronald Li acted out of self-interest during the market crash of 1987, he and other stock exchange officials were arrested for taking bribes from companies seeking a listing. Recriminations and finger pointing continued through mid-1988, all the while further damaging Hong Kong's reputation.

Reforms and Uncertainties

In response to the fading fortunes of the Hong Kong futures market, the colonial government went into action, making sweeping changes to the regulatory system. The Securities and Futures Commission was established and given broad powers to pursue market abuse. The pendulum swung nearly 180 degrees, and while reforms were sorely needed, some brokers, bankers, and lawyers in Hong Kong have complained that market regulation is now too tight.

Aside from stricter colony-wide controls—including the right of entry into firms' offices to check accounting practices, and the elimination of a person's right to remain silent to questions asked by market regulators—the Securities and Futures Commission was empowered with a direct watchdog role over the Hong Kong Futures Exchange (HKFE). With much input from the commission, as well as members and outside consultants, the HKFE was thoroughly reorganized, patterned on some of the best features of more established futures exchanges.

Stricter membership requirements have shifted the exchange's emphasis toward bigger players. Minimum firm capital—as little as HK$2 million (US$260,000) before the market crash—has been raised to a range of HK$10 million up to HK$25 million for clearing membership. More detailed and frequent financial reporting requirements have also been established.

The previously independent clearing house has been brought under the HKFE's domain. In March 1989, the HKFE Clearing Corporation (HKCC) began its operation and combined the clearing and guarantee functions which were previously done semi-independently. Members are likely to be more responsible, as they are now shareholders of the clearing corporation. A further safeguard is a HK$200 million reserve fund operated by the HKCC. Of the HK$200 million, half is cash, $50 million is in the form of insurance, and the remaining $50 million is a bank guarantee facility.

The exchange counts on more than just member's accountability to prevent another default. Rules and enforcement procedures have been upgraded to international standards. Most important is the switch to gross margins. Member's previous tendency not to collect full margins from their clients was a primary cause of the 1987 default. Now both initial and variation margins for all open positions must be deposited in the clearing house. The exchange officials believe the new market structure will serve members and customers for the long term.

The new HKFE constitution was approved in early May 1989, and restored some confidence in the market. Buoyant Hong Kong equities in early 1989 revived interest in Hang Seng index futures, and the exchange began making plans for new products.

At around the same time in May 1989, however, massive student demonstrations in China were clouding Hong Kong's political future, culminating with June's brutal suppression in Tiananmen Square. Hong Kong stocks were battered almost as severely as were hopes for democracy in China, with the Hang Seng index losing over 50 percent and probing its lows from the market crash of 1987. It seemed that Asia's freewheeling economic dynamo may never regain its prominence in regional financial markets.

However, unlike October 1987, the HKFE remained open throughout the crisis, performing a valuable risk transferal and price discovery function, thus restoring a degree of confidence in the exchange's integrity and independence. During May 1989, large international institutional investors significantly increased their use of Hang Seng index futures as a hedging vehicle. For instance, in May 1989, the average daily turnover was over 2000 contracts—a 90% increase from the previous month. During the first six months of 1989, the trading volume averaged about 1,160 lots a day, up over 55 percent from the same period in 1988. Open interest at one point rebounded to over 2,500 contracts.

However, the turnover of Hang Seng index futures declined gradually after June 1989 and dropped during the first six months of 1990 as the Hong Kong equity market went into doldrums after the Tiananmen massacre. During the first six months of 1990, average daily turnover was less than 600 contracts. The second half of the year was strong and activity almost twice the year-earlier level. Daily average volume was over 1200 lots.

By early 1991, the Hang Seng trading volume surged and was approaching 2,000 lots a day. This level of activity, however, still remains small compared to the daily volume of over 15,000 lots in 1987, and has only recently become adequate to accommodate international institutional trading strategies.

Moving Forward

Cleaning up after 1987's defaults and the subsequent restructuring required the total effort of the HKFE's new management. Only in 1989 were they able to shift their energies to developing an overall business strategy. The new structure may be the potential foundation for rebuilding, but the HKFE must both convince institutions to reenter the market and redefine its regional niche.

The exchange's stated mission is to "assert itself as one of the top Asian exchanges, while concentrating on local commercial needs." Because of Hong Kong's political status and location, it must also build a close association with China. As China's trade and investment activities expand, their business entities will become more exposed to market risks. Their hedging needs are potentially enormous, particularly in the agricultural sector, and the exchange hopes to serve them as their sophistication grows.[1] In the near term, however, most of HKFE's opportunities remain with its traditional user groups—local and foreign financial institutions in Hong Kong. Understanding this, the HKFE listed 3-month HIBOR (Hong Kong Interbank Offered Rate) futures for the local banking and corporate sectors in early 1990.

Hong Kong Equity Futures Contract

The exchange's major test is to revitalize Hang Seng index futures. Individual speculators, which made up almost 50 percent of 1987's trading volume, have virtually abandoned the market. Most have simply given up on futures, and many have completely withdrawn from the stock market to pursue investment and emigration plans outside the colony.

Institutions, including HKFE member firms, are still reluctant to participate in a meaningful way. Even when they are ready to do so, it will be difficult because as Hang Seng index futures volume remains light. One detriment to higher volume had been the "Special Levy" on transactions designed to pay back brokers who lent to the "lifeboat fund," which was created to prevent the futures market from going default during the market crash of 1987. This levy was a heavy burden on the contract until mid-October 1990, when it was reduced by over 80 percent. A surge in trading volume followed almost immediately. But the real problem is an underlying lack of faith in the exchange due to lingering memories of 1987. For instance, the American Commodity Futures Trade Commission has not given a regulatory approval for the HSI contract, and currently, U.S. pension fund managers are not permitted to trade HSI futures.

The contract's greatest potential is derived from the inability of most investors to short stock in the cash market. In addition to the latent demand for a hedging and speculative vehicle, the HSI contract itself is well-designed. The 33-share Hang Seng index is the most popular barometer of the colony's stock market—it is familiar to both the old "amah" investing her hard-earned HK$5,000 and to the investment manager with a HK$500 million portfolio.

Furthermore, it it relatively simple to construct a basket of stocks which accurately tracks the small index, making cash/futures arbitrage—and occasional market manipulation—attractive. Market participants think a critical mass of 2,000-3,000 lots/day would be adequate to draw major institutions back to the market.

The HKFE's continuous trading during the Stock Exchange's dislocations in May and June of 1989 restored a degree of confidence. Market participants appreciated the futures exchange as an alternative trading facility to the Stock Exchange of Hong Kong during the crisis.

By late 1989, there was a renewed interest in the HKFE from large international institutions, including Japanese securities houses and American investment banks. The Bank of China was also rumored to be taking active steps to enter the market through some of its brokerage and corporate holdings in the colony.

In late 1990, the HKFE began to offer discount memberships to the members of the Stock Exchange of Hong Kong. The membership, which is nontransferable and carries no voting rights, costs only HK$100,000, compared with the usual HK$500,000 to HK$600,000. In return, firms are expected to trade a minimum daily volume.

One reason for the new signs of interest is the exchange's plans to list options on HSI futures. In many ways, options would be more attractive than the futures because, at least for option buyers, the risk including the exposure to another exchange default is limited. Such a product will serve the extensive hedging needs of the local international investment community without the perceived high-risk profile of futures. The HKFE is negotiating with the Stock Exchange of Hong Kong over the options' format, with a 1992 target for listing. Hopes for a successful options launch, however, are somewhat dependent on the further revitalization of Hang Seng index futures, but are also expected to increase interest in the futures.

In addition to the options, the HKFE has implemented its plans for Hang Seng sub-index futures on four sub-sectors of the 33-share index. The first one is on the Commerce and Industry Sub-Index. The other three, the Hang Seng Properties Sub-Index, Finance Sub-Index, and Utilities Sub-Index followed shortly after. Contract specifications and trading hours are identical to the Hang Seng Index Futures.

Hang Seng Index Futures

Contract Size: HK$50 multiplied by the level of the Hong Seng index. For instance, if the HS Index is at the level of 1,000, the contract value is equivalent to HK$50,000. See Appendix III for a list of the Hang Seng Index's constituent shares and their relative weightings in the Index.

Trading Hours: 10:00 A.M. to 12:30 P.M., 2:30 P.M. to 3:45 P.M.

Delivery Months: March, June, September, December, spot and next month.

Minimum Price Fluctuation: Prices are quoted in terms of the level of the Hang Seng index. The minimum fluctuation is one index point, that is, HK$50.

Daily Price Limit: 300 points per trading session or 600 points per day from the previous settlement price where appropriate. No limit is imposed on the spot month.

Last Trading Day: The last permitted day for trading is the business day preceding the last business day of the delivery month.

Delivery: Cash settlement. All long and short contracts in existence at the close of trading on the last permitted day for trading is settled by the clearing house at the index value for cash settlement.

Price for Cash Settlement: The average derived from the index's position at five-minute intervals rounded down to the nearest whole number on the last trading day.

Initial Margin: HK$18,750 (subject to variation).

Table 1A: Trading Volume of Hang Seng Index Futures

	1986	1987	1988	1989	1990	1991
January	n/l*	185,380	15,471	12,049	11,876	27,163
February	n/l	222,859	12,130	18,764	17,170	37,509
March	n/l	323,381	14,388	20,569	9,336	40,703
April	n/l	276,529	16,247	21,484	8,603	48,052
May	31,070	293,001	17,268	40,703	11,710	64,204
June	38,039	340,994	13,718	25,231	12,592	34,996
July	64,848	420,505	9,416	17,059	19,012	
August	82,300	483,389	7,902	21,687	53,679	
September	118,182	601,005	7,537	11,308	22,039	
October	185,414	399,606	9,776	23,552	27,328	
November	154,182	47,194	10,383	13,386	21,027	
December	151,244	17,486	5,919	10,187	21,631	
Average	103, 160	300,944	11,680	19,665	19,667	
Total	825, 279	3,611,329	140,155	235,979	236,003	

Table 1B: Open Interest of Hang Seng Index Futures

	1986	1987	1988	1989	1990	1991
January	n/l*	13,788	561	787	1,571	4,308
February	n/l	14,619	503	2,151	1,013	3,978
March	n/l	20,122	747	2,767	1,733	4,447
April	n/l	18,878	701	2,454	983	4,662
May	1,891	17,274	783	1,566	2,664	5,133
June	2,314	19,519	600	809	1,172	4,932
July	3,404	17,930	726	1,199	3,413	
August	5,042	23,927	601	904	4,189	
September	6,391	24,946	498	1,008	3,876	
October	7,689	23,010	558	1,164	2,929	
November	7,906	1,928	336	1,180	5,003	
December	9,667	532	399	1,006	2,508	
Average	5,538	16,373	584	1,416	2,588	

*Not Listed

(1) Trading of Hang Seng index futures started in May 1986.
(2) Open Interest is as of the end of each month.
(3) Open Interest of an expiring contract month is included up to the day preceding the settlement date of that contract month.
(4) Open Interest is calculated by counting the net number of futures contracts which remain to be liquidated by additional offsetting transactions or by physical delivery after taking account of matched but as yet unsettled bought and sold contracts.
(5) Beginning May 1990, figures are for Month-End Gross Open Interest

Source: The Hong Kong Futures Exchange

Hong Kong Money Market Futures Contract

Hong Kong's capital market investment opportunities are primarily in equities. Funding activity in the money market, however, is vibrant. Numerous international firms float commercial paper and bonds in Hong Kong to finance regional operations. The unrestricted flow of information and accumulated financial know-how also mean that most loans to Asian countries are syndicated in the colony. Hong Kong dollar debt frequently offers yields well above prevailing international rates without a currency risk, since the Hong Kong dollar is formally pegged to the U.S. dollar. Hong Kong interest rates, however, fluctuate more than Eurodollar rates.

Consequently, the Hong Kong Futures Exchange has always wanted to broaden its appeal beyond equity-oriented products. As the cornerstone of this strategy, it launched a new contract designed specifically for the local corporate and banking sectors in February 1990. Futures on short-term Hong Kong dollar interest rates, 3-month HIBOR futures, were the HKFE's first new contract in almost four years.

A number of Hong Kong banks continuously quote bid-offer rates for three month deposits, the minimum of which is HK$5 million. HIBOR (Hong Kong Interbank Offered Rate) is the offered rate on these quotes. Although the interbank market quotes on overnight, 7-day, 30-day, 3-month and 6-month rates, the 3-month HIBOR is widely accepted as the leading indicator of short-term interest rates in the Hong Kong money market, and also, is the basis for 3-month HIBOR futures. HKFE officials hope that the new product will attract a different class of participants, and thus improve the market's activity and image.

Hong Kong interest rates are volatile, due to the usual economic factors, and also because the government uses its monetary powers to discipline those speculating on a revaluation of the colony's currency and to accommodate trade flows. Hong Kong interest rates are uniquely dependent on the relationship between the Hong Kong dollar and U.S. dollar. Because the Hong Kong government is determined to preserve its currency's 7.8-to-1 peg to the U.S. dollar, variations in currency flows have to be accommodated by adjusting interest rates. Therefore, a serious outflow of the HK dollars results in an increase in interbank rates. When the U.S. dollar is weak, the reverse occurs.

Thus, banks and companies in Hong Kong face substantial variations in short-term rates and have a need to hedge against adverse movements. Chinese business entities have also been assuming more interest rate risk as they increasingly establish joint venture agreements, and as a result, are also potential users.

The Hong Kong clearing banks and large American banks were enthusiastic about the new contract and have been supportive since they have a significant need for such a hedging tool. Companies issuing debt in the colony should also find uses for the contract. While Forward Rate Agreements have long been available in Hong Kong, their use and trading have been limited—hampered by extremely wide bid/offer spreads. HIBOR futures could greatly improve the environment for short-dated hedging instruments and also narrow the spread in both interbank quotes and over-the-counter instruments.

The contract specifications are similar to Eurodollar futures, with a size of HK$1 million quoted as 100 less the interest rate. Each tick of 1 basis point is worth HK$25, with a price limit of 125 basis points. The contract size was reduced from HK$10 million just before the launching to the disappointment of banks and corporations. Rates of twelve reference banks are used to compute the cash settlement price with the highest and lowest two quotes discarded.

Since inception, the trading of the HIBOR contract has been moderately active, but well below initial expectations. In its first six months of trading, HIBOR futures averaged about 550 lots/day with open interest fluctuating between 1,400 and 2,000. While institutions are participating, these activity levels indicate that they were not doing the bulk of their hedging at the HKFE. Commission reductions and other incentives have not yet been enough to attract the full range of participants needed for a successful contract. The situation deteriorated by the end of 1990, with turnover levels sinking to double digits, and open interest plummeting. By early 1991 the contract was barely alive.

Three Month Hong Kong Interbank Offered Rate (HIBOR) Futures

Contract Size: HK$1,000,000

HIBOR: A number of Hong Kong banks continuously quote bid-offer rates for three month deposits, the minimum of which is HK$5 million. HIBOR is the offered rate on these quotes.

Price Quotation: 100 minus the yield. For instance, the yield of 12 percent means a futures price of 88.00.

Trading Hours: 9:00 A.M. to 3:30 P.M. – on the last trading day, the trading of the spot month contract ends at 12:30 P.M.

Delivery Months: March, June, September, December – up to two years ahead.

Maturity Period: Three months.

Minimum Fluctuation: HK$25

Daily Fluctuation Limit: 125 basis point above and below the previous closing price. 125 basis points are equivalent to a move in the underlying interest rate of 1.25 percent.

Expanded Fluctuation Limit: Once the daily fluctuation limit is reached, an expanded fluctuation limit, which is 200 percent of the daily fluctuation limit (250 basis points), is used for the following three trading days.

Table 2A: Trading Volume of HIBOR Futures

	1986	1987	1988	1989	1990	1991
January	n/l*	n/l	n/l	n/l	n/l	582
February	n/l	n/l	n/l	n/l	17,756	174
March	n/l	n/l	n/l	n/l	14,407	268
April	n/l	n/l	n/l	n/l	5,393	60
May	n/l	n/l	n/l	n/l	3,173	23
June	n/l	n/l	n/l	n/l	4,704	18
July	n/l	n/l	n/l	n/l	3,385	
August	n/l	n/l	n/l	n/l	1,751	
September	n/l	n/l	n/l	n/l	1,446	
October	n/l	n/l	n/l	n/l	3,296	
November	n/l	n/l	n/l	n/l	1,106	
December	n/l	n/l	n/l	n/l	344	
Average	n/l	n/l	n/l	n/l	5,160	
Total	n/l	n/l	n/l	n/l	56,761	

Table 2B: Open Interest of HIBOR Futures

	1986	1987	1988	1989	1990	1991
January	n/l*	n/l	n/l	n/l	n/l	396
February	n/l	n/l	n/l	n/l	1,914	296
March	n/l	n/l	n/l	n/l	1,978	252
April	n/l	n/l	n/l	n/l	1,094	251
May	n/l	n/l	n/l	n/l	2,309	251
June	n/l	n/l	n/l	n/l	1,042	101
July	n/l	n/l	n/l	n/l	1,457	
August	n/l	n/l	n/l	n/l	1,946	
September	n/l	n/l	n/l	n/l	612	
October	n/l	n/l	n/l	n/l	701	
November	n/l	n/l	n/l	n/l	790	
December	n/l	n/l	n/l	n/l	6	
Average	n/l	n/l	n/l	n/l	1,259	

*Not Listed
(2) Open Interest is as of the end of each month.
(3) Open Interest of an expiring contract month is included up to the day preceding the contract month. settlement date of that
(4) Open Interest is calculated by counting the net number of futures contracts which remain to be liquidated by additional offsetting transactions or by physical delivery after taking account of matched but as yet unsettled bought and sold contracts.
(5) Figures from May 1990 are for Month-End Gross Open Interest

Source: The Hong Kong Futures Exchange

Expanded Fluctuation Limit Period: Three business days.

No Limit: Last five trading days of the spot month.

Settlement Price: The exchange delivery settlement price (EDSP) is derived from twelve randomly chosen participating bank quotations for three month Interbank offered rates. After the highest and lowest two are discarded, an arithmetic mean of the remaining eight is calculated for the ESDP.

Initial Margin: HK$1,500

Future Expectations

Despite high levels of optimism about the HIBOR contract, little synergy developed between it and the Hang Seng index futures. Nevertheless, HKFE officials still hope that future successes will open up the possibilities for both HSI and HIBOR options. Market participants stress, however, that much greater activity in the underlying futures contracts is needed before the options have a chance of success. The HKFE would have to be sure that the market environment is favorable to listing the options contracts before launching a major educational and marketing program.

One other financial product area is being considered, and is slated for introduction in 1992. The HKFE has long wanted to list currency futures, citing Hong Kong's vibrant foreign trade, the opportunities are slim. The colony's banks offer a variety of sophisticated foreign exchange products; Singapore has an established six year old currency futures market; Tokyo has listed a similar contract; and the GLOBEX electronic trading system—which has received regulatory approval in Hong Kong—will prominently feature currency futures.

Nevertheless, the HKFE is planning to introduce screen-traded currency futures on the British pound, Japanese Yen, and Deutschemark. The contract specifications have not been finalized, but may set price quotes in the interbank format (number of currency units per U.S. dollar). The exchange is also looking to commodities for future growth. The HKFE gold contract is not considered significant and is kept alive by a daily cross by exchange members of 20 to 30 lots. Hong Kong's "Loco-London" cash market in gold is Asia's largest, and is extremely liquid. Major bullion dealers and traders move easily in and out of this market. Furthermore, the Hong Kong Gold and Silver Society trades *tael*—a traditional Asian measurement—units priced in Hong Kong dollars. This wild and unregulated market is a favorite of Hong Kong Chinese speculators, who have little incentive to switch to futures.

The HKFE hopes to garner new business by offering a wider range of agricultural commodities which have a Chinese connection. Hong Kong currently trades futures on soybeans and sugar, priced in U.S. dollars, and traded by the Japanese call method. Most participants are local trading houses, commercial users or Japanese grain dealers.

The first new contract with a Chinese connection may be rice, but it faces numerous infrastructural hurdles regarding delivery and quality. Wheat futures and an energy complex have also been discussed with Chinese officials, but never made much progress. Nevertheless, the HKFE is assisting authorities in Shanghai to develop a grain futures market.

Because of its tarnished international reputation, the Hong Kong Futures Exchange had no choice but to abandon its grandiose expansion plans. It has made the necessary transition away from aggressive competition with other regional exchanges and toward a complementary focus on its home environment. It is now striving to carve out a valued niche for itself in the continually buoyant regional futures environment.

The HKFE leaders stress the importance of serving the "mother market" when they define Hong Kong's "natural products." For the foreseeable future, the exchange will have its hands full with Hang Seng index futures, sub-index futures, HIBOR futures, Hang Seng index options, and China-related commodities. If it can build active markets in these areas, the exchange will be well on its way toward putting the market crash of 1987 behind it and preparing for a future under Chinese sovereignty.

Endnotes

1.   Currently, the Hong Kong Futures Exchange lists three commodity contracts: gold, soybean, and sugar futures.

NEW ZEALAND –
SIGNIFICANCE BEYOND ITS SIZE

Overview of the New Zealand Futures and Options Market

Introduction

The New Zealand Futures and Options Exchange (NZFOE) is one of the smaller regional markets, but has led the way in automation. Founded in 1985, the exchange has never had a trading floor but instead provides computer-based electronic dealing facilities to its members. The market is primarily the domain of New Zealand financial institutions, however, most of its products have relevance for international investors.

New Zealand's capital markets are at the economic and geographic periphery of the world's financial markets. Yet in both respects they play a role proportionately larger than their small size. They are the first market to open each trading day in the Asian-Pacific region, and thus, the first to react to overnight and over-weekend news not only of the region but also from Europe and North America.

The New Zealand debt market also attracted substantial foreign participation due to its historically high yields. In the 1980s, the debt instruments of New Zealand frequently yielded ten percentage points over those of major industrial countries. With the high yields, however, came volatile exchange and interest rates which were caused by the nation's budgetary and political situation. This subsequently resulted in a rising demand for risk management tools. As the Reserve Bank of New Zealand's struggle against inflation began to bear fruit in 1990, interest rates dropped dramatically, and by early 1991, were approaching American and Canadian levels. While some international investors lost interest in New Zealand bonds, others were attracted by rising prices and the central bank's new credibility. The rapidly changing environment helped create another surge in debt futures and options activity on the NZFOE.

Foreign institutions are also involved in New Zealand equities, even though the market comprises a minuscule 0.27 percent of the Morgan Stanley Capital International EAFE (Europe, Australia and Far East) Index at the end of 1990. There are a number of world class companies listed in Auckland, and they have attracted significant investors from the U.K., U.S., and Japan.

The impetus for foreign participation in New Zealand—and the spark that unleashed domestic financial innovation—was the liberalization of the country's economy and capital markets. The liberalization process began in 1984 and set off a market rally of almost 100 percent a year until the international stock market crash of 1987—before the crash, New Zealand was one of the best performing markets in the world. Prior to the liberalization process, New Zealand was a tightly controlled financial backwater with little foreign portfolio investment. This reorientation ended the isolation of the domestic economy, which had been sheltering its deteriorating terms of trade.

The government chose instead to reduce its day-to-day involvement in economic affairs through extensive privatization and market liberalization. The abolition of foreign exchange controls and deregulation of the banking and brokerage industries paved the way for the development of a futures exchange.

Table 1: Currently-Traded Financial Futures Contracts of the NZFOE

Equity Contracts	Inception
Barclays Share Price Index Futures	1/87
Barclays Share Price Index Futures Options	2/89
Interest Rate Contracts	
5-Year Government Stock No. 2 Futures	2/86
5-Year Government Stock No. 2 Futures Options	12/88
90-Day Bank Accepted Bill Futures	12/86
90-Day Bank Accepted Bill Futures Options	6/89
Currency Contracts	
U.S. Dollar Futures	1/85
New Zealand Dollar Futures	1/88
New Zealand Dollar Futures Options	12/88

Since then, almost every sector of the New Zealand economy has used the futures and options markets to offset the increased financial risk associated with the open economy. (See TABLE 1 for the currently traded future and options contracts of the NZFOE.)

Computerized Beginnings

The creation and growth of the New Zealand Futures and Options Exchange (NZFOE) was innovative from the start. The exchange founders chose a completly electronic marketplace because of lower startup costs and in response to geographic realities. None of the country's three major cities—Auckland, Wellington, and Christchurch—had enough commercial activity to support a market independently. The exchange developed its Automated Trading System (ATS) with the International Commodity Clearing House Ltd. (ICCH), which also clears all trades for the NZFOE.

ATS functions by matching the buy and sell orders which members enter into computer terminals in their offices throughout New Zealand. If no exact opposite position is available, the system queues orders according to the dealer's instructions. The computer also generates all the documentation and accounting records for brokers, and provides continuously updated information on transaction prices and trading volume. The ICCH has since used ATS software for the London Futures and Options Exchange (London Fox). In July 1988, ATS Mk II which provides an enhanced dealing facility and multi-currency settlement capability was launched. The system is so advanced that it was used as the backbone for the Automated Pit Trading System of the London International Financial Futures Exchange (LIFFE). The ATS MKII software was upgraded in 1990, improving the system's reponsiveness and efficiency by a factor of 10.

The NZFOE and ICCH have made no secret that around-the-clock operation is possible in the future. The ATS system can easily accommodate expanded trading hours. The exchange frequently holds additional trading sessions when important economic announcements are imminent, particularly concerning the New Zealand government budget. Once GLOBEX begins operating in the Asia-Pacific timezone, the NZFOE will likely expand its trading hours.

Exchange Structure

There are three types of membership at the NZFOE: Trading Members, Affiliate Members, and Introducing Broker Members. The changes in the membership ranks have reflected the fact that futures trading has become an integral part of corporate and banking treasury operations in New Zealand. The membership includes most of New Zealand's major financial institutions, many National Statutory Boards, and a significant number of foreign bank affiliates and international futures brokers — see Appendix II for the complete membership list.

Trading Members are all shareholders of the exchange and have direct access to ATS terminals. All business on the exchange must be transacted through one of eighteen Trading Members, who are directly liable to the clearing house. The number of Trading Memberships is limited to seventeen, and can only be acquired by the transfer from an existing member at a price negotiated between the two parties. Also, the transfer of Trading Membership is subject to the final approval of the Board of Exchange and Trading Members in General Meeting.

Affiliate Members are not the NZFOE shareholders and must clear their trades through Trading Members. They do, however, have access to information and some services of the ATS system. They can operate for their own proprietary accounts or on behalf of clients. The number of Affiliate Memberships is not limited. At the end of 1990, there were eleven Affiliate Members. Introducing Broker Members also must process their trades through Trading Members and cannot issue their own statements. There were two such NZFOE members at the end of 1990.

In late 1990, the NZFOE shareholders (Trading Members) unanimously agreed in principle to change the structure of the exchange. These changes, to be developed over several years, would separate the roles of owners and users of the exchange. The restructured NZFOE will be run as a private company which provides centralized trading facilities and regulates trading activities. The oversight function would extend to both principal traders (institutions trading only for their own accounts), and public brokers (who have the right to trade on behalf of others).

Trading access to the Automated Trading System will be made available via the purchase of annual trading permits. Exchange officials believe this move will (1) ensure that the NZFOE grows efficiently on a sound commercial foundation, and (2) provide the widest possible range of products to the users of the market. Thus, under the new structure, both broader participation and greater opportunities to diversify into different product areas are expected.

In mid-1991, the NZFOE was entertaining substantial bids for its purchase by both the London Futures and Options Exchange (London FOX) and the Sydney Futures Exchange. The acceptance of one of the bids would not likely hinder reorganization plans.

Regulation

Beyond the strict membership requirements, the futures trading activity in New Zealand is safeguarded by the exchange self-regulation and the oversight by government authority. New Zealand's Securities Amendment Act of 1988 provides a statutory environment similar to those in the United States and Australia. This legislation governs all trading of futures and options in New Zealand and is guided by the overriding goal of protecting investor interests.

After its regulatory guidelines were upgraded and clarified, the Act has been helping to bring the New Zealand futures industry up to international standards. Under the requirements of the Act, the exchange controls the activities of members and customers through its rules, internal compliance, and surveillance capabilities. Nonetheless, the ultimate oversight responsibility still lies in government hands.

New Zealand Equity Futures and Options Contracts

Introduction

Stock index futures in New Zealand had an impressive rise and precipitous fall since their listing in January 1987. The NZFOE's contract on the Barclays Share Price Index (BSI) grew rapidly in its first nine months to a peak monthly turnover of 17,000 lots in October 1987. The international stock market crash of 1987 hit New Zealand quite hard, and the BSI contract was a prime casualty. During the month of the crash, the New Zealand equity market was one of the worst performing markets in the world, and it has still not fully recovered from the 1987 shock.

The turnover quickly dropped to under 1,000 lots per month and held this low level through early 1989. When New Zealand equities recovered in mid-1989, some interest came back to the futures as well, which subsequently averaged over 1,500 lots per month for the rest of the year. The average, month-end open interest for the period was a thin 190 positions. In 1990, similarly unimpressive activity levels were recorded. The monthly volume was under 1,400, and the open interest usually remained below 200.

The contract is valued at NZ$20 times the index and is cash-settled. Few international investors currently use the BSI contract as a substitute for investment in New Zealand equities because of the country's small weighting in global equity indices — Financial Times-Actuaries World Indices, Morgan Stanley Capital International World Indices, and Salomon-Russell Global Equity Indices. Fund managers with a desire for New Zealand exposure tend to purchase shares directly in Auckland or via American Depositary Receipts (ADR's) listed on U.S. exchanges.

Exchange-traded options on BSI futures were launched in February 1989. The investment community acknowledged the necessity of the contract but has not actively supported its trading. As it could be expected when underlying futures volume is light, options activity has been extremely thin, rarely exceeding 200 lots per month. By late 1990, both monthly turnover and open interest had dropped to double digits. Exchange officials still hope the efforts of a few traders to maintain liquidity in both the futures and options contracts will provide a platform for the future growth when a buoyant activity returns to the physical share market. The NZFOE would then be in a position to attract more pension and trust fund managers to the market.

In October 1990, the NZFOE marked another milestone by launching share options on four popular New Zealand equities. The NZFOE has been the second exchange in the Asia-Pacific region after the Sydney Stock Exchange to trade options on individual shares. After launching share options, the exchange changed its name from the New Zealand Futures Exchange to the New Zealand Futures and Options Exchange. The exchange hopes that share options will open up a new field of risk management for institutional, corporate, and individual investors. Exchange officials and members believe that options on individual shares can reach a much broader spectrum of users than equity index futures and options.

Put and call options on Brierley Investments, Fletcher Challenge, Carter Holt, Harvey and Robert Jones Investments were listed, although the initial activity focused mainly on the first two companies. In the first three months of trading, the total share options volume averaged over 4,000/month, with an open interest of some 3,500. The success of share options will rest heavily on the trading activity and public interest in the specific shares and the New Zealand equity market in general.

Barclays Share Price Index Futures

Contract Unit: A sum of money equal to twenty times the Barclays Share Price Index expressed as New Zealand dollars. (NZ$20).

The Barclays Share Price Index (BSI): BSI consists of 40 leading New Zealand listed public companies, and its base level of 100 began on January 31, 1957. BSI does not include any Australian-based companies whose shares are quoted on the New Zealand Stock Exchange. The companies included in the index are all New Zealand domiciled — see Appendix III for the list of the BSI constituent shares and their relative weightings in the index.

Price for Cash Settlement: The price of cash settlement is announced by the clearing house and will be the closing quotation for the Barclays Share Price Index on the last trading day of the contract month. The closing quotation is adjusted and provided by Barclays New Zealand Limited to the clearing house at 9:00 A.M. on the business day following the last trading day of the contract month.

Cash Settlement: All bought and sold contracts in existence at the close of the last trading day of the contract month are settled by the clearing house at the amount representing the difference between the contract value and cash settlement value.

Prices: Prices are quoted in the same form as the Barclays Share Price Index.

Margin Requirement: Minimum deposits are determined by the clearing house and subject to change from time to time.

Clearing House: International Commodities Clearing House Limited.

Clearing House Fees: NZ$3.00 per contract traded, subject to change from time to time.

Exchange Transaction Fee: NZ$2.00 per contract traded, or as determined from time to time.

Cash Settlement Months: Spot month plus next two consecutive months then financial quarters out for one year.

Table 2A: Trading Volume of Barclays Share Price Index Futures

	1986	1987	1988	1989	1990	1991
January	n/l*	4,393	794	842	1,003	790
February	n/l	9,011	1,146	984	1,458	1,597
March	n/l	10,037	4,379	756	1,290	895
April	n/l	10,627	1,460	995	907	768
May	n/l	12,580	1,388	1,531	1,163	
June	n/l	10,624	740	1,269	558	
July	n/l	13,478	989	1,000	782	
August	n/l	13,150	764	2,447	1,950	
September	n/l	11,645	752	2,490	1,669	
October	n/l	16,691	757	1,865	1,694	
November	n/l	4,515	1,301	1,345	1,288	
December	n/l	2,287	1,536	759	713	
Average	n/l	9,920	1,334	1,357	1,206	
Total	n/l	119,038	16,006	16,283	14,475	

Table 2B: Open Interest of Barclays Share Price Index Futures

	1986	1987	1988	1989	1990	1991
January	n/l	768	365	135	178	125
February	n/l	1,564	615	161	203	264
March	n/l	564	349	52	66	54
April	n/l	1,688	362	134	188	172
May	n/l	2,266	190	207	179	
June	n/l	304	120	77	60	
July	n/l	1,728	193	153	88	
August	n/l	1,235	178	467	225	
September	n/l	926	93	148	130	
October	n/l	526	84	225	171	
November	n/l	399	237	183	152	
December	n/l	336	7	51	8	
Average	n/l	1,025	233	166	137	

*Not Listed
(1) Trading of Barclays Share Price index futures started in January 1987.
(2) Open Interest is as of the end of each month.
(3) Open Interest of an expiring contract month is included up to the day preceding the settlement date of that contract month.
(4) Open Interest is calculated by counting the net number of futures contracts which remain to be liquidated by additional offsetting transactions or by physical delivery after taking account of matched but as yet unsettled bought and sold contracts.

Source: The New Zealand Futures and Options Exchange

Last Day of Trading: The last permitted day for trading will be the second to last business day of the cash settlement month.

Settlement Day: The business day following the last permitted day of trading.

Trading Hours: The trading hours for the contract on the NZFOE's Automated Trading System will be 9:15 A.M. to 3:45 P.M.

Barclays Share Price Index Options

Contract Unit: The value of the Barclays Share Price Index multiplied by NZ$20.

Contract Months: Financial quarters out to six months.

Trading Hours: 9:00 A.M. to 4:50 P.M.

Option Premium: The option premium (contract price) is payable by the buyer of a call or put to the seller on exercise or expiration of the option, not on the purchase of the option.

Premium Quotation: Quoted as the number of points of the Barclays Share Price Index.

Exercise Price: Set at intervals of 50 points of the Barclays Share Price Index.

Exercise: On any business day to expiration.

Expiration Date: At the close of the last trading day for the BSI futures contract, which is the second to last business day of the cash settlement month.

Margin Requirement: The initial margin deposit for long and short options will be the daily-published risk factor multiplied by the initial margin of the underlying futures contract. The initial margin deposit cannot exceed the value of the option premium. Initial margin deposits are reduced for all options and options/futures combinations which include offsetting positions.

Clearing House: International Commodities Clearing House Limited.

Clearing House Fees: As determined by the Clearing House.

Exchange Transaction Fee: NZ$1.50 per contract traded or as determined by the NZFOE.

Table 3A: Trading Volume of Options on Barclays Share Price Index

	1986	1987	1988	1989	1990	1991
January	n/l*	n/l	n/l	n/l	416	5
February	n/l	n/l	n/l	72	184	2
March	n/l	n/l	n/l	12	89	16
April	n/l	n/l	n/l	128	129	95
May	n/l	n/l	n/l	431	231	
June	n/l	n/l	n/l	372	183	
July	n/l	n/l	n/l	292	198	
August	n/l	n/l	n/l	667	73	
September	n/l	n/l	n/l	415	69	
October	n/l	n/l	n/l	230	37	
November	n/l	n/l	n/l	241	21	
December	n/l	n/l	n/l	96	2	
Average	n/l	n/l	n/l	269	136	
Total	n/l	n/l	n/l	2,956	1,632	

Table 3B: Open Interest of Options on Barclays Share Price Index

	1986	1987	1988	1989	1990	1991
January	n/l	n/l	n/l	n/l	252	5
February	n/l	n/l	n/l	53	385	7
March	n/l	n/l	n/l	2	8	15
April	n/l	n/l	n/l	85	99	59
May	n/l	n/l	n/l	303	237	
June	n/l	n/l	n/l	216	71	
July	n/l	n/l	n/l	389	232	
August	n/l	n/l	n/l	754	265	
September	n/l	n/l	n/l	149	8	
October	n/l	n/l	n/l	266	30	
November	n/l	n/l	n/l	325	44	
December	n/l	n/l	n/l	0	0	
Average	n/l	n/l	n/l	231	136	

*Not Listed
(1) Trading of options on Barclays Share Price Index futures started in February 1989.
(2) Open Interest is as of the end of each month.
(3) Open Interest of an expiring contract month is included up to the day preceding the settlement date of that contract month.
(4) Open Interest is calculated by counting the net number of futures contracts which remain to be liquidated by additional offsetting transactions or by physical delivery after taking account of matched but as yet unsettled bought and sold contracts.

Source: The New Zealand Futures and Options Exchange Futures

New Zealand Bond Futures and Options Contracts

Introduction

The NZFOE lists diverse contracts on bond, equity, foreign exchange and agricultural products.[1] However, activity has been dominated by the futures and options contracts on New Zealand government bonds. Turnover in the bond contracts grew steadily since 1986, to over 300,000 contracts per year for both 1989 and 1990. Although these levels are small by international standards, they are significant from the perspective of the New Zealand futures industry. The dollar value of trading in each year since 1987 has been nearly equal or above the country's Gross National Product.

The Five Year Government Stock Contract (GSC), listed in February 1986, is the NZFOE's most successful contract, accounting for over half of the exchange turnover from late 1987 to mid-1990. Since mid-1990, the exchange's short-term Bank Bill futures surpassed the longer term contract. These medium-term government bond futures were designed to allow corporate borrowers, lenders, and institutional investors to manage their substantial interest rate risk in New Zealand. The contract was revised in May 1988 and reissued as Five Year Government Stock No. 2 Contract (GSC), which has a lower coupon rate of 10 percent for a face value of NZ$100,000. This adjustment was elicited by the reduction of the coupon rate from 14 percent to 10 percent by the New Zealand government.

New Zealand financial institutions are very active in trading this contract, both to adjust their bond holdings and arbitrage the pricing discrepancy in the futures and underlying cash markets. Foreigners with New Zealand dollar fixed-income investments use this contract to lock in high yields. In 1989, the daily average volume for Five Year Government Stock Contract (GSC) was close to 2,000 lots per day. The open interest surged in 1989, peaking at 17,000 positions. This indicated a healthy market depth. The trading activity consolidated at these levels in 1990, with the daily average turnover of over 1,500 contracts and the open interest generally above 10,000 contracts.

Options on Five Year Government Stock No. 2 Contract (GSO) were successfully launched in December 1988, along with an extensive marketing and educational program. The exchange hoped that more risk-adverse corporations would be attracted to the fixed-cost of hedging with options, while institutions welcomed the new trading vehicle. Since then, the GSO quickly became the NZFOE's most active option contract.

In September 1989, the NZFOE launched another bond contract, on 3-year Government Stock. The contract was designed to enhance users' risk management flexibility along the yield curve. Although it seemed promising, the contract began fading a year after its introduction, and by the end of 1990, its activity had become moribund, with only 941 lots traded for the entire year. Three Year Government Stock options are also listed, but did not trade at all in 1990.

Five Year Government Stock No. 2 Contract

Contract Unit: New Zealand Government Stock with (1) a face value of NZ$100,000, (2) a coupon rate of 10 percent per annum, and (3) a term to maturity of five years.

Contract Price: Yield per annum per NZ$100 face value in multiples of 0.01 percent.

Prices: Prices are quoted as one hundred minus the price. For instance, a price of 85.53 on the NZFOE represents a yield or interest rate of 14.47 percent.

Margin Requirement: Deposit requirements are determined from time to time by the Clearing House and are subject to change from time to time.

Clearing House: International Commodities Clearing House Limited.

Clearing House Fee: As determined by the Clearing House.

Exchange Transaction Fee: NZ$2.00 per contract traded or as determined by the NZFOE.

Delivery Months: Financial quarters out to one year.

Last Day of Trading: The last day of trading is the first Wednesday after the ninth day of the cash settlement month. Trading ceases in the cash settlement month at 12:00 P.M. on the last day of trading.

Settlement Day: One business day following the last trading day of the contract month.

Mandatory Cash Settlement: All bought and sold contracts in existence at the close of trading in the contract month are settled by the clearing house at the cash settlement price. No provision for physical delivery exists.

Cash Settlement Price: The cash settlement price is declared by the clearing house and calculated as follows.

On the last trading day of the contract month, the clearing house obtains the quotes of the bid/offer yields from the government stock dealers on the Approved Settlement List. Upon the request of the Clearing House, each government stock dealer offers the bid/offer yields at which it would buy/sell at 11:30 A.M. that day New Zealand Government Stock with (1) a face value of NZ$1,000,000, (2) a coupon rate of 10 percent, and (3) a five year to maturity from the last trading day of the cash settlement month.

After discarding those quoted bid/offer yields with a spread of more than 0.15 per annum, the clearing house randomly selects the quotes of ten dealers. The quotes of the randomly selected dealers with the two highest and two lowest mid-rates will be discarded, and the arithmetic average of the mid-rates of the remaining six quotes will be the cash settlement price. The clearing house will announce the cash settlement price at no later than 3:00 P.M. on the last trading day of the contract month.

Table 4A: Trading Volume of 5-Year Government Stock No. 2 Futures

	1986	1987	1988	1989	1990	1991
January	n/l**	5,956	11,825	15,869	24,731	15,180
February	201	12,249	28,430	24,774	19,116	18,336
March	1,091	14,545	33,129	24,758	28,837	27,556
April	3,592	15,081	23,844	12,001	11,871	15,746
May	6,083	18,932	31,243	27,379	22,610	
June	4,970	17,133	28,365*	14,918	27,970	
July	7,395	24,538	32,801	25,740	27,196	
August	6,147	13,446	22,604	37,537	40,391	
September	9,990	9,796	19,674	42,877	28,133	
October	8,404	13,344	14,477	43,022	27,395	
November	18,102	17,551	34,355	50,403	29,112	
December	15,557	13,594	25,933	29,384	20,867	
Average	7,412	14,680	25,557	30,254	25,686	

Table 4B: Open Interest of 5-Year Government Stock No. 2 Futures

	1986	1987	1988	1989	1990	1991
January	n/l	2,274	2,470	5,779	6,454	6,682
February	n/a***	3,785	5,664	7,685	7,589	8,677
March	n/a	3,172	4,609	4,735	5,438	7,368
April	n/a	3,798	6,248	6,176	7,151	9,851
May	n/a	6,441	6,535	6,786	9,527	
June	n/a	5,144	4,552*	4,215	6,821	
July	1,016	6,656	6,346	8,361	10,428	
August	1,289	6,238	6,134	13,762	16,350	
September	2,199	1,118	4,382	11,437	7,423	
October	2,534	2,955	5,558	16,952	10,520	
November	3,959	2,714	10,571	15,371	12,649	
December	2,455	1,279	2,891	7,817	4,995	
Average	2,242	3,798	5,497	9,391	8,779	

*The contract was revised and reissued in May 1988, and the June volume and open interest reflect the new contract's turnover. The contract name changed from 5-year Government Stock futures to 5-year Government Stock No. 2 futures.

**Not Listed
***Not Available
(1) Trading of 5-year Government Stock futures started in February 1986.
(2) Open Interest is as of the end of each month.
(3) Open Interest of an expiring contract month is included up to the day preceding the settlement date of that contract month.
(4) Open Interest is calculated by counting the net number of futures contracts which remain to be liquidated by additional offsetting transactions or by physical delivery after taking account of matched but as yet unsettled bought and sold contracts.

Source: The New Zealand Futures and Options Exchange

Options on Five Year Government Stock No. 2 Contract (GSO)

Contract Unit: One futures contract on 5-year Government Stock with NZ$100,000 face value and 10 percent coupon for a specified contract month on the NZFOE.

Exercise Prices: Set at intervals of 0.25 percent per annum yield.

Exercise: On any buisness day to expiration.

Trading Months: Financial quarters out to six months.

Table 5A: Trading Volume of Options on 5-Year Government Stock Futures

	1986	1987	1988	1989	1990	1991
January	n/l*	n/l	n/l	775	688	750
February	n/l	n/l	n/l	58	711	640
March	n/l	n/l	n/l	421	1,211	2,218
April	n/l	n/l	n/l	595	550	1,117
May	n/l	n/l	n/l	500	1,145	
June	n/l	n/l	n/l	1,270	677	
July	n/l	n/l	n/l	3,000	1,030	
August	n/l	n/l	n/l	5,673	1,642	
September	n/l	n/l	n/l	2,998	624	
October	n/l	n/l	n/l	5,373	456	
November	n/l	n/l	n/l	6,933	578	
December	n/l	n/l	526	460	152	
Average	n/l	n/l	526	2,480	789	
Total	n/l	n/l	526	28,056	9,464	

Table 5B: Open Interest of Options on 5-Year Government Stock Futures

	1986	1987	1988	1989	1990	1991
January	n/l	n/l	n/l	720	1,362	541
February	n/l	n/l	n/l	669	1,744	1,146
March	n/l	n/l	n/l	350	661	1,996
April	n/l	n/l	n/l	852	1,053	2,117
May	n/l	n/l	n/l	1,219	1,597	
June	n/l	n/l	n/l	1,143	599	
July	n/l	n/l	n/l	2,480	1,225	
August	n/l	n/l	n/l	4,765	1,928	
September	n/l	n/l	n/l	3,353	540	
October	n/l	n/l	n/l	5,181	920	
November	n/l	n/l	n/l	5,542	1,240	
December	n/l	n/l	92	946	241	
Average	n/l	n/l	92	2,409	1,093	

*Not Listed
(1) Trading of options on Government Stock futures started in December 1988.
(2) Open Interest is as of the end of each month.
(3) Open Interest of an expiring contract month is included up to the day preceding the settlement date of that contract month.
(4) Open Interest is calculated by counting the net number of futures contracts which remain to be liquidated by additional offsetting transactions or by physical delivery after taking account of matched but as yet unsettled bought and sold contracts.

Source: The New Zealand Futures and Options Exchange.

Expiration Date: At 12:00 P.M. on the last trading day of the underlying contract month—the first Wednesday after the ninth day of the cash settlement month.

Margin Requirement: The initial margin deposit for long and short options will be the daily-published risk factor multiplied by the initial margin of the underlying futures contract. The initial margin deposit cannot exceed the value of the option premium. The initial margin deposit is reduced for all options and option futures combinations which include offsetting positions.

Clearing House: International Commodities Clearing House Limited.

Clearing House Fees: As determined by the Clearing House.

Exchange Transaction Fee: NZ$1.50 per contract traded or as determined by the NZFOE.

New Zealand Short-Term Interest Rate and Currency Futures and Options

Introduction

The New Zealand Futures and Options Exchange's other highly popular contract is 90-day Bank Accepted Bill futures. It was listed in December 1986 to replace an existing short-term interest rate contract on Prime Commercial Paper. In 1990 it became the exchange's most active contract. The Bank Bill contract is used to control risk associated with New Zealand's volatile call money, 30-day, and 90-day rates. The emergence of sophisticated interest rate management tools such as FRA's, Caps, Collars, and Cylinders has been fostered by the NZFOE's short-term rate futures.

The contract has a unit value of NZ$500,000 and is cash-settled, based on the quotes from fifteen approved bill dealers. In mid-1989, the Bank Bill futures were averaging 400 to 500 lots per day, with a relatively deep open interest of 4,300. Since then, the Bank Bill contract activity has grown steadily, with the daily average trading volume surging over 1,000 lots by early 1990 and close to 1,500 later in the year. Open interest also grew rapidly and has not fallen below

10,000 lots since June 1990. The Bank Bill contract now rivals the Government Stock futures in both breadth and depth of users.

Options on Bank Bill futures (BBO) got off to a slow start in June 1989, and have rarely traded more than 500 lots a month since then. The open interest grew steadily, and by the end of 1990 hovered around 1,000 lots. Considering the huge success of the Bank Bill futures during this period, BBO should be achieving a higher turnover, particularly in relation to the Government Stock options. Nevertheless, they remain NZFOE's second most popular options contract.

The volatile Kiwi dollar forces many institutions and corporations to use foreign exchange risk management tools. Currency futures should therefore fare well in New Zealand. U.S. Dollar futures (USD) were the first contract to be listed on the NZFOE, in January 1985. USD was initially rather successful but never won widespread acceptance. This has been due to the competition from the interbank forward market and, also, because the contract is quoted in U.S. dollar terms which are unfamiliar to major dealers. The USD volume was around 200 lots a month in 1989, and rose to about 350 lots a month in 1990. The open interest has been between 200 and 300 lots since mid-1990.

Hoping to boost currency trading, in late-1988 the exchange added New Zealand dollar futures (KWI) with a contract size of NZ$100,000. Although the Kiwi contract's format is more familiar to forex dealers and the general public, it has yet to attract wide interest. The USD contract still remains more active. KWI turnover never exceeded 400 lots, and the trading activity dropped sharply in 1990.

90-Day Bank Accepted Bill Futures

Contract Unit: NZ$500,000 face-valued 90-Day Bank Accepted Bills of Exchange complying with the Bills of Exchange Act 1908.

Cash Settlement Months: Spot month plus next two consecutive months, and then financial quarters out to two years.

Trading Hours: 8:10 A.M. to 4:50 P.M.

Contract Price: Yield per annum per NZ$100 face value in multiples of 0.01 percent.

Price Quotation: One hundred minus price.

Cash Settlement Price: At 10:00 A.M. on the last trading day of the cash settlement month, the clearing house will obtain the quotes of the bid and offer yields for NZ$500,000 of Bank Accepted Bills of the basis type from the Bank Accepted Bills dealers on the Approved Settlement list.

After discarding those with a spread of more than 0.25 per annum, the clearing house will randomly select the quotes of ten dealers. The quotes of the randomly selected dealers with the two highest and two lowest mid-rates will be discarded and the arithmetic average of the mid-rates of the remaining six quotes will be the cash settlement price.

The clearing house will announce the cash settlement price at 1:30 P.M. on the last trading day of the contract month.

Mandatory Settlement: All short and long contracts in existence at the close of the last trading day of the contract month are settled by the clearing house at the cash settlement price. There is no provision for physical delivery.

Margin Requirement: As determined by the clearing house, and subject to change from time to time.

Commission: By negotiation between client and Trading or Affiliate Member.

Clearing House: International Commodities Clearing House Ltd.

Clearing House Fees: NZ$3.00 per contract traded, or as determined from time to time by the clearing house.

Exchange Transaction Fee: NZ$2.00 per contract traded, or as determined from time to time by the Exchange.

Last Day of Trading: The first Wednesday after the ninth day of the cash settlement month. Trading ceases at 12:30 P.M. on the last trading day of the contract month.

Settlement Day: First business day following the last trading day of the contract month.

Table 6A: Trading Volume of 90-Day Bank Accepted Bill Futures

	1986	1987	1988	1989	1990	1991
January	n/l*	2,229	2,663	2,476	15,160	26,222
February	n/l	2,504	4,572	4,493	11,711	24,919
March	n/l	2,340	4,755	5,953	12,372	29,609
April	n/l	2,584	7,109	4,352	7,596	29,259
May	n/l	3,168	8,801	7,317	20,293	
June	n/l	2,989	6,829	6,263	15,673	
July	n/l	2,671	5,378	9,133	30,505	
August	n/l	2,271	7,278	17,661	35,159	
September	n/l	3,296	4,526	17,187	30,719	
October	n/l	4,940	5,285	22,819	38,713	
November	n/l	5,492	4,863	12,431	38,877	
December	2,793	3,290	1,749	8,267	24,407	
Average	2,793	3,148	5,317	9,863	23,432	
Total	2,793	37,774	63,808	118,352	281,185	

Table 6B: Open Interest of 90-Day Bank Accepted Bill Futures

	1986	1987	1988	1989	1990	1991
January	n/l	861	1,892	1,808	5,415	15,197
February	n/l	1,364	1,935	2,877	7,933	22,208
March	n/l	1,206	2,149	2,462	5,764	14,522
April	n/l	1,644	2,546	3,403	5,961	16,267
May	n/l	2,028	2,634	4,624	12,539	
June	n/l	1,759	2,134	2,462	7,152	
July	n/l	2,158	2,296	4,388	11,786	
August	n/l	2,331	2,855	7,670	18,566	
September	n/l	1,707	1,738	5,088	11,953	
October	n/l	2,347	2,413	7,645	19,048	
November	n/l	2,165	2,767	8,932	24,226	
December	1,097	1,636	880	3,977	10,509	
Average	1,097	1,767	2,187	4,611	11,738	

*Not Listed
(1) Trading of 90-day Bank Accepted Bill futures started in December 1986.
(2) Open Interest is as of the end of each month.
(3) Open Interest of an expiring contract month is included up to the day preceding the settlement date of that contract month.
(4) Open Interest is calculated by counting the net number of futures contracts which remain to be liquidated by additional offsetting transactions or by physical delivery after taking account of matched but as yet unsettled bought and sold contracts.

Source: The New Zealand Futures and Options Exchange

Options on 90-Day Bank Accepted Bill Futures

Contract Unit: One NZ$500,000 face value, 90-Day Bank Bill futures contract of a specified month.

Option Premium: The option premium, which is the price of the contract, should be payed by the buyer of a call or put to the seller on exercise or expiration of the options, but not on purchase. The value of the premium is calculated by the following formula:

$$\text{Premium} = \left[\frac{(500,000 \times 365)}{\left(365 + \dfrac{(e \times 90)}{100}\right)} - \frac{(500,000 \times 365)}{365 + \dfrac{((e + 0.01) \times 90)}{100}} \right]$$

e = 100 - Exercise Price
p = (premium in yield percent per annum) x 100

Premium Quotation: Premiums are quoted in yield percent per annum in multiples of 0.01 per cent multiplied by 100.

Exercise Price: Set at intervals of 0.25 percent per annum yield.

Exercise: On any business day to expiration.

Cash Settlement: Financial quarters out to six months.

Expiration Date: At the close of the last trading day of the underlying futures contract (the first Wednesday after the ninth business day of the cash settlement month).

Trading Hours: Same as the 90-Day Bank Bill Futures—8:10 A.M. to 4:50 P.M.

Margin Requirement: The initial margin deposit for long and short options will be the daily-published risk factor multiplied by the initial margin of the underlying futures contract. The initial margin deposit cannot exceed the value of the option premium. The initial margin deposit is reduced for all options and option futures combinations which include offsetting positions.

Clearing House: International Commodities Clearing House Limited.

Clearing House Fee: As determined by the Clearing House.

Exchange Transaction Fee: NZ$1.50 (plus gross sales tax) per contract traded or as determined by the NZFOE.

Table 7A: Trading Volume of Options on 90-Day Bank Bill Futures

	1986	1987	1988	1989	1990	1991
January	n/l*	n/l	n/l	n/l	102	350
February	n/l	n/l	n/l	n/l	0	330
March	n/l	n/l	n/l	n/l	0	610
April	n/l	n/l	n/l	n/l	360	547
May	n/l	n/l	n/l	n/l	460	
June	n/l	n/l	n/l	17	20	
July	n/l	n/l	n/l	374	250	
August	n/l	n/l	n/l	312	123	
September	n/l	n/l	n/l	1,060	90	
October	n/l	n/l	n/l	222	556	
November	n/l	n/l	n/l	310	461	
December	n/l	n/l	n/l	140	580	
Average	n/l	n/l	n/l	348	250	
Total	n/l	n/l	n/l	2,435	3,002	

Table 7B: Open Interest of Options on 90-Day Bank Bill Futures

	1986	1987	1988	1989	1990	1991
January	n/l	n/l	n/l	n/l	280	1,211
February	n/l	n/l	n/l	n/l	280	1,461
March	n/l	n/l	n/l	n/l	0	840
April	n/l	n/l	n/l	n/l	280	1,327
May	n/l	n/l	n/l	n/l	380	
June	n/l	n/l	n/l	0	40	
July	n/l	n/l	n/l	275	240	
August	n/l	n/l	n/l	371	363	
September	n/l	n/l	n/l	252	160	
October	n/l	n/l	n/l	212	706	
November	n/l	n/l	n/l	182	1,122	
December	n/l	n/l	n/l	180	861	
Average	n/l	n/l	n/l	210	393	

*Not Listed
(1) Trading of options on 90-day Bank Bill futures started in June 1989.
(2) Open Interest is as of the end of each month.
(3) Open Interest of an expiring contract month is included
   up to the day preceding the settlement date of that contract month.
(4) Open Interest is calculated by counting the net number of futures contracts which
   remain to be liquidated by additional offsetting transactions or by physical delivery after
   taking account of matched but as yet unsettled bought and sold contracts.

Source: The New Zealand Futures and Options Exchange

U.S. Dollar Futures

Contract Unit: U.S.$50,000

Delivery Months: Spot months plus the next three consecutive months, and then financial quarters out to one year.

Quotation: Prices are quoted in New Zealand dollars per U.S. dollar in multiples of 0.0001.

Mandatory Close-Out: All contracts in existence at the close of the last trading day of the cash settlement month are settled in New Zealand dollars.

Rate of Exchange for Mandatory Close-Out: The rate of exchange for mandatory close-out will be announced by the Clearing House and be calculated as follows:

On the last trading day for the cash settlement, the clearing house obtains a quote from six licensed foreign exchange dealers in New Zealand (of whom at least two will be trading banks) of the bid and offer quotations for the spot exchange of U.S. dollars vis-a-vis New Zealand dollar at 2:30 P.M.

The quotes of the selected dealers with the highest and lowest mid-rates will be discarded and the arithmetic average of the mid-rates of the remaining four quotes will be the settlement rate.

Margin Requirement: The margin requirement is determined by the clearing house, and is subject to change from time to time.

Clearing House: International Commodities Clearing House Clearing Limited.

House Fees: NZ$3.00 per contract traded or as determined from time to time by the clearing house.

Commission: By negotiation between client and Trading or Affiliate Member.

Exchange Transaction Fee: NZ$2.00 per contract or as determined from time to time by the Exchange.

Last Day of Trading: The permitted last trading day of the contract month is first Wednesday after the ninth day of the cash settlement month or such other day determined by the Board of the NZFOE.

Settlement Day: Two business days following the last trading day of the cash settlement month.

Table 8A: Trading Volume of U.S. Dollar Futures

	1985	1986	1987	1988	1989	1990	1991
January	231	1,327	640	1,657	253	12	512
February	1,579	1,235	381	1,445	43	612	533
March	2,640	823	817	1,465	43	424	301
April	1,698	923	623	1,664	55	34	157
May	1,971	1,050	2,366	1,357	1,304	32	
June	1,808	1,014	1,441	753	420	87	
July	2,878	789	2,186	639	600	353	
August	1,538	820	484	1,821	434	111	
September	1,568	1,350	934	3,157	178	448	
October	1,709	876	2,957	2,412	213	565	
November	1,287	1,193	1,822	840	0	590	
December	1,209	1,538	1,540	274	1,000	592	
Average	1,676	1,078	1,349	1,457	379	322	
Total	20,116	12,938	16,191	17,484	4,543	3,860	

Table 8B: Open Interest of U.S. Dollar Futures

	1985	1986	1987	1988	1989	1990	1991
January	106	n/a	253	54	12	12	261
February	276	n/a	345	363	36	12	268
March	296	n/a	405	227	19	224	241
April	133	n/a	490	468	36	20	214
May	189	n/a	1,353	353	259	31	
June	197	n/a	490	201	163	59	
July	368	294	549	297	49	227	
August	313	188	523	785	55	174	
September	279	529	104	387	129	209	
October	177	289	326	672	1	310	
November	212	649	171	229	1	292	
December	n/a	598	286	83	0	438	
Average	212	212	441	343	63	167	

(1) Trading of U.S. dollar futures started in January 1985.
(2) Open Interest is as of the end of each month.
(3) Open Interest of an expiring contract month is included up to the day preceding the settlement date of that contract month.
(4) Open Interest is calculated by counting the net number of futures contracts which remain to be liquidated by additional offsetting transactions or by physical delivery after taking account of matched but as yet unsettled bought and sold contracts.

Source: The New Zealand Futures and Options Exchange

New Zealand Dollar Futures

Contract Unit: One hundred thousand New Zealand dollars (NZ$100,000).

Delivery Months: Spot months plus the next two consecutive months, and then financial quarters out to one year.

Quotation: Prices are quoted in United States dollars per New Zealand dollar in multiples of 0.0001.

Mandatory Close-Out: All short and long contracts in existence at the close of the last trading day of the cash settlement month are settled in U.S. dollars by the clearing house at the rate of exchange for mandatory close-out. There is no provision for physical delivery.

Rate of Exchange for Mandatory Close Out: The rate of exchange for mandatory close-out is announced by the clearing house, and is calculated as follows.

On the last trading day for the cash settlement, the Clearing House obtains a quote from each licensed foreign exchange dealer on the Approved Settlement List of the bid and offer quotations for the spot exchange of New Zealand dollars vis-a-vis United States dollars at 11:30 A.M.

After discarding those bid/ask quotes with a spread of more than 0.15 percent per annum, the clearing house will randomly select the quotes of ten dealers. The quotes of the randomly selected dealers with the two highest and two lowest mid-rates will be discarded and the arithmetic average of the mid-rates of the remaining six quotes will be the settlement rate.

Margin Requirement: The margin requirement is determined by the clearing house, and is subject to change from time to time.

Clearing House: International Commodities Clearing House Limited.

Clearing House Fees: As determined from time to time by the clearing house.

Exchange Transaction Fee: NZ$2.00 per contract or as determined from time to time by the Exchange.

Last Day of Trading: The permitted last trading day of the contract month is two business days before the third Wednesday of the cash settlement month. Trading in the cash settlement month ceases at 2:30 P.M. on the last trading day of the contract month.

Settlement Day: One business day following the last trading day of the cash settlement month.

Table 9A: Trading Volume of New Zealand Dollar Futures

	1986	1987	1988	1989	1990	1991
January	n/l*	n/l	n/l	251	67	1
February	n/l	n/l	n/l	308	68	1
March	n/l	n/l	n/l	154	2	0
April	n/l	n/l	n/l	196	8	0
May	n/l	n/l	n/l	322	9	
June	n/l	n/l	n/l	190	5	
July	n/l	n/l	n/l	229	2	
August	n/l	n/l	n/l	168	4	
September	n/l	n/l	n/l	142	5	
October	n/l	n/l	n/l	106	210	
November	n/l	n/l	111	39	216	
December	n/l	n/l	137	91	1	
Average	n/l	n/l	124	183	50	
Total	n/l	n/l	248	2,196	597	

Table 9B: Open Interest of New Zealand Dollar Futures

	1986	1987	1988	1989	1990	1991
January	n/l	n/l	n/l	124	0	1
February	n/l	n/l	n/l	173	0	0
March	n/l	n/l	n/l	80	0	0
April	n/l	n/l	n/l	124	8	0
May	n/l	n/l	n/l	84	11	
June	n/l	n/l	n/l	72	0	
July	n/l	n/l	n/l	47	1	
August	n/l	n/l	n/l	57	2	
September	n/l	n/l	n/l	27	5	
October	n/l	n/l	n/l	26	215	
November	n/l	n/l	42	37	6	
December	n/l	n/l	60	19	0	
Average	n/l	n/l	51	73	21	

*Not Listed
(1) Trading of New Zealand dollar futures started in November 1988.
(2) Open Interest is as of the end of each month.
(3) Open Interest of an expiring contract month is included up to the day preceding the settlement date of that contract month.
(4) Open Interest is calculated by counting the net number of futures contracts which remain to be liquidated by additional offsetting transactions or by physical delivery after taking account of matched but as yet unsettled bought and sold contracts.

Source: The New Zealand Futures and Options Exchange

Options on New Zealand Dollar Futures

Contract Unit: One NZ$100,000 New Zealand Dollar futures contract of a specified contract month.

Delivery Months: Financial quarters out to six months.

Premium: Quoted in minimum fluctuations of 0.0001 U.S. dollars per one New Zealand dollar, which is referred to as one point. The premium of the options is quoted in points.

Exercise Prices: Set at multiples of 50 points or 0.005 U.S. dollars per one NZ dollar.

Exercise: On any business day to expiration.

Expiration Date: At 2:30 P.M. on the last trading day of the underlying futures contract (two business days before the third Wednesday of the cash settlement month).

Margin Requirement: The initial margin deposit for long and short options will be the daily-published risk factor multiplied by the initial margin of the underlying futures contract. The initial margin deposit cannot exceed the value of the option premium. The initial margin deposit is reduced for all options and option futures combinations which include offsetting positions.

Clearing House: International Commodities Clearing House Limited.

Clearing House Fee: As determined by the Clearing House.

Exchange Transaction Fee: $1.50 per contract traded or as determined by the NZFOE.

Table 10A: Trading Volume of Options on New Zealand Dollar Futures

	1986	1987	1988	1989	1990	1991
January	n/l*	n/l	n/l	18	0	0
February	n/l	n/l	n/l	7	0	0
March	n/l	n/l	n/l	13	0	0
April	n/l	n/l	n/l	0	0	0
May	n/l	n/l	n/l	0	2	
June	n/l	n/l	n/l	6	0	
July	n/l	n/l	n/l	1	0	
August	n/l	n/l	n/l	25	0	
September	n/l	n/l	n/l	4	0	
October	n/l	n/l	n/l	0	0	
November	n/l	n/l	n/l	0	0	
December	n/l	n/l	17	0	0	
Average	n/l	n/l	17	6	0	
Total	n/l	n/l	17	74	2	

Table 10B: Open Interest of Options on New Zealand Dollar Futures

	1986	1987	1988	1989	1990	1991
January	n/l	n/l	n/l	9	0	0
February	n/l	n/l	n/l	7	0	0
March	n/l	n/l	n/l	11	0	0
April	n/l	n/l	n/l	6	0	0
May	n/l	n/l	n/l	6	2	
June	n/l	n/l	n/l	6	0	
July	n/l	n/l	n/l	7	0	
August	n/l	n/l	n/l	32	0	
September	n/l	n/l	n/l	0	0	
October	n/l	n/l	n/l	0	0	
November	n/l	n/l	n/l	0	0	
December	n/l	n/l	17	0	0	
Average	n/l	n/l	17	7	0	

*Not Listed
(1) Trading of options on New Zealand dollar futures started in December 1988.
(2) Open Interest is as of the end of each month.
(3) Open Interest of an expiring contract month is included up to the day preceding the settlement date of that contract month.
(4) Open Interest is calculated by counting the net number of futures contracts which remain to be liquidated by additional offsetting transactions or by physical delivery after taking account of matched but as yet unsettled bought and sold contracts.

Source: The New Zealand Futures and Options Exchange

Looking Forward

Although it is a regional innovator and serves a vital and growing domestic risk transferal role, the New Zealand Futures and Options Exchange has yet to achieve prominence in the Pacific Basin financial arena. Instead of rushing to launch new products to gain worldwide attention, the exchange intends to build on its existing strengths. These include an advanced, proven trading system and a geographical location at the start of the Asian-Pacific trading day. In addition, the exchange is placing a particular emphasis on education of members, corporate customers, and individual investors. Furthermore, options, both on futures and individual shares, remain a top priority of the exchange.

The restructuring of the NZFOE will likely occur by late 1992. Improved access to full trading privileges for a broader group of users should greatly benefit both the exchange and the New Zealand futures industry. These gains will be enhanced by the generally improving economic conditions in the country.

The NZFOE appears well positioned to grow along with New Zealand's financial sector and to pursue expansion on the domestic front. As its markets develop, institutional users worldwide should find the NZFOE an increasingly attractive venue for hedging and asset allocation strategies.

Endnote

1. Agricultural contracts played a vital role in the genesis of the New Zealand futures industry, but have since become virtually inactive. Wool futures volume dried up in 1987 and 1988, while wheat futures did not last through their first year of trading. The exchange launched a revised wool futures contract and options on wool futures in May 1991.

EMERGING ASIAN FUTURES AND OPTIONS MARKETS —

Bold Initiatives for a Promising Future

Introduction

A dramatic financial evolution is spreading throughout the Asia-Pacific region, particularly outside of the region's major international financial centers. Recently, the expansion of capital market activities and structural liberalizations have often been more extensive in the less-developed regional financial centers. Furthermore, as discussed in Chapter 1, international fund managers from the developed world, who were able to enhance returns and reduce market risks by investing in the more-established Asian equity markets in the 1980s, are aggressively venturing into the emerging markets of the region in the 1990s. As a result, the less-developed Asian financial centers will be able to deepen their capital markets and will seek to develop risk management tools in order to further accelerate incoming foreign investment as well as domestically-generated investment. This chapter discusses some of the numerous changes that are bringing these emerging markets closer to the development of significant derivative market activity.

The emerging Asian financial markets have little in common except for geographical proximity. Some, like Taiwan and Korea, are on the threshold of building capital markets of international standard, while others, like Mongolia and Vietnam, are decades away. In addition, their significance to regional derivative markets is varied. For instance, financial centers such as Korea and Taiwan have the potential to become a major source of business for regional or international exchanges in the near term. In the long term, a number of these financial markets could develop both vibrant futures and options markets at home, and send significant activity abroad.

In viewing these markets, it is essential to note that capital market development will be the basic prerequisite for financial futures activity. Although many countries in the region, such as Vietnam and China, are still on the lower portion of the development curve, the rapid economic growth in the region has greatly accelerated capital market development in the countries that are further up on the learning curve. As recently as the mid-1980s, it would have been unimaginable to consider financial futures markets in countries such as the Philippines and Malaysia. However, the Philippines established a financial futures exchange in 1990, and Malaysia is on the verge of doing so. Thus, even though it still strains one's imagination to envisage active financial derivative markets in countries such as Thailand and Indonesia, the dynamic metamorphosis of the region has surprised many observers before. Both of these countries could have derivative markets by the second half of the decade.

The common thread between the following countries is therefore more than geographical. Most of the Asian emerging financial markets can be characterized as demonstrating increasing awareness of derivative products, and possessing major long term potential as either markets or sources of activity.

In this chapter, markets and financial developments in the Philippines, Malaysia, Taiwan, Korea, Thailand, Indonesia, China, Mongolia, and Vietnam are discussed. As mentioned above, the Philippines has a functioning financial futures market, and Malaysia will soon have one. The near-term prospect for Taiwan and Korea are uncertain but it will not be a surprise to see them trade financial futures and options in their domestic markets by the mid-1990s. Thailand and Indonesia both have rapidly maturing capital markets, and are likely to follow closely behind Taiwan and Korea in their emergence on the derivatives scene. China, Mongolia and Vietnam still need to establish very basic infrastructures for capital markets based upon free market principles, and their development of financial futures and options lies on the distant horizon. However, given the rapid collapse of communism in Eastern Europe and the Soviet Union, upcoming regulatory and financial reforms in these three countries will likely be extensive. The financial terrain is certain to change dramatically during the 1990s.

Part 1: The Philippines

Although it is neither the largest nor most significant Asian-Pacific emerging financial center, the Philippines has already established an financial futures exchange. The Manila International Futures Exchange (MIFE) started trading commodity futures in 1986, and has since expanded its range of products to the interest rate and currency complexes. It now lists a total of eight contracts, four of which are financial futures. (See TABLE 1.) The others are contracts on copra, coffee, sugar and soybeans.

The MIFE has 13 Full Trading Members, all of whom are Philippine-registered companies. In addition, there are 13 foreign Trade Affiliated Members. (See TABLE 2 for a list of Full Trading members.) The exchange is regulated by the Philippine Securities and Exchange Commission, and the Central Bank of the Philippines also has oversight for financial futures trading. The MIFE has its own clearing facilities, The Manila International Futures Clearing House Inc., which acts as the ultimate guarantor of all trades on the exchange.

In October 1990, MIFE launched its 91-day Philippine Treasury bill interest rate futures, and in March 1991, began trading futures on US$/Yen, US$/Deutschemark, and British Pound/US$ foreign exchange rates. Both the interest rate and currency contracts are traded on the MIFE floor, but through very different trading methods.

The three currency contracts are traded by traditional open outcry, whereas the interest rate futures use a unique combination of two different methods. Four times a day, the Peso rate contract trades through a "one-price group trading system," which gathers all buyers and sellers who indicate their orders, in a manner similar to the London gold fix. When supply and demand is equalized, a single price is reached, and all orders transact at that price. At other times of the day, the short-term Peso interest rate contract trades — infrequently — through a board-trading system.

Trading on these new contracts is light, averaging less than 700 per day for all of the currencies in May 1991, and about 100 lots per day for the interest rate contract in the same month. On active days, however, currency volume can surge to over 1000 lots. Open interest for the interest rate contract averages

---

Table 1:   Currently Traded Financial Futures Contracts at the MIFE

Financial Futures	Inception
91-Day Philippines Treasury Bill Futures	10/90
British Pound/U.S. Dollar Futures	3/91
U.S. Dollar/Yen Futures	3/91
U.S. Dollar/Deutschemark Futures	3/91

Source: The Manila International Futures Exchange

Table 2: Corporate Full Trading Members of MIFE

Billion Gold Futures, Inc.
C.B. Master Commodities Futures, Inc.
C & T Global Futures, Inc.
Everich International Commodities, Inc.
Golden Commodities Corporation
Goldwell Commodity Traders, Inc.
Imperial Commodities, Inc.
Kingly Commodities Traders & Multi-Resources, Inc.
Pan-Asia International Commodities, Inc.
Queensland-Tokyo Commodities, Inc.
Solidlink Futures, Inc.
Trustcom Futures, Inc.
Uniwell Commodities, Inc.

Source: The Manila International Futures Exchange

about 2000 positions, while the currency contracts achieved an impressive total open interest of 5,800 positions by their third month of trading. Of the currency contracts, the U.S. Dollar/Yen is the most active. (See TABLE 3A and 3B for volume and open interest figures.) Financial futures participants are predominantly Philippine financial institutions and corporations, with a small amount of activity emanating from Singapore, Hong Kong, Taiwan and Indonesia.

In the near future, MIFE hopes to introduce a Philippine stock index contract, but has a number of substantial hurdles to overcome. Aside from the need to secure regulatory approval from both the Central Bank and the Securities and Exchange Commission, MIFE must convince stock exchange officials and members to support the market, and will need to attract international members. There should be a natural core group of interested foreign participants for a Philippine stock index futures contract as Philippine equities have gained popularity with international fund managers.

In its very short experience with financial futures, MIFE has succeeded in attracting regional, as well as local, user bases for its currently traded contracts. This growing critical mass could serve as the foundation of liquidity for upcoming contracts such as Philippine stock index futures.

Table 3A: Monthly Trading Volumes of MIFE's Financial Futures

	Interest Rate	Sterling	Yen	Deutschemark
10/90	1,134	n/l*	n/l	n/l
11/90	2,756	n/l	n/l	n/l
12/90	2,292	n/l	n/l	n/l
1/91	2,826	n/l	n/l	n/l
2/91	2,550	n/l	n/l	n/l
3/91	2,372	2,828	2,884	2,852
4/91	2,258	3,262	3,508	3,446
5/91	2,154	4,314	4,972	4,292

*Not Listed
Source: The Manila International Futures Exchange

Table 3B: Month-end Open Interest of MIFE's Financial Futures

	Interest Rate	Sterling	Yen	Deutschemark
10/90	816	n/l*	n/l	n/l
11/90	2,392	n/l	n/l	n/l
12/90	2,518	n/l	n/l	n/l
1/91	2,876	n/l	n/l	n/l
2/91	3,338	n/l	n/l	n/l
3/91	3,222	1,250	1,216	1,258
4/91	2,852	1,594	1,674	1,656
5/91	1,974	2,082	2,842	2,106

*Not Listed
Source: The Manila International Futures Exchange

91-Day Philippine Treasury Bill Futures

Contract Unit: The weighted average of interest rates of the 91-day Treasury bills issued by the Central Bank of the Philippines.

Trading Month: Spot month plus three trading months.

Trading Hours: 9:30 A.M. to 11:30 A.M.
1:30 P.M. to 3:30 P.M.
(Manila time)

Contract Size: The contract price multiplied by 10,000 Pesos.

Last Day of Trading: The third Thursday of the trading month.

Settlement Day: The Monday immediately following the last trading day.

Settlement: All open positions will be settled by the cash settlement price on the settlement day.

Settlement Price: The weighted average of interest rates of the 91-day Treasury bills determined by the Central Bank of the Philippines on the third Friday auction of the trading month will be the basis for calculating cash settlement price.

U.S. Dollar/Japanese Yen Futures

Contract Unit: 12,500,000 Yen

Trading Month: Spot month plus three consecutive months

Trading Hours: 8:30 A.M. to 11:30 A.M.
2:00 P.M. to 5:00 P.M.
9:00 P.M. to 4:00 A.M.
(Manila time)

Last Day of Trading: The third Tuesday of the trading month.

*Settlement Day:*The business day immediately following the last trading day.

Settlement: All open positions will be settled in Philippine Pesos.

Settlement Price: The average to the second decimal point (not rounded-up) of four hourly spot U.S. Dollar/Yen quotations by the banks and institutions designated by the Executive Committee on the last trading day.

U.S. Dollar/Deutschemark Futures

Contract Unit: 125,000 Deutschemark.

Trading Month: Spot month plus three consecutive months.

Trading Hours: 8:30 A.M. to 11:30 A.M.
2:00 P.M. to 5:00 P.M.
9:00 P.M. to 4:00 A.M.
(Manila time)

Last Day of Trading: The third Tuesday of the trading month.

Settlement Day: The business day immediately following the last trading day.

Settlement: All open positions will be settled in Philippine Pesos.

Settlement Price: The average to the fourth decimalpoint (not rounded-up) of four hourly spot U.S. Dollar/Deutschemark quotations by the banks and institutions designated by the Executive Committee on the last trading day.

British Pound/U.S. Dollar Futures

Contract Unit: 62,500 British Pounds.

Trading Month: Spot month plus three consecutive months.

Trading Hours: 8:30 A.M. to 11:30 A.M.
2:00 P.M. to 5:00 P.M.
9:00 P.M. to 4:00 A.M.
(Manila time)

Last Day of Trading: The third Tuesday of the trading month.

Settlement Day: The business day immediately following the last trading day.

Settlement: All open positions will be settled in Philippine Pesos.

Settlement Price: The average to the fourth decimal point (not rounded-up) of four hourly spot British Pound/U.S. Dollar quotations by the banks and institutions designated by the Executive Committee on the last trading day.

Part 2: Malaysia

Beginning of a New Era

In 1990, the International Monetrary Fund (IMF) told Bank Negara, the central bank of Malaysia, that its capital markets are not yet ready for financial futures. The Kuala Lumpur Commodity Exchange (KLCE) has gone nowhere with its professed intention to list financial contracts. The Kuala Lumpur Stock Exchange (KLSE) is preoccupied with refining its clearing and settlement system and has done little to develop options market. This would not appear to be a conducive environment for a bold initiative for establishing derivative trading in Malaysia.

Yet, a group of well-connected Malaysian firms are trying to lead their capital markets to a new era of financial futures and options. With the implicit backing from the Ministry of Finance, the Kuala Lumpur Options and Financial Futures Exchange (KLOFFE) is currently being set up to enhance the growth of the Malaysian capital markets. The organizers of the exchange have ambitious goals and an optimistic timetable. If the plans remain on track, the KLOFFE may launch Malaysian stock index futures by late 1991 or early 1992.

KLOFFE will be the stepchild of necessity — or at least perceived necessity. Malaysia'a former Finance Minister, Datuk Paduka Daim Zainuddin, was committed to increasing Kuala Lumpur's potential as a financial center, not in order to capture international activity, but to support the country's economic development. The Malaysian government has major privatization plans in the works and recognizes the need to develop liquidity in its capital markets. Futures and options markets are integral to such an objective. When hedging and asset allocation facilities exist, investors can hold larger debt and equity positions and as a result, enhance the liquidity of the market.

Bold Move by Private Organizers

Since some of Malaysia's biggest privatization issues such as Telekoms and the National Electricity Board are slated for the near future, the agility in developing the derivative market is a high priority. Daim stated that "KLCE officials were dragging their feet" in bringing about needed changes, and he was widely known to disapprove of the way in which the KLSE handled the surge of volume after Malaysian shares were officially delisted from Singapore in 1989. Daim's well-known preference for shock therapy was apparent when, in December 1990, the Ministry of Finance and the Capital Issues Committee granted "approval in principle" to the private sector organizers of the KLOFFE for both futures and options trading.

The government's move stunned Kuala Lumpur Commodity Exchange officials who had always taken for granted that new financial contracts would be listed on the KLCE. Even the Ministry of Primary Industries, which oversees commodity trading, was taken by surprise. However, their shock is difficult to justify, considering that they had over three years to develop financial futures markets, and neither ideas nor actions had been forthcoming from them.

Clearly, there were different interpretations of the IMF report. After the IMF ruled out the KLCE, a group of five private institutional organizers of the KLOFFE decided to look into it themselves. Renong Bhd., the New Straits Times Press, Rashid Hussain Bhd., and Zalik Securities commissioned a M$100,000 feasibility study on the prospects for the Malaysian financial futures and options markets. Renong Bhd. in conjunction with its partially-owned subsidiary, the New Straits Times Press, will likely hold a controlling interest in the Kuala Lumpur Options and Financial Futures Exchange. Renong's chairman, Halim Saad, is considered by many observers to have represented Daim's viewpoint within the KLOFFE organizing group.

The Plan

The initial feasibility study was conducted by Commerce International Merchant Bankers Bhd. and relied heavily on outside consultants, especially from the existing foreign exchanges. The Stockholm Options Market (OM) is one such contributor. The first phase of the study was completed in early 1991, and its conclusions have sufficiently bolstered KLOFFE's organizers to move ahead with the project. Specific proposals were then submitted to the Ministry of Finance.

The organizers have set realistic goals for the exchange and have no starry-eyed vision of becoming a major regional futures trading center. According to the head of a Malaysian securities house with close ties to the organizers, KLOFFE's priority is to develop a derivative market that complements the Malaysian equity market. The organizers are also attempting not to make the same mistake that the KLSE made by modeling itself on the world's largest exchanges. They are looking at smaller exchanges as their role models, not to Chicago or London.

While the trading systems of both the New Zealand Futures and Options Exchange and the Swiss Options and Financial Futures Exchange (SOFFEX) have been studied, KLOFFE is planning to use Stockholm OM technology. The Swedish exchange organization has already successfully transferred its system to

London and other financial centers and is rapidly expanding its international activities. The second phase of the study addresses more complex technical and legal aspects of KLOFFE's development. From these early plans, one can discern the rough contours of the market.

The exchange will be structured as an independent, profit-making company, with the aforementioned Malaysian organizing institutions as its main shareholders. It has not yet been decided whether memberships will represent partial ownership in the exchange, or simply convey the right to trade in the markets. It is also unclear whether membership will have tiered categories and privileges.

Membership is expected to be open to any firm which meets exchange requirements, which are yet to be formulated. This, however, does not guarantee that foreign firms can join KLOFFE independently. Foreigners may have to form joint-ventures with local banks or brokerage houses as they must for the Malaysian stock market. A high level member of the organizing group states that the KLSE members will be among the first to join the new exchange. Skeptics have noted, however, that KLOFFE is infringing on the stock exchange's turf, and that some members may be less than eager to join the new exchange.

Regulatory turf is also being contested. It remains undecided whether KLOFFE will be supervised directly by the Ministry of Finance or through a reorganized Commodity Trading Commission. So far, the Commissioner of the commodity regulatory board appears to be out of the decision-making loop. This issue may remain unresolved until other legal changes are enacted, but the Ministry of Finance holds most of the political cards.

The organizers have decided upon an automated trading system for more than the obvious overhead savings that come from not having a trading floor. A proven, off-the-shelf system will save software development costs and, moreover, will not be prone to costly and time-consuming debugging. KLOFFE will probably use a modified version of the Stockholm OM technology. The system will enable KLOFFE to establish an electronic trading system for futures and cash or futures options, with integrated clearing facilities. Furthermore, the Swedish system can accommodate telephone-based block orders, which could be built into the KLOFFE system or added at a later date when volume or type of contract necessitates it. The organizers see screen-based systems as more viable for the size of the Malaysian market, and also regards it as the wave of the future.

The Products

KLOFFE intends to concentrate on equity-related products at the onset. This meshes with the government's privatization and capital market plans and is expected to attract the broadest possible group of users. The relative familiarity of stock index futures will also smooth the KLOFFE's major educational and marketing tasks.

South-east Asian equity markets have attracted significant regional and foreign interest, but the region needs local risk management products. For instance, many overseas fund managers fear liquidity drying up in the local markets and thus long for a viable hedging mechanism. Local index futures will lessen this fear, and consequently, enhance the inflow of investment.

While in many ways index futures are the logical place to start, it also will require numerous changes in existing legal and market structures if KLOFFE is to succeed. Liquidity in Malaysian derivatives — and the added liquidity that would flow into the cash market — is only possible if arbitrageurs and market makers can operate freely in both markets.

This means having to take short positions in the KLSE, which is currently prohibited. Arbitrageurs' difficulty in shorting stock has greatly handicapped the recovery of the Hong Kong Futures Exchange's Hang Seng index futures contract after the stock market crash of 1987. Regulators from Tokyo to Jakarta are naturally wary of relinquishing the control that they feel prevents speculators from driving markets down. However, they do not realize that they are hobbling the long-term development of genuine liquidity.

The KLOFFE organizers have recognized the need for changes in the cash market. According to an official at an organizing firm, the third phase of the feasibility study provides detailed recommendations on modifications for the stock market. One organizer states that KLSE restrictions on short selling need to be addressed and solved, preferably before they launch the contract.

The KLOFFE promoters are not waiting for the government machinery to act on their requests. They have brought in international lawyers with futures regulation expertise to prepare a proposal for modifying the existing Malaysian laws. The organizers then intends to submit their proposal and founding charter as a single package to the Parliament, backed by their ties to the government. This process is targeted for late 1991. Hence, the optimistic early-1992 target for commencement of trading is a distinct possibility. However, many other issues must be tackled well before then.

For instance, the authorities justifiably fear manipulation of an index in either direction — although there is a clear preference for upward movement. Also, the KLOFFE feasibility study indicates a need to find an appropriate index on which to base the futures contract. Malaysian market analysts and the exchange's organizers agree that the current benchmark for the KLSE—the New Straits Times Industrials (NSTI)—is inadequate. With only 30 components, it is subject to manipulation and does not reflect the overall Malaysian market. Even a senior official at the New Straits Times Press, which compiles the index, admits the shortcomings of the widely-followed NSTI. While the KLSE has a broader-based index, the KLOFFE organizers have indicated that they may create their own all-share index.

Regardless of the benchmark index that is to be eventually chosen, stock index futures are almost certain to be KLOFFE's first product. Even if their are teething pains, index futures will eventually enable institutional investors to rapidly hedge or adjust their Malaysian equity positions, and thus make them more willing to take larger holdings. These same risk management needs might also increase their appetite for options.

KLOFFE's "approval in principle" from the Ministry of Finance includes the right to list options on stocks as well. Just as the complacent Malaysian commodity industry had assumed that it would be given the chance to list financial futures, the Kuala Lumpur Stock Exchange always thought that options were its domain. But the authorities thought otherwise. KLOFFE is now giving a high priority to options on stocks as well as stock index futures. The initial study and inclination of the organizers favor options on a handful of the highest market capitalization and most actively-traded equities.

The exchange's proposed start-up plans—attracting members, educational programs, marketing efforts, launching index futures, and eventually options—are highly ambitious. Nevertheless, KLOFFE's organizers are looking beyond this first stage of development. Even though the August 1990 IMF report which cautioned against the early introduction of financial futures included interest rate and currency futures among the instruments that were not yet viable, it is in this direction that KLOFFE intends to eventually move. Products under consideration for the mid-1990s include: medium or long-term bond futures; short-term ringgit interest rate futures; the Malaysian ringgit/the U.S. dollar currency futures; and possibly the ringgit/the yen and the ringgit/the Singapore dollar contracts. Bond and interest rate futures would dovetail with the Ministry of Finance's efforts to cultivate active and sophisticated markets for government and corporate bonds, and commercial paper.

Potential Obstacles

The linkage between the development goals for KLOFFE and Malaysia's capital markets — along with the backing of the Ministry of Finance — should provide a solid foundation for the new exchange. KLOFFE is intended to play an integral part in the growth of Malaysia's domestic markets. Furthermore, the government's bold privatization plans should work to its advantage. However, establishing active futures and options markets will be substantially more difficult than attracting investors into the equity market.

Although a successful modification of the trading restrictions for the cash market would remove a major structural hurdle for KLOFFE and allow arbitrageurs to trade both sides, many traders question whether an active stock index future market can develop in Malaysia. Liquidity requires market makers and substantial pools of risk capital in addition to arbitrageurs.

The KLOFFE decision to opt for a screen-based system, while cost effective, may inhibit the development of market depth. Electronic trading tends to function smoothly in normal market environments, but it exhibits a serious structural weakness at times of market stress. The presence of the on-screen market makers with their bids and offers cannot be guaranteed in a wildly volatile market. This has been demonstrated by the frequent pauses in trading — and occasional lock-ups — in Japan's Nikkei and Topix stock index futures and options contracts.

In contrast, the Singapore International Monetary Exchange's (SIMEX) Nikkei 225 futures trade continuously even during the most violent sessions. The difference is the constant bids and offers on the trading floor by "locals" who risk their own capital on a minute-by-minute basis. It has taken SIMEX much time and effort to build its own pool of locals, but it now stands as one of the exchange's major achievements and sources of strength. Also, SIMEX has long desired to launch Singapore stock index futures, and the KLOFFE's debut may hasten that moment.

KLOFFE, however, does not have time to develop a pool of locals. It might have to concentrate on getting as many market makers as possible and encourage arbitrageurs with clearing fee rebates and other incentives. But will Kuala Lumpur become an environment conducive to developing a futures market expertise?

Much depends on how open the KLOFFE truly is to foreign membership and participation. One reason Singapore has become a center of derivative expertise is that SIMEX strongly encourages foreign membership. This facilitates the transfer of hedging, trading, and market-making technologies. On this issue, Kuala Lumpur should look to its neighbor for a successful example.

KLOFFE Moves Ahead

Is Malaysia ready for a financial futures and options markets? In 1990, the IMF said "not yet." Or did they only mean that the KLCE was not yet ready for derivative trading, as a Renong official implied in January of 1991? Whatever the conclusion of the IMF report—which is now gathering dust on a bookshelf of the central bank of Malaysia—was, KLOFFE is currently sprinting ahead with the Ministry of Finance's endorsement.

"Sure, it's a bold move to grab the derivative turf from the KLCE and KLSE, but how else will it happen here?," a foreign broker in Kuala Lumpur. There are bigger stakes involved, particularly the government's economic goals, and they are clearly a top priority.

So far, KLOFFE's organizers have taken an impressively realistic approach toward setting up the market. They have done their homework and are not aiming too high as other regional futures exchanges did in the mid-1980s. With strong underlying fundamentals and firm political support, KLOFFE could soon be another well-known acronym on the lips of Asian market participants.

Part 3: Taiwan

By some measures, Taiwan is Asia's second richest country, and it has the fourth largest equity market of the region after Japan, Korea, and Australia. According to the Emerging Market Indices of International Finance Corporation, the total market capitalization of Taiwan was US$100 billion at the end of 1990. The country also has an extraordinarily high level of public speculation. Over 20% of the population has a stock trading account and the Taipei Stock Exchange has the world's second highest turnover, even after its 64% drop between February and July of 1990. This volatility has sparked a recognition of the need for risk management tools, but has equally elicited a greater public appetite for new speculative vehicles.

Until a government crackdown in 1989 and 1990, a huge, underground futures trading environment existed in Taiwan, generating over US$1 billion in daily activity. Trading took place mostly at night since the illegal trades tended to price off of Chicago and New York markets. As many as 30,000 to 50,000 orders were sent abroad daily, and many more orders — 100,000 to 150,000 — never left Taiwan. These latter trades took place in "bucket shops," so named because most of the orders never made it to the exchanges, but were thrown into the house's "bucket" and netted off each other. As recently as early 1991, another type of bucketing activity was prevalent. Known as "Trading in the Air," brokers would accept bets on the future price movement of the local stock index or individual shares.

The government has closed down the biggest brokers in these activities, and forced others — many of whom have legal stockbroking operations — to curtail their business. A new law, sponsored by the Ministry of Economic Affairs, that will clarify the status of the futures industry and set up a regulatory structure, is now working its way through the Yuan (Taiwan's legislature), and will have its reading in the spring of 1992. The bill gained the support from various Taiwan business associations, securities firms, and overseas exchanges. Futures trading in Taiwan will thus be legalized by the end of 1992.

If the new law passes in its current form, Asian and U.S. futures industry leaders expect greatly increased Taiwanese business to flow to regional futures exchanges. Trading activity will be initially directed to the markets which are familiar to Taiwanese investors, such as Hong Kong, Singapore, Japan and the U.S. Taiwanese equity investment in those countries is expected to continue expanding, as well as investment in Thailand, Malaysia, Indonesia, and even the infant stock exchanges in China.

Futures brokerage firms from the U.S. and Japan have begun exploratory operations in Taipei, and their number is expected to grow. A few firms have already established joint ventures with local financial brokers or institutions.

Although the pending legislation is designed first to regulate futures brokerage activity in Taiwan which is geared to outward order flows, the development of domestic futures activity is likely to occur by the middle of the decade. Stock Exchange officials, Taiwan academics, and brokerage officials have all initiated research on a local stock index future, and there can be little doubt that Taiwan's risk-loving investors would welcome such a product. Any financial community that can devise and sustain "trading in the air," is certainly a ripe market for exchange-listed equity derivatives.

Furthermore, under a major infrastructure and financial development plan announced in early 1991, Taiwan set a timetable for broad reforms to make the island one of Asia'a main banking centers. Eased restrictions on foreign banks, internationalization of the New Taiwan dollar, and the establishment of a gold market have been proposed. The Finance Ministry also plans to develop Taiwan's bond market by floating over US$40 billion in bond issues by 1996, and privatizing scores of state-run enterprises.

These major capital market reforms, as well as the public's huge demand for speculative activity in the equity and commodity markets, will ensure a strong underlying foundation for the growth of Taiwan's derivative markets. By the end of the decade, Taiwan's financial strength will be close to catching up with its industrial prowess.

Part 4: Korea

As the Korean equity market declined over 23% between 1989 and 1990 after a rise of about 550% between 1985 and 1988, sharp volatility occured in the Korean securities such as closed-end country funds, investment trusts, convertible bonds and bonds with warrants. These Korean securities have been the only investment vehicles available to international investors who wish to participate in the Korean equity market — direct access to the Korean market by international investors will not be possible until early 1992.

The Korea Fund listed on the New York Stock Exchange — a brainchild of the International Finance Corporation in Washington, D.C. — was the first exchange-traded, close-end country fund ever created, and has been quite popular among international investors since its inception in August 1984 as the Korean equity boomed in the second half of the 1980s. Other funds, such as the Korea Europe Fund and the Korea Asia Fund followed quickly behind.

From March to June of 1989, the Korean market fell some 15%. This kind of volatility convinced international investors the need for risk management tools for their Korean investment, and the American Stock Exchange (AMEX) explored the feasibility of listing options on the Korea Fund in 1990. However, the insufficient daily trading volume of the Fund presented a problem of market manipulation, and options on the Korea Fund were never listed.

The Koreans themselves have begun to recognize the need for risk management tools after their market demonstrated that stock prices can also come down. The Korean Ministry of Finance announced its plan in 1990 to establish a stock index futures market and made its plan more specific in 1991 by including Korean stock index futures in its five year capital market restructuring plan. However, the Ministry's projected establishment of financial futures market faces a number of obstacles.

In case of stock index futures, the Korean government must be able to convince itself that the equity market should be driven by free market forces. The Korean government has sought to prop up the market on a number of occasions since 1989 without much success. An efficient stock index futures market cannot be formed if the government tries to boost the cash market whenever the underlying market heads substantially southward. At the end of 1989, the Korean government persuaded the three largest Korean investment companies to purchase declining Korean equities by offering them low interest US$3 billion bank loans. Despite the injection of US$3 billion, the Korean equity market fell 23% in 1990 and incurred huge losses to the three investment companies — Korea Investment Trust, Daehan Investment Trust and Citizens' Investment Trust. These losses are known to have put these three investment companies under serious financial stress despite the fact that they were considered blue chip firms throughout the 1980s.

The Korean Ministry of Finance has yet to deregulate interest rates and foreign exchange trading. These liberalizations will be the first steps toward establishing futures on interest rates and currencies. The complete deregulation of domestic interest rates and foreign exchange trading is not expected until the mid-1990s.

Furthermore, in order to establish futures markets, the education of the Korean financial community will be essential. However, the Korean securities houses and institutional investors are not currently allowed to trade financial futures overseas. Instead, Korean corporations have been permitted to trade commodity and currency futures in international futures markets for hedging purpose only since 1975. Currently, five foreign-owned and one Korean-owned commodity brokerage firms are operating in Korea: Gerald Commodities Ltd., Korean Commodities Inc., Cargill Investor Services Korea, Paribas Commodities Inc., Credit Lyonnais Rouse and MG Commodities.

Korean corporations are required to report their international futures positions to the Ministry of Finance. Despite this disclosure requirement, it is well known that Korean corporations have been speculating in international currency derivative markets. For instance, a bank located in Southwestern Korea wiped out two thirds of its total net worth by taking reckless positions in international currency derivative markets during the two year span between 1989 and 1990. Since then, the Ministry of Finance has been taking more cautious steps in allowing Korean institutions to trade in international futures markets. This will further delay the entry of Korean financial institutions into international futures markets.

In 1990 Korean economy was the 15th largest in the world in terms of GNP. As the Korean economy completes its transformation into an industrialized nation in the 1990s, its capital markets need to catch up with the prowess of the Korean manufacturers in order to support their continuing growth. After the Iraqi invasion of Kuwait in 1990, Korea, which relies heavily on imported oil, purchased a substantial amount of crude oil at its peak price (over US$40/barrel) at the end of 1990, anticipating a further surge in the oil price. Although the Gulf crisis ended in the spring of 1991 and oil prices declined to pre-war levels (US$20/barrel), in May 1991 Korea was still taking the delivery of oil priced in late 1990. Korean industrial companies cannot maintain its competitiveness against their foreign counterparts if they have to consume higher priced oil. This energy fiasco has further convinced Korean institutions of the need for sophisticated hedging operations.

Korea faces a number of problems which it must overcome in order to establish a financial and commodity futures industry and markets. However, it seems to have recognized the importance of developing them in order to nurture a balanced economy. The Ministry of Finance and Korean securities houses have been patiently studying international futures markets since the mid-1980s. Korean industrial companies have rapidly overcome many obstacles in a short period of time on a number of occasions to become world class steel manufacturer, ship builders, computer chip markers and automobile manufacturers. Furthermore, in a four year period between 1985 and 1989 the Korean equity market saw its total market capitalization grow approximately 1,900 percent to US$141 billion from US$7 billion in 1985, and became the tenth largest equity market in the world, surpassing Switzerland. Thus it would not be surprising if Korea develops significant financial and commodity futures activity and markets by the mid-1990s.

Part 5: Thailand

In the mid-1980s, Thailand was one of the Asian emerging financial markets whose readiness for a domestic financial futures market was highly questionable. While the development of such markets still lies in the distant future, it is now a much more realistic possibility than would have been believed just a few years ago. Substantial growth and maturation is anticipated for the Thai capital markets in the 1990s, and this could lay the foundation for financial futures and options. Furthermore, as the economic growth of the country continues its remarkable progress, Thai financial futures market could play a significant role.

Fueled by stellar economic growth throughout the 1980s, the Thai equity market boomed and attracted both domestic and international investors. According to the Emerging Market Indices of the International Finance Corporation, at the end of 1990 Thailand's total market capitalization was US$24 billion. This represented a 1,200 percent growth in five years from US$1.9 billion in 1985, yet there is still much room for further expansion. Upcoming government privatization plans will continue to increase market capitalization and broaden the base of shareholders in Thailand. The widely discussed liberalization of investment guidelines for domestic institutions should also deepen the equity market.

The Ministry of Finance is expected to authorize stock warrants and convertible bonds in late 1991 or early 1992. These are the first steps toward equity derivative activity. Other steps include the Stock Exchange of Thailand's development research into both index futures and stock options. Overseas derivative exchanges have been approached for consultation and feasibility studies..

The Ministry of Finance has also expressed its desire to expand the ability of financial institutions and corporations to issue debt, and to nurture the development of the secondary bond market. These efforts to create a favorable infrastructure for capital formation will include tax reform and the lifting of asset allocation restrictions on life insurance companies and mutual funds. As capital market development proceeds, it will create domestic demand for risk management tools, and might open the way for both equity and bond futures trading in Thailand.

The path toward derivative activity in Thailand is not clear, and is strewn with many political and economic uncertainties, such as the February 1991 military coup. However, the country's phenomenal economic growth, increasing financial strength, and active role in the South-east Asian economic development, will likely make it a key economic force in the Asian-Pacific region in the coming years. Thailand's hosting of the World Bank/IMF annual meeting in 1991 is only the first indication of its emerging prominence within the world financial community.

Part 6: Indonesia

The Indonesian financial markets have made enormous strides since the sweeping liberalization of October 1988, known as "Pakto." The reforms allowed new banks and foreign joint venture banks to open for the first time in 20 years, and liberalized foreign exchange trading and offshore borrowing. As a result, both the number of banks and the level of deposits have more than doubled.

Capital market activities have grown even more dramatically. New listings on the Jakarta Stock Exchange (JSE) boomed, with over 150 companies going public since the reforms took effect. According to the Emerging Market Indices of the International Finance Corporation, Indonesian equity market capitalization surged from US$117 million in 1985 to to just over US$8 billion at the end of 1990.

There have been numerous dislocations resulting from this rush to liberalize and modernize. Major foreign exchange trading losses at banks with inadequate risk control mechanisms and horrendous settlement problems at the Stock Exchange were two of the most prominent problems. Yet, the worst of the indigestion appears to be over, and Indonesia's financial and capital market growth is expected to reaccelerate in the near future.

In early 1991, Indonesia's Central Bank and Finance Ministry began pushing through new rules and guidelines to strengthen the country's financial structure. This will both promote a more stable system, and ease foreign participant's anxiety due to the uncertainty about regulatory controls.

The first major area of reform is related to the new Banking Bill. It establishes higher capital adequacy standards for banks, and requires them to demonstrate a minimum of competence before speculating in the foreign exchange markets. This Bill will also authorize pension funds to invest in equities and bonds.

The second major upcoming area of reform concerns the equity market. The JSE will be privatized in 1992, and will move to fully computerized settlement. The current Capital Markets Supervisory Agency, or BAPEPAM, which now owns the JSE, will become simply a market supervisor and a regulator, but will have expanded jurisdiction over new investment vehicles.

The move toward more sophisticated capital-raising vehicles has already begun, with the first equity warrants issued in 1990 and the first convertible Eurobond floated in early 1991. This trend will likely accelerate as Indonesia's market structure becomes more clearly defined in the coming years.

Indonesia has one of the largest and youngest populations in the world, and a rapidly expanding economy. By the middle of this decade, the country's financial markets will — at minimum — reach the stage that Thailand and Malaysia reached in the mid-1980s. The bond, equity and money markets will be substantially stronger and healthier, and in a position to serve a vital role in Indonesia's economic development. Just as with its South-east Asian neighbors such as the Philippines and Malaysia, it is inevitable that one day, Indonesian derivative markets will be established in order to make the capital markets more liquid and efficient.

Part 7: China

China, the world's most populous nation, has always sparked dreams of the bountiful "China Market" of a billion customers. The People's Republic's economic reforms have moved in fits and starts since the early 1980s, and its political development has certainly not progressed nearly as far. However, slowly but surely, the basic elements of financial and commodity markets are developing in the Middle Kingdom, and thus, any discussion of the Pacific Rim capital markets would be incomplete if it did not briefly touch upon China.

Since 1988, "grey market" share trading has taken place in Shenzhen, the Special Economic Zone closest to Hong Kong. Shanghai, the site of China's pre-Communist stock market, also began unofficial trading in the late 1980s under the careful guidance of state economists. In December 1990, stock trading in Shanghai became official, and since then, Shanghai has listed 8 shares. Beginning in May 1990, the more freewheeling Shenzhen bourse has also begun its semi-official trading — under local authorization — of its first 5 listed companies.

The Shenzhen Securities Exchange officially opened in July 1991, with six shares listed, and as many as 15 companies may be trading by early 1992. There are already over 10 securities firms in Shenzhen, and a few Hong Kong firms are also participating. In fact, Sun Hung Kai Securities of Hong Kong has been instrumental in helping the exchange with numerous technical hurdles.

The future growth of Chinese financial markets depend heavily on local and national government authorities, who have been relatively pragmatic in their development. The Central Bank no longer intends to subsidize the thousands of state enterprises, and hopes to tap the estimated US$130 billion in cash holdings and savings accounts of the nation's citizens. But it cannot access the population's cash horde without forming more structured and efficient capital markets through which its citizens' investment and savings will be channeled into Chinese industrial companies.

The Central Bank is also drafting a major program which will set up a regulatory framework and establish guidelines for foreign portfolio investment. Chinese authorities have also intensively researched futures markets, particularly for agricultural commodities. They worked with the Chicago Board of Trade on feasibility studies for such markets, and also received assistance from the Hong Kong Futures Exchange. In late 1990 and early 1991, provincial cash grain markets opened in several parts of China. The first, The Zhengzhou Grain Wholesale Market, opened in October 1990 featuring wheat trading. Jiangxi and Anhui provinces have followed with rice markets, and Jilin has opened a corn market.

In early 1991, the Communist Party's Central Committee recommended the establishment of grain wholesale and futures markets, giving official support to the provincial undertakings. The already formed cash markets will soon be ready to develop into futures markets, particularly since standardized contract terms and auction price discovery mechanisms have been being introduced.

In addition, a number of Chinese state and province- owned companies are known to be active in the Hong Kong futures market, and the Bank of China and CITIC (China International Trust and Investment Corporation) have also participated in international financial futures markets. The activity level of Chinese entities is expected to increase sharply as 1997 approaches, both within and beyond the Hong Kong futures market.

Despite this impressive growth of market activity, the development of financial futures markets in China is a long way off, probably not until the next century. However, China's higher profile in regional financial futures markets is certain to become a significant factor during this decade.

Part 8: Mongolia

China's neighbor to the north, Mongolia, has taken some of the most dramatic steps toward a free market in recent years. Asia's second oldest Communist state has embarked on a sweeping reform process, spearheaded by its prime minister. If all goes according to plan, by the end of 1993, 70% of state-owned assets will have been privatized, and Mongolians might pay as much attention to Ulan Batur's stock exchange as they do to the capital's renowned Yak races.

All of Mongolia's 2 million citizens will be entitled to vouchers which will enable them to bid on the shares of state-owned companies. International investors will be allowed to buy up to 100% of Mongolian firms, currency restrictions will be eliminated, and the financial system will be revamped along Western, free market standards.

Financial futures activity is unlikely, but that does not diminish the extent of the changes Asia's second oldest communist state has adapted. If Mongolia can take such dramatic steps as setting up its stock exchange in a former children's entertainment center that still sports a mural of Bugs Bunny perhaps commodity futures trading should not be ruled out.

Part 9: Vietnam

Although it is one of the poorest countries in the Asian-Pacific region — and with an economy suffering from years of Communist mismanagement — Vietnam has a large, young, and (at least in the South) entrepreneurial population. Before the end of the decade, the country could be fully reintegrated into regional trade and investment flows, and provide financial opportunities for international investors.

Even before the implementation of needed regulatory and structural changes to the economy, a few bold institutions have launched specialized funds for investment in Vietnam. In mid-1991, the Vietnamese government approved two investment funds. The first, the US$30 million Vietnam Fund, which is managed by Lloyds Bank of Britain and Asia Securities of Taiwan, will invest predominantly in foreign/Vietnamese joint-ventures. The other is a US$100 million fund managed by the Hong Kong subsidiary of Credit Lyonnais Securities. The Credit Lyonnais fund will be structured more like a traditional country fund, with investments in local enterprises. It evisages the proposed Vietnamese stock market as its route for cashing out its investments.

These first tentative steps for foreign investment inflow might encourage other international investors to keep an eye on Vietnam, particularly as a boom in foreign investment and economic growth is expected when the U.S.-led economic embargo is lifted. This could lay the foundation for a Vietnamese capital market.

Part 10: Conclusion

As illustrated in this chapter, developments within Asian emerging financial markets are occurring at diverse speeds and have different levels of significance for international investors and futures traders. However, if the history of rapid development in the major Pacific Rim financial centers provides any single overarching lesson, it is that once a regional financial community commits itself to reform such as the creation of futures markets, the changes can be dramatic and the growth, spectacular.

Market participants have already witnessed this dynamism in Japan, Australia, Singapore, Hong Kong and New Zealand, and are beginning to see signs of it in the Philippines and Malaysia. International market users will surely witness some of the same dramatic changes in Taiwan and Korea, and eventually, Thailand and Indonesia. By early in the next century, not only will the economic size of the Pacific Rim far exceed that of either Europe or North America, but the region may also generate more futures and options activity than anywhere else in the world.

Directory of World Futures & Options Exchanges

Australia

Australian Options Market Pty. Ltd. (AOM)
Australian Stock Exchange Ltd.
20 Bond St., Second Level
Sydney, N.S.W. 2000, Australia
61-2-227-0000; fax 61-2-251-5525

Established in 1976 with calls only; puts were introduced in 1982. The exchange currently trades options on 27 underlying stocks and clears through the Options Clearing House Pty. Ltd.

Sydney Futures Exchange Ltd. (SFE)
Grosvenor St.
Sydney, N.S.W. 2000, Australia
61-2-256-0555; fax 61-2-256-0666
Telex: AA126713

Established in 1960, the SFE has expanded rapidly in recent years and now trades a wide range of futures contracts including All Ordinaries Share Price Index futures, 90-day bankbills, 10-year and three-year Australian Treasury bonds and Australian dollars. In 1989, it developed an after-hours screen dealing system.

Belgium

Bourse de Bruxelles (Brussels Stock Exchange)
Rue Henri Maus 2
Brussels, Belgium 1000
32-2-509-12-11; fax 32-2-511-95-00
Telex: 21374 BOURS B

Brazil

Bolsa Brasileira de Futuros (Brazilian Futures Exchange) (BBF)
Rua do Mercado 11-6 Andar
Rio de Janeiro, Brazil 20010
55-21-224-6062; fax 55-21-231-1635

The BBF opened on Nov. 30, 1984, with a 250-gram gold futures contract. Exchange members are banks, stockholders, commodity brokers and locals. After the BBF and Bolsa Mercantil & de Futuros (BM&F) agreement for clearing and simultaneous trading, BM&F's clearinghouse is the independent clearinghouse for BBF.

Bolsa de Mercadorias de São Paulo (São Paulo Commodities Exchange) (BMSP)
Rua Libero Badaro, 471 Fourth Floor
S/227o Paulo, Brazil 01009
55-11-32-3101; fax 55-11-32-4244

The São Paulo Commodities Exchange was founded in 1917. In 1988, it launched the Adjusted Future Market for coffee, cattle and gold. The BMSP presently trades arabic coffee, live cattle and cotton.

Bolsa Mercantil & de Futuros (BM&F)
Praca Antonio Prado, 48
São Paulo, Brazil 01010
55-11-239-5511; 55-11-36-6183

The BM&F, which was founded by the São Paulo Stock Exchange, is the leading futures exchange in Brazil, trading more than 67,500 contracts daily. The most liquid contracts are gold options and spot, U.S. dollar futures, Government Treasury Bonds futures and stock index futures.

Canada

Montreal Exchange (ME)
800 Square Victoria, Fourth Floor
Montreal, Quebec, Canada H4Z 1A9
(514) 871-2424; fax (514) 871-3559

The ME is Canada's leading futures and options market with international exposure. The exchange trades futures contracts on Government of Canada bonds and Canadian Bankers' Acceptances as well as options on Canadian equities, Canada bonds and gold bullion. Its options and futures are cleared by Trans Canada Options Inc.

Toronto Futures Exchange (TFE)
2 First Canadian Place
The Exchange Tower
Toronto, Ontario Canada M5X IJ2
(416) 947-4487; fax (416) 947-4585

The TFE, formed in early 1984, lists futures on the Toronto 35 Stock Index and options on silver buillion.

Toronto Stock Exchange (TSE)
2 First Canadian Place
The Exchange Tower
Toronto, Ontario Canada M5X IJ2
(416) 947-4700; fax (416) 947-4662

The TSE trades equity options as well as index options based on the Toronto 35 Stock Index.

Vancouver Stock Exchange (VSE)
609 Granville St.
Stock Exchange Tower
Vancouver, B.C., Canada V7Y 1H1
(604) 689-3334; fax (604) 688-6051

The VSE, founded in 1907, is primarily a marketplace for raising venture capital. About 30% of listings are high technololgy and junior industrial companies. In 1982, the VSE became a part of the International Options Clearing Corp. (IOCC), and trades gold and silver options through the IOCC. In 1984, the VSE expanded into equity options, which are cleared by the Trans Canada Options Inc. Currently, 21 option classes are traded on the VSE.

The Winnipeg Commodity Exchange
500 Commodity Exchange Tower
360 Main St., Winnipeg, Manitoba
Canada R3C 3Z4
(204) 949-0495; fax (204) 943-5448

Canada's largest and one of North Anerica's oldest futures exchanges, the WCE trades Canadian agricultural futures. It presently offers trading in canola, flaxseed, oats, rye, domestic feed wheat, domestic feed barley and Western domestic feed barley. Options on canola futures are planned for early 1991.

Denmark

Copenhagen Stock Exchange
Nikolaj Plads 6, Box 1040
DK-1007 Copenhagen, Denmark
45-33-93-33-66; fax 45-33-12-86-13
Telex: 16496 COSTEX DK

Options and futures at the Copenhagen Stock Exchange are traded and quoted with an electronic trading system.

Guarantee Fund for Danish Options and Futures (FUTOP)
Kompagnistrade 15, Box 2017
DK-1012 Copenhagen, Denmark
45-33-93-33-11; fax 45-33-93-44-80

The Guarantee Fund is a nonprofit fund established in 1987 by the Central Bank, the Danish Bankers' Association and the Association of Danish Stock Broking Companies. The fund has 29 clearing members comprising major banks, saving banks and stock broking companies. It operates an integrated registration, real-time margining and clearing system technically operated by the Danish Securities Centre.

Finland

Finnish Options Market (FOM)
P.O. Box 926
SF-00101 Helsinki, Finland
358-0-13-12-11; fax 358-0-13-12-12-11

Finnish Options Market is a marketplace and a clearing house jointly owned by the market participants. Trading is arranged via two systems, electronic and telephone. Founded in 1987, Finnish Options Market began trading stock index futures and options on May 2, 1988.

France

France Matif Automatique (FMA)
52 Ave des Champs Elysees
75008 Paris, France
33-1-42-25-66-25; fax 33-1-42-25-72-45
Telex: 650-563

Marche a Terme International de France (MATIF)
176 rue Montmartre
75002 Paris, France
33-1-40-28-82-82; fax 33-1-40-28-80-01
Telex: 218-362

The MATIF offers a wide range of financial products including long-term and short-term interest rates, notional bonds futures and options, and CAC 40 Stock Index futures. The long-term ECU bond was launched in October 1990. The MATIF also offers futures trading on white sugar, coffee, cocoa and potatoes.

Germany

Deutsche Terminböerse (DTB)
Grueneburgweg 102, Postfach 17 02 03
D-6000 Frankfurt 1, Germany
49-69-15303-0; fax 49-69-5574-92
Telex: 417-5953 DTB

The Deutsch Terminböerse GmbH, established in August 1988, is introducing futures on the German Stock Index (DAX-Future) and a German government bond future (Bund-Future). The exchange will be fully computerized with an itnegrated clearinghouse.

Hong Kong

Hong Kong Futures Exchange Ltd. (HKFE)
Room 911, Ninth Floor
New World Tower, 16-18 Queen's Road
Hong Kong
852-525-1005; fax 852-810-5089

The HKFE offers futures contracts on sugar, soybeans, gold, Hang Seng Stock Index and three-month HIBOR. The HIBOR, launched Feb. 7, 1990, provides Hong Kong's substantial capital markets with a tool for offsetting interest rate risk. The HKFE plans to introduce other financial contracts in the near future.

Ireland

Irish Futures and Options Exchange (IFOX)
Segrave House, Earlsfort Tce.
Dublin 2, Ireland
353-1-767413; fax 353-1-614645

IFOX commenced trading in 1989. It trades futures and options on domestic (Irish pound-demoninated) instruments, using an automated trading system. The IFOX contracts include gilt futures and ISEQ Index futures.

Japan

Nagoya Stock Exchange (NSE)
3-17 Sakae, 3-chome
Naka-Ku, Nagoya, 460 Japan
52-262-3172; fax 52-241-1527

Osaka Securities Exchange (OSE)
8-16 Kitahama, 1-chome, Chuo-ku
Osaka 541, Japan
81-6-229-8643; fax 81-6-231-2639

The OSE trades the Osaka Stock Futures 50 contract, the first stock index futures traded in Japan. The exchange launched the Nikkei Stock Average on Sept 3, 1988. Trading in Nikkei Stock Average options started on June 12, 1989, the first stock index options traded in Japan.

Tokyo Commodity Exchange (TCE)
10-8 Nihonbashi Horidomecho
1-chome, Chuo-ku
Tokyo 103, Japan
81-3-661-9191; fax 81-03-661-7568

The Tokyo Commodity Exchange was organized on Nov. 1, 1984, by consolidating the Tokyo Gold Exchange, the Tokyo Rubber Exchange and the Tokyo Textile Commodities Exchange. TCE contracts include futures on gold, silver, platinum, rubber, cotton yarn and wool yarn.

Tokyo International Financial Futures Exchange (TIFFE)
NTT Data Otemachi Bldg.
2-2-2 Otemachi, Chiyoda-ku
Tokyo 100, Japan
81-3-275-2400; fax 81-3-275-2862

The TIFFE began trading on June 30, 1989. The exchange enables financial institutions, investors and corporations to manage exchange and interest rate risk.

Tokyo Stock Exchange (TSE)
2-1 Nihombashi-Kabuto-Cho
Chuo-ku, Tokyo 103, Japan
81-3-666-0141; fax 81-3-663-0625
Telex: 02522759

The present form of the TSE was established in April 1949. The TFE trades futures on 10- and 20-year Japanese government bonds and the Tokyo Stock Price Index (TOPIX). It also trades TOPIX options.

Malaysia

Kuala Lumpur Commodity Exchange
Fourth Floor, Citypoint
Komplex Dayabumi
Jalan Sultan Hishamuddin
P.O. Box 11260
50740 Kuala Lumpur, Malaysia
6-03-2936822; fax 6-03-2742215
Telex: MA31472 KLCE

The exchange was established in July 1980 as a company limited by guarantee. In 1985, the exchange went through a major restructuring involving changes of its membership, trading system, and clearing and guaranteeing arrangements. A new clearinghouse was set up; the exchange and its clearing members own 70% of the equity with the balance owned by a consortium of banks.

Netherlands

European Options Exchange (EOE)
Rokin 65, Amsterdam
1012 KK, The Netherlands
31-20-5504550; fax 31-20-230012
Telex: 14596 EOEPR NL

The EOE lists options on stocks, the EOE Stock Index, the FTA Bullet Index, Dutch Government bonds and, as part of the International Options Clearing Corp (IOCC) network, on gold and silver as well as the U.S. dollar and British pound. The EOE also lists options on the Major Market Index (XMI), fungible with the XMI options on the American Stock Exchange and cleared by the Options Clearing Corp.

Financiële Termijnmarkt Amsterdam N.V. (FTA)
Nes 49, Amsterdam
1012 KD, The Netherlands
31-20-550455; fax 31-20-245416

The FTA, a wholly owned subsidiary of the Eurpoean Options Exchange, lists three types of futures—guilder bond, EOE Stock Index and Dutch Top 5 Index futures. The guilder bond future is based on a notional bond of Dfl 250,000 nominal with a 7% coupon.

New Zealand

New Zealand Futures & Options Exchange Ltd. (NZFOE)
P.O. Box 6734, Wellesley St.
10th Level, Stock Exchange Centre
Auckland, New Zealand
64-9-398-308; fax 64-9-398-817

The fully computerized NZFOE is the first exchange in the world to open each day and trades five financial futures contracts; Barclays Share Price Index futures, four options on futures and options on four New Zealand equities. The NZFOE operates with 16 trading members and 18 affiliate members located in New Zealand, Australia and the U.K. International Commodities Clearing House serves as the clearinghouse and operates the trading system.

Norway

Norwegian Options Market (NOM)
P.O. Box 1494 Vika
Tordenskioldsgt. 8-10
Oslo 1, Norway N-0116
47-2-331550; fax 47-2-332793

The NOM was established Oct. 1, 1987, and is owned by major Norwegian banks, insurance companies and stockholders. The NOM offers trading in stock options.

Philippines

Manila International Futures Exchange Inc. (MIFE)
7/F Producer's Bank Centre
Paseo de Roxas
Makati 1200, The Philippines
63-2-818-5496; fax 63-2-818-5529

The MIFE was incorporated in 1984. It started trading sugar and soybean futures in 1986 and coffee and copra futures in 1988. The MIFE is the only futures exchange to trade copra futures contracts. Financial futures were launched in 1990.

Singapore

Singapore International Monetary Exchange Ltd. (SIMEX)
1 Raffles Place, #07-00
OUB Centre, Singapore 0104
65-535-7382; fax 65-535-7282
Telex: RS 38000 SINMEX

SIMEX, the first financial futures exchange in Asia, is also the first exchange involved in mutual offset trading with another exchange, the Chicago Mercantile Exchange. SIMEX introduced Japanese Stock Index futures (Nikkei Stock Average) and energy futures to the Asia-Pacific region. SOMEX trades futures and options on Eurodollars, Euroyen, Japanese yen and Deutsche marks plus futures on Nikkei Stock Index, Euromark, British pound, gold, fuel oil and Dubai crude oil.

Spain

Mercado de Futuros Financieros S.A. (MEFF)
Via Layetana 60-62
08003 Barcelona, Spain
(34) 3-412-11-28; fax (34) 3-412-48-26

The MEFF, Spain's first futures market, started trading March 16, 1990, with futures on three-year government notional bonds. MIBOR, 90-day interest rate, futures were launched in October 1990. The MEFF is a fully automated exchange and currenmtly has 34 full members and 11 associate members. The shareholders and the majority of members must be agents of the Sistema de Deuda Publica en Anotaciones en Cuenta (book entry government debt system).

OM Iberica S.A. (OMIB)
Torre Picasso, Planta 26
28020 Madrid, Spain
(34) 1-585-08-00; fax (34) 1-571-95-42

A branch of the Stockholm Options Market, OMIB opened Nov. 8, 1989. It offers cash options on government securities with MIBOR and Treasury bill contracts planned.

Sweden

Stockholm Options Market (OM)
Brunkebergstorg 2, Box 16305
103 26 Stockholm, Sweden
46-8-700-06-00; fax 46-8-723-10-92
Telex: 15394 OPTION S

Stockholm Options Market is an options and futures exchange with integrated clearing facilities based on an electronic trading system combined with telephone-based block order handling. The OM started in June 1985 and opened for foreign trading in August 1987. It is owned by banks and brokers active on the exchange plus a number of Swedish institutions. In a link arrangement with OM London, OM trades OMX and stock futures and options.

Switzerland

Swiss Options and Financial Futures Exchange AG (SOFFEX)
Neumattstrasse 7
8953 Dietikon, Switzerland
41-1-740-30-20; fax 41-1-740-17-76
Telex: 828392 SOFX CH

Founded in 1986, Soffex started trading options on 11 Swiss stocks in May 1988. SOFFEX offers trading in options on 13 Swiss stocks plus futures and options on the Swiss Market Index (SMI). All trading and clearing is fully automated.

United Kingdom

London Grain Futures Market
24-28 St. Mary Axe
London, England EC3A 8EP
44-71-626-7985; fax 44-71-623-2917
Telex: 916434 BALFUT G

The exchange began trading as the London Corn Trade Association in 1929 and merged in 1971 with the Cattle Food Trade Association. Originally, business was confined to imported grains, but that changed after World War II to homegrown barley and wheat and, subsequently, to the present European Economic Community barley and wheat futures and options.

London Meat Futures Exchange
24-28 St. Mary Axe
London, England EC3A 8EP
44-71-626-7985; fax 44-71-623-2917
Telex: 916434 BALFUT G

Cash-settled pig and live cattle futures are offered.

London Potato Futures Market
24-28 St. Mary Axe
London, England EC3A 8EP
44-71-626-7985; fax 44-71-623-2917
Telex: 916434 BALFUT G

Trading in potato futures and options.

International Petroleum Exchange of London Ltd. (IPE)
International House
1 St. Katherine's Way
London, England E1 9UN
44-71-481-0643; fax 44-71-481-8485
Telex: 927479

IPE opened in April 1981 with a gas oil futures contract. The exchange now trades futures on Brent and Dubai crude oil, gas oil and heavy fuel oil as well as options on gas oil and Brent crude oil.

London Futures and Options Exchange (FOX)
1 Commodity Quay
St. Katherine Docks
London, England E1 9AX
44-71-481-2080; fax 44-71-702-9923

The London FOX trades futures and options on soft commodities, enabling commercial users to hedge risk. In 1987, various organizational changes took place: the introduction of "locals"; a Traded Options Market, and the launch of an automated trading system (ATS). Rubber and the MGMI (base metal index) began trading in 1990. White sugar, rubber and MGMI are traded on the fast automated screen trading (FAST) system.

In 1991, FOX merged with the Baltic Futures Exchange, adding pig, lamb, potatoes, grain, soybean meal and BIFFEX freight futures to the contracts traded.

London International Financial Futures Exchange (LIFFE)
The Royal Exchange
London, England EC3V 3PJ
44-71-623-0444; fax 44-71-588-3624
Telex: 893893

LIFFE's nearly 200 members deal in UK, U.S., Japanese and German government bonds, UK, U.S. and European short-term interest rates and the Financial Times-Stock Exchange 100 Index. In 1990, Euromark options were launched and a New York office was opened. Plans for 1991 include merger with the London Traded Options Market and revision of the Japanese government bond futures contract.

London Metal Exchange (LME)
Plantation House, Frenchurch St.
London, England EC3M 3AP
44-71-626-3311; fax 44-71-626-1703
Telex: 8951367

Established in 1877, the LME is the leading international futures market for base metals trading in copper, lead, tin, aluminum, nickel and zinc. The LME accounts for over one-fourth of all the futures trading in London. All market transactions are recorded on a centralized clearing system operated by the International Commodities Clearing House Ltd. (ICCH).

London Traded Options Market (LTOM)
Old Broad St.
London, England EC2N 1HP
44-71-588-2355; fax 44-71-374-0451
Telex: 886557

The London Traded Options Market, part of the International Stock Exchange, offers traded options on 68 equities and restricted life options plus the Financial Times-Stock Exchange (FT-SE) 100 Index. The LTOM was established in 1978.

United States

American Stock Exchange
86 Trinity Place
New York, NY 10006
(212) 306-1000; fax (212) 306-1802

The American Stock Exchange is a uniquely balanced marketplace incorporating a primary equities market and a principal options market trading options on listed and over-the-counter stocks and stock indexes. AMEX's Major Market Index (XMI) is the only U.S. index option listed in Europe; it trades on the European Options Exchange in Amsterdam. The LT-20 Index, long-term options on the SMI, is approved for trading.

Amex Commodity Corp.
86 Trinity Place
New York, NY 10006
(212) 306-8940; fax (212) 306-8934

Chicago Board of Trade (CBOT)
141 W. Jackson St.
Chicago, IL 60604
(312) 435-3500; fax (312) 341-3306

The world's oldest and largest futures exchange trades agricultural and financial futures and options on futures.

Chicago Board Options Exchange (CBOE)
400 S. LaSalle St.
Chicago, IL 60605
(312) 786-5600; (800) OPTIONS
Fax: (312) 786-7409; (312) 786-7413

CBOE, the world's largest options marketplace, offers options contracts on the S&P 100 and 500 stock indexes, 238 stocks, short-term and long-term interest rates, and on U.S. Treasury bonds and notes.

Chicago Mercantile Exchange (CME)
30 S. Wacker Drive
Chicago, IL 60606
(312) 930-1000; fax (312) 930-3439

The CME has the world's largest facility for futures and options trading. The exchange has 2,724 members divided into the CME, the International Monetary Market (IMM) and the Index and Option Market (IOM). In 1989, over 104 million contracts were traded with Eurodollar futures the most active. Eurodollar open interest increased 15% from 1988 to 1989 and by mid 1990 reached nearly 750,000 open positions. The CME trades 36 futures and options contracts including foreign currencies, stock indexes (foreign and domestic), short-term interest rates, Euro-rate differentials and livestock.

Chicago Rice & Cotton Exchange (CRCE)
141 W. Jackson Blvd.
Chicago, IL 60604
(312) 341-3078

The CRCE, an affiliate of the MidAmerica Commodity Exchange, offers a rough rice futures contract, which is traded on the floor of the Chicago Board of Trade.

The Citrus Associates of the New York Cotton Exchange
(See New York Cotton Exchange)
4 World Trade Center
New York, NY 10048
(212) 938-2702; fax (212) 839-8061

Coffee, Sugar & Cocoa Exchange Inc. (CSCE)
4 World Trade Center
New York, NY 10048
(212) 938-2800; (800) HEDGEIT
Fax: (212) 524-9863

The Coffee, Sugar & Cocoa Exchange Inc. is the world's leading marketplace for futures and options trading in these three international commodities. The CSCE also offers a futures contract based on white refined sugar in addition to its raw sugar contracts. In May 1989, it expanded its presence in the international markets by offering a futures contract based on the International Market Index (IMI).

Commodity Exchange Inc. (COMEX)
4 World Trade Center
New York, NY 10048
(212) 938-2900; fax (212) 432-1154

COMEX, the world's most active metals market, offers opportunity to trade gold, silver, copper and aluminum futures and options on gold, silver and copper futures.

Financial Instrument Exchange (FINEX)
4 World Trade Center
New York, NY 10048
(212) 938-2634; fax (212) 432-0294

MidAmerica Commodity Exchange (MidAm)
141 W. Jackson Blvd.
Chicago, IL 60604
(312) 341-3000; fax (312) 341-3027

The MidAm, an affiliate of the Chicago Board of Trade, offers futures on grain, livestock, metals, financial instruments and foreign currencies, as well as options on wheat, soybeans and gold futures.

Minneapolis Grain Exchange
400 S. Fourth St.
Minneapolis, MN 55415
(612) 338-6212; fax (612) 339-1155

MGE trades futures and options on hard red spring wheat futures, hard red spring wheat options (European-style and American-style exercise). White wheat, oats, high fructose corn syrup futures also trade.

New York Cotton Exchange (NYCE)
4 World Trade Center
New York, NY 10048
(212) 938-2702; fax (212) 839-8061

The NYCE, founded in 1870, is the oldest futures exchange in New York. It offers cotton futures, cotton options and, under the Citrus Associates of the New York Cotton Exchange Inc., frozen concentrated orange juice (FCOJ) futures and options. U.S. Dollar Index (USDX) futures and options, European Currency Unit futures, five-year U.S. Treasury note FYTR) futures and options, and two-year U.S. Treasury note futures are traded on the Financial Instrument Exchange (FINEX). The New York Futures Exchange is affiliated with the New York Cotton Exchange.

New York Futures Exchange (NYFE)
20 Broad St., New York, NY 10005
(212) 656-4949; (800) 221-7722
Fax: (212) 656-2925

The NYFE lists futures and options on the NYSE Composite Index and Commodity Research Bureau Futures Price Index, and a futures contract on U.S. Treasury Bonds.

New York Mercantile Exchange (NYMEX)
4 World Trade Center
New York, NY 10048
(212) 938-2222; fax (212) 938-2985

Established in 1872, NYMEX maintains a marketplace for energy and metals futures and options contracts. Its energy complex, the largest in the world, includes futures on crude oil, heating oil, unleaded gasoline, residual fuel oil, propane and natural gas as well as options on crude oil, heating oil and unleaded gasoline. It also offers platinum and palladium futures.

New York Stock Exchange (NYSE)
11 Wall St., New York, NY 10005
(212) 656-8533; (800) 692-6973
Fax: (212) 656-8534

Listing exchange for options on the NYSE Composite Index (NYA), on 50 listed and 7 OTC equities.

Pacific Stock Exchange (PSE)
301 Pine St., San Francisco, CA 94104
(415) 393-4000; fax (415) 393-4202

The PSE has equity trading floors in Los Angeles and San Francisco and an options trading floor in San Francisco. It trades about 1,600 securities and offers options on more than 150 underlying securities, including one index: the Financial News Composite Index (FNCI).

Philadelphia Stock Exchange (PHLX)/Philadelphia Board of Trade (PBOT)
1900 Market St.
Philadelphia, PA 19103
(215) 496-5337; (800) THE-PHLX
Fax: (215) 496-5653

PHLX, the nation's oldest securities exchange, trades more than 1,800 equity securities, 161 stock options, eight foreign currency options and four index options (Value Line European-style, National OTC, Gold-Silver and Utility). The PBOT is the futures subsidiary of the Philadelphia Stock Exchange. The foreign currency options program, started in 1982, is the largest of its kind and offers options and futures on Australian dollars, Deutsche marks, Swiss francs, Canadian dollars, British pounds, Japanese yen, French francs and European Currency Units.

Twin Cities Board of Trade (TCBOT)
430 First Ave. North
Minneapolis, MN 55415
(612) 333-6742; (800) 627-0267
Fax: (612) 333-8728

New futures and options exchange awaiting start of trading. Currency cross-rate futures pending CFTC approval.

A. Corporate Members of Pacific Rim Futures and Options Exchanges

as of Dec 31 1990

NAME OF MEMBER (CATEGORY)	REGISTERED ADDRESS	TEL NO
ALPHA BEST COMMODITIES CO. LTD. (FCM)	10/F., GRANDVIEW COMMERCIAL CENTRE, 29-31 SUGAR ST., CAUSEWAY BAY, HONG KONG.	8905033
ANDERSON MAN FUTURES LTD. (FCM)	RM. 2302 ADMIRALTY CENTRE, TOWER II, 18 HARCOURT RD., HONG KONG.	5200666
ASIA EQUITY FUTURES LIMITED (FCM)	28/F., TWO EXCHANGE SQUARE, 8 CONNAUGHT PLACE, C., HONG KONG.	8424555
ASIAN OCEANIC COMMODITIES LTD. (FCM)	12/F., EAST TOWER, BOND CENTRE, 89 QUEENSWAY, HONG KONG	8467333
BARING FUTURES (HONG KONG) LIMITED (FCM)	8/F., THREE EXCHANGE SQUARE, 8 CONNAUGHT PLACE, CENTRAL, HONG KONG.	8488488
BERITA LTD. (FCM)	21/F., CIRCLE PLAZA, 497-499, HENNESSY ROAD, CAUSEWAY BAY, HONG KONG.	8342399
BONSAR LTD. (FCM)	2108-2109, ALEXANDRA HOUSE, 16-20 CHATER ROAD, C., HONG KONG.	5252373
BUMPER TRADING LIMITED (FCM)	A 9/F., LIN FOOK HOUSE, 3 JARDINE'S CRESCENT, CAUSEWAY BAY, HONG KONG	8952766
CAMPBELL FUTURES LIMITED (FCM)	ROOM 1104A, TOWER I, ADMIRALTY CENTRE, HONG KONG	8660886

CHART TOP LTD. (FCM)	C/O 19/F., FLAT C, 4 CHI FU ROAD, CHI FU FA YUEN, HONG KONG.	8342399
CHEERFUL COMMODITIES COMPANY LIMITED (FCM)	RM. 2105 WORLDWIDE HOUSE, 19 DES VOEUX ROAD, CENTRAL, HONG KONG	5236131
CHENG SEE MOK (TRADING AS YICK HING COMMODITIES CO.) (FB)	3703-5 WEST TOWER, BOND CENTRE, 89 QUEENSWAY, CENTRAL, HONG KONG.	8682287
CHINA SEA COMMODITY CO. LTD. (FCM)	27/F., TUNG WAI COMMERCIAL BLDG., 109-112 GLOUCESTER ROAD, C., HONG KONG.	8912733
CHINA TOP COMMODITIES AND FUTURES LTD. (FCM)	6/F., LIU CHONG HING BANK BLDG., 24 DES VOEUX ROAD, C., HONG KONG.	8682222
CHOW SANG SANG COMMODITIES LTD. (FCM)	1/FL., CHOW SANG SANG BLDG., 229 NATHAN ROAD, KOWLOON.	7351202
CHUNG MAO COMMODITIES & FUTURES LTD. (FB)	ROOM 201, FAR EAST CONSORTIUM BLDG., 121 DES VOEUX ROAD C., HONG KONG	5418877
CITICORP VICKERS HONG KONG FUTURES LIMITED(FCM)	42/FL., ONE EXCHANGE SQUARE, 8 CONNAUGHT PLACE, CENTRAL, HONG KONG.	8435777
CORPORATE COMMODITIES AGENCY LTD. (FCM)	5/FL., ALLIED CAPITAL RESOURCES BLDG., 32-38, ICE HOUSE STREET, CENTRAL, HONG KONG.	5262525
DAO HENG COMMODITIES LTD. (FCM)	15/F., WHEELOCK HOUSE, 20 PEDDER STREET, CENTRAL, HONG KONG.	5255091
EMPEROR FUTURES LIMITED (FCM)	7TH FLOOR, INTERNATIONAL BULD., 141 DES VOEUX ROAD, CENTRAL, HONG KONG	8544606
FAIRGAIN INVESTMENTS LIMITED	7/F., THE CHINESE BANK BLDG., 61-65 DES VOEUX ROAD, CENTRAL, HONG KONG	8448789
FOREGROUND COMMODITIES CO. LTD. (FB)	RM. 1302-1304, CHIYU BANK BLDG., 78-80 DES VOEUX ROAD, C., HONG KONG.	5252718

FRANKWELL COMMODITIES LTD. (FCM)	RM. 814-820, 8/FL., TOWER B, NEW MANDARIN PLAZA, 14 SCIENCE MUSEUM ROAD, TST EAST, KOWLOON.	7221178
FUJI HONG KONG COMMODITIES CO. LTD. (FCM)	RM. 1203-1204, SINGGA COMMERCIAL CENTRE, 144-151 CONNAUGHT ROAD, WEST, HONG KONG.	5591041
FULLYTEX INVESTMENTS LTD. (FCM)	17/FL., FAR EAST FINANCE CENTRE, 16 HARCOURT RD., C., HONG KONG.	8617777
HASE FUTURES LIMITED (FCM)	HANG SENG BANK BLDG., 2/FL., 77 DES VOEUX ROAD, CENTRAL, HONG KONG.	8255615
HENCHMAN FUTURES LTD. (FCM)	22ND FLOOR, EURO TRADE CENTRE, 13-14 CONNAUGHT ROAD, CENTRAL, HONG KONG.	5254422
HOARE GOVETT ASIA FUTURES LTD. (FCM)	30TH FLOOR, EDINBURGH TOWER, THE LANDMARK, CENTRAL, HONG KONG.	8680368
HON HING FUTURES LIMITED (FORMERLY TRIVEST TRADERS LTD.) (FCM)	23/F., WING ON HOUSE, COMMODITIES 71 DES VOEUX ROAD, CENTRAL, HONG KONG.	8456722
HONFIRST INVESTMENT LIMITED (FCM)	8/F., CHEKIANG FIRST BANK BLDG., 60 GLOUCESTER ROAD, HONG KONG.	8236400
HONOUR FUTURES LIMITED (FCM)	45/F., SUN HUNG KAI CENTRE, HARBOUR ROAD, WANCHAI, HONG KONG.	8912111
I.C.A. ENTERPRISE CO., LTD. (FCM)	UG/F., FLAT C, HOP HING IND. BLDG., 704 CASTLE PEAK RD., KOWLOON.	7852681
INFAST FUTURES LTD. (FCM)	29/F., VICWOOD PLAZA, 199 DES VOEUX ROAD, CENTRAL, HONG KONG.	8156118
JAMES CAPEL FAR EAST FUTURES LTD. (FCM)	39/F., TWO EXCHANGE SQUARE, CONNAUGHT PLACE, CENTRAL, HONG KONG.	8439111
JARDINE FLEMING FUTURES LTD. (FCM)	46/FL., JARDINE HOUSE, 1 CONNAUGHT PLACE, HONG KONG.	8438888

KEVIN FUTURES LIMITED (FCM)	ROOM 1604, FAR EAST EXCHANGE BUILDING, 8 WYNDHAM STREET, CENTRAL, HONG KONG	5259191
KING FOOK COMMODITIES CO. LTD. (FCM)	6/FL., KING FOOK BUILDING 30-32 DES VOEUX ROAD, C., HONG KONG.	5235111
KONGSON COMMODITIES LIMITED (FCM)	ROOM 401, UNITED CHINESE BANK BLDG., 31-37 DES VOEUX ROAD, CENTRAL, HONG KONG	8108382
L & D COMMODITIES LIMITED (FCM)	9/F., SING PO CENTRE, 8 QUEEN'S ROAD, CENTRAL, HONG KONG	5232399
LEE FUNG HONG GOLD, SILVER & JEWELLERY CO. LTD. (FCM)	RM. 1501, WING HANG BANK BLDG., 161 QUEEN'S ROAD, C., HONG KONG.	5421128
MERRILL LYNCH FUTURES (H.K.) LTD. (FCM)	12/FL., ST. GEORGE'S BLDG., 2 ICE HOUSE ST., C., HONG KONG.	8445678
MIN XIN COMMODITY LTD. (FCM)	18/FL., FAIRMONT HOUSE, 8 COTTON TREE DRIVE, C., HONG KONG.	5215671
MONTGOMERY COMMODITIES LTD. (FB)	2/F., TAI SANG BANK BLDG., 130-132 DES VOEUX RD., CENTRAL, HONG KONG.	5418988
MONTLAKE FUTURES LIMITED (FCM)	7TH FLOOR, INTERNATIONAL BLDG., 141 DES VOEUX ROAD, CENTRAL, HONG KONG	8544606
NEW CENTURY FINANCIAL FUTURES LTD. (FCM)	29TH FLOOR, INTERNATIONAL BLDG., 141 DES VOEUX ROAD, CENTRAL, HONG KONG.	5434988
NOMURA FUTURES (HONG KONG) LTD. (FCM)	46-48TH FLOORS, FAR EAST FINANCE CENTRE, 16 HARCOURT ROAD, HONG KONG.	5201811
O & S (COMMODITIES) LTD. (FB)	RM. 2106, WING ON HOUSE, 71 DES VOEUX ROAD, CENTRAL, HONG KONG.	5259268
OKACHI (HONG KONG) CO. LTD. (FCM)	RM. 910-912, MELBOURNE PLAZA, 33 QUEEN'S ROAD, CENTRAL, HONG KONG.	8680968
ONG COMMODITIES (H.K.) LTD. (FCM)	RM. 1916-1917, HUTCHISON HOUSE, 10 HARCOURT ROAD, HONG KONG	8016288

PAINEWEBBER INTERNATIONAL FUTURES (ASIA) LIMITED (FCM)	19/F., ST. GEORGE'S BUILDING, 2 ICE HOUSE STREET, HONG KONG	5265533
PASCAL FUTURES COMPANY LIMITED (FCM)	RM. 1204, ASIA STANDARD TOWER, 59-65 QUEEN'S ROAD, CENTRAL, H.K.	5216354
PEREGRINE FUTURES HONG KONG (FCM)	22/F., NEW WORLD TOWER, 16-18 QUEEN'S ROAD, CENTRAL, HONG KONG	8251888
REPUBLIC CLEARING (HK) LTD. (FB)	RM. 607 JARDINE HOUSE, ONE CONNAUGHT PLACE, C., HONG KONG.	5266941
RESIDENTS INTERNATIONAL LTD. (FCM)	RM. 1901A, RUTTONJEE HOUSE, 11 DUDDELL STREET, C., HONG KONG.	5258207
RING KUN CO. LTD. (FCM)	RMS. 1104-6, KINCHENG BANK BLDG., 51-57 DES VOEUX RD., C., HONG KONG.	5230738
ROCTEC FUTURES TRADING COMPANY LIMITED (FCM)	ROOM 47,NEW HENRY HOUSE, 10 ICEHOUSE STREET HONG KONG	5213630
SCHRODERS ASIA FUTURES LTD. (FCM)	25/FL., TWO EXCHANGE SQUARE, 8 CONNAUGHT PLACE, CENTRAL, HONG KONG.	5211633
SEAPOWER FUTURES LIMITED (FCM)	14/F., EURO TRADE CENTRE, 13 CONNAUGHT ROAD, CENTRAL, HONG KONG.	8474888
SEIO COMMODITIES TRADERS (HK) LTD. (FB)	56/F., BANK OF CHINA TOWER, ONE GARDEN ROAD, CENTRAL, H.K. HONG KONG.	5262141
SHACOM FUTURES LTD. (FCM)	12 QUEEN'S ROAD, CENTRAL, HONG KONG.	8415283
SOUTH CHINA COMMODITIES LTD. (FCM)	28/F., BANK OF CHINA TOWER, NO. 1 GARDEN ROAD, CENTRAL, HONG KONG	8206333
STANDARD CHARTERED FUTURES (HK) LTD (FCM)	10/F., STANDARD CHARTERED BANK BUILDING, 4-4A DES VOEUX ROAD, CENTRAL, HONG KONG	8211665
SUN HUNG KAI COMMODITIES LTD. (FCM)	3/FL., ADMIRALTY CENTER, HONG KONG.	8225678

SUN HUNG KAI INTERNATIONAL COMMODITIES LTD. (FCM)	3/FL., ADMIRALTY CENTRE, HONG KONG.	8225678
SUN WING YUEN FUTURES LIMITED (FCM)	ROOM 1205-1207, INTERNATIONAL BUILDINGS, 141 DES VOEUX ROAD, CENTRAL, HONG KONG	5413821
SUN'S INVESTMENT CO. LTD. (FCM)	ROOMS NO. 401-403, SUNNY HOUSE, 12-16 LI YUEN STREET, WEST, CENTRAL, HONG KONG	5222072
TAI YIP COMMODITIES & FUTURES LTD. (FCM)	304-307 INTERNATIONAL BLDG., 141 DES VOEUX RD., C., HONG KONG.	5421322
TAK FUNG COMMODITIES LTD. (FCM)	8/FL., WAH YUEN BLDG., 145-149 QUEEN'S ROAD, C., HONG KONG.	5439382
THE SOUTH-SEAS INVESTMENT CO. LTD. (FB)	WORLD-WIDE HOUSE, 12TH FLOOR, 19 DES VOEUX ROAD, CENTRAL, HONG KONG.	8440000
TUNG SHING FUTURES LIMITED (FCM)	3/FL., THE BANK OF EAST ASIA BLDG., 10 DES VOEUX ROAD, CENTRAL, HONG KONG	8454575
U. B. FUTURES LTD. (FCM)	5TH FLOOR, ASIA STANDARD TOWER, 59-65 QUEEN'S RD., CENTRAL, HONG KONG.	8680331
UNION SHINE COMMODITIES LTD. (FCM)	65TH FLOOR, BANK OF CHINA TOWER, NO. 1, GARDEN ROAD, CENTRAL, HONG KONG.	8773228
WARDLEY-THOMSON FUTURES H.K. LTD. (FCM)	3RD FL., HUTCHISON HOUSE, 10 HARCOURT ROAD, HONG KONG.	5211661
WOCOM LIMITED (FCM)	RM. 2701, WING ON CENTRE, 111 CONNAUGHT ROAD, CENTRAL, H.K.	8530111
YU ON COMMODITIES CO. LTD. (FCM)	11/FL., V. HEUN BLDG., 138 QUEEN'S ROAD, C., HONG KONG.	5433255
YUEN CHOW INTERNATIONAL INVESTMENT LTD. (FCM)	3703-5 WEST TOWER, BOND CENTRE, 89 QUEENSWAY, CENTRAL, HONG KONG.	8682287

ZEE KWOH KUNG (TRADING AS   RM. 2502, ADMIRALTY CENTRE,   5200111
NEW SHUN LOONG   TOWER I, 18 HARCOURT ROAD,
COMMODITIES CO.)   HONG KONG
(FT)

	NUMBER OF	FLOOR TRADER	(FT) :	1
		FLOOR BROKER	(FB) :	8
		FUTURES COMMISSION MERCHANT	(FCM) :	68
		MERCHANT TRADER	(MT) :	0
TOTAL NUMBER OF HKFE MEMBER ------------------				77

II

B. The Nagoya Stock Exchange

as of June, 1990

Regular Members (45 companies)

Securities Companies	Address
Aizawa	10-24, Higashisakura 1-chome, Higashi-ku, Nagoya 461
Ando	23-21, Nishiki 3-chome, Naka-ku, Nagoya 460
Ark	5-11, Sakae 2-chome, Naka-ku, Nagoya 460
Chiyoda	15-22, Nishiki 2-chome, Naka-ku, Nagoya 460
Cosmo	11-35, Sakae 3-chome, Naka-ku, Nagoya 460
Dai-ichi	2-1, Sakae 2-chome, Naka-ku, Nagoya 460
Daiman	8-5, Sakae 2-chome, Naka-ku, Nagoya 460
Daitoku	7-30, Sakae 3-chome, Naka-ku, Nagoya 460
Daiwa	15-30, Nishiki 3-chome, Naka-ku, Nagoya 460
Ichiyoshi	1-26, Sakae 3-chome, Naka-ku, Nagoya 460
Izumi	16-30, Nishiki 3-chome, Naka-ku, Nagoya 460
Kimura	3-17, Sakae 3-chome, Naka-ku, Nagoya 460
Kokusai	25-11, Nishiki 3-chome, Naka-ku, Nagoya 460
Kosei	28-12, Meieki 3-chome, Nakamura-ku, Nagoya 450
Kotobuki	7-2, Sakae 3-chome, Naka-ku, Nagoya 460
Kyokuto	7-23, Meieki 4-chome, Nakamura-ku, Nagoya 450
Kyosai	6-12, Sakae 2-chome, Naka-ku, Nagoya 460
Maruhachi	4-28, Sakae 3-chome, Naka-ku, Nagoya 460
Maruman	4-21, Sakae 3-chome, Naka-ku, Nagoya 460
Marusan	19-18, Nishiki 2-chome, Naka-ku, Nagoya 460
Matsuhiko	7-26, Sakae 3-chome, Naka-ku, Nagoya 460
Meiko	2-12, Sakae 2-chome, Naka-ku, Nagoya 460
Mito	26-25, Meieki 4-chome, Nakamura-ku, Nagoya 450
Naigai	8-13, Sakae 3-chome, Naka-ku, Nagoya 460
National	19-1, Nishiki 2-chome, Naka-ku, Nagoya 460
New Japan	3-1, Sakae 2-chome, Naka-ku, Nagoya 460
Nikko	2-3, Sakae 3-chome, Naka-ku, Nagoya 460
Nippon Kangyo Kakuma-ru	15-8, Sakae 3-chome, Naka-ku, Nagoya 460
Nomura	19-22, Nishiki 2-chome, Naka-ku, Nagoya 460
Okachi	7-29, Sakae 3-chome, Naka-ku, Nagoya 460
Okasan	25-22, Meieki 4-chome, Nakamura-ku, Nagoya 450
Sanyo	10-27, Meieki 4-chome, Nakamura-ku, Nagoya 450

List of Members (continued)

Securities Companies	Address
Tachibana	25-3, Meieki 3-chome, Nakamura-ku, Nagoya 450
Taiheiyo	4-1, Sakae 2-chome, Naka-ku, Nagoya 460
Takagi	21-7, Meieki 3-chome, Nakamura-ku, Nagoya 450
Tokai	20-20, Nishiki 2-chome, Naka-ku, Nagoya 460
Tokyo	22-13, Nishiki 3-chome, Naka-ku, Nagoya 460
Towa	13-26, Nishiki 1-chome, Naka-ku, Nagoya 460
Toyo	1-1, Sakae 4-chome, Naka-ku, Nagoya 460
Universal	15-15, Nishiki 2-chome, Naka-ku, Nagoya 460
Wako	6-35, Nishiki 3-chome, Naka-ku, Nagoya 460
World	14-21, Nishiki 2-chome, Naka-ku, Nagoya 460
Yamaichi	22-20, Nishiki 3-chome, Naka-ku, Nagoya 460
Yamatane	4-22, Sakae 3-chome, Naka-ku, Nagoya 460
Yutaka	7-1, Sakae 3-chome, Naka-ku, Nagoya 460

Special Participants (20 companies)

Securites company	Address
Ace	6-11, Honmachi 2-chome, Chuo-ku, Osaka 541
Baring	3-2, Kasumigaseki 3-chome, Chiyoda-ku, Tokyo 100
Chuo	7-8, Nihonbashi-Kabuto-cho, Chuo-ku, Tokyo 103
Daika	1-7, Imabashi 3-chome, Chuo-ku, Osaka 541
Daito	4-3, Nihonbashi-Kabuto-cho, Chuo-ku, Tokyo 103
Goldman Sachs	12-32, Akasaka 1-chome, Minato-ku, Tokyo 107
Hinode	3-9, Koraibashi 2-chome, Chuo-ku, Osaka 541
Hiraoka	6-19, Imabashi 1-chome, Chuo-ku, Osaka 541
Kaisei	13-2, Nihonbashi-Kabuto-cho, Chuo-ku, Tokyo 103
Kaneyama	11-8, Nihonbashi-Koami-cho, Chuo-ku, Tokyo 103
Kyoritsu	7-3, Nihonbashi 2-chome, Chuo-ku, Tokyo 103
Misawaya	5-4, Nihonbashi-Hakozaki-cho, Chuo-ku, Tokyo 103
Morgan Stanley	1-3, Otemachi 1-chome, Chiyoda-ku, Tokyo 100
Nakai	1-21, Kitahama 1-chome, Chuo-ku, Osaka 541
Nichiei	10-7, Nihonbashi-Koami-cho, Chuo-ku, Tokyo 103
Nippon	4-2, Koraibashi 1-chome, Chuo-ku, Osaka 541
Salomon Brothers	12-32, Akasaka 1-chome, Minato-ku, Tokyo 107
Shinyei Ishinop	27, Naniwa-cho, Chuo-ku, Kobe 650
UBS Phillips & Drew	1-7, Uchisaiwai-cho 1-chome, Chiyoda-ku, Tokyo 100
Yamaka	13-10, Nihonbashi 2-chome, Chuo-ku, Tokyo 103

C. The New Zealand Futures and Options Exchange

As of 31 March 1991

TRADING MEMBERS

ANZ BANKING GROUP NEW ZEALAND LTD
New Zealand Treasury
PO Box 1492, 215-229 Lambton Quay, WELLINGTON
Fax: 04 496 8639
Phone: 04 731 960

BAIN REFCO COMMODITIES LIMITED
PO Box 1797, Level 8, Barclays House,
36 Customhouse Quay, WELLINGTON
Fax: 04 712 638
Phone: 04 731 920

BANK OF NEW ZEALAND
PO Box 2392, Financial Markets
Level 21, BNZ Centre, 1 Willis Street, WELLINGTON
Fax: 04 746 446
Phone: 04 746 999

BARCLAYS BANK PLC
PO Box 574, 11th Floor, Treasury Department
Barclays House, 36 Custom House Quay, WELLINGTON
Fax: 04 730 457
Phone: 04 726 926

BT FUTURES NEW ZEALAND LIMITED
PO Box 6900, Wellesley Street
9th Floor, Stock Exchange Centre
191 Queen Street, AUCKLAND
Fax: 09 303 1851
Phone: 09 309 3226

BUTTLE WILSON FUTURES LIMITED
PO Box 45, Level 23, Stock Exchange Centre
191 Queen Street, AUCKLAND
Fax: 09 307 4888
Phone: 09 307 4800 / 307 4910

CITIFUTURES NEW ZEALAND LIMITED
PO Box 3429, Citibank Centre,
23 Custom Street East, AUCKLAND Fax 09 302 1688
Phone: 09 302 3128

CS FIRST BOSTON NEW ZEALAND FUTURES LIMITED
PO Box 3394, 9th Floor, Caltex House
282-292 Lambton Quay, WELLINGTON
Fax: 04 712 331
Phone: 04 744 400

EGDEN WIGNALL & COMPANY FUTURES LIMITED
PO Box 2335, Exchange House
112 Hereford Street, CHRISTCHURCH
Fax: 03 791 196
Phone: 03 792 600

**EGDEN WIGNALL & COMPANY FUTURES LIMITED - AUCKLAND OF-
FICE**
C/-Stock Exchange Centre, Ground Floor
191 Queen Street, AUCKLAND
Fax: 09 308 9661
Phone: 09 308 9680

ELDERBANK LIMITED
PO Box 882, Level Two, Windsor Court
136 Parnell Road, AUCKLAND
Fax: 09 307 2747
Phone: 09 307 3920

FAY RICHWHITE FUTURES LIMITED
PO Box 10085, Level 12, 89 The Terrace, WELLINGTON
Fax: 04 498 7099 / 04 498 7045
Phone: 04 498 7000

NZI BANK LIMITED
Private Bag, 7th Floor, NZI Bank House
115 Queen Street, AUCKLAND
Fax: 09 307 6699
Phone: 09 796 099

ORD WESTPAC FUTURES -NZ- LIMITED
PO Box 744, Level 15, Stock Exchange Centre
191 Queen Street, AUCKLAND
Fax: 09 792 119
Phone: 09 309 3553

TRUST BANK NEW ZEALAND LIMITED
PO Box 2260, Levels 14 & 15, Trust Bank Centre
125 The Terrace, WELLINGTON
Fax: 04 711 981
Phone: 04 732 807

THE NATIONAL BANK OF NEW ZEALAND LIMITED
PO Box 1791, 170-186 Featherston Street
WELLINGTON
Fax: 04 732 422
Phone: 04 729 459

THE NATIONAL BANK OF NEW ZEALAND DEALING ROOM
PO Box 540, 10th Floor, Southpac House
1 Victoria Street, WELLINGTON
Fax: 04 734 928
Phone: 04 735 787

WESTPAC BANKING CORPORATION
PO Box 691, 4th Floor, Westpac House
318-324 Lambton Quay, WELLINGTON
Fax: 04 737 879
Phone: 04 498 1275

AFFILIATE MEMBERS

ASB BANK LIMITED
PO Box 35, ASB Building
Cnr Queen & Wellesley Streets, AUCKLAND
Fax: 09 307 8010
Phone: 09 309 2072

AUSTRALIAN MUTUAL PROVIDENT SOCIETY
PO Box 1290, 95 Customhouse Quay, WELLINGTON
Fax: 04 498 8821
Phone: 04 781 705

BANQUE INDOSUEZ NEW ZEALAND LIMITED
PO Box 10112, Indosuez House, 169 The Terrace, WELLINGTON
Fax: 04 726 096
Phone: 04 724 131

BNZ FINANCE LIMITED
PO Box 401, Norwich Insurance House
Hunter Street, WELLINGTON
Fax: 728 970
Phone: 04 724 306

ELECTRICITY CORPORATION OF NEW ZEALAND LIMITED
Rutherford House, 23 Lambton Quay
PO Box 930, WELLINGTON
Fax: 04 733 189
Phone: 04 742 322

NATIONAL AUSTRALIA BANK NZ LIMITED
Private Bag, 9th Floor BNZ Tower
125 Queen Street, AUCKLAND
Fax: 09 307 0758
Phone: 09 307 0740 / 771 489

NATIONAL PROVIDENT FUND
PO Box 606, 95 Customhouse Quay, WELLINGTON
Fax: 04 498 7239
Phone: 04 732 752

NEW ZEALAND DAIRY BOARD
PO Box 417, Level 3 Petrocorp House
Lambton Quay, WELLINGTON
Fax: 04 729 087
Phone: 04 718 300

THE RURAL BANK LIMITED
PO Box 5046, 11th Floor, Rural Bank House
34-42 Manners Street, WELLINGTON
Fax: 04 828 190
Phone: 04 828 188

STATE BANK OF SOUTH AUSTRALIA
PO Box 5021, Wellesley Street
Level 17, BNZ Tower, 125 Queen Street, AUCKLAND
Fax: 09 309 1801
Phone: 09 309 1420

THE HONGKONG AND SHANGHAI BANKING CORPORATION
PO Box 5947, Wellesley Street
4th Floor, Prudential Building
Cnr Queen & Wellesley Street, AUCKLAND
Fax: 09 309 6681
Phone: 09 309 3800

INTRODUCING BROKER MEMBERS

A W GILLION
43 Roseneath Terrace
Roseneath WELLINGTON
Fax: 04 733 695
Phone: Bus 04 720 358 ex 787

HANSEATIC NZ LIMITED
PO Box 3256, Auckland
Level 3, 82 Symonds Street, Auckland
Fax: 09 309 9670 Phone 09 307 6625

D. The Osaka Securities Exchange

Members (94 companies)   **As of April 1, 1990**

Securities Companies	Address
Ace	6-11, Honmachi 2-chome, Chuo-ku, Osaka 541
Aizawa	1-7, Honmachi 4-chome, Chuo-ku, Osaka 541
Akane	1-3, Bingomachi 4-chome, Chuo-ku, Osaka 541
Ando	2-17, Imabashi 2-chome, Chuo-ku, Osaka 541
Ark	1-7, Imabashi 2-chome, Chuo-ku, Osaka 541
Century	6-10, Koraibashi 2-chome, Chuo-ku, Osaka 541
Chiyoda	5-11, Minami-semba 3-chome, Chuo-ku, Osaka 542
Chuo	3-10, Hiranomachi 3-chome, Chuo-ku, Osaka 541
Cosmo	8-12, Imabashi 1-chome, Chuo-ku, Osaka 541
Daichu	6-4, Koraibashi 2-chome, Chuo-ku, Osaka 541
Daiichi	2-5, Koraibashi 2-chome, Chuo-ku, Osaka 541
Daika	1-7, Imabashi 3-chome, Chuo-ku, Osaka 541
Dainana	2-3, Kitahama 4-chome, Chuo-ku, Osaka 541
Daito	2-8, Honmachi 3-chome, Chuo-ku, Osaka 541
Daiwa	13-20, Sonezaki-shinchi 1-chome, Kita-ku, Osaka 530
Dojima	14-10, Nishitenma 5-chome, Kita-ku, Osaka 530
Eiwa	7-22, Imabashi 1-chome, Chuo-ku, Osaka 541
Fukuyama*	9-4, Hacchobori 4-chome, Chuo-ku, Tokyo 103
Hikari	4-2, Kano-cho 3-chome, Chuo-ku, Kobe 650
Hinode	3-9, Koraibashi 2-chome, Chuo-ku, Osaka 541
Hiraoka	6-19, Imabashi 1-chome, Chuo-ku, Osaka 541
Hirota	1-24, Kitahama 1-chome, Chuo-ku, Osaka 541
Ichiyoshi	1-3, Koraibashi 3-chome, Chuo-ku, Osaka 541
Imagawa	3-6, Kitahama 2-chome, Chuo-ku, Osaka 541
Ishizuka	1-14, Kitahama 2-chome, Chuo-ku, Osaka 541
Issei	1-6, Honmachi 3-chome, Chuo-ku, Osaka 541
Iwai	5-5, Kitahama 1-chome, Chuo-ku, Osaka 541
Izumi	2-22, Kitahama 2-chome, Chuo-ku, Osaka 541
Jyujiya*	6-17, Nihombashi Kayaba-cho 1-chome, Chuo-ku, Tokyo 103
Kaisei	4-19, Minamimorimachi 1-chome, Kita-ku, Osaka 530
Kaneju*	7-15, Nihombashi Kabuto-cho, Chuo-ku, Tokyo 103
Kaneyama*	11-8, Nihombashi Koami-cho, Chuo-ku, Tokyo 103
Kaneyoshi	1-26, Kitahama 2-chome, Chuo-ku, Osaka 541

Members (continued)

Securities Companies	Address
Kimura*	3-17, Sakae 3-chome, Naka-ku, Nagoya 460
Kokusai	8-15, Azuchimachi 1-chome, Chuo-ku, Osaka 541
Kosei	4-33, Kitahama Higashi, Chuo-ku, Osaka 540
Kurokawa Kitoku	6-10, Koraibashi 1-chome, Chuo-ku, Osaka 541
Kyokuto	5-7, Honmachi 3-chome, Chuo-ku, Osaka 541
Kyoritsu*	7-3, Nihombashi 2-chome, Chuo-ku, Tokyo 103
Kyosei*	2-6, Yaesu 1-chome, Chuo-ku, Tokyo 103
Maruhachi*	4-28, Sakae 3-chome, Naka-ku, Nagoya 460
Maruki	16-3, Nishitenma 5-chome, Kita-ku, Osaka 530
Marukuni*	10-2, Nihombashi Koami-cho, Chuo-ku, Tokyo 103
Maruman	1-1, Minami-honmachi 2-chome, Chuo-ku, Osaka 541
Marusan	7-15, Minami-honmachi 1-chome, Chuo-ku, Osaka 541
Maruso*	9-14, Nihombashi Kabuto-cho, Chuo-ku, Tokyo 103
Meiko	7-18, Imabashi 1-chome, Chuo-ku, Osaka 541
Misawaya*	5-4, Nihombashi Hakozaki-cho, Chuo-ku, Tokyo 103
Mito	2-7, Honmachi 2-chome, Chuo-ku, Osaka 541
Morgan Stanley*	1-3, Ohte-machi 1-chome, Chiyoda-ku, Tokyo 100
Naigai	7-3, Nihombashi Kabuto-cho, Chuo-ku, Tokyo 103
Naito	5-9, Koraibashi 1-chome, Chuo-ku, Osaka 541
Nakahara*	1-10, Nihombashi Kabuto-cho, Chuo-ku, Tokyo 103
Nakai	1-21, Kitahama 1-chome, Chuo-ku, Osaka 541
Nakano	7-14, Imabashi 1-chome, Chuo-ku, Osaka 541
National	5-9, Koraibashi 1-chome, Chuo-ku, Osaka 541
New Japan	1-1, Minami-honmachi 4-chome, Chuo-ku, Osaka 541
Nichiei	12-12, Minami-semba 4-chome, Chuo-ku, Osaka 542
Nihon Kangyo Kakumaru	6-10, Kawaramachi 1-chome, Chuo-ku, Osaka 541
Nihon Kyoei	3-10, Kitahama 2-chome, Chuo-ku, Osaka 541
Nikko	11-8, Sonezaki 2-chome, Kita-ku, Osaka 530
Nippon	4-2, Koraibashi 1-chome, Chuo-ku, Osaka 541
Nissan*	7-6, Nihombashi Kabuto-cho, Chuo-ku, Tokyo 103
Nomura	5-4, Kitahama 2-chome, Chuo-ku, Osaka 541
Ogawa	9-15, Kitahama 1-chome, Chuo-ku, Osaka 541
Okachi*	7-29, Sakae 3-chome, Naka-ku, Nagoya 460
Okasan	8-7, Imabashi 1-chome, Chuo-ku, Osaka 541
Otsuka	3-7, Kitahama 2-chome, Chuo-ku, Osaka 541
Ryoko	2-15, Bakurocho 4-chome, Chuo-ku, Osaka 541
Salomon Brothers Asia*	12-32, Akasaka 1-chome, Minato-ku, Tokyo 107
San-ei*	12-7, Kyobashi 3-chome, Chuo-ku, Tokyo 103
Sankyo	7-10, Bingomachi 1-chome, Chuo-ku, Osaka 541
Sanyo	6-9, Kitahama 1-chome, Chuo-ku, Osaka 541
Shinyei Ishino	1-3, Kitahama 2-chome, Chuo-ku, Osaka 541
Tachibana	16-19, Sonezaki 2-chome, Kita-ku, Osaka 530
Taiheiyo	6-6, Doshomachi 2-chome, Chuo-ku, Osaka 541
Takagi	1-30, Kitahama 1-chome, Chuo-ku, Osaka 541
Tokai*	20-20, Nishiki 2-chome, Naka-ku, Nagoya 460

Members (continued)

Securities Companies	Address
Tokyo	1-2, Hiranomachi 2-chome, Chuo-ku, Osaka 541
Towa	2-2, Imabashi 2-chome, Chuo-ku, Osaka 541
Toyo	6-17, Kitahama 2-chome, Chuo-ku, Osaka 541
Tsukamoto	8-14, Imabashi 1-chome, Chuo-ku, Osaka 541
Tsuyama	5-5, Kitahama 1-chome, Chuo-ku, Osaka 541
Universal	4-10, Imabashi 2-chome, Chuo-ku, Osaka 541
Utsumiya	2-7, Kawaramachi 2-chome, Chuo-ku, Osaka 541
Wako	6-22, Kitahama 2-chome, Chuo-ku, Osaka 541
World	16-20, Minami-semba 1-chome, Chuo-ku, Osaka 541
Yamagen	6-9, Koraibashi 2-chome, Chuo-ku, Osaka 541
Yamaichi	2-7, Koraibashi 3-chome, Chuo-ku, Osaka 541
Yamaka*	13-10, Nihombashi 2-chome, Chuo-ku, Tokyo 103
Yamamaru*	11, Nihombashi Kabuto-cho 3-chome, Chuo-ku, Tokyo 103
Yamatane	4-4, Koraibashi 2-chome, Chuo-ku, Osaka 541
Yamawa*	1-3, Nihombashi Kabuto-cho, Chuo-ku, Tokyo 103
Yutaka	2-12, Kitahama 3-chome, Chuo-ku, Osaka 541

*Out-of-Town Members

*Out-of-Town Members

Special Participants (8 companies)

Securities Companies	Address
Baring	3-2, Kasumigaseki 3-chome, Chiyoda-ku, Tokyo 100
BT Asia	2-1, Marunouchi 2-chome, Chiyoda-ku, Tokyo 100
CRT	4-1, Kanda 1-chome, Chiyoda-ku, Tokyo 101
Goldman Sachs	12-32, Akasaka 1-chome, Minato-ku, Tokyo 107
Merrill Lynch	2-14, Kawaramachi 4-chome, Chuo-ku, Osaka 541
Shearson Lehman Hutton	12-32, Akasaka 1-chome, Minato-ku, Tokyo 107
Smith Barney	5-2, Marunouchi 2-chome, Chiyoda-ku, Tokyo 100
Société Générale	5-5, Shiba-Daimon 2-chome, Minato-ku, Tokyo 105

E. The Singapore International Monetary Exchange

SIMEX CLEARING MEMBERS AS OF
10 JANUARY 1991

ABC FUTURES & BULLION PTE LTD
50 RAFFLES PLACE
#14-00 SHELL TOWER
SINGAPORE 0104
TEL: 224 2977   TLX: RS 28989 ABCSNG
FAX: 225 0440

ACB BULLION & FUTURES PTE LTD
60 ROBINSON ROAD
#08-00
SINGAPORE 0106
TEL: 222 8222   TLX: RS 21911/ 23116 ASI
FAX: 225 3493

BA FUTURES, INCORPORATED
78 SHENTON WAY
#19-00
SINGAPORE 0207
TEL: 320 3389   TLX: RS 29159 BAFSIN
FAX: 320 3390

BABCOCK FULTON PREBON FUTURES (SINGAPORE) LTD
50 ROBINSON ROAD
#15-00 MNB BUILDING
SINGAPORE 0106
TEL: 223 0777   TLX: RS 22939/20107 FULS
FAX: 224 9186/ 225 8249

BT FUTURES (SINGAPORE) LTD
50 RAFFLES PLACE
#26-01/06 SHELL TOWER
SINGAPORE 0104
TEL: 222 2988/ 535 3539   TLX: RS 28626 BANKERS
FAX: 225 5552/535 2272

CHASE MANHATTAN FUTURES CORPORATION
50 RAFFLES PLACE
#08-00 SHELL TOWER
SINGAPORE 0104
TEL: 530 4478   TLX: RS 26051 CMFCSP
FAX: 530 4477

CHEMICAL FUTURES INC
C/O CHEMICAL BANK
150 BEACH ROAD
#23-00 GATEWAY WEST
SINGAPORE 0718
TEL: 291 1298   TLX: RS 23022 CHEMBNK
FAX: 290 1756

CITICORP FUTURES LIMITED
5 SHENTON WAY
#26-02 UIC BUILDING
SINGAPORE 0106
TEL: 225 9422   TLX: RS 29260 CITICF
FAX: 225 8924

CM & M FUTURES (SINGAPORE) PTE LTD
20 COLLYER QUAY
#11-03 TUNG CENTRE
SINGAPORE 0104
TEL: 225 7322   TLX: RS 55102 CMMSIN
FAX: 225 7079/ 220 117

CONTINENTAL FIRST OPTIONS, INC
10 COLLYER QUAY
#20-08 OCEAN BUILDING
SINGAPORE 0104
TEL: 535 6466   TLX: RS 22030 CONSING
FAX: 533 8329

CREDIT LYONNAIS ROUSE (PTE) LTD
50 RAFFLES PLACE
#13-03 SHELL TOWER
SINGAPORE 0104
TEL: 221 3380　　　　　TLX: RS 22368 ROUSE　　　FAX: 226 1538

DAIWA FUTURES PTE LTD
6 SHENTON WAY
#39-01/02 DBS BUILDING
SINGAPORE 0106
TEL: 220 3666　　　　　TLX: RS 21126 DAIWA　　　FAX: 225 3797

DBS TRADING PTE LTD
6 SHENTON WAY, DBS BUILDING
2ND STOREY TOWER BLOCK
SINGAPORE 0106
TEL: 223 3064/223 3067　　TLX: RS 24850 DBSDEAL　　FAX: 225 7464

DISCOUNT CORPORATION OF NEW YORK FUTURES PTE LTD
20 COLLYER QUAY
#07-03 TUNG CENTRE
SINGAPORE 0104
TEL: 226 3900/ 226 3911　　TLX: RS 23251 DCNYS
FAX: 226 2922/ 225 1767

FUJI FUTURES (SINGAPORE) PTE LTD, THE
1 RAFFLES PLACE
#20-00 OUB CENTRE
SINGAPORE 0104
TEL: 534 3500　　　　　TLX: RS 24670 FUJISP　　　FAX: 532 7310

GOLDMAN SACHS (SINGAPORE) PTE LTD
50 RAFFLES PLACE
#29-01 SHELL TOWER
SINGAPORE 0104
TEL: 222 0177　　　　　TLX: RS 25510 GOLSIN　　　FAX: 222 4994

INDOSUEZ CARR FUTURES PTE LTD
3 SHENTON WAY
#22-04 SHENTON HOUSE
SINGAPORE 0106
TEL: 221 5377　　　　　TLX: RS 43280 CARRS　　　FAX: 224 4946

J P MORGAN FUTURES INC
6 SHENTON WAY
#30-01 DBS BUILDING
SINGAPORE 0106
TEL: 225 1011   TLX: RS 22770 MFCSIN
FAX: 225 9138

MERRILL LYNCH FUTURES (S) PTE LTD
50 RAFFLES PLACE
#27-01 SHELL TOWER
SINGAPORE 0104
TEL: 221 0555   TLX: RS 21800
FAX: 225 3895

NIKKO FUTURES (SINGAPORE) PTE LTD, THE
6 BATTERY ROAD #28-01 STANDARD CHARTERED BANK BLDG
SINGAPORE 0104
TEL: 223 3390   TLX: RS 35089 NIKOMB
FAX: 225 2854

NOMURA FUTURES (SINGAPORE) PTE LTD
6 BATTERY ROAD
#39-01 STANDARD CHARTERED BANK BLDG
SINGAPORE 0104
TEL: 220 8766   TLX: RS 21198 SINGNOM
FAX: 224 0966

OCBC BULLION & FUTURES LIMITED
65 CHULIA STREET
#11-00 OCBC CENTRE
SINGAPORE 0104
TEL: 535 7222   TLX: RS 24444 OCBCBU
FAX: 532 6007 ONG

FIRST CHICAGO FUTURES PTE LTD
76 SHENTON WAY
#10-00 ONG BUILDING
SINGAPORE 0207
TEL: 221 7455   TLX: RS 24279 AURIC
FAX: 223 9890

OUB BULLION & FUTURES LTD
1 RAFFLES PLACE
#15-00 OUB CENTRE
SINGAPORE 0104
TEL: 530 2350   TLX: RS 22373 OUBANK   FAX: 533 2360

PHILLIP COMMODITIES (PTE) LTD
95 SOUTH BRIDGE ROAD
#11-17 PIDEMCO CENTRE
SINGAPORE 0105
TEL: 535 1155   TLX: RS 20188 PILSEC
FAX: 533 0593

PRUDENTIAL-BACHE SECURITIES ASIA PACIFIC LTD
5 SHENTON WAY
26TH FLOOR UIC BUILDING
SINGAPORE 0106
TEL: 224 6122   TLX: RS 22107 BACHECO
FAX: 224 5640

RCC FUTURES (SINGAPORE) LTD
143 CECIL STREET
#01-00 GB BUILDING
SINGAPORE 0106
TEL: 224 0077   TLX: RS 20237 RNBSIN
FAX: 225 5769

REFCO (SINGAPORE) PTE LTD
8 SHENTON WAY
#11-02 TREASURY BUILDING
SINGAPORE 0106
TEL: 225 3628   TLX: RS 40183/ 40184 REF
FAX: 225 7373

ROTHSCHILD BULLION & FINANCIAL FUTURES PTE LTD
9 BATTERY ROAD
#01-02 STRAITS TRADING BUILDING
SINGAPORE 0104
TEL: 535 8311   TLX: RS 36269 NMRS
FAX: 534 2407

SASSOON FINANCIAL FUTURES PTE LTD
1 RAFFLES PLACE
#43-01 OUB CENTRE
SINGAPORE 0104
TEL: 534 1966   TLX: RS 23475 SFFDLR
FAX: 533 4889

SECURITY PACIFIC ASIA FUTURES INC
2 D'ALMEIDA STREET
#06-01 BHARAT BUILDING
SINGAPORE 0104
TEL: 535 6311   TLX: RS 42716/ 50446 SPA
FAX: 533 3035/ 533 3027

SHEARSON LEHMAN BROTHERS PTE LTD
4 SHENTON WAY
#12-01/08 SHING KWAN HOUSE
SINGAPORE 0106
TEL: 222 8366   TLX: RS 20212 SAES
FAX: 224 9779

STANDARD CHARTERED FUTURES (S) PTE LTD
6 BATTERY ROAD
#09-03/04 STANDARD CHARTERED BANK BLDG
SINGAPORE 0104
TEL: 227 7113   TLX: RS 43042 SCFSIN
FAX: 222 0368/ 225 9136

SUN HUNG KAI BULLION & FUTURES PTE LTD
20 COLLYER QUAY
#18-01 TUNG CENTRE
SINGAPORE 0104
TEL: 224 1688   TLX: RS 20327 SHKSEC
FAX: 222 8330

TLB BULLION & FUTURES PTE LTD
63 MARKET STREET
#09-06/10 TAT LEE BANK BLDG
SINGAPORE 0104 T
EL: 535 6811   TLX: RS 20647 TLGOLD   FAX: 533 1043

UOB BULLION & FUTURES LIMITED
1 BONHAM STREET
UOB BUILDING
SINGAPORE 0104
TEL: 533 9898   TLX: RS 21539 TYEHUA   FAX: 534 3028

WARDLEY-THOMSON FUTURES SINGAPORE PTE LTD
21 COLLYER QUAY
#20-02 HONGKONG BANK BUILDING
SINGAPORE 0104
TEL: 225 4007   TLX: RS 22129 WTFSIN   FAX: 224 9201

WINALL INVESTMENTS PTE LTD
200 CANTONMENT ROAD
#15-00 SOUTHPOINT
SINGAPORE 0208
TEL: 225 0411   TLX: RS 36874 KIBPL
FAX: 224 3040

YAMAICHI FUTURES PTE LTD
138 ROBINSON ROAD
#20-01/21-01 HONG LEONG CENTRE
SINGAPORE 0106
TEL: 225 0688   TLX: RS 22571 YAMASP
FAX: 225 0075

SIMEX CORPORATE NON-CLEARING MEMBERS AS OF 10 JANUARY 1991

BARING FUTURES (SINGAPORE) PTE LTD
10 COLLYER QUAY
#16-01 OCEAN BUILDING
SINGAPORE 0104
TEL: 535 3688   TLX: RS 26881/ 26882 BAR
FAX: 532 5592

BOT FUTURES (SINGAPORE) PTE LTD
16 RAFFLES QUAY
#01-06 HONG LEONG BUILDING
SINGAPORE 0104
TEL: 223 3987   TLX: RS 23593 BTFXSPR
FAX: 224 8538

CIC UNION EUROPEENNE, INTERNATIONAL ET CIE
36 ROBINSON ROAD
#11-01 CITY HOUSE
SINGAPORE 0106
TEL: 225 0333   TLX: RS 29070 CICSGP
FAX: 224 4939

CRT ASIA, INC
c/o CHICAGO RESEARCH & TRADING GROUP
440 SOUTH LASALLE STREET,
SUITE 330, IL 60605, CHICAGO
SINGAPORE USA
TEL: (312) 922 4200   TLX: 433 0469 CRT CGO
FAX: (312) 431 3089

CZARNIKOW FUTURES PTE LTD
6 BATTERY ROAD,
#16-01 STANDARD CHARTERED BANK BLDG
SINGAPORE 0104
TEL: 225 3939   TLX: RS 21329/ 21021 CZA
FAX: 224 5493

DAIWA BK FINANCIAL FUTURES SINGAPORE PTE LTD
8 SHENTON WAY
#30-01 TREASURY BUILDING
SINGAPORE 0106
TEL: 220 1791   TLX: RS 22123 DAIWABK
FAX: 224 6840

DIAMOND FUTURES (SINGAPORE) PTE LTD
20 COLLYER QUAY
#01-02 TUNG CENTRE
SINGAPORE 0104
TEL: 220 5666   TLX: RS 21913/ 219914 BI
FAX: 225 4739

DKB FUTURES (SINGAPORE) PTE LTD
1 RAFFLES PLACE
#47-00 OUB CENTRE
SINGAPORE 0104
TEL: 533 2626   TLX: RS 21622 DKBSP
FAX: 533 2190

DMT FUTURES (ASIA) PTE LTD
101 CECIL STREET
#22-11 TONG ENG BUILDING
SINGAPORE 0106
TEL: 223 9066   TLX: RS 34138 DMTINT   FAX: 224 9974

FCT SINGAPORE (PTE) LTD
c/o 50 RAFFLES PLACE
#13-03 SHELL TOWER
SINGAPORE 0104
TEL: 221 3380   TLX: RS 22368 ROUSE   FAX: 226 1538

FIMAT FUTURES ASIA PTE LTD
105 CECIL STREET
THE OCTAGON #12-01
SINGAPORE 0106
TEL: 227 8214   TLX: 24558 FIMSIN   FAX: 225 4562

GOLDEN HOPE COMMODITIES PTE LTD
49 BEACH ROAD
#03-03 HEXAGON HOUSE SINGAPORE 0718
TEL: 339 5344   TLX: RS 34510 KOGINPO
FAX: 339 3315

IBJ FUTURES PTE LTD
6 SHENTON WAY
#14-01 DBS BUILDING
SINGAPORE 0106
TEL: 220 0133   TLX: RS 21880 KOGINPO
FAX: 224 1777

J BALLAS FUTURES PTE LTD
9 BATTERY ROAD
#19-06 STRAITS TRADING BLDG
SINGAPORE 0104
TEL: 535 3677/ 532 4633   TLX: 21718 JBFPL
FAX: 534 1313

KYOWA FINANCIAL FUTURES (SINGAPORE) PTE LTD
24 RAFFLES PLACE
#12-01/06 CLIFFORD CENTRE
SINGAPORE 0104
TEL: 535 4822   TLX: RS 22059 KYOWASP
FAX: 533 1462

LTCB FUTURES (SINGAPORE) PTE LTD
65 CHULIA STREET
#32-00 OCBC CENTRE
SINGAPORE 0104
TEL: 534 1977   TLX: RS 23813 LTCBSIN
FAX: 532 6048

MACRON FUTURES PTE LTD
70 ANSON ROAD
#23-00 APEX TOWER
SINGAPORE 0207
TEL: 221 2777   TLX: RS 55010 MACRON
FAX: 221 2219

MITSUI TAIYO KOBE FINANCIAL FUTURES (SINGAPORE) PTE LTD
16 RAFFLES QUAY
#01-04 HONG LEONG BUILDING
SINGAPORE 0104
TEL: 321 7250/ 220 9761   TLX: RS 21319 MITKBK
FAX: 225 0962

MITSUI TRUST FUTURES (SINGAPORE) PTE LTD
6 SHENTON WAY
#35-01 DBS BUILDING
SINGAPORE 0106
TEL: 224 9988/ 224 9989   TLX: RS 20653 MTBSPR
FAX: 225 0605

MOCATTA & GOLDSMID LIMITED
6 BATTERY ROAD
#14-08 STANDARD CHARTERED BANK BLDG
SINGAPORE 0104
TEL: 226 2603   TLX: RS 21530 MOCATS
FAX: 226 3756

MORGAN GRENFELL ASIA FUTURES PTE LTD
36 ROBINSON ROAD
#13-01 CITY HOUSE
SINGAPORE 0106
TEL: 225 8080   TLX: RS 23147 MGASIA
FAX: 222 5993

OKACHI FUTURES PTE LTD
138 CECIL STREET
#08-01/02 CECIL COURT
SINGAPORE 0106
TEL: 225 5744/ 225 5319   TLX: RS 29333 OKACHI
FAX: 224 4662

PANIN FUTURES PTE LTD
108 MIDDLE ROAD
#09-01 BRIGHT CHAMBERS
SINGAPORE 0718
TEL: 336 8933   TLX: RS 34750 PANINS
FAX: 338 0880 10

PEREGRINE FUTURES SINGAPORE PTE LTD
COLLYER QUAY OCEAN BUILDING #12-02
SINGAPORE 0104
TEL: 535 2818   TLX: RS RS 23415
FAX: 533 9698

PHIBRO ENERGY FUTURES PTE LTD
101 THOMSON ROAD
#16-03 UNITED SQUARE
SINGAPORE 1130
TEL: 250 6088   TLX: RS 24374 PHIBRO
FAX: 250 6124

SAITAMA FINANCIAL FUTURES (SINGAPORE) PTE LTD
1 RAFFLES PLACE
#14-00 OUB CENTRE
SINGAPORE 0104
TEL: 533 3334   TLX: RS 20359/20371 SAIG
FAX: 533 3244

SANWA FUTURES (SINGAPORE) PTE LTD
50 RAFFLES PLACE
#25-00 SHELL TOWER
SINGAPORE 0104
TEL: 224 9822   TLX: RS 28573 SNWSGP
FAX: 225 1444

SBCI FUTURES INC
c/o SWISS BANK CORPORATION
6 BATTERY ROAD
#35-01 STANDARD CHARTERED BANK BLDG
SINGAPORE 0104
TEL: 224 2200   TLX: RS 24140 SINSUIS
FAX: 539 7415

SIMBL INVESTMENTS PTE LTD
65 CHULIA STREET
#47-01 OCBC CENTRE
SINGAPORE 0104
TEL: 535 3411   TLX: RS 28146
FAX: 534 3917

SIN HUAT BULLION (S) PTE LTD
141 CECIL STREET
#07-01/04 TUNG ANN ASSOCIATION BUILDING
SINGAPORE 0106
TEL: 223 8118/ 223 3178   TLX: RS 25133 SHGOLD
FAX: 223 5675

SING BULLION & FUTURES PTE LTD
96 ROBINSON ROAD
#02-00 SIF BUILDING SINGAPORE 0106
TEL: 221 9998/ 225 9798   TLX: RS 20083 SING
FAX: 225 3267

SMITH BARNEY, HARRIS UPHAM (SINGAPORE) PTE LTD
150 BEACH ROAD
#19-05/08 GATEWAY WEST
SINGAPORE 0718
TEL: 296 6288   TLX: RS 23615 SBSING
FAX: 291 9620

STB FINANCIAL FUTURES (SINGAPORE) PTE LTD
5 SHENTON WAY
#35-00 UIC BUILDING
SINGAPORE 0106
TEL: 224 9055   TLX: RS 20717 SMTRST
FAX: 224 2873

SUMITOMO FINANCIAL FUTURES (S) PTE LTD
6 SHENTON WAY
#17-01 DBS BUILDING
SINGAPORE 0106
TEL: 220 0610   TLX: RS 20830 SUMTSX
FAX: 225 9647

TAKUGIN FINANCIAL FUTURES (SINGAPORE) PTE LTD
65 CHULIA STREET
#48-01 OCBC CENTRE
SINGAPORE 0104
TEL: 533 2155   TLX: RS 24414   FAX: 535 4047

TOKAI FINANCIAL FUTURES (SINGAPORE) PTE LTD
24 RAFFLES PLACE
#22-01/06 CLIFFORD CENTRE
SINGAPORE 0104
TEL: 535 8222   TLX: RS 26289 TOKAIS   FAX: 532 5453

TOKYO FOREX AND TULLETT (FUTURES) PTE LTD
10 ANSON ROAD
#16-11 INTERNATIONAL PLAZA
SINGAPORE 0207
TEL: 224 8077/ 535 6898   TLX: RS 28571 KTD FX
FAX: 224 1021/ 535 7828

UBS (FUTURES)
SINGAPORE PTE LTD
50 RAFFLES PLACE
#38-01 SHELL TOWER
SINGAPORE 0104
TEL: 530 7780   TLX: RS 21549 UBS
FAX: 224 1839

WOCOM COMMODITIES PTE LTD
150 CECIL STREET
#16-00 WING ON LIFE BUILDING
SINGAPORE 0106
TEL: 220 1477/ 225 5988   TLX: RS 23278 WOLASCO
FAX: 225 8890

YTB FINANCIAL FUTURES (SINGAPORE) PTE LTD
50 RAFFLES PLACE
#16-02 SHELL TOWER
SINGAPORE 0104
TEL: 223 7266   TLX: RS 29308 YTBSFX
FAX: 224 4365

SIMEX COMMERCIAL ASSOCIATE MEMBERS AS AT 10 JANUARY 1991

BP SINGAPORE PTE LTD
BP HOUSE
1 PASIR PANJANG ROAD
SINGAPORE 0511
TEL: 475 6633   TLX: RS 55788/ 21240 BEE
FAX: 273 7897/ 475 9273

C ITOH INTERNATIONAL PETROLEUM CO (SINGAPORE) PTE LTD
16 RAFFLES QUAY
#14-02B HONG LEONG BUILDING
SINGAPORE 0104
TEL: 321 8581   TLX: RS 21275 CITOH
FAX: 225 9809

CALTEX (ASIA) LIMITED 210 JALAN BUROH
SINGAPORE 2260
TEL: 660 8451   TLX: RS 21207 CALTEX
FAX: 265 9140

CALTEX TRADING PTE LTD
302 ORCHARD ROAD
#12-01 TONG BUILDING
SINGAPORE 0923
TEL: 734 7373   TLX: RS 36051 CXTRAD
FAX: 732 7382

HIN LEONG TRADING (PTE) LTD
1 PLAYFAIR ROAD
SINGAPORE 1336
TEL: 284 9134   TLX: RS 35549 HINOIL
FAX: 288 2653

MARUBENI INTERNATIONAL PETROLEUM (S) PTE LTD
16 RAFFLES QUAY
#40-01A HONG LEONG BUILDING
SINGAPORE 0104
TEL: 224 0446   TLX: RS 21245 MARBENI
FAX: 221 5458

MITSUI & CO LTD
16 RAFFLES QUAY
#17-00 HONG LEONG BUILDING
SINGAPORE 0104
TEL: 321 3150   TLX: RS 21272 MITSUI
FAX: 224 3458/ 224 7289

MOBIL SALES AND SUPPLY CORPORATION
18 PIONEER ROAD
SINGAPORE 2282
TEL: 660 6000   TLX: RS 21327 MOBOIL
FAX: 264 1693

PETRO-DIAMOND
SINGAPORE (PTE) LTD
51 BRAS BASAH ROAD
#06-02/03 PLAZA BY THE PARK
SINGAPORE 0718
TEL: 338 2000   TLX: RS 50118 PDS
FAX: 338 8287

SHELL EASTERN TRADING (PTE) LTD
50 RAFFLES PLACE
#43-00 SHELL TOWER
SINGAPORE 0104
TEL: 224 7777   TLX: 21251/ 21271 SHELL
FAX: 224 00739

F. The Sydney Futures Exchange

FLOOR MEMBER

as of February 1991

ANZ McCaughan Futures Limited
Level 3, 70 Phillip Street
Sydney, NSW 2000
Phone (02) 257 6170
Facsimile (02) 251 5961
Telex AA 72059

Australian Interdealer Brokers Pty Limited
Level 7, 114-120 Castlereagh Stree
Sydney, NSW 2000
Phone (02) 267 9922
Facsimile (02) 261-8481

Bain Refco Commodities Limited
19th Level, Grosvenor Place
225 George Street, Sydney, NW 2000
Phone Dealing (02) 258 1222
Administration (02) 258 1259
Facsimile (02) 258 1133.1134
Telex AA73745

Barclays de Zoete Wedd Australia Futures Pty Limited
Level 24, 255 George Street
Sydney, NSW 2000
Phone (02) 247 7188
Facsimilie (02) 259 5808
Telex AA 27467

BNY Australia Limited
15 Castlereagh Street, Sydney, NSW 2000
Phone (02) 237 2844
Facsimilie (02) 235 0836

BT Australia Limited
38th Floor, Australia Square Tower
Sydeny, NSW 2000
Phone (02) 259 3555
Facsimilie (02) 235 2882
Telex AA121821

C., A. & L. Bell Commodities Corporation Pty Limited
225 George Street, Sydney, NSW 2000
Phone (02) 251 5577
Facsimile (02) 251 6992
Telex AA71568

Capel Court Corporation Limited
Level 19, 60 Margaret Street
Sydney, NSW 2000
Phone (02) 231 2133
Facsimile (02) 251 5901
Telex AA170424

CitiFutures Limited
Level 12, Citibank Centre
1 Margaret Street
Sydney, NSW 2000
Phone (02) 239 9100
Facsimile (02) 239 9690
Telex AA24161

Commonwealth Bank of Australia
Group Treasury
Cnr Pitt Street and Martin Place
Sydney, NSW 2000
Phone (02) 227 5902
Facsimile (02) 227 5259
Telex AA70778

Credit Lyonnaise Rouse Australia Pty Limited
Level 17, 9-13 Castlereagh Street
Sydney, NSW 2000
Phone (02) 220 8090
Facsimile (02) 220 8091
Telex AA26881

CS First Boston Australian Futures Pty Ltd
Level 21, 60 Margaret Street
Sydney, NSW 2000
Phone (02) 251-4939
Facsimile (02) 232 2090
Telex AA176875

HKBA Futures Limited
14th Floor, 20 Bond Street
Sydney, NSW 2000
Phone (02)252 2211
Facsimile (02) 255 2408
Telex AA24856

Fay, Richwhite Futures Australia Limited
Level 29, Capital Centre, 9 Castlereagh Street Sydney, NSW 2000
Phone (02) 232 1255
Facsimile (02) 221 1188
Telex AA20673

LCF Limited
C/- Priestley & Morris
1 York Street, Sydney, NSW 2000
Phone (02) 247 3333
Facsimile (02) 237 3590
Telex AA122246

McIntosh Risk Management Ltd
Level 25, Rialto
525 Collins Street, Melbourne, Vic. 3000
Phone (03) 614 5133
Facsimile (03) 614 5707
Telex AA30701

Merrill Lynch, Pierce, Fenner, Smith & Co. (Brokers and Dealers) Limited
Level 17, State Bank Centre,
52 Martin Place, Sydney, NSW 2000
Phone (02) 251 8791
Facsimile (02) 225 6655
Telex AA24498

Midland Montagu Australia Futures Limited
Level 6, Grosvenor Place
225 George Street, Sydney, NSW 2000
Phone (02) 258 2000
Facsimile (02) 258 2099
Telex AA22553

J.P. Morgan Australia Limited
Level 20, 52 Martin Place
Sydney, NSW 2000
Phone (02) 239 6111
Facsimile (02) 239 6122 or 232 6881
Telex AA120953

National Australia Bank
29th Floor, National Australia Bank House
255 George Street, Sydney, NSW 2000
Phone (02) 237 1528/29
Facsimile (02) 237 1512 and 237 1155
Telex AA26951

Ord Westpac Futures Limited
Level 25, Grosvenor Place
225 George Street, Sydney, NSW 2000
Phone (02) 220 1555
Facsimile (02) 220 1316
Telex AA27780

SBV Futures Pty Limited
23rd Floor, 9 Castlereagh Street
Sydney, NSW 2000
Phone (02) 239 6370
Facsimile (02) 239 6388
Telex AA20393

Schroders Australia Limited
31st Floor, Grosvenor Place
225 George Street, NSW 2000
Phone (02) 258 9500
Facsimile (02) 251 5353
Telex AA73404

State Bank of New South Wales
Level 40, Grosvenor Place
225 George Street, Sydney, NSW 2000
Phone (02) 259 4503
Facsimile (02) 251 8009
Telex AA122263

Tullett & Tokyo (Australia) Pty Ltd
Level 2A, Hunter Connection
7-13 Hunter Street
Sydney, NSW 2000
Phone (02) 223 1255
Facsimile (02) 223 6577
Telex AA170567

J.B. Were Futures Pty Ltd
Level 1, 4 Bligh Street
Sydney, NSW 2000
Phone (02) 239 8777
Facsimile (02) 223 7319
Melbourne Office
Phone (03) 618 1222
Facsimile (03) 614 3076
Contact Mr G. Gibson

G. The Tokyo International Financial Futures Exchange

as of August 1st, 1990

CLEARING MEMBERS

THE ASHIKAGA BANK, LTD.
ADDRESS: 1-25 Sakura 4-Chome, Utsunomiya, Tochigi
TELEPHONE NUMBER: 0286-22-0111
FACSIMILE NUMBER: 03-201-0417

THE BANK OF FUKUOKA, LTD.
ADDRESS: 13-1, Tenjin 2-Chome, Chuo-Ku, Fukuoka
TELEPHONE NUMBER: 092-723-2131
FACSIMILE NUMBER: 03-242-6918

BANK OF KINKI, LTD.
ADDRESS: 4-27, Shiromi 1-Chome, Chuo-Ku, Osaka
TELEPHONE NUMBER: 06-945-2121
FACSIMILE NUMBER: 03-552-7399

THE BANK OF KYOTO, LTD.
ADDRESS: 700 Yakushimae-Cho, Karasuma-Dori, Matsubara-Agaru,
  Shimogyo-Ku, Kyoto
TELEPHONE NUMBER: 075-361-2211
FACSIMILE NUMBER: 03-281-8026

THE BANK OF NAGOYA, LTD.
ADDRESS: 19-17, Nishiki 3-Chome, Naka-Ku, Nagoya
TELEPHONE NUMBER: 052-951-5911
FACSIMILE NUMBER: 03-277-1083

THE BANK OF OSAKA, LTD.
ADDRESS: 4-1, Nishi-Hommachi 1-Chome, Nishi-Ku, Osaka
TELEPHONE NUMBER: 06-538-1021
FACSIMILE NUMBER: 03-274-3083

THE BANK OF TOKYO, LTD.
ADDRESS: 3-2, Nihombashi Hongokucho 1-Chome, Chuo-Ku, Tokyo
TELEPHONE NUMBER: 03-245-1111
FACSIMILE NUMBER: 03-246-0328

THE BANK OF YOKOHAMA, LTD.
ADDRESS: 47, Honcho 5-Chome, Naka-Ku, Yokohama
TELEPHONE NUMBER: 045-201-2211
FACSIMILE NUMBER: 03-271-0950

CHASE MANAHATTAN SECURITIES (C.I.) LIMITED
ADDRESS: 2-1, Marunouchi 1-Chome, Chiyoda-Ku, Tokyo
TELEPHONE NUMBER: 03-287-4300
FACSIMILE NUMBER: 03-287-4376

THE CHIBA BANK, LTD.
ADDRESS: 1-2, Chiba-Minato, Chiba City
TELEPHONE NUMBER: 0472-45-1111
FACSIMILE NUMBER: 03-244-1227

THE CHUGOKU BANK, LIMITED
ADDRESS: 10-13, 1-Chome, Marunouchi, Okayama
TELEPHONE NUMBER: 0862-23-3111
FACSIMILE NUMBER: 03-242-4071

THE CHUO TRUST & BANKING CO., LTD.
ADDRESS: 7-1, 1-Chome, Kyobashi, Shou-Ku, Tokyo
TELEPHONE NUMBER: 03-567-1451
FACSIMILE NUMBER: 03-535-6417

CITICORP FUTURES CORPORATION
ADDRESS: 2-2-1, Ohtemachi, Chiyoda-Ku, Tokyo
TELEPHONE NUMBER: 03-273-6904
FACSIMILE NUMBER: 03-279-6515

CONTINENTAL FIRST OPTIONS, INC.
TOKYO BRANCH
ADDRESS: Mitsui Seimei Building 2f 2-3, Ohtemachi 1-Chome,
Chiyoda-Ku, Tokyo
TELEPHONE NUMBER: 03-213-0400
FACSIMILE NUMBER: 03-213-1727

COSMO SECURITIES CO., LTD.
ADDRESS: 16-10, Nihonbashi 1-Chome, Chuo-Ku, Tokyo
TELEPHONE NUMBER: 03-273-8768
FACSIMILE NUMBER: 03-273-0641

CREDITY LYONNAIS
ADDRESS: Hibiya Park Bldg. 7th Floor, 1-8-1, Yurakucho, Chiyoda-Ku, Tokyo
TELEPHONE NUMBER: 03-214-4559
FACSIMILE NUMBER: 03-214-0886

CS FIRST BOSTON (JAPAN) LIMITED
ADDRESS: Asahi Seimei Hibiya Building 5-1, Yurakucho 1-Chome,
Chiyoda-Ku, Tokyo
TELEPHONE NUMBER: 03-508-4200
FACSIMILE NUMBER: 03-504-1573

THE DAI-ICHI KANGYO BANK, LIMITED
ADDRESS: 1-5, Uchisaiwaicho 1-Chome, Chiyoda-Ku, Tokyo
TELEPHONE NUMBER: 03-596-1111
FACSIMILE NUMBER: 03-596-5363

DAI-ICHI SECURITIES CO., LTD.
ADDRESS: 1-6-2, Nihonbashi-Muromachi, Chuo-Ku, Tokyo
TELEPHONE NUMBER: 03-244-2600
FACSIMILE NUMBER: 03-279-4080

THE DAISHI BANK, LTD.
ADDRESS: 1048, 6-Bancho, Higashibori-Dori, Niigata
TELEPHONE NUMBER: 025-223-6611
FACSIMILE NUMBER: 03-270-5694

THE DAIWA BANK, LTD.
ADDRESS: 1-8, Bingo Machi 2-Chome, Chuo-Ku, Osaka
TELEPHONE NUMBER: 06-271-1221
FACSIMILE NUMBER: 03-243-0062

DAIWA SECURITIES CO., LTD.
ADDRESS: 6-4, 2-Chome, Otemachi, Chiyoda-Ku, Tokyo
TELEPHONE NUMBER: 03-243-2111
FACSIMILE NUMBER: 03-279-2275

THE EIGHTEENTH BANK, LIMITED
ADDRESS: 1-11, Doza-Machi, Nagasaki City, Nagasaki
TELEPHONE NUMBER: 0958-24-1818
FACSIMILE NUMBER: 03-535-0156

THE FUJI BANK, LIMITED
ADDRESS: 1-5-5, Otemachi, Chiyoda-Ku, Tokyo
TELEPHONE NUMBER: 03-216-2211
FACSIMILE NUMBER: 03-212-0036

THE FUKUI BANK, LTD.
ADDRESS: 1-1, Junka 1-Chome, Fukui
TELEPHONE NUMBER: 0776-24-2030
FACSIMILE NUMBER: 03-273-9726

THE FUKUOKA CITY BANK, LTD.
ADDRESS: 4-21, Yaesu 1-Chome, Chuo-Ku, Tokyo
TELEPHONE NUMBER: 03-272-2757
FACSIMILE NUMBER: 03-272-7355

THE FUKUTOKU BANK, LTD.
ADDRESS: 5-9, Higashi-Shinsaibashi 1-Chome, Chuo-Ku, Osaka
TELEPHONE NUMBER: 06-252-1101
FACSIMILE NUMBER: 03-535-7319

GOLDMAN SACHS (JAPAN) CORP.
ADDRESS: Ark Mori Building 10F 12-32, Akasaka 1-Chome,
  Minato-Ku, Tokyo
TELEPHONE NUMBER: 03-589-7000
FACSIMILE NUMBER: 03-588-6489

THE GUNMA BANK, LTD.
ADDRESS: 194 Motosojamachi, Maebashi, Gunma
TELEPHONE NUMBER: 0272-52-1111
FACSIMILE NUMBER: 03-231-3676

THE HACHIJUNI BANK, LTD.
ADDRESS: 1-22, Nihonbashi Muromachi 4-Chome, Chuo-Ku, Tokyo
TELEPHONE NUMBER: 03-277-0141
FACSIMILE NUMBER: 03-246-4675

THE HIGO BANK, LTD.
ADDRESS: 1 Renpei-Cho, Kumamoto-Shi
TELEPHONE NUMBER: 096-325-2111
FACSIMILE NUMBER: 03-561-3156

THE HIROSHIMA BANK, LTD.
ADDRESS: 3-8, Kamiya-Cho 1-Chome, Naka-Ku, Hiroshima
TELEPHONE NUMBER: 082-247-5151
FACSIMILE NUMBER: 03-272-3837

THE HOKKAIDO BANK, LTD.
ADDRESS: 1, Nishi 4-Chome, Odori, Chuo-Ku, Sapporo
TELEPHONE NUMBER: 011-261-7111
FACSIMILE NUMBER: 03-275-0420

THE HOKKAIDO TAKUSHOKU BANK, LTD.
ADDRESS: 7, Odori Nishi 3-Chome, Chuo-Ku, Sapporo
TELEPHONE NUMBER: 011-271-2111
FACSIMILE NUMBER: 03-281-6082

THE HOKKOKU BANK, LTD.
ADDRESS: 1 Shimotsutumi-Cho, Kanazawa, Ishikawa
TELEPHONE NUMBER: 0762-63-1111
FACSIMILE NUMBER: 03-274-0554

THE HOKURIKU BANK, LTD.
ADDRESS: 2-26, Tsutsumicho-Dori 1-Chome, Toyama-Shi
TELEPHONE NUMBER: 0764-23-7111
FACSIMILE NUMBER: 03-279-2544

THE HYAKUGO BANK, LTD.
ADDRESS: 21-27, Iwata, Tsu, Mie
TELEPHONE NUMBER: 0592-27-2151
FACSIMILE NUMBER: 03-281-0513

THE HYAKUJUSHI BANK, LTD.
ADDRESS: 5-1, Kamei-Cho, Takamatsu, Kagawa
TELEPHONE NUMBER: 0878-31-0114
FACSIMILE NUMBER: 03-297-9063

THE HYOGO BANK, LTD.
ADDRESS: 1-2-1, Iwamoto-Cho, Chiyoda-Ku, Tokyo
TELEPHONE NUMBER: 03-864-4701
FACSIMILE NUMBER: 03-864-6976

THE INDUSTRIAL BANK OF JAPAN, LIMITED
ADDRESS: 3-3, Marunouchi 1-Chome, Chiyoda-Ku, Tokyo
TELEPHONE NUMBER: 03-214-1111
FACSIMILE NUMBER: 03-201-2346

THE IYO BANK, LTD.
ADDRESS: 1, Minami-Horibata-Cho, Mastuyama
TELEPHONE NUMBER: 0899-41-1141
FACSIMILE NUMBER: 03-278-8495

THE JOHNAN SHINKIN BANK
ADDRESS: 7-2-3, Nishigotanda, Shinagawa-Ku, Tokyo
TELEPHONE NUMBER: 03-493-8111
FACSIMILE NUMBER: 03-493-2479

THE JOYO BANK, LTD.
ADDRESS: 7-2, Yaesu 2-Chome, Chuo-Ku, Tokyo
TELEPHONE NUMBER: 03-273-5245
FACSIMILE NUMBER   03-242-3726

J.P. MORGAN SECURITIES ASIA LIMITED
ADDRESS: Shinyurakucho Bldg., 1-12-1, Yurakucho, Chiyoda-Ku, Tokyo
TELEPHONE NUMBER: 03-287-6502
FACSIMILE NUMBER: 03-216-4364

THE JUROKU BANK, LTD.
ADDRESS: 8-26, Kandamachi, Gifushi
TELEPHONE NUMBER: 0582-65-2111
FACSIMILE NUMBER: 03-231-7875

THE KAGOSHIMA BANK, LTD.
ADDRESS: 6-6, Kinsei-Cho, Kagoshima-City
TELEPHONE NUMBER: 0992-25-3111
FACSIMILE NUMBER: 03-272-3947

THE KEIYO BANK, LTD.
ADDRESS: 11-11, Fujimi 1-Chome, Chiba
TELEPHONE NUMBER: 0472-22-2121
FACSIMILE NUMBER: 03-279-6087

THE KIYO BANK, LTD.
ADDRESS: 35, Honmachi 1-Chome, Wakayama
TELEPHONE NUMBER: 0734-23-9111
FACSIMILE NUMBER: 03-295-5217

KOKUSAI SECURITIES CO., LTD.
ADDRESS: (Tokyo-Sumitomo Twin Building East) 27-1, Shinkawa 2-Chome,
Chuo-Ku, Tokyo
TELEPHONE NUMBER: 03-297-2111
FACSIMILE NUMBER: 03-297-9564

THE KYOWA BANK, LTD.
ADDRESS: 1-2, Otemachi 1-Chome, Chiyoda-Ku, Tokyo
TELEPHONE NUMBER: 03-287-2111
FACSIMILE NUMBER: 03-287-3250

THE LONG-TERM CREDIT BANK OF JAPAN, LTD.
ADDRESS: 2-4, Otemachi 1-Chome, Chiyoda-Ku, Tokyo
TELEPHONE NUMBER: 03-211-5111
FACSIMILE NUMBER: 03-214-4364

MARUSAN SECURITIES CO., LTD.
ADDRESS: 2-5-2, Nihonbashi, Chuo-Ku, Tokyo
TELEPHONE NUMBER: 03-272-5211
FACSIMILE NUMBER: 03-271-5840

THE MITSUBISHI BANK, LTD.
ADDRESS: 7-1, Marunouchi 2-Chome, Chiyoda-Ku, Tokyo
TELEPHONE NUMBER: 03-240-1111
FACSIMILE NUMBER: 03-240-3217

THE MITSUBISHI TRUST AND BANKING CORPORATION
ADDRESS: 4-5, Marunouchi 1-Chome, Chiyoda-Ku, Tokyo
TELEPHONE NUMBER: 03-212-1211
FACSIMILE NUMBER: 03-214-0265

THE MITSUI TAIYO KOBE BANK, LTD.
ADDRESS: 3-1, Kudan Minami 1-Chome, Chiyoda-Ku, Tokyo
TELEPHONE NUMBER: 03-230-3111
FACSIMILE NUMBER: 03-595-2986

THE MITSUI TRUST AND BANKING COMPANY, LIMITED
ADDRESS: 1-1, Nihonbashi-Muromachi 2-Chome, Chuo-Ku, Tokyo
TELEPHONE NUMBER: 03-270-9511
FACSIMILE NUMBER: 03-279-3853

MORGAN STANLEY JAPAN LTD.
ADDRESS: Ote Center Building 1-3, Otemachi 1-Chome, Chiyoda-Ku, Tokyo
TELEPHONE NUMBER: 03-286-9000
FACSIMILE NUMBER: 03-286-9664

THE NANTO BANK. LTD.
ADDRESS: 16, Hashimoto-Cho, Nara
TELEPHONE NUMBER: 0742-22-1131
FACSIMILE NUMBER: 03-213-1796

NEW JAPAN SECURITIES CO., LTD.
ADDRESS: 3-11, Kanda-Surugadai, Chiyoda-Ku, Tokyo
TELEPHONE NUMBER: 03-219-1111
FACSIMILE NUMBER: 03-292-6922

THE NIKKO SECURITIES CO., LTD.
ADDRESS: 3-1, Marunouchi 3-Chome, Chiyoda-Ku, Tokyo
TELEPHONE NUMBER: 03-283-2211
FACSIMILE NUMBER: 03-5566-4936

THE NIPPON CREDIT BANK, LTD.
ADDRESS: 13-10, Kudan Kita 1-Chome, Chiyoda-Ku, Tokyo
TELEPHONE NUMBER: 03-263-1111
FACSIMILE NUMBER: 03-222-0158

**THE NIPPON KANGYO KAKGYO KAKUMARU
SECURITIES CO., LTD.**
ADDRESS: Marunouchi Center Building, 1-6-1 Marunouchi,
Chiyoda-Ku, Tokyo
TELEPHONE NUMBER: 03-286-7111
FACSIMILE NUMBER: 03-212-0665

NIPPON TRUST BANK, LIMITED
ADDRESS: 1-8, Nihonbashi 3-Chome, Chuo-Ku, Tokyo
TELEPHONE NUMBER: 03-245-8111
FACSIMILE NUMBER: 03-271-3308

THE NISHI-NIPPON BANK, LTD.
ADDRESS: 3-6, Hakata-Ekimae 1-Chome, Hakata-Ku, Fukuoka
TELEPHONE NUMBER: 092-476-2525
FACSIMILE NUMBER: 03-564-3570

THE NOMURA SECURITIES CO., LTD.
ADDRESS: 1-9-1, Nihonbashi, Chuo-Ku, Tokyo
TELEPHONE NUMBER: 03-211-1811
FACSIMILE NUMBER: 03-281-1560

THE NORINCHUKIN BANK
ADDRESS: 8-3, Otemachi 1-Chome, Chiyoda-Ku, Tokyo
TELEPHONE NUMBER: 03-279-0111
FACSIMILE NUMBER: 03-245-0563

THE OGAKI KYORITSU BANK, LTD.
ADDRESS: 98, Kuruwamachi 3-Chome, Ogaki, Gifu
TELEPHONE NUMBER: 0584-74-2111
FACSIMILE NUMBER: 03-555-8439

OKASAN SECURITIES CO., LTD.
ADDRESS: 1-17-6, Nihonbashi, Chuo-Ku, Tokyo
TELEPHONE NUMBER: 03-272-2211
FACSIMILE NUMBER: 03-272-3994

THE SAITAMA BANK, LTD.
ADDRESS: 7-4-1, Tokiwa, Urawa, Saitama
TELEPHONE NUMBER: 03-276-6471
FACSIMILE NUMBER: 03-271-4398

SALOMON BROTHERS ASIA LIMITED
ADDRESS: ARK Mori Building 9F, 12-32, Akasaka 1-Chome,
 Minato-Ku, Tokyo
TELEPHONE NUMBER: 03-589-9111
FACSIMILE NUMBER: 03-589-9988

THE SAN-IN GODO BANK, LTD.
ADDRESS: 18, Shirakata-Honmachi, Matsue
TELEPHONE NUMBER: 0852-26-7111
FACSIMILE NUMBER: 03-297-3168

THE SANWA BANK, LIMITED
ADDRESS: 3-5-6, Fushimi-Machi, Chuo-Ku, Osaka
TELEPHONE NUMBER: 06-202-2281
FACSIMILE NUMBER: 03-212-2393

SANYO SECURITIES CO., LTD.
ADDRESS: 8-1, 1-Chome, Kayaba-Cho, Nihonbashi, Chuo-Ku, Tokyo
TELEPHONE NUMBER: 03-666-1233
FACSIMILE NUMBER: 03-669-3529

SHEARSON LEHMAN HUTTON ASIA, INC.
ADDRESS: ARK Mori Bldg. 36F, 12-32, Akasaka 1-Chome, Minato-Ku, Tokyo
TELEPHONE NUMBER: 03-505-9000
FACSIMILE NUMBER: 03-505-5725

THE SHIGA BANK, LTD.
ADDRESS: 1-38, Hamamachi, Otsu, Shiga
TELEPHONE NUMBER: 0775-24-2141
FACSIMILE NUMBER: 03-663-4199

THE SHIZUOKA BANK, LTD.
ADDRESS: 10, Gofukucho 1-Chome, Shizuoka-Shi, Shizuoka
TELEPHONE NUMBER: 0542-61-3131
FACSIMILE NUMBER: 03-246-0443

THE SHOKO CHUKIN BANK
ADDRESS: 10-17, 2-Chome, Yaesu, Chuo-Ku, Tokyo
TELEPHONE NUMBER: 03-272-6111
FACSIMILE NUMBER: 03-274-3910

SOCIETE GENERALE TOKYO BRANCH
ADDRESS: Hibiya Central Building 2-9, Nishi-Shinbashi 1-Chome,
Minato-Ku, Tokyo
TELEPHONE NUMBER: 03-503-9781
FACSIMILE NUMBER: 03-592-8567

THE SUMITOMO BANK, LIMITED
ADDRESS: 3-2, Marunouchi 1-Chome, Chiyoda-Ku, Tokyo
TELEPHONE NUMBER: 03-282-5111
FACSIMILE NUMBER: 03-282-8339

THE SUMITOMO TRUST AND BANKING COMPANY, LIMITED
ADDRESS: 5-33, Kitahama 4-Chome, Chuo-Ku, Osaka
TELEPHONE NUMBER: 06-220-2121
FACSIMILE NUMBER: 03-286-8380

THE SURUGA BANK, LTD.
ADDRESS: 23, Tohriyoko-Cho, Numazu, Shizuoka
TELEPHONE NUMBER: 0559-62-0080
FACSIMILE NUMBER: 03-242-3284

THE 77 BANK, LTD.
ADDRESS: 3-20, Chuo 3-Chome, Aoba-Ku, Sendai, Miyagi
TELEPHONE NUMBER: 022-267-1111
FACSIMILE NUMBER: 03-670-0770

TAIHEIYO SECURITIES CO., LTD.
ADDRESS: 1-17-10, Kyobashi, Chuo-Ku, Tokyo
TELEPHONE NUMBER: 03-566-4511
FACSIMILE NUMBER: 03-5695-3523

THE TOHO BANK, LTD.
ADDRESS: 3-25, Ohmachi, Fukushima
TELEPHONE NUMBER: 0245-23-3131
FACSIMILE NUMBER: 03-271-5429

THE TOKAI BANK, LIMITED
ADDRESS: 6-1, Otemachi 2-Chome, Chiyoda-Ky, Tokyo
TELEPHONE NUMBER: 03-242-2111
FACSIMILE NUMBER: 03-241-0678

TOKYO SECURITIES CO., LTD.
ADDRESS: 7-3, Marunouchi 2-Chome, Ciyoda-Ku, Tokyo
TELEPHONE NUMBER: 03-214-3211
FACSIMILE NUMBER: 03-5695-5650

THE TOKYO SOWA BANK, LTD.
ADDRESS: 6-16, 1-Chome, Akasaka, Minato-Ku, Tokyo
TELEPHONE NUMBER: 03-586-3111
FACSIMILE NUMBER: 03-585-9745

THE TOKYO TOMIN BANK, LTD.
ADDRESS: 3-11, Roppongi 2-Chome, Minato-Ku, Tokyo
TELEPHONE NUMBER: 03-582-8251
FACSIMILE NUMBER: 03-589-6662

THE TOKYO TRUST AND BANKING COMPANY, LIMITED
ADDRESS: 4-3, Marunouchi 1-Chome, Chiyoda-Ku, Tokyo
TELEPHONE NUMBER: 03-287-2211
FACSIMILE NUMBER: 03-212-0843

UNIVERSAL SECURITIES CO., LTD.
ADDRESS: 4-3, Marunouchi 1-Chome, Chiyoda-Ku, Tokyo
TELEPHONE NUMBER: 03-287-2211
FACSIMILE NUMBER: 03-212-0843

UNIVERSAL SECURITIES CO., LTD.
ADDRESS: 4-2, 3-Chome, Marunouchi, Chiyoda-Ku, Tokyo
TELEPHONE NUMBER: 03-284-3511
FACSIMILE NUMBER: 03-284-1602

WAKO SECURITIES CO., LTD.
ADDRESS: 6-1, Nihonbashi-Koamicho, Chuo-Ku, Tokyo
TELEPHONE NUMBER: 03-667-8111
FACSIMILE NUMBER: 03-662-6578

THE YAMAGUCHI BANK, LTD.
ADDRESS: 2-36, 4-Chome, Takezaki-Cho, Shimonoseki, Yamaguchi-Pref.
TELEPHONE NUMBER: 0832-23-3411
FACSIMILE NUMBER: 03-242-9340

YAMAICHI SECURITIES COMPANY, LIMITED
ADDRESS: 2-4-1, Yaesu, Chuo-Ku, Tokyo
TELEPHONE NUMBER: 03-276-3181
FACSIMILE NUMBER: 03-664-2109

THE YAMANASHI CHUO BANK, LTD.
ADDRESS: 20-8, Marunouchi 1-Chome, Kofu, Yamanashi
TELEPHONE NUMBER: 0552-33-2111
FACSIMILE NUMBER: 03-255-2096

YAMATANE SECURITIES CO., LTD.
ADDRESS: 7-12, Kabuto-Cho, Nihonbashi, Chuo-Ku, Tokyo
TELEPHONE NUMBER: 03-669-3211
FACSIMILE NUMBER: 03-669-5202

THE YASUDA TRUST AND BANKING COMPANY, LIMITED
ADDRESS: 2-1, Yaesu 1-Chome, Chuo-Tokyo
TELEPHONE NUMBER: 03-278-8111
FACSIMILE NUMBER: 03-273-6327

THE ZENSHINREN BANK
ADDRESS: 4-1, Nihonbashi-Honcho 3-Chome, Chuo-Ku, Tokyo
TELEPHONE NUMBER: 03-5255-9640
FACSIMILE NUMBER: 03-5255-9655

H. The Tokyo Stock Exchange

Member List (124 companies)   **As of April, 1990**

Member Securities Companies	Address	Tel.
(Domestic)		
ACE*	2-12, Nihombashi-Kayaba-cho, Chuo-ku, Tokyo 103	5695-5153
Aizawa*	20-3, Nihombashi 1-chome, Chuo-ku, Tokyo 103	272-3111
Akagiya	7-1, Nihombashi 2-chome, Chuo-ku, Tokyo 103	271-0011
Ando	10-3, Nihombashi-Kabuto-cho, Chuo-ku, Tokyo 103	666-1471
ARK	Shuwa Daini-Sakurabashi Bldg. 8-2, Hacchobori 4-chome, Chuo-ku, Tokyo 104	297-5811
Century*	Itopia Nihombashi-Honcho Bldg. 7-1, Nihombashi-Honcho 2-chome, Chuo-ku, Tokyo 103	667-0371
Chiyoda*	2-15, Nihombashi-Muromachi 3-chome, Chuo-ku, Tokyo 103	271-2311
Chuo*	7-8, Nihombashi-Kabuto-cho, Chuo-ku, Tokyo 103	660-4700
Cosmo*	16-10, Nihombashi 1-chome, Chuo-ku, Tokyo 103	272-4611
Daiichi*	6-2, Nihombashi-Muromachi 1-chome, Chuo-ku, Tokyo 103	244-2600
Dainana	10-9, Ginza 3-chome, Chuo-ku, Tokyo 104	545-9111
Daisei	1-10, Nihombashi-Kabuto-cho, Chuo-ku, Tokyo 103	661-6006
Daito*	4-3, Nihombashi-Kabuto-cho, Chuo-ku, Tokyo 103	660-4311
Daiwa*	6-4, Ohtemachi 2-chome, Chiyoda-ku, Tokyo 100	243-2111
Fukuyama	9-4, Hacchobori 4-chome, Chuo-ku, Tokyo 104	297-2980
Hinode*	Shuwa Higashi Yaesu Bldg. 9-1, Hacchobori 2-chome, Chuo-ku, Tokyo 104	297-5111
Hiraoka	6-6, Nihombashi-Kobuna-cho, Chuo-ku, Tokyo 103	667-7676
Hirota	7-3, Nihombashi-Kayaba-cho 1-chome, Chuo-ku, Tokyo 103	667-1181
Ichiyoshi*	14-1, Hacchobori 2-chome, Chuo-ku, Tokyo 104	555-6200
Imagawa	10-1, Nihombashi 2-chome, Chuo-ku, Tokyo 103	273-7788
Issei	Dainichi Yaesu Bldg., 8-5, Yaesu 2-chome, Chuo-ku, Tokyo 104	273-9111
Iwai	Yaesu Kato Bldg., 15-12, Nihombashi-Kabuto-cho, Chuo-ku, Tokyo 103	662-7151
Izumi*	17-24, Shinkawa 1-chome, Chuo-ku, Tokyo 104	555-4811
Jujiya	6-17, Nihombashi-Kayaba-cho 1-chome, Chuo-ku, Tokyo 103	666-0101

Member List (continued)

Member Securities Companies	Address	Tel.
Kaisei*	13-2, Nihombashi-Kabuto-cho, Chuo-ku, Tokyo 103	666-1431
Kaneju	7-15, Nihombashi-Kabuto-cho, Chuo-ku, Tokyo 103	666-0191
Kaneman	3-8, Nihombashi-Kabuto-cho, Chuo-ku, Tokyo 103	666-1191
Kaneyama	11-8, Nihombashi-Koami-cho, Chou-ku, Tokyo 103	668-3111
Kanto	8-1, Kanda-Ogawa-cho, 1-chome, Chiyoda-ku, Tokyo 103	253-6721
Kokusai*	27-1, Shinkawa 2-chome, Chuo-ku, Tokyo 104	297-2111
Kosei*	Nihon Bldg., 6-2, Ohtemachi 2-chome, Chiyoda-ku, Tokyo 100	246-0811
Kurokawa Kitoku	16-3, Nihombashi 1-chome, Chuo-ku, Tokyo 103	278-7800
Kyokuto*	4-7, Nihombashi-Kayaba-cho, 1-chome, Chuo-ku, Tokyo 103	667-9171
Kyoritsu	7-3, Nihombashi 2-chome, Chuo-ku, Tokyo 103	272-3361
Kyowa	8-3, Nihombashi-Kabuto-cho, Chuo-ku, Tokyo 103	666-1381
Maruhachi	15-12, Nihombashi-Kabuto-cho, Chuo-ku, Tokyo 103	639-0808
Maruichi	13-1, Nihombashi-Koami-cho, Chuo-ku, Tokyo 103	666-0411
Marukin	7-9, Nihombashi-Kakigara-cho, 1-chome, Chuo-ku, Tokyo 103	668-8381
Marukuni	10-2, Nihombashi-Koami-cho, Chuo-ku, Tokyo 103	666-2291
Maruko	3-3, Nihombashi-Kabuto-cho, Chuo-ku, Tokyo 103	666-2431
Maruman*	1-10, Nihombashi 2-chome, Chuo-ku, Tokyo 103	272-6011
Marusan*	5-2, Nihombashi 2-chome, Chuo-ku, Tokyo 103	272-5211
Maruso	9-14, Nihombashi-Kabuto-cho, Chuo-ku, Tokyo 103	666-7901
Maruwa	8-2, Nihombashi 3-chome, Chuo-ku, Tokyo 103	274-5341
Matsui	20-7, Nihombashi 1-chome, Chuo-ku, Tokyo 103	281-3111
Meiko*	14-1, Nihombashi-Koami-cho, Chuo-ku, Tokyo 103	666-5211
Meiwa	7-15, Nihombashi-Kabuto-cho, Chuo-ku, Tokyo 103	666-2541
Miki	20-9, Nihombashi 1-chome, Chuo-ku, Tokyo 103	278-1111
Misawaya	5-4, Nihombashi-Hakozaki-cho, Chuo-ku, Tokyo 103	667-4411
Mito*	13-5, Nihombashi 3-chome, Chuo-ku, Tokyo 103	274-6111
Murosei	1-10, Nihombashi-Kabuto-cho, Chuo-ku, Tokyo 103	666-1451
Naigai*	7-3, Nihombashi-Kabuto-cho, Chuo-ku, Tokyo 103	665-4321
Naito	10-1, Nihombashi-Ningyo-cho 3-chome, Chuo-ku, Tokyo 103	668-2090
Nakahara	1-10, Nihombashi-Kabuto-cho, Chuo-ku, Tokyo 103	666-0241
Naruse	4-2, Nihombashi-Kabuto-cho, Chuo-ku, Tokyo 103	666-2101
National*	6-7, Nihombashi-Kabuto-cho, Chuo-ku, Tokyo 103	666-0321
New Japan*	11, Kanda-Surugadai 3-chome, Chiyoda-ku, Tokyo 101	219-1111
Nichiei	10-7, Nihombashi-Koami-cho, Chuo-ku, Tokyo 103	667-3181
Nihon Kyoei	2-18, Nihombashi-Kayaba-cho 1-chome, Chuo-ku, Tokyo 103	668-2211
Nikko*	3-1, Marunouchi 3-chome, Chiyoda-ku, Tokyo 100	283-2211
Nippon Kangyo Kakumaru*	6-1, Marunouchi 1-chome, Chiyoda-ku, Tokyo 100	286-7111

Member List (continued)

Member Securities Companies	Address	Tel.
Nippon*	9-10, Nihombashi-Horidome-cho 1-chome, Chuo-ku, Tokyo 103	668-0311
Nissan	7-6, Nihombashi-Kabuto-cho, Chuo-ku, Tokyo 103	666-3151
Nomura*	9-1, Nihombashi 1-chome, Chuo-ku, Tokyo 103	211-1811, 3811
Okachi	3-12, Nihombashi-Kayaba-cho 1-chome, Chuo-ku, Tokyo 103	668-3661
Okasan*	17-6, Nihombashi 1-chome, Chuo-ku, Tokyo 103	272-2211
Osawa	2-13, Nihombashi-Kayaba-cho 1-chome, Chuo-ku, Tokyo 103	666-0311
Ryoko*	17-12, Nihombashi 1-chome, Chuo-ku, Tokyo 103	246-5711
Sanei	12-7, Kyobashi 3-chome, Chuo-ku, Tokyo 104	562-3321
Sanyo*	8-1, Nihombashi-Kayaba-cho 1-chome, Chuo-ku, Tokyo 103	666-1233
Shinei-Ishino	15-1, Nihombashi 1-chome, Chuo-ku, Tokyo 103	271-5661
Tachibana	13-14, Nihombashi-Kayaba-cho 1-chome, Chuo-ku, Tokyo 103	669-3111
Taiheiyo*	17-10, Kyobashi 1-chome, Chuo-ku, Tokyo 104	566-4511
Takagi*	12-11, Nihombashi 1-chome, Chuo-ku, Tokyo 103	281-3231
Tokai	8-8, Yaesu 2-chome, Chuo-ku, Tokyo 104	274-3441
Tokyo*	7-3, Marunouchi 2-chome, Chiyoda-ku, Tokyo 100	214-3211
Tokyo Rengo	7-6, Nihombashi-Kayaba-cho 3-chome, Chuo-ku, Tokyo 103	667-2085
Towa*	16-7, Nihombashi 1-chome, Chuo-ku, Tokyo 103	278-1511
Toyo*	20-5, Nihombashi 1-chome, Chuo-ku, Tokyo 103	274-0211
Universal*	4-2, Marunouchi 3-chome, Chiyoda-ku, Tokyo 100	284-3511
Utsumiya	12-4, Nihombashi-Kayaba-cho 1-chome, Chuo-ku, Tokyo 103	661-8855
Wako*	6-1, Nihombashi-Koami-cho, Chuo-ku, Tokyo 103	667-8111
World*	Sumitomo Real Estate Hakozaki Bldg., 16-9, Nihombashi-Hakozaki-cho, Chuo-ku, Tokyo 103	661-0241
Yamabun	18-3, Nihombashi-Koami-cho, Chuo-ku, Tokyo 103	666-1121
Yamaichi*	4-1, Yaesu 2-chome, Chuo-ku, Tokyo 104	276-3181
Yamaka	13-10, Nihombashi 2-chome, Chuo-ku, Tokyo 103	273-8681
Yamakichi	1-7, Nihombashi-Kabuto-cho, Chuo-ku, Tokyo 103	666-2281
Yamamaru	3-11, Nihombashi-Kabuto-cho, Chuo-ku, Tokyo 103	668-0211
Yamani	4-1, Nihombashi-Kabuto-cho, Chuo-ku, Tokyo 103	666-1151
Yamatane*	7-12, Nihombashi-Kabuto-cho, Chuo-ku, Tokyo 103	669-3211
Yamawa	1-3, Nihombashi-Kabuto-cho, Chuo-ku, Tokyo 103	668-5411
Yutaka	10-14, Nihombashi-Horidome-cho 1-chome, Chuo-ku, Tokyo 103	668-3621

Member List (continued)

Member Securities Companies	Address	Tel.
(admitted to be regular members in or after November, 1990)		
Daika	11-5, Nihombashi-Koami-cho, Chuo-ku, Tokyo 103	668-5531
Kimura	22-11, Hacchobori 3-chome, Chuo-ku, Tokyo 104	5566-0881
Kokyo	14-9, Nihombashi-Kabuto-cho, Chuo-ku, Tokyo 103	669-0121
Maeda	Futabakaikan Bldg. 1F, 16-5, Nihombashi-Kabuto-cho, Chuo-ku, Tokyo 103	662-2667
Marufuku	Yokokawa Bldg. 7F, 17-27, Shinkawa 1-chome, Chuo-ku, Tokyo 104	297-9111
Yahata	Koura Bldg. 4F, Nihombashi-Kayaba-cho, Chuo-ku, Tokyo 103	669-2429
Yamagen	1-17, Nihombashi-Ningyo-cho 3-chome, Chuo-ku, Tokyo 103	662-4451
(Foreign)		
Baring*	Shin-Kasumigaseki Bldg. 10F, 3-2, Kasumigaseki 3-chome, Chiyoda-ku, Tokyo 100	595-8811
Citicorp Scrimgeour Vickers*	Ark Mori Bldg. 24F, 12-32, Akasaka 1-chome, Minato-ku, Tokyo 107	589-7400
County Natwest*	AIU Bldg., 1-3, Marunouchi 1-chome, Chiyoda-ku, Tokyo 100	285-1300
DB Capital Markets*	Ark Mori Bldg. 22F, 12-32, Akasaka 1-chome, Minato-ku, Tokyo 107	589-1986
Dresdner-ABD*	Shionogi Honcho Kyodo Bldg. 5F, 7-2, Nihombashi-Honcho 3-chome, Chuo-ku, Tokyo 103	662-3450
First Boston*	Asahi Seimei Hibiya Bldg., 5-1, Yurakucho 1-chome, Chiyoda-ku, Tokyo 100	508-4200
Goldman Sachs*	Ark Mori Bldg. 10F, 12-32, Akasaka 1-chome, Minato-ku, Tokyo 107	589-7000
Jardine Fleming*	Yamato Seimei Bldg., 1-7, Uchisaiwai-cho 1-chome, Chiyoda-ku, Tokyo 100	508-0261
Kidder Peabody*	Tokyo Kaijo Bldg. Shinkan, 2-1, Marunouchi 1-chome, Chiyoda-ku, Tokyo 100	213-6111
Kleinwort Benson*	Kokusai Bldg. 810, 1-1, Marunouchi 3-chome, Chiyoda-ku, Tokyo 100	284-0647
Merrill Lynch*	Ote Center Bldg. 11F, 1-3, Otemachi 1-chome, Chiyoda-ku, Tokyo 100	213-7000
Morgan Stanley*	Ote Center Bldg. 8F, 1-3, Otemachi 1-chome, Chiyoda-ku, Tokyo 100	286-9000
Prudential-Bache*	Sumitomo Shibadaimon Bldg., 5-5, Shibadaimon 2-chome, Minato-ku, Tokyo 105	578-0505
Salomon Brothers*	Ark Mori Bldg. 9F, 12-32, Akasaka 1-chome, Minato-ku, Tokyo 107	589-9111

Member List (continued)

Member Securities Companies	Address	Tel.
SBCI*	Shin-Kasumigaseki Bldg. 19F, 3-2, Kasumigaseki 3-chome, Chiyoda-ku, Tokyo 100	595-4300
Schroder*	Ark Mori Bldg. 17F, 12-32, Akasaka 1-chome, Minato-ku, Tokyo 107	587-6800
S. G. Warburg*	New Edobashi Bldg., 7-2, Nihombashi-Honcho 1-chome, Chuo-ku, Tokyo 103	246-4111
Shearson Lehman Hutton*	Ark Mori Bldg. 36F, 12-32, Akasaka 1-chome, Minato-ku, Tokyo 107	505-9000
Smith Barney*	Mitsubishi Bldg., 5-2, Marunouchi 2-chome, Chiyoda-ku, Tokyo 100	201-3101
Société Générale*	Sumitomo Shimbadaimon Bldg. 12F, 5-5, Shibadaimon 2-chome, Minato-ku, Tokyo 105	459-6841
UBS Phillips & Drew*	Yamato Seimei Bldg., 1-7, Uchisaiwaicho 1-chome, Chiyoda-ku, Tokyo 100	595-0211
W. I. Carr*	Yaesu Dai-Bldg. 4F, 1-1, Kyobashi 1-chome, Chuo-ku, Tokyo 104	278-4600

(admitted to be regular members in or after November, 1990)

Barclays de Zoete*	Sin-Kasumigaseki Bldg. 18F, 3-2, Kasumigaseki 3-chome, Chiyoda-ku, Tokyo 100	591-0890
Crédit Lyonnais*	Sumitomo-Fudosan-Hibiya Bldg. 5F, 8-6, Nishi-Shimbashi 2-chome, Minato-ku, Tokyo 105	504-3932
James Capel Pacific*	Kokusai Bldg. 7F, 1-1, Marunouchi 3-chome, Chiyoda-ku, Tokyo 100	282-0111

Note: *"Integrated" securities companies.

A. Component Stocks and Weighting of Asian-Pacific Stock Indices

Companies on ASX Indices as of December 31, 1990

The Alphabetical List of Index companies on the following pages shows the Base Index for each company as well as the Composite Groups to which each stock belongs. The ANZ Bank for example is included in the Index samples for Banks (Group 16), All Ordinaries (Group 30), 20 Leaders (Group 26) and 50 Leaders (Group 31.)

The following table provides a complete list of index numbers and names, with the % weight of each group in the All Ordinaries Index as of December 31, 1990 and the number of companies in each Index sample.

No.	Group	(1) Industry Groups as % of all Ords Index 12/31/90	Co's in each Index 12/31/90
1	Gold	5.8	30
2	Other Metals	13.4	18
3	Solid Fuels	1.1	5
27	All Mining	20.3	53
4	Oil & Gas	4.7	17
5	Diversified Resources	12.8	4
28	All Resources	37.8	74
6	Developers & Contractors	2.8	12
7	Building Materials	7l5	11
8	Alcohol & Tobacco	1.3	5
9	Food & H/Hold Goods	2.9	6
10	Chemicals	1.0	4
11	Engineering	1.6	10
12	Paper & Packaging	3.5	5
13	Retail	3.0	14
14	Transport	3.9	4
15	Media	1.6	4

Companies on ASX Indices as of December 31, 1990 (continued)

No.	Group	(1) Industry Groups as % of all Ords Index 12/31/90	Co's in each Index 12/31/90
16	Banks & Finance	9.9	9
17	Insurance	0.6	2
18	Entrepreneurial Investors	1.1	7
19	Investment & Financial Services	1.7	20
20	Property Trusts	3.6	13
21	Miscellaneous Services	1.5	15
22	Miscellaneous Industrials	1.9	15
23	Diversified Industrial	12.8	12
29	All Industrials	62.2	168
30	All Ordinaries	100.0	242
26	Twenty Leaders	55.4	20
31	Fifty Leaders	80.2	50

ASX Code	Company Name	Base Index	Composite Group			20 Ldrs/ 50 Ldrs	
ABF	Aberfoyle Limited	2	27	28	30		
AGO	ACM Gold Limited	1	27	28	30		
ANH	Action Holdings Limited	13	39	30			
ABC	Adelaide Brighton Cement Holdings Limited	7	29	30			
AST	The Adelaide Steamship Company Limited	18	29	30			
ABA	Advance Bank Australia Limited	16	29	30			
AFG	AFP Group Plc	18	29	30			
AGN	Agen Limited	22	29	30			
ALC	Alcan Australia Limited	2	27	28	30		
AMC	Amcor Limited	12	29	30			31
AMX	Ampol Exploration Limited	4	28	30			
ANZ	Australia & New Zealand Banking Group Ltd.	16	29	30		26	31
ARG	Argo Investments Limited	19	29	30			
ARA	Ariadne Australia Limited	18	29	30			
ARM	Arimco N.L.	1	27	28	30		
ARJ	Armstrong Jones Prime Investment Fund	19	29	30			
ARN	Arnotts Limited	9	29	30			31
ARF	Arrowfield Group Limited	22	29	30			
ACO	Asarco Australia Limited	1	27	28	30		
ASH	Ashton Mining Limited	2	27	28	30		
AKC	Atkins Carlyle Limited	21	29	30			
AEE	Atlas Steels Limited	11	29	30			
AAG	Australian Agricultural Company Limited	22	29	30			
ACH	Australian Chemical Holdings Limited	10	29	30			
AFI	Australian Foundation Investment Co. Ltd.	19	29	30			
AGL	The Australian Gas Light Company	4	28	30			
ANI	Australian National Industries Limited	11	29	30			31
AZT	Aztec Mining Company Limited	1	27	28	30		
AUC	Australian Consolidated Investments Limited	18	29	30			
ACM	Australian Consolidated Minterals Limited	1	27	28	30		
AOG	Australian Oil and Gas Corporation Limited	4	28	30			
AWA	A W A Limited	22	29	30			
BAB	The Ballarat Brewing Company Limited	21	29	30			
BML	Bank of Melbourne Limited	16	29	30			
BQD	Bank of Queensland Limited	16	29	30			
BRM	Barrack Mines Limited	1	27	28	30		

ASX Code	Company Name	Base Index	Composite Group			20 Ldrs/ 50 Ldrs	
BHG	BHP Gold Mines Limited	1	27	28	30		
BOR	Boral Limited	7	29	30		26	31
BOC	Bougainville Copper Limited	2	27	28	30		
BIL	Brambles Industries Limited	14	29	30		26	31
BSH	Brash Holdings Limited	13	29	30			
BKW	Brickworks Limited	19	29	30			
BRG	Bridge Oil Limited	4	28	30			
BRY	Brierley Investments Limited	18	29	30			31
BTE	BT Australian Equity Management Limited	19	29	30			
BTG	BT Global Asset Management Limited	19	29	30			
BTR	BTR Nylex Limited	23	29	30		26	31
BBS	Bundaberg Sugar Company Limited	22	29	30			
BUN	Bunnings Limited	7	29	30			
BPC	Burns, Philp & Company Limited	23	29	30			31
BSD	Burswood Property Trust	21	29	30			
BHM	Broken Hill Metals N.L.	1	27	28	30		
BHP	The Broken Hill Proprietary Company Limited	5	28	30		26	31
CTX	Caltex Australia Limited	21	29	30			
CPY	Capcount Property Trust	20	29	30			
CPL	Capital Property Trust	20	29	30			
CIN	Carlton Investments Limited	19	29	30			
CCL	Coca-Cola Amatil Limited	9	29	30			31
CPM	Central Pacific Minerals N.L.	4	28	30			
CLG	Challenge Bank Limited	16	29	30			
CLY	Clyde Industries Limited	11	29	30			
CMF	Colonial Mutual Australian Property Fund	20	29	30			
CNA	Coal & Allied Industries Limited	3	27	28	30		
CML	Coles Myer Limited	13	29	30		26	31
CDA	Comada Energy Limited	4	28	30			
CMC	Comalco Limited	2	27	28	30		31
CPS	Compass Holdings Limited	14	29	30			
CPH	Command Petroleum Holdings N.L.	4	28	30			
CPW	Computer Power Group Limited	21	29	30			
COM	Comrealty Limited	6	29	30			
CTY	Country Road Limited	13	29	30			
CYG	Coventry Group Limited	23	29	30			
CRA	C R A Limited	2	27	28	30	26	31
CRG	C.E. Crane Holdings Limited	11	29	30			
CSD	Crusader Limited	4	28	30			
CSR	C S R Limited	7	29	30		26	31
CUD	Cudgen R.Z. Limited	2	27	28	30		
CAP	The Cities of Australia Property Trust	20	29	30			

ASX Code	Company Name	Base Index	Composite Group			20 Ldrs/ 50 Ldrs	
CNG	Central Norseman Gold Corporation Limited	1	27	28	30		
CRT	Consolidate Rutile Limited	2	27	28	30		
DAV	Charles Davis Limited	13	29	30			
DFM	Defiance Mills Limited	9	29	30			
DGD	Delta Gold N.L.	1	27	28	30		
DHU	Denehurst Limited	2	27	28	30		
DOM	Dominion Mining Limited	1	27	28	30		
ERL	Elders Resources NZFP Limited	12	29	30			31
EML	Email Limited	22	29	30			31
EMP	Emperor Mines Limited	1	27	28	30		
ENT	E N T Limited	15	29	30			
EQK	Equitilink Limited	19	29	30			
ERA	Energy Resources of Australia Limited	3	27	28	30		
EXI	Exicom Limited	22	29	30			
FAI	FAI Insurances Limited	17	29	30			
FHF	F.H. Faulding & Company Limited	21	29	30			
FLC	Fletcher Challenge Limited	12	29	30			31
FOA	Foodland Associated Limited	13	29	30			
FRG	Forrestania Gold N.L.	1	27	28	30		
FBG	Foster's Brewing Group Limited	23	29	30		26	31
FCL	Futuris Corporation Limited	22	29	30			
FNT	First National Resource Trust	2	27	28	30		
GLG	Galore Group (The) Limited	13	29	30			
GZL	Gazal Corporation Limited	22	29	30			
GPT	General Property Trust	20	29	30			31
GCI	Gibson Chemical Industries Limited	10	29	30			
GMF	Goodman Fielder Wattie Limited	9	29	30			31
GOW	Gowing Bros. Limited	13	29	30			
GWC	Gwalia Consolidated Limited	1	27	28	30		
GMK	Gold Mines of Kalgoorlie Limited	1	27	28	30		
GUD	G.U.D. Holdings Limited	22	29	30			
HAH	James Hardie Industries limited	7	29	30			31
HVN	Harvey Norman Holdings Limited	13	29	30			
HDH	Hawker De Havilland Limited	11	29	30			
HCL	Helm Corporation Limited	19	29	30			
HLG	Highlands Gold Limited	1	27	28	30		
HIL	Hills Industries Limited	22	29	30			
HSG	Homestake Gold of Australia Limited	1	27	28	30		
HCO	Hudson Conway Limited	19	29	30			
HDC	Hastings Deering Corporation Limited	21	29	30			
ICI	I C I Australia Limited	10	29	30			31
ICT	Incitec Limited	10	29	30			
IHL	Independent Holdings Limited	13	29	30			
IRP	International Petroleum Corporation	4	28	30			
JDL	Darrell James Limited	13	29	30			

ASX Code	Company Name	Base Index	Composite Group			20 Ldrs/ 50 Ldrs	
JEN	Jennings Group Limited	6	29	30			
JNP	Jennings Properties Limited	6	29	30			
JOD	David Jones Limited	13	29	30			
JPT	Jupiters Trust	20	29	30			
JDE	Jupiters Development Limited	6	29	30			
KLZ	Kalamazoo Holdings Limited	21	29	30			
KRN	Kern Corporation Limited	6	29	30			
KPF	Kern Property Fund	20	29	30			
KGM	Kidston Gold Mines Limited	1	27	28	30		
KUP	Peter Kurts Properties Limited	6	29	30			
LDA	Leda Limited	6	29	30			
LEI	Leighton Holdings Limited	6	29	30			
LLC	Lend Lease Corporation Limited	6	29	30			31
MQP	MacQuarie Property Trust	20	29	30			
MAH	MacMahon Holdings Limited	6	29	30			
MAG	Magellan Petroleum Australia Limited	4	28	30			
MRK	Markalinga Trust	21	29	30			
MAY	Mayne Nickless Limited	14	29	30			31
MSL	McIntosh Securities Limited	19	29	30			
MCP	McPherson's Limited	23	29	30			
MKA	Meekatharra Minerals Limited	3	27	28	30		
MET	Memtec Limited	22	29	30			
MMF	Metal Manufactures Limited	23	29	30			
MWB	Metway Bank Limited	16	29	30			
MLD	Mildara Wines Limited	8	29	30			
MLT	Milton Corporation Limited	19	29	30			
MIN	Minora Resources N.L.	4	28	30			
MNP	Minproc Holdings Limited	5	28	30			
MRV	Mirvac Limited	6	29	30			
MIM	M.I.M. Holdings Limited	2	27	28	30	26	31
NAB	National Australia Bank Limited	16	29	30		26	31
NCI	National Can Industries Limited	12	29	30			
NCL	National Consolidated Limited	11	29	30			
NMP	National Mutual Property Trust	20	29	30			
NEW	Newmont Australia Limited	1	27	28	30		31
NCP	The News Corporation Limited	15	29	30		26	31
NRN	Nicron Resources Limited	2	27	28	30		
NNA	Nine Network Australia Limited	15	29	30			
NML	Niugini Mining Limited	1	27	28	30		
NDR	Normandy Resources N.L.	1	27	28	30		
NBH	North Broken Hill Peko Limited	5	28	30		26	31
NFM	North Flinders Mines Limited	1	27	28	30		
OAK	Oakbridge Limited	3	27	28	30		
OSH	Oil Search Limited	4	28	30			
OPS	O P S Industries Limited	21	29	30			
OEC	Orbital Engine Corporation Limited	22	29	30			31

ASX Code	Company Name	Base Index	Composite Group			20 Ldrs/ 50 Ldrs	
PMU	Pacific Mutual Australia Limited	19	29	30			
PBB	Pacific BBA Limited	11	29	30			
PDP	Pacific Dunlop Limited	23	29	30		26	31
PTM	Palmer Tube Mills Limited	11	29	30			
PAM	Pan Australia Mining Limited	1	27	28	30		
PCM	Pancontinental Mining Limited	5	28	30			
PGN	Paragon Resources N.L.	1	27	28	30		
PHH	Parbury Henty Holdings Limited	22	29	30			
PAS	Pasminco Limited	2	27	28	30		31
PMT	Permanent Trustee Company Limited	19	29	30			
PNI	Pioneer International Limited	7	29	30		26	31
PLP	Placer Pacific Limited	1	27	28	30	26	31
PLU	Plutonic Resources Limited	1	27	28	30		
POS	Poseidon Limited	1	27	28	30		31
PGO	Poseidon Gold Limited	1	27	28	30		
PBC	Power Brewing Company Limited	8	29	30			
PMV	Premier Investments Limited	19	29	30			
PSL	Petersville Sleigh Limited	23	29	30			
PPT	Perpetual Trustees Australia Limited	19	29	30			
QBE	Q B E Insurance Group Limited	17	29	30			
QRL	QCT Resources Limited	3	27	28	30		31
QDL	QDL Limited	13	29	30			
QIW	QIW Retailers Limited	13	29	30			
QCL	Queensland Cement Limited	7	29	30			
QMC	Queensland Metals Corporation Limited	2	27	28	30		
QUF	Q.U.F. Industries Limited	9	29	30			
RMT	Ramtron Holdings Limited	21	29	30			
REH	Reece Australia Limited	7	29	30			
RTH	Rothmans Holdings Limited	8	29	30			31
RUP	Rural Press Limited	15	29	30			
RGC	Renison Goldfields Consolidated Limited	2	27	28	30		31
SAG	Sagasco Holdings Limited	4	28	30			
STO	Santos Limited	4	28	30		26	31
SCI	Schroders International Property Fund	20	29	30			31
SWD	Sea World Property Trust	21	29	30			
SID	Siddons Ramset Limited	11	29	30			
SMI	Howard Smith Limited	23	29	30			31
SGW	Sons of Gwalia N.L.	1	27	28	30		
SOL	Washington H. Soul Pattinson & Co. Limited	19	29	30			
SPP	Southern Pacific Petroleum N.L.	4	28	30			
SCP	Spicers Paper Limited	12	29	30			
SPS	Spotless Services Limited	21	29	30			
SPT	Spotless Group Limited	21	29	30			

ASX Code	Company Name	Base Index	Composite Group			20 Ldrs/ 50 Ldrs	
SCB	Standard Chartered Bank Australia Limited	16	29	30			
SST	Steamships Trading Company Limited	21	29	30			
SGP	Stockland Trust Group	20	29	30			31
STK	Stroika Limited	18	29	30			
SBG	S.A. Brewing Holdings Limited	23	29	30			31
TGG	Templeton Global Growth Fund Limited	19	29	30			
TNT	T N T Limited	14	29	30		26	31
TTH	Tooth & Company Limited	19	29	30			
TAD	Triad Minerals N.L.	2	27	28	30		
TMA	Tubemakers of Australia Limited	11	29	30			
TYC	Tyco Investments (Australia) Limited	23	29	30			
TYA	Tyndall Australia Limited	19	29	30			
VGS	Vamgas Limited	4	28	30			
VRL	Village Roadshow Limited	22	29	30			
WAC	Waco International Limited	7	29	30			
WYL	Wattyl Limited	7	29	30			
WES	Wesfarmers Limited	23	29	30			31
WTC	Western Capital Limited	18	29	30			
WMC	Western Mining Corporation Holdings Limited	2	27	28	30	26	31
WSF	Westfield Holdings Limited	6	29	30			
WFT	Westfield Trust	20	29	30			31
WEG	George Weston Foods Limited	9	29	30			
WBC	Westpac Banking Corporation	16	29	30		26	31
WSL	Westralian Sands Limited	2	27	28	30		
WFI	Westralian Forest Indutries Limited	7	29	30			
WBW	Wolf Blass Wines Limited	8	29	30			
WPL	Woodside Petroleum Limited	4	28	30			31
WHW	W.D. & H.O. Wills Holdings Limited	8	29	30			
ZAP	Zapopan N.L.	1	27	28	30		

Source: The Sydney Futures Exchange

B. The Barclays Share Price Index

as of April 18, 1991

Companies	Weighting	Price
Fletcher Challenge	25.40	$3.94
Goodman Fielder Wattie	14.06	$2.50
Brierley Investments	12.10	$1.11
Carter Holt Harvey	8.55	$1.80
Lion Nathan	7.01	$3.35
Bank of New Zealand	5.82	$0.67
Magnum Corporation	4.26	$2.73
Air New Zealand Ltd.	2.57	$1.73
Independent News	2.50	$4.15
Wilson and Horton	2.20	$5.90
Robt Jones Inv.	2.07	$0.50
Fernz Corporation	1.36	$5.45
New Zealand Refining	1.12	$8.80
Corporate Investments	1.04	$1.08
Fay Richwhite & Co Ltd	1.03	$0.62
Wilson Neill	0.97	$0.54
Fisher and Paykel	0.94	$1.89
BNZ Finance Ltd	0.89	$1.15
Countrywide	0.76	$2.38
Sanford Limited	0.74	$2.20
Ceramco Ltd	0.59	$1.15
Fortex Group Ltd	0.50	$1.89
City Realties Ltd	0.47	$0.24
Donaghys Industries	0.41	$2.35
Shortland Properties	0.40	$0.70
Jarden Morgan	0.38	$0.27
Cavalier Corporation	0.28	$1.73
Steel and Tube	0.24	$0.53
Ernest Adams Ltd	0.22	$3.40
Owens Group Limited	0.18	$0.77
Mainzeal Group	0.17	$0.21
Reid Farmers Ltd	0.14	$0.60

Companies	Weighting	Price
Air Astley	0.13	$0.63
Amuri Corporation Ltd	0.10	$0.30
Salmond Smith Bio Ltd	0.10	$0.72
Lasercorp Hldgs Ltd	0.09	$0.17
Kupe Group Ltd	0.07	$0.09
Kingsgate	0.07	$0.05
Rendue Corp Ltd	0.05	$0.03
Smiths City Group	0.02	$0.04
	100.0000	

Source: The New Zealand Futures and Options Exchange

C. The Hang Seng Index

as of November 1, 1990

Stock/Index	Close ($)	% Change since last week	% Change since last year	Dividend Yield (%)	P/E Ratio (Times)	Sensitivity Factor #	Market Capital- lization Weighting (%)
Bank East Asia	15.100	+0.67	+2.03	4.14	12.41	0.18	0.89
Hang Seng Bank	23.800	+3.93	+3.93	4.20	12.92	0.64	4.97
Hongkong Bank	4.625	−2.12	−2.12	8.26	6.17	1.04	6.31
Jard Strategic	14.800	+2.07	−1.33	1.69	7.40	0.47	2.26
Finance Sub-index	1787.04	+0.72	+0.27	5.58	8.09	—	14.43
China Light	15.700	−1.26	−0.63	4.59	11.21	1.07	5.49
HK China Gas	10.000	−1.96	−1.96	2.25	20.35	0.35	2.30
HK Electric	9.850	−1.50	−0.51	5.53	11.66	0.65	4.20
HK Telecom	6.200	−0.80	0.00	4.52	15.86	3.60	14.59
K M Bus	5.550	0.00	−0.89	8.65	8.81	0.13	0.47
Utilities Sub-index	4140.23	−1.09	−0.39	4.57	13.97	—	27.05
Cheung Kong	13.200	+4.76	+3.94	2.88	10.48	1.42	6.12
Great Eagle Hldgs	2.100	−4.55	0.00	4.19	2.84	0.23	0.63
Hang Lung	5.400	+4.85	+8.00	7.59	6.26	0.37	1.30
Henderson Land	8.500	−1.16	0.00	4.12	7.80	0.51	2.86
HK Land Holdgs	7.150	+1.42	+1.42	6.71	12.12	0.85	3.95
Hopewell	3.200	−3.03	−1.54	7.50	7.62	0.24	1.01
Hysan	1.130	−2.59	−0.88	7.52	10.97	0.28	1.03
New World Dev	7.550	−1.31	−1.95	8.08	8.39	0.43	2.11
SHK Prop.	15.300	+2.68	+3.38	5.03	9.94	1.11	5.55

Hang Seng Index® Constituent Stocks, November 1, 1991 (continued)

Stock/Index	Close ($)	% Change since last week	% Change since last year	Dividend Yield (%)	P/E Ratio (Times)	Sensitivity Factor #	Market Capital- lization Weighting (%)
Properties Sub-index	4929.01	+1.60	+2.07	5.24	8.95	—	24.57
Cathay Pacific	7.150	0.00	+2.88	5.87	6.17	0.92	4.32
Cavendish Int'l	3.550	0.00	0.00	5.92	10.14	0.47	2.17
Dairy Farm Int'l	10.600	0.00	0.00	2.83	16.69	1.05	3.65
HK Aircraft	14.800	−0.67	+1.37	5.00	9.93	0.12	0.58
HK Hotels	4.000	−3.03	−4.19	4.25	10.81	0.16	0.83
Hut Whampoa	12.600	+2.44	+5.00	4.29	12.60	1.97	8.10
Jardine Hldg	26.800	−3.94	−4.63	3.54	9.08	0.41	3.60
Lai Sun Int'l	1.430	−0.69	0.00	9.79	5.50	0.08	0.39
Mandarin Oriental	4.200	−4.00	−3.45	9.29	5.50	0.08	0.39
Miramar	5.100	−4.14	−4.14	3.33	26.70	0.17	0.57
Swire Pac (A)	15.500	+4.03	+5.44	5.16	7.98	0.63	3.17
TV Broadcasts	5.650	0.00	0.00	10.62	6.65	0.14	0.50
Wharf (Hldgs)	7.800	+1.96	+5.41	5.58	11.87	0.63	3.24
Winsor	7.100	0.00	+0.71	11.27	7.47	0.08	0.39
World Int'l	4.250	+2.41	+4.94	4.47	9.91	0.33	1.84
Com & Ind Sub-index	2775.98	+0.57	+2.03	4.89	9.80	—	33.95
Hang Seng Index®	3058.37	+0.39	+1.12	4.99	10.07	—	100.00

Notes: (1) Historical figures are used in computing yield and P/E ratio.
(2) # Change in HSI (points) per spread change in stock price.

Source: The Hong Kong Futures Exchange

D. The Japan Index

as of April 29, 1991

Air Transport:
All Nippon Airways Co. Ltd.

Banking:
Bank of Tokyo Ltd.
Dai Ichi Kangyo Bank Ltd.
Fuji Bank Ltd.
Mitsubishi Bank Ltd.
Mitsubishi Trust and Banking Corp.
Mitsui Taiyo Kobe Bank Ltd.
Mitsui Trust and Banking Co. Ltd.
Sumitomo Bank Ltd.

Chemicals:
Asahi Denka Kogyo K.K.
Denki Kagaku Kogyo K.K.
Fuji Photo Film Co. Ltd.
Kanegafuchi Chemical Industry Co.
Konica Corporation
Kyowa Hakko Kogyo Co. Ltd.
Mitsubishi Kasei Corporation
Mitsui Toatsu Chemicals Inc.
Nippon Carbide Industries Co. Inc.
Nippon Chemical Industrial Co. Ltd.
Nippon Kayaku Co. Ltd.
Nippon Oil and Fats Co. Ltd.
Nippon Soda Co. Ltd.
Nippon Synthetic Chemical Industry
Nissan Chemical Industries Ltd.
Rasa Industries Ltd.
Shin Etsu Chemical Co. Ltd.
Showa Denko K.K.
Sumitomo Chemical Co. Ltd.

Toagosei Chemical Industry
Tosoh Corporation

Clay and Glass:
Asahi Glass Co. Ltd.
NGK Insulators Ltd.
Nihon Cement Co. Ltd.
Nippon Carbon Co. Ltd.
Nippon Sheet Glass Co. Ltd.
Noritake Co. Ltd.
Onoda Cement Co. Ltd.
Shinagawa Refractories Co. Ltd.
Tokai Carbon Toto Ltd.

Communications:
Nippon Telegraph and Telephone Corporation*

Construction:
Daiwa House Industry Co. Ltd.
Fujita Corporation Kajima Corporation
Ohbayashi Corporation
Sato Kogyo Co. Ltd.
Shimizu Corporation Taisei Corp.
Tekken Construction Toa Corporation
Tobishima Corp.

Drugs:
Dainippon Pharmaceutical Co. Ltd.
Sankyo Co. Ltd.
Takeda Chemical Industries
Yamanouchi Pharmaceutical

*Nippon Tel. & Tel. (Par 50,000 Yen) Prices to be scaled down by 1,000 to yield equivalent of 50 yen par value

Electric Equipment:
Fuji Electric Co. Ltd.
Fujitsu Ltd.
Hitachi Cable Ltd.
Hitachi Ltd.
Matsushita Electric Industrial
Meidensha Corporation
Mitsubishi Electric Corporation
NEC Corporation
Nippondenso Co. Ltd.
Oki Electric Industry Co. Ltd.
Sanyo Electric Co. Ltd.
Sharp Corporation
Sony Corporation
Toshiba Corp.
Yokogawa Electric
Yuasa Battery

Electric Power:
Kansai Electric Power Co.**
Tokyo Electric Power**

Foods:
Ajinomoto Co.
Inc. Asahi Breweries Ltd.
Godo Shusei Co. Ltd.
Kikkoman Corporation
Kirin Brewery Co. Ltd.
Meiji Milk Products Co. Ltd.
Meiji Seika Kaisha Ltd.
Morinaga and Co. Ltd.
Nichirei Corporation
Nippon Beet Sugar Manufacturing Co.
Nippon Flour Mills Co. Ltd.
Nisshin Flour Milling Co. Ltd.
Nisshin Oil Mills Ltd.
Sapporo Breweries Ltd.

Gas Services:
Tokyo Gas

Insurance:
Taisho Marine and Fire Insurance
Tokio Marine and Fire Insurance
Yasuda Fire and Marine Insurance

Iron & Steel:
Japan Steel Works Ltd.
Mitsubishi Steel Manufacturing Co.
Nippon Denko Co. Ltd.
Nippon Metal Industry Co. Ltd.
Nippon Stainless Steel Co. Ltd.
Nippon Yakin Kogyo Sumitomo Metal
Industries Ltd.

Machinery:
Chiyodo Corporation
Ebara Corporation Komatsu Ltd.
Kubota Corporation
Nachi Fujikoshi Corporation
Niigata Engineering Co. Ltd.
Nippon Seiko K.K.
NTN Corporation
Okuma Machinery Works Ltd.

Marine Products:
Kyokuyo Co. Ltd.
Nichiro Corporation
Nippon Suisan Kaisha Ltd.

Metal Products:
Dowa Mining Co. Ltd.
Fujikura Ltd.
Furukawa Co. Ltd.
Furukawa Electric Co. Ltd.
Mitsubishi Metal Corporation
Mitsui Mining and Smelting Co. Ltd.
Nippon Light Metal Co. Ltd.
Nippon Mining Co. Ltd.
Shimura Kako Co. Ltd.
Showa Electric Wire and Cable Co. Ltd.
Sumitomo Electric Industries Ltd.
Sumitomo Metal Mining Co. Ltd.
Toho Zinc Tokyo Rope Mfg.
Toyo Seikan Kaisha

Mining:
Mitsui Mining Co. Ltd.
Sumitomo Coal Mining Co. Ltd.
Teikoku Oil

**Tokyo Electric Power, Kansai Electric Power, Toho Co. (Par 500 Yen) Prices to be scaled down by 10 to yield equivalent of 50 yen par value

Motor Vehicles:
Hino Motors Ltd.
Honda Motor Co. Ltd.
Isuzu Motors Ltd.
Mazda Motor Corporation
Nissan Motor Co. Ltd.
Suzuki Motor Co. Ltd.
Toyota Motor Corp.

Other Manufacturing:
Dai Nippon Printing Co. Ltd.
Toppan Printing
Yamaha Corporation
Yamaha Motor

Paper & Pulp:
Hokuetsu Paper Mills Ltd.
Honshu Paper Co. Ltd.
Jujo Paper Co. Ltd.
Mitsubishi Paper Mills Ltd.
Oji Paper Co. Ltd.
Sanyo Kokusaku Pulp Co. Ltd.

Petroleum:
Mitsubishi Oil Co. Ltd.
Nippon Oil Co. Ltd.
Showa Shell Sekiyu K.K.
Tonen Corporation

Precision Instruments:
Canon Inc. Citizen Watch Co. Ltd.
Nikon Corporation Ricoh Co. Ltd.

Railroad Transport:
Keihin Electric Express Railway Co.
Keio Teito Electric Railway Co. Ltd.
Keisei Electric Railway Co. Ltd.
Kinki Nippon Railway Co. Ltd.
Odakyu Electric Railway
Tobu Railway
Tokyu Corp.

Real Estate:
Heiwa Real Estate Co. Ltd.

Mitsubishi Estate Co. Ltd.
Mitsui Real Estate Development Co.

Retail Stores:
Maruzen Co. Ltd.
Matsuzakaya Co. Ltd.
Mitsukoshi Ltd.
Takashimaya Co.
Tokyu Department Store

Rubber Products:
Bridgestone Corporation
Yokohama Rubber

Sea Transport:
Kawasaki Kisen Kaisha Ltd.
Mitsui O.S.K. Lines Ltd.
Nippon Yusen K.K.
Showa Line Ltd.

Securities/Finance:
Daiwa Securities Co. Ltd.
Japan Securities Finance Co. Ltd.
Nikko Securities Co. Ltd.
Nippon Shinpan Co. Ltd.
Nomura Securities Co. Ltd.

Services:
Korakuen Co. Ltd.
Shochiku Co. Ltd.
Toei Co.
Toho Co.**

Shipbuilding:
Hitachi Zosen Corporation
Ishikawajima Harima Heavy Industries
Mitsubishi Heavy Industries
Mitsui Engineering and Shipbuilding

Textile Products:
Asahi Chemical Industry Co. Ltd.
Daito Woolen Spinning and Weaving
    Co.
Fuji Spinning Co. Ltd.
Japan Wool Textile Co. Ltd.
Kanebo Ltd.

**Tokyo Electric Power, Kansai Electric Power, Toho Co. (Par 500 Yen) Prices to be scaled down by 10 to yield equivalent of 50 yen par value

Katakura Industries Co. Ltd.
Kuraray Co. Ltd.
Nisshinbo Industries Inc.
Nitto Boseki Co. Ltd.
Teikoku Sen I Co. Ltd.
Toho Rayon Toray Industries
Toyobo Co.

Trade:
C. Itoh & Co. Ltd.
Iwatani International Corporation
Marubeni Corporation
Mitsubishi Corporation Mitsui and Co.
    Ltd.
Sumitomo Corporation

Transport Equipment:
Nippon Sharyo Ltd.

Trucking:
Nippon Express Co. Ltd.

Warehousing:
Mitsubishi Warehouse and Transporta-
    tion
Mitsui Warehouse Co., Inc.

SYM	NAME	WEIGHT
1301	KYOKUYO CO. LTD.	0.36%
1331	NICHIRO CORPORATION	0.21%
1332	NIPPON SUISAN KAISHA LTD.	0.24%
1501	MITSUI MINING CO. LTD.	0.36%
1503	SUMITOMO COAL MINING CO. LTD.	0.36%
1601	TEIKOKU OIL	0.39%
1801	TAISEI CORPORATION	0.38%
1802	OBAYASHI CORPORATION	0.46%
1803	SHIMIZU CORPORATION	0.61%
1804	SATO KOGYO CO. LTD.	0.55%
1805	TOBISHIMA CORPORATION	0.51%
1806	FUJITA CORPORATION	0.44%
1812	KAJIMA CORPORATION FL	0.60%
1815	TEKKEN CONSTRUCTION	0.45%
1885	TOA CORPORATION FL	0.34%
1925	DAIWA HOUSE INDUSTRY CO. LTD. FL	0.77%
2001	NIPPON FLOUR MILLS CO. LTD.	0.29%
2002	NISSHIN FLOUR MILLING CO. LTD.	0.57%
2108	NIPPON BEET SUGAR MANUFACTURING CO.	0.31%
2201	MORINAGA AND CO. LTD.	0.27%
2202	MEIJI SEIKA KAISHA LTD.	0.30%
2261	MEIJI MILK PRODUCTS CO. LTD.	0.30%
2501	SAPPORO BREWERIES LTD.	0.50%
2502	ASAHI BREWERIES LTD.	0.53%
2503	KIRIN BREWERY CO. LTD. FL	0.61%
2533	GODO SHUSEI CO. LTD.	0.44%
2602	NISSHIN OIL MILLS LTD.	0.41%
2801	KIKKOMAN CORPORATION	0.45%
2802	AJINOMOTO CO. INC. FL	0.62%
2871	NICHIREI CORPORATION FL	0.34%
3001	KATAKURA INDUSTRIES CO. LTD.	0.90%
3101	TOYOBO CO. FL	0.21%
3102	KANEBO LTD. FL	0.24%
3104	FUJI SPINNING CO. LTD.	0.28%
3105	NISSHINBO INDUSTRIES INC.	0.40%
3110	NITTO BOSEKI CO. LTD.	0.25%
3201	JAPAN WOOL TEXTILE CO. LTD.	0.67%
3202	DAITO WOOLEN SPINNING AND WEAVING CO	0.43%
3302	TEIKOKU SEN I CO. LTD.	0.65%
3402	TORAY INDUSTRIES	0.25%
3403	TOHO RAYON	0.34%
3405	KURARAY CO. LTD.	0.58%
3407	ASAHI CHEMICAL INDUSTRY CO. LTD.	0.31%

SYM	NAME	WEIGHT
3702	SANYO KOKUSAKU PULP CO. LTD.	0.26%
3861	OJI PAPER CO. LTD.	0.36%
3862	HONSHU PAPER CO. LTD.	0.50%
3863	JUJO PAPER CO. LTD.	0.28%
3864	MITSUBISHI PAPER MILLS LTD.	0.28%
3865	HOKUETSU PAPER MILLS LTD.	0.43%
4001	MITSUI TOATSU CHEMICALS INC.	0.21%
4004	SHOWA DENKO K.K.	0.20%
4005	SUMITOMO CHEMICAL CO. LTD.	0.22%
4010	MITSUBISHI KASEI CORPORATION	0.23%
4021	NISSAN CHEMICAL INDUSTRIES LTD.	0.29%
4022	RASA INDUSTRIES LTD.	0.35%
4041	NIPPON SODA CO. LTD.	0.36%
4042	TOSOH CORPORATION	0.25%
4045	TOAGOSEI CHEMICAL INDUSTRY	0.30%
4061	DENKI KAGAKU KOGYO K.K.	0.23%
4063	SHIN ETSU CHEMICAL CO. LTD.	0.65%
4064	NIPPON CARBIDE INDUSTRIES CO. INC.	0.30%
4092	NIPPON CHEMICAL INDUSTRIAL CO. LTD.	0.51%
4118	KANEGAFUCHI CHEMICAL INDUSTRY CO.	0.28%
4151	KYOWA HAKKO KOGYO CO. LTD.	0.52%
4201	NIPPON SYNTHETIC CHEMICAL INDUSTRY	0.40%
4272	NIPPON KAYAKU CO. LTD. FL	0.35%
4401	ASAHI DENKA KOGYO K.K.	0.41%
4403	NIPPON OIL AND FATS CO. LTD. FL	0.34%
4501	SANKYO CO. LTD. FL	0.98%
4502	TAKEDA CHEMICAL INDUSTRIES FL	0.67%
4503	YAMANDUCHI PHARMACEUTICAL	1.16%
4506	DAINIPPON PHARMACEUTICAL CO. LTD.	0.85%
4901	FUJI PHOTO FILM CO. LTD. FL	1.40%
4902	KONICA CORPORATION FL	0.41%
5001	NIPPON OIL CO. LTD. FL	0.42%
5002	SHOWA SHELL SEKIYU K.K.	0.56%
5004	MITSUBISHI OIL CO. LTD.	0.45%
5005	TONEN CORPORATION	0.66%
5108	BRIDGESTONE CORPORATION FL	0.43%
5201	ASAHI GLASS CO. LTD. FL	0.56%
5202	NIPPON SHEET GLASS CO. LTD. FL	0.27%
5231	NIHON CEMENT CO. LTD. FL	0.38%
5233	ONODA CEMENT CO. LTD. FL	0.27%
5301	TOKAI CARBON	0.32%
5302	NIPPON CARBON CO. LTD.	0.29%
5331	NORITAKE CO. LTD.	0.57%

SYM	NAME	WEIGHT
5332	TOTO LTD.	0.72%
5333	NGK INSULATORS LTD.	0.46%
5351	SHINAGAWA REFRACTORIES CO. LTD.	0.47%
5405	SUMITOMO METAL INDUSTRIES LTD.	0.20%
5478	NIPPON STAINLESS STEEL CO. LTD.	0.34%
5479	NIPPON METAL INDUSTRY CO. LTD.	0.28%
5480	NIPPON YAKIN KOGYO	0.39%
5563	NIPPON DENKO CO. LTD.	0.30%
5631	JAPAN STEEL WORKS LTD.	0.28%
5632	MITSUBISHI STEEL MANUFACTURING CO.	0.49%
5701	NIPPON LIGHT METAL CO. LTD.	0.38%
5706	MITSUI MINING AND SMELTING LTD.	0.22%
5707	TOHO ZINC	0.33%
5711	MITSUBISHI MATERIALS CORPORATION	0.28%
5712	NIPPON MINING CO. LTD.	0.23%
5713	SUMITOMO METAL MINING CO. LTD.	0.50%
5714	DOWA MINING CO. LTD.	0.29%
5715	FURUKAWA CO. LTD.	0.35%
5721	SHIMURA KAKO CO. LTD.	0.35%
5801	FURUKAWA ELECTRIC CO. LTD.	0.32%
5802	SUMITOMO ELECTRIC IND. LTD.	0.57%
5803	FUJIKURA LTD.	0.38%
5805	SHOWA ELECTRIC WIRE AND CABLE CO LTD	0.32%
5812	HITACHI CABLE LTD.	0.42%
5901	TOYO SEIKAN KAISHA	1.70%
5981	TOKYO ROPE MFG.	0.48%
6011	NIIGATA ENGINEERING CO. LTD.	0.29%
6103	OKUMA CORPORATION	0.52%
6301	KOMATSU LTD.	0.35%
6326	KUBOTA CORPORATION FL	0.31%
6361	EBARA CORPORATION FL	0.65%
6366	CHIYODA CORPORATION	1.10%
6471	NIPPON SEIKO K.K.	0.32%
6472	NTN CORPORATION	0.31%
6474	NACHI FUJIKOSHI CORPORATION	0.33%
6501	HITACHI LTD. FL	0.48%
6502	TOSHIBA CORPORATION LTD. FL	0.32%
6503	MITSUBISHI ELECTRIC CORPORATION	0.31%
6504	FUJI ELECTRIC CO. LTD. FL	0.34%
6508	MEIDENSHA CORPORATION	0.52%
6701	NEC CORPORATION FL	0.62%
6702	FUJITSU LTD.	0.46%
6703	OKI ELECTRIC INDUSTRY CO. LTD. FL	0.30%
6752	MATSUSHITA ELECTRIC INDUSTRIAL	0.68%

SYM	NAME	WEIGHT
6753	SHARP CORPORATION FL	0.62%
6758	SONY CORPORATION FL	2.46%
6764	SANYO ELECTRIC CO. LTD. FL	0.24%
6841	YOKOGAWA ELECTRIC	0.55%
6902	NIPPONDENSO CO. LTD.	0.68%
6933	YUASA BATTERY	0.47%
7003	MITSUI ENG. AND SHIPBUILDING FL	0.24%
7004	HITACHI ZOSEN CORPORATION FL	0.25%
7011	MITSUBISHI HEAVY INDUSTRIES	0.30%
7013	ISHIKAWAJIMA HARIMA HEAVY IND.	0.29%
7102	NIPPON SHARYO LTD.	0.60%
7201	NISSAN MOTOR CO. LTD. FL	0.31%
7202	ISUZU MOTORS LTD.	0.19%
7203	TOYOTA MOTOR CORP. FL	0.73%
7205	HINO MOTORS LTD.	0.38%
7261	MAZDA MOTOR CORPORATION	0.24%
7267	HONDA MOTOR CO. LTD. FL	0.53%
7269	SUZUKI MOTOR CORPORATION	0.28%
7272	YAMAHA MOTOR	0.35%
7731	NIKON CORPORATION	0.53%
7751	CANON INC. FL	0.63%
7752	RICOH CO. LTD. FL	0.30%
7762	CITIZEN WATCH CO. LTD.	0.40%
7911	TOPPAN PRINTING FL	0.59%
7912	DAI NIPPON PRINTING CO. LTD.	0.65%
7951	YAMAHA CORPORATION	0.71%
8001	C ITOH AND CO. LTD.	0.27%
8002	MARUBENI CORPORATION	0.26%
8031	MITSUI AND CO. LTD.	0.30%
8053	SUMITOMO CORPORATION	0.44%
8058	MITSUBISHI CORPORATION	0.52%
8088	IWATANI INTERNATIONAL CORPORATION	0.37%
8231	MITSUKOSHI LTD.	0.50%
8232	TOKYU DEPARTMENT STORE	0.55%
8233	TAKASHIMAYA CO.	0.86%
8235	MATSUZAKAYA CO. LTD.	1.54%
8236	MARUZEN CO. LTD.	0.44%
8311	DAI ICHI KANGYO BANK LTD.	0.92%
8313	BANK OF TOKYO LTD.	0.55%
8314	MITSUI TAIYO KOBE BANK LTD.	0.78%
8315	MITSUBISHI BANK LTD.	1.07%
8317	FUJI BANK LTD.	1.06%
8318	SUMITOMO BANK LTD.	0.93%
8401	MITSUI TRUST AND BANKING CO. LTD.	0.60%

SYM	NAME	WEIGHT
8402	MITSUBISHI TRUST AND BANKING CORP.	0.74%
8511	JAPAN SECURITIES FINANCE CO. LTD.	0.72%
8583	NIPPON SHINPAN CO. LTD.	0.44%
8601	DAIWA SECURITIES CO. LTD.	0.52%
8603	NIKKO SECURITIES CO. LTD.	0.40%
8604	NOMURA SECURITIES CO. LTD.	0.84%
8751	TOKIO MARINE AND FIRE INSUR. CO.	0.53%
8752	MITSUI MARINE AND FIRE INSUR. CO LTD	0.40%
8755	YASUDA FIRE AND MARINE INSURANCE CO.	0.37%
8801	MITSUI REAL ESTATE DEVELOP. CO.	0.59%
8802	MITSUBISHI ESTATE CO. LTD.	0.60%
8803	HEIWA REAL ESTATE CO. LTD. FL	0.42%
9001	TOBU RAILWAY	0.34%
9005	TOKYU CORP. FL	0.62%
9006	KEIHIN ELECTRIC EXPRESS RAILWAY CO.	0.38%
9007	ODAKYU ELECTRIC RAILWAY	0.42%
9008	KEIO TEITO ELECTRIC RAILWAY CO. LTD.	0.38%
9009	KEISEI ELECTRIC RAILWAY CO. LTD. FL	0.67%
9041	KINKI NIPPON RAILWAY CO. LTD.	0.34%
9062	NIPPON EXPRESS CO. LTD. FL	0.36%
9101	NIPPON YUSEN K.K. FL	0.24%
9104	MITSUI O.S.K. LINES LTD. FL	0.23%
9107	KAWASAKI KISEB KAISHA LTD. FL	0.20%
9126	SHOWA LINE LTD.	0.22%
9202	ALL NIPPON AIRWAYS CO. LTD. FL	0.56%
9301	MITSUBISHI WAREHOUSE AND TRANSPORT.	0.62%
9302	MITSUI WAREHOUSE CO. LTD.	0.39%
9432	NIPPON TEL AND TEL FL	0.37%
9501	TOKYO ELECTRIC POWER FL	0.15%
9503	KANSAI ELECTRIC POWER CO. INC. FL	0.11%
9531	TOKYO GAS CO. LTD.	0.24%
9601	SHOCHIKU CO. LTD.	1.21%
9602	TOHO CO.	0.96%
9605	TOEI CO.	0.42%
9681	TOKYO DOME CORPORATION	1.26%

Source: The American Stock Exchange

III E. The Nagoya Option 25 Index

Company name	Business line	Stock price (C) (yen)	No. of listed shares (unit: 1,000)	Market value (A) (unit: 1 mill. yen)	Trading volume		A / B	C / D
					Jan. to Dec. '87	Jan. '85 to Dec. '87		
Kajima Corporation	Construction	1,270	842,218	1,069,616	769,985	2,872,955	1.78%	3.81%
Kirin Brewery Co., Ltd.	Foods	1,880	903,340	1,698,279	564,636	1,701,440	2.83	5.64
Toray Industries, Inc.	Textiles	680	1,309,070	890,167	1,709,522	3,593,921	1.48	2.04
Oji Paper Co., Ltd.	Pulp and Paper	1,050	566,002	594,302	738,107	1,790,924	0.99	3.15
Sumitomo Chemical Co., Ltd.	Chemicals	880	1,573,607	1,384,774	2,964,449	5,275,867	2.31	2.64
Takeda Chemical Industries, Ltd.	Chemicals	2,850	785,910	2,239,843	498,963	1,395,337	3.74	8.54
Nippon Oil Co., Ltd.	Oil and Coal Products	1,040	1,046,628	1,088,493	677,691	2,198,326	1.82	3.12
Asahi Glass Co., Ltd.	Glass & Ceramics Products	1,660	1,133,992	1,882,426	516,856	925,293	3.14	4.98
Nippon Steel Corporation	Iron and Steel	359	6,636,705	2,382,577	29,241,292	41,150,124	3.98	1.08
Mitsubishi Metal Corporation	Nonferro Metals	722	602,610	435,084	2,001,761	2,920,177	0.73	2.17
Komatsu Ltd.	Machinery	580	862,098	500,016	586,382	1,095,133	0.83	1.74
Hitachi, Ltd.	Electric Machinery	1,150	2,913,440	3,350,456	3,413,462	6,561,653	5.59	3.45
NEC Corporation	Electric Machinery	1,870	1,462,134	2,734,190	1,525,186	3,171,065	4.56	5.61
Matsushita Electric Industrial Co., Ltd.	Electrical machinery	2,030	1,860,284	3,776,376	1,787,006	3,192,058	6.30	6.09

Source: The Nagoya Stock Exchange

F. The Nikkei Stock Average

The Nikkei Stock Average

	(A)*	(B)*	(C)*	(D)*	(E)*	(F)*	(G)*	(H)*	(I)*
Foods									
1. Nippon Flour Mills	865	0.2849%	1577	433	2.40	41.50	2.41	0.69	1.10
2. Nisshin Flour Mills	1490	0.4908%	3039	130	−3.90	26.43	3.78	0.47	0.99
3. Taito	1470	0.4842%	729	81	26.70	155.08	0.64	0.34	0.31
4. Nippon Beef Sugar	1290	0.4249%	1977	1062	63.90	94.14	1.06	0.39	0.97
5. Morinaga	838	0.2760%	2222	661	0.40	111.10	0l90	0.60	0.82
6. Meiji Deika	906	0.2984%	3528	722	−7.60	50.40	1.98	0.66	0.91
7. Meiji Milk Products	836	0.2754%	2346	412	−10.10	80.89	1.24	0l72	1.09
8. Sapporo Breweries	1500	0l4941%	5005	532	−11.80	111.22	0.90	0.33	1.05
9. Asahi Breweries	1810	0.5962%	7201	705	−11.50	120.01	0.83	0.44	1.29
10. Kirin Brewery	1500	0.5105%	15535	1081	−14.40	53.20	1.88	0.48	1.46
11. Takara Shuzo	930	0.3063%	1964	500	3.30	78.55	1.27	0.65	0.91
12. Godo Shusei	1880	0.6192%	890	145	16.00	329.45	0.30	0.27	0.59
13. Sanraku	1130	0.3722%	1615	258	−11.00	89.74	1.11	0.44	0.62
14. Honen	935	0.3080%	777	223	7.50	7776.54	0.13	0.55	0.70
15. Nisshin Oil Mills	1170	0.3854%	1621	456	13.60	54.05	1.85	0.60	0.75
16. Kikkoman	1320	0.4348%	2237	301	14.80	111.86	0.89	0.53	1.09
17. Ajinomoto	1900	0.6258%	12295	597	−32.90	76.84	1.30	0.53	1.09
18. Nichirei	1010	0.3327%	3110	989	−11.40	81.84	1.22	.059	1.15
Textile Products									
1. Katakura Industries	5000	1.6469%	1754	45	85.90	167.00	0.60	0.16	0.99
2. Toyobo	630	0.2075%	4351	1697	−30.80	58.01	1.72	0.79	1.46
3. Kanebo	685	0.2256%	3402	861	−18.90	100.05	1.00	0.73	0.84
4. Unitika	610	0.2009%	2903	1120	−23.40	87.98	1.14	0.82	1.19
5. Fuji Spinning	736	0.2424%	795	275	−4.30	83.67	1.20	0.68	0.50
6. Nisshinbo Industries	1200	0.3953%	2811	580	−13.70	46.85	2.13	0.58	1.46
7. Nitto Boseki	675	0.2223%	1672	596	−14.70	79.61	1.26	0.96	0.93

The Nikkei Stock Average (continued)

	(A)*	(B)*	(C)*	(D)*	(E)*	(F)*	(G)*	(H)*	(I)*
8. Japan Wool Textile	2160	0.7115%	2067	121	24.90	76.54	1.31	0.27	1.51
9. Daito Wool Spinning	1430	0.4710%	429	86	58.90	NA	NA	0.00	0.93
10. Teikoku Sen-I	2130	0.7016%	574	59	145.40	NA	NA	0.00	0.11
11. Teijin	700	0.2306%	6747	2760	−19.10	32.13	3.11	1.00	1.15
12. Toray Industries	715	0.2355%	9909	3098	−27.00	33.03	3.03	1.05	1.28
13. Toho Rayon	900	0.2964%	818	457	−3.20	109.07	0.92	0.56	0.92
14. Mitsubishi Rayon	610	0.2009%	3807	1753	−26.90	66.79	1.50	0.82	1.05
15. Kuraray	1470	0.4842%	3947	858	16.70	56.38	1.77	0.41	0.75
16. Asahi Chemical Ind.	805	0.2651%	10928	2206	−39.90	33.12	3.02	1.12	1.14

Paper and Pulp

	(A)*	(B)*	(C)*	(D)*	(E)*	(F)*	(G)*	(H)*	(I)*
1. Sanyo-Kokusaku Pulp	650	0.2141%	2918	1200	−46.30	32.42	3.08	1.15	1.21
2. Oki Paper	1000	0.3294%	6072	1447	−49.50	26.40	3.79	0.85	1.35
3. Honshu Paper	1710	0.5632%	5708	2006	67.60	190.26	0.53	0.35	0.80
4. Jujo Paper	730	0.2404%	3483	826	−44.30	30.29	3.30	0.96	1.13
5. Mitsunishi Paper	849	0.2796%	2734	648	−39.80	32.55	3.07	0.94	0.86
6. Hokuetsu Paper Mills	980	0.3228%	1217	232	−16.20	33.82	2.96	0.71	0.86

Chemicals

	(A)*	(B)*	(C)*	(D)*	(E)*	(F)*	(G)*	(H)*	(I)*
1. Mitsui Toatsu Chemical	661	0.2177%	5009	2730	−43.70	41.74	2.40	0.91	1.59
2. Showa Denko	659	0.2171%	6835	2536	−44.20	42.72	2.34	0.91	1.31
3. Sumitomo Chemical	630	0.2075%	10214	1955	−41.70	46.23	2.15	0.95	1.59
4. Mitsunishi Kasei	700	0.2306%	9847	1576	−42.10	54.70	1.83	0.86	1.47
5. Nissan Chemical Ind.	1030	0.3393%	1426	1143	21.50	95.06	1.05	0.49	0.71
6. Rasa Industries	931	0.3066%	519	405	21.40	97.98	1.02	0.53	0.86
7. Nippon Soda	900	0.2964%	756	476	1.10	88.94	1.12	0.56	1.07
8. Tosoh	605	0.1993%	2749	1313	−39.20	54.98	1.82	0.83	1.35
9. Toagosei Chemical	841	0.2770%	1758	506	−25.70	35.51	2.82	0.71	1.33
10. Denki Kagaku Kogyo	646	0.2128%	3070	1142	−40.20	51.16	1.95	0.93	1.42
11. Shin-Etsu Chemical	1490	0.4908%	4780	881	−24.70	40.86	2.45	0.49	1.08
12. Nippon Carbide Ind.	899	0.2961%	595	194	5.50	77.46	1.29	0.68	0.74
13. Nippon Chemical Ind.	2340	0.7707%	1755	701	141.20	168.75	0.59	0.13	0.75

The Nikkei Stock Average (continued)

	(A)*	(B)*	(C)*	(D)*	(E)*	(F)*	(G)*	(H)*	(I)*
14. Kyowa Hakko Kogyo	1300	0.4282%	5801	609	-16.10	52.47	1.91	0.46	1.54
15. Nippon Synthetic	1100	0.3623%	799	194	11.40	57.07	1.75	0.45	0.62
16. Ube Industries	618	0.2036%	5141	1215	-33.50	64.27	1.56	0.81	1.37
17. Nippon Kayaku	1060	0.3491%	1928	1119	-15.20	38.56	2.59	0.71	1.15
18. Asahi Denka Kogyo	1200	0.3953%	877	309	22.40	67.44	1.48	0.42	0.54
19. Nippon Oil and Fats	980	0.3228%	2132	449	-16.90	62.71	1.59	0.61	1.14
20. Fuji Photo Film	3910	1.2879%	16556	2500	23.20	20.19	4.95	0.38	0.50
21. Konica	1400	0.4611%	4991	1082	30.80	55.46	1.80	0.71	0.69
Drugs									
1. Sankyo	2150	0.7082%	7683	1108	-10.40	65.67	1.52	0.35	1.31
2. Takeda Chemical Ind.	1750	0.5764%	15268	830	-28.60	41.26	2.42	0.57	1.29
3. Yamanouchi Pharmaceutical	2620	0.8630%	7655	519	-27.00	31.90	3.14	0.38	0.62
4. Dainippon Pharmaceutical	2530	0.8333%	3797	193	14.00	63.28	1.58	0.30	0.58
Petroleum									
1. Nippon Oil	1050	0.3458%	12814	3112	-34.80	116.49	0.86	0.57	0.92
2. Showa Shell Sekiyu	1180	0.3887%	3222	344	-15.70	53.71	1.86	0.51	1.01
3. Mitsubishi Oil	955	0.3146%	3299	1965	-25.40	54.99	1.82	0.63	0.97
4. Tonen	1580	0.5204%	10215	377	-11.20	56.75	1.76	1.58	0.61
Rubber									
1. Yokohama Rubber	1200	0.3953%	2925	731	12.10	37.50	2.67	0.50	0.69
2. Bridgestone	1420	0.4677%	10898	2297	-4.70	23.19	4.31	0.85	0.92
Clay and Glass									
1. Asahi Glass	1730	0.5698%	20150	1236	-24.50	42.87	2.33	0.52	0.87
2. Nippon Sheet Glass	851	0.2803%	3713	1607	-17.40	33.75	2.96	0.71	0.98
3. Nihon Cement	920	0.3030%	2992	675	-31.30	49.87	2.01	0.65	1.17
4. Sumitomo Cement	680	0.2240%	2081	718	-31.30	39.27	2.55	0.88	1.12
5. Onoda Cement	705	0.2322%	3266	982	-37.10	48.03	2.08	0.78	1.56
6. Mitsubishi Mining	650	0.2141%	2937	928	-35.60	36.71	2.72	0.92	1.21
7. Tokai Carbon	850	0.2800%	1335	650	-13.10	111.28	0.90	0.59	0.82
8. Nippon Carbon	831	0.2737%	983	1135	7.90	409.70	0.24	0.24	0.97
9. Noritake	1480	0.4875%	2084	288	22.30	69.46	1.44	0.54	0.73
10. Toto	1980	0.6522%	6647	858	-0.05	39.10	2.56	0.45	1.05

The Nikkei Stock Average (continued)

	(A)*	(B)*	(C)*	(D)*	(E)*	(F)*	(G)*	(H)*	(I)*
11. MGK Insulators	1310	0.4315%	4624	1119	−22.00	51.38	1.95	0.61	0.70
12. Shinagawa Refractory	1690	0.5566%	1115	256	20.70	202.80	0.49	0.30	0.77

Iron and Steel

1. Nippon Steel	520	0.1713%	35812	15969	−44.40	35.81	2.79	1.15	1.40
2. Kawasaki Steel	519	0.1709%	16874	8747	−43.70	42.19	2.37	1.16	1.29
3. NKK	500	0.1647%	17614	7694	−44.40	58.71	1.70	1.20	1.41
4. Sumitomo Metal Ind.	539	0.1775%	16621	14765	−36.00	46.46	2.15	1.11	1.34
5. Kobe Steel	555	0.1828%	15637	7736	−38.00	62.55	1.60	1.08	1.10
6. Nippon Stainless	930	0.3063%	885	347	−36.70	32.19	3.11	0.54	0.56
7. Nippon Metal Ind.	879	0.2895%	1400	594	−24.90	51.87	1.93	0.58	0.50
8. Nippon Yakin Kogyo	750	0.2470%	1245	687	−49.70	49.78	2.01	0.67	0.93
9. Nippon Denko	915	0.3014%	1040	456	−21.10	104.00	0.96	0.55	0.44
10. Japan Steel Works	753	0.2480%	2797	1705	−35.10	17.48	5.72	0.53	1.09
11. Mitsubishi Steel Mfg	1450	0.4776%	2088	417	−40.30	696.01	0.14	0.00	0.74

Metal products

1. Nipponlight Metal	780	0.2569%	3436	1094	−12.00	49.08	2.04	0.64	1.07
2. Mitsui Mining & Smelting	668	0.2200%	3246	2790	−28.00	43.29	2.31	0.60	0.80
3. Toho Zinc	985	0.3244%	985	382	23.10	42.64	2.35	0.51	0.60
4. Mitsubishi Metal	770	0.2536%	5274	3748	−31.30	47.95	2.09	0.78	1.12
5. Nippon Mining	799	0.2632%	7054	4002	−20.00	70.54	1.42	0.63	1.15
6. Sumitomo Metal-mining	1290	0.4249%	6447	3870	−9.20	67.87	1.47	0.54	1.04
7. Dowa Mining	910	0.2997%	2209	1628	−3.10	81.82	1.22	0.55	0.88
8. Furukawa	872	0.2872%	2143	1175	−9.80	47.62	2.10	0.69	0.92
9. Shimura Kako	1580	0.5204%	646	336	122.80	248.29	0.40	0.00	0.32
10. Shimitomo Electric	725	0.2388%	4731	3057	−38.60	63.08	1.59	0.83	1.48
11. Sumitomo Electric	1400	0.4611%	9847	1368	−10.80	61.54	1.62	0.54	1.02
12. Fujikura	850	0.2800%	2835	883	−36.10	65.93	1.52	0.76	1.01
13. Showa Electric Wire	929	0.3060%	1971	1008	−28.00	65.71	1.52	0.65	1.03
14. Toyo Seikan	3400	1.1199%	5715	213	42.30	32.66	3.06	0.22	0.68
15. Tokyo Rope Mfg.	1440	0.4743%	2037	331	−38.70	185.19	0.54	0.35	0.58

Machinery

1. Niigata Engineering	746	0.2457%	2488	820	−16.00	138.20	0.72	0.54	1.07

The Nikkei Stock Average (continued)

	(A)*	(B)*	(C)*	(D)*	(E)*	(F)*	(G)*	(H)*	(I)*
2. Okuma Machinery Works	1546	0.5092%	2042	426	13.20	40.03	2.50	0.42	0.45
3. Komatsu	1030	0.3393%	10183	1990	-27.00	59.90	1.67	0.78	0.83
4. Kubota	920	0.3030%	12954	1318	-27.60	66.43	1.51	0.71	1.23
5. Ebara	1670	0.5501%	4742	2641	-8.20	105.38	0.95	0.51	0.91
6. Chiyoda	2470	0.8136%	4822	1595	83.00	241.10	0.41	0.16	0.33
7. Nippon Piston Ring	1260	0.4150%	807	111	17.80	120.45	0.83	0.40	0.38
8. Nipponseiko	1120	0.3689%	6205	2578	6.70	53.95	1.85	0.71	0.54
9. NTV	948	0.3122%	4357	1014	-2.50	44.46	2.25	0.95	0.48
10. Koyo Seiko	1250	0.4117%	2442	390	7.80	42.11	2.37	0.56	0.11
11. Nachi-Fujikoshi	1020	0.3360%	2317	622	-4.70	68.16	1.47	0.59	0.30
Electric Equipment									
1. Hitachi	1590	0.5237%	51188	6076	10.60	44.51	2.25	0.69	0.51
2. Toshiba	1060	0.3491%	33592	10549	-10.20	37.32	2.68	0.94	1.07
3. Mitsubishi Electric	970	0.3195%	20708	4987	-8.50	37.65	2.66	1.03	0.82
4. Fuji Electric	900	0.2964%	6382	2262	-25.00	60.78	1.65	0.78	1.04
5. Meidensha	1170	0.3854%	2361	615	0.90	73.32	1.36	0.51	0.89
6. NEC	2120	0.6983%	32170	3062	22.50	46.62	2.14	0.47	0.43
7. Fujitsu	1480	0.4875%	26649	3364	5.00	36.51	2.74	0.61	0.63
8. Oki Electric Ind.	1050	0.3458%	6239	2303	10.50	38.99	2.56	0.67	0.75
9. Matsushita Elect. Ind.	2150	0.7082%	44636	2549	-10.80	31.21	3.20	0.47	0.69
10. Sharp	1770	0.5830%	18548	4502	36.20	40.81	2.05	0.62	0.40
11. Sony	8000	2.6350%	26446	2182	19.20	40.69	2.46	0.63	0.33
12. Sanyo Electric	825	0.2717%	15720	4154	-11.20	68.35	1.46	0.97	0.90
13. Yokogawa Electric	1630	0.5369%	4213	890	-3.60	46.82	2.14	0.46	0.46
14. Nippondenso	2020	0.6653%	16539	822	8.90	35.19	2.84	0.64	0.36
15. Yuasa Battery	1070	0.3524%	1909	823	-18.30	119.34	0.84	0.46	0.62
Shipbuilding									
1. Mitsui Engine & Ship	780	0.2569%	5952	4715	-14.70	297.61	0.34	0.51	1.07
2. Hitachi Zosen	745	0.2454%	7466	4085	2.50	746.64	0.13	0.00	1.01
3. Mitsubishi Heavy Ind.	870	0.2866%	29090	10281	-23.70	37.79	2.58	0.80	1.22
4. Kawasaki Heavy Ind	720	0.2372%	9584	8468	-26.90	95.84	1.04	0.69	1.54
5. Ihi	991	0.3264%	12868	6460	-20.10	116.98	0.85	0.50	1.42
Motor Vehicles									
1. Nissan Motors	1070	0.3524%	26815	2952	-29.60	33.52	2.98	1.31	0.84

The Nikkei Stock Average (continued)

	(A)*	(B)*	(C)*	(D)*	(E)*	(F)*	(G)*	(H)*	(I)*
2. Isuzu Motors	675	0.2223%	6824	1119	−20.80	45.50	2.20	0.74	0.86
3. Toyota Motors	2220	0.7312%	67438	1858	−7.50	18.73	5.34	0.90	0.45
4. Hino Motors	1020	0.3360%	3644	715	−1.90	36.44	2.74	0.74	0.85
5. Mazda Motor	845	0.2783%	9039	1386	−7.40	36.16	2.77	0.89	0.56
6. Honda Motor	1760	0.5797%	16996	1262	−7.40	33.46	2.99	0.80	0.43
7. Suzuki Motor	740	0.2437%	3021	1070	−10.30	35.54	2.81	0.88	0.83
Transportation Equipment									
1. Nippon Sharyo	1450	0.4776%	2116	429	−7.10	72.98	1.37	0.41	0.35
Precision Instrument									
1. Nikon	1450	0.4776%	5315	1136	6.60	53.15	1.88	0.59	0.58
2. Canon	1680	0.5334%	12328	3739	12.00	41.09	2.43	0.74	0.49
3. Ricoh	1120	0.3689%	7179	1296	1.40	39.88	2.51	0.89	0.25
4. Citizen Watch	960	0.3162%	2962	1255	−5.90	37.98	2.63	0.86	0.22
Other Manufacturing									
1. Toppan Printing	1840	0.6061%	11807	1023	−4.70	39.75	2.52	0.54	0.76
2. Dai Nippon Print-ing	1870	0.6159%	13954	642	−18.30	40.45	2.47	0.53	0.86
3. Yamaha	1740	0.5731%	3410	417	4.20	79.30	1.26	0.56	0.85
Marine Products									
1. Kyokuyo	1310	0.4315%	1484	1211	78.20	247.33	0.40	0.23	1.24
2. Nichino	691	0.2276%	1137	779	−10.10	378.90	0.26	0.00	1.45
3. Nippon Suisan	669	0.2204%	1983	678	−20.30	132.22	0.76	0.75	0.99
Mining									
1. Mitsui Mining	1060	0.3491%	1613	727	−1.90	268.80	0.37	0.00	0.90
2. Sumitomo Coal Mining	1100	0.3623%	840	305	37.50	101.24	0.99	0.45	1.14
Construction									
1. Taiski	1180	0.3887%	12014	3132	−39.20	53.40	1.87	0.76	1.18
2. Ohbayashi	1430	0.4710%	10619	4105	−24.30	45.19	2.21	0.49	1.26
3. Shimizu	1740	0.5731%	13652	2363	−25.30	53.54	1.87	0.63	1.14
4. Sato Kagyo	2300	0.7576%	5678	2265	−7.30	157.72	0.63	0.26	0.11
5. Tobishima	1150	0.5105%	3567	507	−0.60	118.91	0.84	0.48	−0.19
6. Fujita	1650	0.5435%	7386	2338	−24.70	73.86	1.35	0.55	1.20
7. Kajima	1660	0.5468%	15859	1812	−30.80	61.00	1.64	0.66	1.36
8. Tekken Construc-tion	1710	0.5632%	2662	1278	9.60	166.36	0.60	0.44	0.21
9. Toa	1060	0.3491%	1878	366	−23.70	117.40	0.85	0.47	1.17
10. Daiwa House In-dustry	1980	0.6522%	9256	2803	−1.00	28.92	3.46	0.85	1.29

The Nikkei Stock Average (continued)

	(A)*	(B)*	(C)*	(D)*	(E)*	(F)*	(G)*	(H)*	(I)*
Trade									
1. C. Itoh	728	0.2398%	10324	3953	−34.70	57.35	1.74	0.69	1.60
2. Marubeni	700	0.2306%	10346	5862	−27.60	60.86	1.64	0.71	1.36
3. Mitsui	850	0.2800%	12987	3520	−29.80	61.84	1.62	0.71	1.67
4. Sumitomo	1120	0.3689%	11846	3243	−13.20	34.84	2.87	0.71	1.39
5. Mistubishi	1240	0.4084%	19346	2367	−22.50	48.36	2.07	0.73	1.74
6. Iwatani	1090	0.3590%	2576	783	7.90	95.41	1.05	0.46	1.18
Retail Stores									
1. Mitsukoshi	1630	0.5369%	7830	842	−31.80	116.86	0.86	0.37	1.54
2. Tokyu Depart-ment	1400	0.4611%	3845	1884	3.00	67.45	1.48	0.57	1.00
3. Takashimaya	2950	0.9717%	6537	194	2.80	78.76	1.27	0.36	1.12
4. Matsuzakaya	6870	2.2628%	10686	46	19.50	159.50	0.63	0.14	0.51
5. Maruzen	1430	0.4710%	1443	431	40.20	131.21	0.76	0.52	0.96
Banks									
1. Dai-Ichi Kangyo Bank	2370	0.7806%	73946	490	−24.30	47.71	2.10	0.36	1.05
2. Bank of Tokyo	1350	0.4447%	26918	520	−20.60	48.94	2.04	0.59	1.09
3. Mitsui Taiyo Kobe	2150	0.7082%	40564	399	−5.70	62.41	1.60	0.40	1.16
4. Mitsubishi Bank	2500	0.8234%	71830	569	−15.30	51.31	1.95	0.34	1.07
5. Fuji Bank	2940	0.9684%	85027	549	−10.80	53.14	1.88	0.29	0.97
6. Sumitomo Bank	2620	0.8630%	82498	833	−22.20	45.83	2.18	0.32	1.40
7. Mitsui Trust & Bank	1580	0.5204%	18926	322	−24.80	33.20	3.01	0.54	1.61
8. Mitsubishi Trust & Bank	1800	0.5929%	23427	311	−34.50	30.03	3.33	0.47	2.22
Other Financial Services									
1. Nippon Shinpan	1120	0.3689%	3479	1029	−14.50	31.62	3.16	0.94	1.48
Securities									
1. Japan Securities Finance	2100	0.6917%	2599	354	39.10	28.88	3.46	0.29	1.64
2. Nikko Securities	1250	0.4117%	18299	590	−33.50	14.64	6.83	1.12	2.14
3. Nomura Securities	2170	0.7147%	42505	1552	−36.90	20.24	4.94	0.71	2.11
Insurance									
1. Tokio Marine & Fire	1400	0.4611%	21615	1723	−29.00	51.47	1.94	0.57	1.72
2. Taisho Marine & Fire	980	0.3228%	6754	1119	−25.20	42.21	2.37	0.71	1.65
3. Yasuda Fire & Marine	980	0.3228%	8693	2703	−27.40	52.68	1.90	0.71	1.63

The Nikkei Stock Average (continued)

	(A)*	(B)*	(C)*	(D)*	(E)*	(F)*	(G)*	(H)*	(I)*
Real Estate									
1. Mitsui Real Estate	1650	0.5435%	13125	3601	-35.00	47.73	2.10	0.61	2.07
2. Mitsubishi Estate	1530	0.5039%	19526	1456	-41.60	45.94	2.18	0.56	1.89
3. Heiwa Real Estate	1460	0.4809%	1563	416	-20.50	77.35	1.29	0.41	1.48
Railroad Transport									
1. Tobu Railway	970	0.3195%	7790	2452	-41.20	165.76	0.60	0.52	1.66
2. Tokyu	1580	0.5204%	17203	6541	-7.60	256.76	0.39	0.32	1.46
3. Keihin Electric Railway	1030	0.3393%	5060	688	-44.00	167.54	0.60	0.49	1.52
4. Odakyu Electric Railway	1080	0.3557%	7087	1386	-32.50	181.71	0.55	0.46	1.29
5. Keio Teito Railway	1000	0.3294%	5875	818	-28.60	172.81	0.58	0.50	1.51
6. Keisei Electric Railway	1690	0.5566%	4591	1963	-37.40	167.38	0.60	0.24	1.18
Trucking									
1. Nippon Express	1000	0.3294%	10690	3264	-35.90	80.38	1.24	0.60	1.45
Sea Transport									
1. Nippon Yusen	820	0.2701%	9396	4554	-15.00	156.61	0.64	0.49	1.61
2. Mitsui O.S.K. Lines	785	0.2586%	8228	3489	-14.70	182.83	0.55	0.51	1.37
3. Navix Line	921	0.3034%	3610	1482	12.90	164.10	0.61	0.00	0.91
4. Kawasaki	780	0.2569%	4567	3336	-2.50	130.48	0.77	0.00	1.01
5. Showa	1210	0.3985%	3309	1441	39.10	66.18	1.51	0.00	0.62
Air Transport									
1. All Nippon Airways	1600	0.5270%	21977	1031	-10.10	137.36	0.73	0.31	0.92
Warehousing									
1. Mitsubishi Warehouse	1620	0.5336%	2705	365	-3.60	60.79	1.65	0.37	1.13
2. Mitsui Warehouse	1300	0.4282%	1799	253	-0.80	138.41	0.72	0.46	1.26
Communications									
1. NIT	1160000	0.3821%	180960	4492	-25.20	76.68	1.30	0.52	0.87
Electric Power									
1. Tokyo Electric Power	3920	0.1291%	52501	8867	-33.90	58.33	1.71	1.28	0.95
2. Kansai Electric Power	3120	0.1028%	30210	7819	-29.30	50.35	1.99	1.60	1.02

The Nikkei Stock Average (continued)

	(A)*	(B)*	(C)*	(D)*	(E)*	(F)*	(G)*	(H)*	(I)*
Gas Services									
1. Tokyo Gas	720	0.2372%	20221	3208	−33.90	80.88	1.24	0.69	0.92
2. Osaka Gas	580	0.1910%	14632	2189	−30.00	73.16	1.37	0.86	0.97
Services									
1. Shociku	4380	1.4427%	2671	67	34.80	667.78	0.15	0.11	0.65
2. Toho	38500	1.2681%	5407	138	72.20	117.54	0.85	0.26	0.88
3. Toki	1200	0.3953%	1768	723	10.10	73.66	1.36	0.50	1.35
4. Nittatsu	521	0.1716%	1260	1459	17.80	NA	NA	0.00	0.97
5. Korakuen	3700	1.2187%	5373	183	−7.30	103.32	0.97	0.32	0.83

*(A) Closing price as of 3/30/90
(B) Weight in index
(C) Market value as of 3/30/90
(D) Average daily volume 4/89 to 3/90 (1000 shares)
(E) Annual return from 4/89 to 3/90
(F) Price to earnings ratio (3/30/90)
(G) 1/Per
(H) Dividend Yield as of 3/30/90
(I) Beta as of 3/30/90

Source: The Chicago Mercantile Exchange

G. The Tokyo Stock Price Index

as of July 3, 1990

Company Name	Market Value (000s Yen)	As a % of Index
FISHING AND FORESTRY		
Kyokuyo Co	150,665,060	0.03%
Nichiro Corp	116,460,336	0.02%
Nippon Suisan	256,103,145	0.05%
Taiyo Fishery Co	208,500,000	0.04%
Hoko Fishing Co	51,000,000	0.01%
Hohsui Corporation	46,928,700	0.01%
		0.17%
MINING		
Mitsui Mining Co	167,373,800	0.03%
Sumitomo Coal Mng	82,666,440	0.02%
Nittetsu Mining Co	160,083,000	0.03%
Mitsui Matsushima	57,050,994	0.01%
Teikoku Oil Co	319,440,000	0.07%
Arabian Oil Co	477,388,000	0.10%
Kanto Natural Gas	106,723,750	0.02%
		0.28%
CONSTRUCTION		
Taisei Corporation	1,364,741,760	0.28%
Ohbay Ashi Road	1,605,912,480	0.33%
Shimizu Corp	1,658,303,860	0.34%
Sato Kogyo Co	478,156,800	0.10%
Tobishima Corp	409,802,790	0.08%
Fujita Corporation	712,183,260	0.15%
Haseko Corp	543,317,430	0.11%
Fujikura	38,949,900	0.01%
Matsui Const Co	55,600,000	0.01%
Kajima Corporation	1,874,240,200	0.38%
Fudo Construction	139,104,000	0.03%
Daisue Const	135,069,120	0.03%
Tekken Const	254,638,080	0.05%
Ando Construction	138,145,500	0.03%

Company Name	Market Value (000s Yen)	As a % of Index
Katsumura Const	49,500,000	0.01%
Nissan Const	98,206,500	0.02%
Taihei Kogyo Co	129,600,000	0.03%
Nishimatsu Const	380,293,200	0.08%
Mitsui Const	264,274,300	0.05%
Daiho Construction	80,085,720	0.02%
Sumitomo Const Co	230,283,200	0.05%
Maeda Corporation	359,116,160	0.07%
Sata Construction	56,212,200	0.01%
Nakanogumi Corp	81,383,250	0.02%
Okazaki Industries	50,116,000	0.01%
Okumura Corp	475,215,360	0.10%
Odakyu Const	59,295,600	0.01%
totetsu Kogyo	46,500,000	0.01%
Dai Nippon Const	125,136,830	0.03%
Hazama Corporation	452,669,220	0.09%
Magara Const	62,348,750	0.01%
Tokai Kogyo Co	126,614,240	0.03%
Asanuma Corp	114,452,800	0.02%
Arai Gumi	130,800,000	0.03%
Tokyu Construction	249,200,640	0.05%
Toda Construction	561,517,860	0.11%
Kumagai Gumi Co	773,259,720	0.16%
Komatsu Const	31,536,000	0.01%
Kitano Const Corp	119,379,420	0.01%
Uekigumi Co	39,625,600	0.01%
Nichiei Const	158,046,300	0.03%
Nippon Hodo Co	391,130,220	0.08%
Toa Doro Kogyo Co	64,012,040	0.01%
Maeda Road Const	294,395,400	0.06%
Nippon Road Co	194,799,200	0.04%
Toa Corp	193,148,000	0.04%
Aoki Corporation	482,892,000	0.10%
JDC Corporation	186,754,770	0.04%
Wakachiku Const	175,896,600	0.04%
Saeki Construction	51,000,000	0.01%
Toyo Construction	178,745,170	0.04%
Daito Kogyo Co	50,150,900	0.01%
Penta-Ocean Const	370,621,140	0.08%
Taisei Road Const	133,152,000	0.03%
Ohbay Ashi Corp	60,249,700	0.01%
Seikitokyu Kogyo	67,681,150	0.01%
Fukuda Corporation	72,395,880	0.01%
Kobori Juken Co	121,296,000	0.02%
Shokusan Jutaku Co	177,240,540	0.04%
Tomoegumi Iron Works	89,428,500	0.02%
Misawa Homes Co	314,938,080	0.06%

Company Name	Market Value (000s Yen)	As a % of Index
Natl House Ind	302,027,300	0.06%
Daiwa House Ind	1,226,300,400	0.25%
Raito Kogyo Co	125,358,970	0.03%
Sekisui House	1,198,489,600	0.25%
Nittoc Const Co	75,835,650	0.02%
Tohoku Elec Const	165,445,780	0.03%
Yondenko Corp	61,925,600	0.01%
Chugoku Elec Const	244,879,400	0.05%
Kandenko Co	429,739,090	0.09%
Daimei Telecom Eng	58,544,500	0.01%
Kinden Corporation	489,676,110	0.10%
Tokyo Denki Komush	65,071,740	0.01%
Toenec Corporation	142,633,440	0.03%
Nippon Comsys Corp	109,603,600	0.02%
Nippon Densetsu	86,643,960	0.02%
Kyowa Densetsu	108,537,300	0.02%
Nippon Koei Co	109,283,040	0.02%
Toyo Tele Const	56,481,600	0.01%
Kyudenko Corp	152,885,590	0.03%
Sanki Engineering	214,844,760	0.04%
JGC Corporation	279,373,500	0.06%
Chugai Ro Co	106,377,780	0.02%
Taihei Chemicals	21,225,600	0.00%
Takasago Thml Eng	245,774,100	0.05%
Hitachi Plant Eng	180,769,820	0.04%
Sanko Metal Indl	60,588,000	0.01%
Asahi Kogyosha Co	55,135,080	0.01%
Taikisha	94,965,800	0.02%
Toshiba Eng + Const	112,145,630	0.02%
Sho-Bond Const Co	52,060,800	0.01%
		5.12%

FOODS

Nippon Flour Mills	156,804,660	0.03%
Nisshin Flour Mill	346,968,300	0.07%
Nitto Flour Milling	37,240,115	0.01%
Showa Sangyo Co	154,449,680	0.03%
Nihon Nosan Kogyo	103,449,930	0.02%
Kyodo Shiryo Co	87,563,790	0.02%
Nippon Form Feed	49,810,068	0.01%
Taito Co	71,896,800	0.01%
toyo Sugar Refining	36,608,000	0.01%
Nippon Beet Sugar	170,114,160	0.03%
Mitsui Sugar Co	61,966,200	0.01%
Morinaga + Co	208,429,275	0.04%
Meiji Seika Kaisha	350,487,900	0.07%
Nakamuraya Co	102,189,230	0.02%

Company Name	Market Value (000s Yen)	As a % of Index
Ezaki Glico Co	150,772,860	0.03%
Meito Sangyo Co	68,595,000	0.01%
Fujiya Co Ltd	149,085,920	0.03%
Yamazaki Baking Co	374,479,400	0.08%
First Baking Co	47,999,952	0.01%
Morozoff	45,976,140	0.01%
Meiji Milk Product	235,738,440	0.05%
Snow Brand Milk	304,036,200	0.06%
Morinaga Milk Ind	215,143,620	0.04%
Yakult Honsha Co	439,882,280	0.09%
Prima Meat Packers	116,955,960	0.02%
Nippon Meat Packers	245,908,640	0.07%
Itoham Foods Inc	267,969,740	0.05%
Hayashikane Sangyo	65,043,000	0.01%
Marudai Food Co	158,863,200	0.03%
Sapporo Breweries	550,786,500	0.11%
Asahi Breweries	714,469,550	0.15%
Kirin Brewery Co	1,864,300,320	0.38%
Takara Shuzo Co	202,713,600	0.04%
Toyo Jozo Co	174,988,300	0.04%
Godo Shusei Co	88,952,200	0.02%
Sanraku Inc	190,941,450	0.04%
Yomeishu Seizo Co	64,020,000	0.01%
Chukyo Coco Cola	86,939,580	0.02%
Mikuni Coca-Cola	158,095,580	0.03%
Calpis Food Ind	92,610,000	0.02%
Pokka Corporation	65,155,750	0.01%
Honen Corporation	85,201,000	0.02%
Nisshin Oil Mills	171,821,160	0.04%
Yoshihara Oil Mill	19,800,000	0.00%
Fuji Oil Co	133,626,000	0.03%
Kikkoman Corp	234,092,160	0.05%
Ajinomoto Co Inc	1,314,173,280	0.27%
Q P Corporation	194,633,280	0.04%
House Food Indl Co	229,334,880	0.05%
Kagome Co	129,977,300	0.03%
Nichirei Corp	323,785,350	0.07%
Kato Works Co	58,136,640	0.01%
Toyo Suisan Kaisha	155,073,490	0.03%
Nissin Food Prods	439,461,760	0.09%
Nagatanien-Honpo	52,719,800	0.01%
		2.60%
TEXTILES		
Katakura Inds	207,200,000	0.04%
Gunze Limited	226,582,650	0.05%
Shinyei Kaisha	30,888,000	0.01%

Company Name	Market Value (000s Yen)	As a % of Index
Kobe Kiito Co	28,019,400	0.01%
Kawashima Textile	121,524,180	0.02%
Toyobo Co	498,200,906	0.10%
Kanebo Ltd	355,059,705	0.07%
Unitika Ltd	328,894,579	0.07%
Fuji Tec	190,080,000	0.04%
Nisshinbo Inds Inc	321,415,700	0.07%
Kurabo Industries	248,707,858	0.05%
Daiwabo Co Ltd	88,488,855	0.02%
Shikibo (Spinning)	91,122,930	0.02%
Nitto Boseki Co	182,042,595	0.04%
Omikenshi Co	495,708,000	0.10%
Tesac Corporation	61,982,660	0.01%
Japan Wool Textile	235,922,500	0.05%
Daito Woolen Spin	43,200,000	0.01%
Toa Wool Spinning	60,258,240	0.01%
Daidoh	63,371,140	0.01%
Miyuki Keori Co	132,132,000	0.03%
Teikoku Sen-I Co	60,371,140	0.01%
Teijin Limited	702,233,896	0.14%
Toray Inds Inc	1,059,599,240	0.22%
Toho Rayon Co	90,978,000	0.02%
Mitsubishi Rayon	420,718,368	0.09%
Kuraray Co	409,533,740	0.08%
Asahi Chemical Ind	1,229,528,475	0.25%
Sakai Textile Mfg	57,680,000	0.01%
Suminoe Textile Co	93,241,780	0.02%
Nippon Felt Co	56,194,560	0.01%
Ichikawa Woolen	38,134,800	0.01%
Japan Vilene Co	116,202,600	0.02%
Nippon Lace Co	35,552,000	0.01%
Nitto Seimo Co	21,300,300	0.00%
Ashimori Industry	110,632,650	0.02%
Atsugi Nylon Indl	340,704,000	0.07%
Dynic Corporation	63,638,690	0.01%
Kyowa Leather	47,150,000	0.01%
Seiren Co	162,414,000	0.03%
Tokai Senko KK	55,404,540	0.01%
Komatsu Seiren Co	70,031,500	0.01%
Fukusuke Corp	84,512,500	0.02%
Wacoal Corp	209,597,760	0.04%
		1.95%
PULP AND PAPER		
Sanyo-Kokusaku Plp	309,558,743	0.06%
Tokai Pulp Co	67,200,000	0.01%
Oji Paper Co	668,353,400	0.14%

Company Name	Market Value (000s Yen)	As a % of Index
Honshu Paper Co	993,899,600	0.20%
Jujo Paper Co	371,319,950	0.08%
Mitsubishi Paper	270,629,520	0.06%
Hokuetsu Paper Mls	137,322,900	0.03%
Kanzaki Paper Mfg	151,708,920	0.03%
Takasaki Paper Mfg	57,350,000	0.01%
Japan Paper Ind Co	56,522,120	0.01%
Nippon Kakoh Seish	108,643,180	0.02%
Daishowa Paper Mfg	716,446,080	0.15%
Chuetsu Pulp Inds	88,560,780	0.02%
Tomoegawa Paper Co	35,036,320	0.01%
Daio Paper Corp	144,705,000	0.03%
Settsu Corporation	245,132,160	0.05%
Chuo Paperboard Co	41,000,960	0.01%
Rengo Co	151,637,030	0.03%
Tomoku Co	57,462,912	0.01%
		0.96%

CHEMICALS

Mitsu Toatsu Chem	527,140,820	0.11%
Nitto Chemical Ind	53,369,280	0.01%
Co-Op Chemical Co	40,152,000	0.01%
Showa Denko KK	747,241,200	0.15%
Sumitomo Chemical	1,083,243,496	0.22%
Nippon Kasei Chem	54,990,000	0.01%
Sumitomo Seika	59,815,020	0.01%
Mitsubishi Kasei	1,037,220,635	0.21%
Nissan Chem Inds	128,752,920	0.03%
Rasa Industries	52,158,720	0.01%
Ishihara Sangyo	200,327,304	0.04%
Tayca Corporation	339,247,780	0.07%
Nippon Soda Co	87,360,000	0.02%
Tosoh Corporation	329,262,168	0.07%
Tokuyama Soda Co	198,811,860	0.04%
Central Glass Co	175,225,772	0.04%
Toagosei Chem Ind	200,651,184	0.04%
Daiso Co	83,828,160	0.02%
Kanto Denka Kogyo	52,827,228	0.01%
Denki Kagaku Kogyo	310,803,690	0.06%
Ibiden	142,281,840	0.03%
Shin-Etsu Chem Co	605,969,120	0.12%
Nippon Carbide Ind	58,951,200	0.01%
Sakai Chemical Ind	136,185,390	0.03%
Teisan KK	138,185,390	0.03%
Daido Sanso KK	52,762,720	0.01%
Hoxan Corporation	65,294,640	0.01%
Osaka Sanso Kogyo	88,983,820	0.02%

Company Name	Market Value (000s Yen)	As a % of Index
Toyo Sanso KK	79,040,000	0.02%
Nippon Sanso KK	79,040,000	0.02%
Nippon Chem Indl	186,750,000	0.04%
Nihon Parkerizing	98,202,920	0.02%
Koatsu Gas Kogyo	62,865,000	0.01%
Titan Kogyo KK	54,277,970	0.01%
Shikoku Chem Corp	60,514,050	0.01%
Toda Kogyo Corp	80,400,000	0.02%
Taiyo Sanso Co	142,871,880	0.03%
Hodogaya Chemcical	46,913,256	0.01%
Nippon Shokubai KK	348,380,250	0.07%
Dainichiseika C+C	90,404,600	0.02%
Kanegafuci Chem	315,448,362	0.06%
Kyowa Hakko Kogyo	607,015,600	0.12%
Mitsubishi Gas Chm	368,652,687	0.08%
Mitsui Petrochem	339,078,290	0.07%
Mitsubishi Petroch	580,510,440	0.12%
Japan Synth Rubber	258,237,900	0.05%
Nippon Synth Chem	85,708,350	0.02%
Daicel Chem Inds	366,878,390	0.08%
Sumitomo Bakelite	171,675,640	0.04%
Sekisui Chemical	847,771,120	0.17%
Nippon Zeon Co	186,695,353	0.04%
Aica Kogyo Company	93,657,870	0.02%
Ube Industries Ltd	546,702,183	0.11%
Toyo Chemical Co	26,014,430	0.01%
Sekisui Jushi Corp	77,206,400	0.02%
Mitsubishi Plastic	225,397,120	0.05%
Showa Highpolymer	46,614,550	0.01%
Takiron Co	65,629,320	0.01%
Asahi Organic Chem	152,003,040	0.03%
Hitachi Chemical	418,407,200	0.09%
Nichiban Co	51,015,480	0.01%
Riken Vinyl Ind Co	68,885,300	0.01%
Okura Industrial	80,359,800	0.02%
Tsutsunaka Plastic	74,993,820	0.02%
Sekisui Plastics	122,338,750	0.03%
Gunze Sangyo Inc	133,852,300	0.03%
Japan Carlit Co	45,000,000	0.01%
Nippon Kayaku Co	207,342,060	0.04%
Asahi Denka Kogyo	86,273,340	0.02%
Nippon Oil Co	293,854,500	0.06%
Miyoshi Oil + Fat	73,467,954	0.02%
Kao Corporation	803,923,210	0.16%
Dai-Ichi Kogyo	47,965,070	0.01%
Sanyo Chemical Ind	227,410,260	0.05%

Company Name	Market Value (000s Yen)	As a % of Index
Sankyo Company Y	921,673,960	0.19%
Takeda Chem Inds	1,474,795,400	0.30%
Yamanouchi Pharm	850,453,320	0.17%
Daiichi Pharm Co	677,780,000	0.14%
Dainippon Pharm	476,948,280	0.10%
Shionogi + Co	516,166,980	0.11%
Tanabe Seiyaku Co	313,384,500	0.06%
Yoshitomi Pharm	254,087,040	0.05%
Fujisawa Pharm Co	653,472,350	0.13%
Wakamoto Pharm	71,693,600	0.01%
Banyu Pharm	327,350,080	0.07%
Nippon Shinyaku Co	106,669,150	0.02%
Toyama Chemical Co	182,710,960	0.04%
Chugai Pharm Co	408,643,860	0.08%
Kaken Pharm	142,861,950	0.03%
Green Cross Corp	359,899,860	0.07%
Eisai Co	434,714,280	0.09%
Rohto Pharm	84,480,000	0.02%
Ono Pharmaceutical	677,250,630	0.14%
Nikken Chemicals	89,438,720	0.02%
Hisamitsu Pharm Co	57,587,370	0.01%
Tokyo Tanabe Co	72,631,600	0.01%
Mochida Pharm Co	374,547,950	0.08%
Taisho Pharm Co	117,815,040	0.02%
Santen Pharm Co	113,607,360	0.02%
SS Pharmaceutical	151,984,920	0.03%
Fuso Pharm	110,618,850	0.02%
Nippon Chemiphar	76,637,400	0.02%
Tsumura + Co	168,083,300	0.03%
Terumo Corporation	328,945,660	0.07%
Fuji Spinning Co	32,251,716	0.01%
Hokuriku Seiyaku	194,137,720	0.04%
Dai Nippon Toryo	96,887,200	0.02%
Nippon Paint Co	280,636,060	0.06%
Naksai Paint Co	297,617,600	0.06%
Toa Paint Co	27,200,000	0.01%
Chugoku Mar Paints	68,096,736	0.01%
Dainippon Ink + Chem	537,691,032	0.11%
Sakata Inx Corp	63,848,960	0.01%
Toyo Ink Mfg Co	230,513,600	0.05%
Fuji Photo Film Co	1,977,455,460	0.40%
Konica Corporation	571,056,000	0.12%
Shiseido Company	682,196,290	0.14%
Lion Corporation	249,537,930	0.05%
Takasago Intl Corp	100,410,000	0.02%
Ihara Chemical Ind	55,283,040	0.01%

Company Name	Market Value (000s Yen)	As a % of Index
Hokko Chemical Ind	31,896,700	0.01%
Kumiai Chem Ind Co	102,632,860	0.02%
Nihon Nohyaku Co	95,679,040	0.02%
		6.75%
OIL AND COAL PRODUCTS		
Nippon Oil + Fats	1,234,376,550	0.25%
Showa Shell Sekiyu	387,773,600	0.08%
Mitsubishi Oil Co	410,866,540	0.08%
Tonen Corporation	1,060,335,440	0.22%
Koa Oil	177,144,000	0.04%
Cosmo Oil Company	546,248,672	0.11%
Fuji Kosan Company	61,442,150	0.01%
Nichireki Chemical	44,622,760	0.01%
General Sekiyu KK	274,051,350	0.06%
		0.86%
RUBBER PRODUCTS		
Yokohama Rubber Co	319,519,480	0.07%
Toyo Tire + Rubber	234,286,360	0.05%
Bridgestone Corp	1,161,649,040	0.24%
Sumitomo Rubber	236,390,400	0.05%
Okamoto Industries	148,601,200	0.03%
Achilles Corp	185,581,980	0.04%
Mitsuboshi Belting	128,765,000	0.03%
Bando Chemical Ind	99,061,875	0.02%
Kinugawa Rubber	48,403,300	0.01%
		0.52%
GLASS AND CERAMIC PRODUCTS		
Asahi Glass Co	2,190,835,440	0.45%
Nippon Sheet Glass	388,419,961	0.08%
Ishizuka Glass Co	41,667,950	0.01%
Yamamura Glass Co	139,047,650	0.03%
Sasaki Glass Co	50,779,680	0.01%
Toshiba Ceramics	169,258,880	0.03%
Nippon Elec Glass	377,611,000	0.08%
Nihon Cement Co	354,775,380	0.07%
sumitomo Cement Co	231,118,335	0.05%
Onoda Cement Co	381,718,000	0.08%
Dai Ichi Cement Co	31,149,180	0.01%
Osaka Cement	148,186,332	0.03%
Chichibu Cement Co	108,891,750	0.02%
Mitsubishi Min + Cem	348,778,792	0.07%
Misawa Resort Co	102,952,800	0.02%
Nippon Hume Pipe	46,955,200	0.01%
Tokai Carbon Co	143,918,520	0.03%
Nippon Carbon Co	106,965,800	0.02%

Company Name	Market Value (000s Yen)	As a % of Index
Noritake Co	236,365,090	0.05%
Toto	744,166,670	0.15%
NGK Insulators	533,473,940	0.11%
NGK Spark Plug Co	319,021,020	0.07%
Inax Corporation	430,702,200	0.09%
Danto Corporation	80,750,000	0.02%
Shinagawa Refract	106,920,000	0.02%
Kurosaki Refractrs	67,953,600	0.01%
Tokyo Ohka Kogyo	295,913,200	0.06%
Ask Corporation	50,544,000	0.01%
Nichias Corp	147,954,320	0.03%
		1.73%
IRON AND STEEL		
Nippon Steel Corp	3,857,502,320	0.79%
Kawasaki Steel Corp	1,876,131,656	0.38%
NKK Corporation	1,708,375,912	0.35%
Sumitomo Metal Ind	1,708,375,912	0.35%
Kobe Steel	1,593,410,175	0.33%
Nisshin Steel Co	894,228,720	0.18%
Nakayama Steel Works	216,524,460	0.04%
Godo Steel	197,477,700	0.04%
Tokyo Steel Mfg	712,224,780	0.15%
Yamato Kogyo Co	233,832,900	0.05%
Tokyo Tekko Co	138,629,700	0.03%
Toa Steel Co	266,922,500	0.05%
Yodogawa Steel Works	282,676,210	0.06%
Toyo Kohan Co	108,864,000	0.02%
Daido Steel Sheet	57,782,860	0.01%
Nippon Pipe Mfg	27,964,450	0.01%
Maruichi Steel Tube	219,290,400	0.04%
Mory Industries	57,453,840	0.01%
Daido Steel Co	373,065,000	0.08%
Nippon Koshuha Stl	64,766,775	0.01%
Nippon Stainless	113,414,140	0.02%
Nippon Metal Ind	146,817,000	0.03%
Nippon Yakin Kogyo	148,498,764	0.03%
Sanyo Spec Steel	143,654,455	0.03%
Aichi Steel Works	167,083,980	0.03%
Hitachi Metals	560,935,160	0.11%
Nippon Kinzoku Co	64,320,000	0.01%
Pacific Metals Co	179,123,220	0.04%
Yahagi Iron Co	22,720,000	0.00%
Japan Metal + Chem	233,920,000	0.05%
Nippon Denko Co	105,719,610	0.02%
Kurimoto	204,298,620	0.04%
Jpan Steel Works	287,140,899	0.06%

Company Name	Market Value (000s Yen)	As a % of Index
Mitsubishi Steel	230,400,000	0.05%
Kanto Special Steel	56,436,080	0.01%
Nichia Steel Works	64,950,610	0.01%
		3.63%
NONFERROUS METALS		
Nippon Light Metal	449,270,220	0.09%
Mitsui Min'g + Smelt	389,286,000	0.08%
Toho Zinc Co	111,000,000	0.02%
Mitsubishi Metal	616,526,937	0.13%
Nippon Mining Co	844,855,080	0.17%
Sumitomo Metal Mng	740,198,320	0.15%
Dowa Mining Co	229,272,110	0.05%
Furukawa Co	268,555,290	0.05%
Shimura Kako Co	58,426,940	0.01%
Osaka Titanium Co	147,047,400	0.03%
Showa Aluminium	203,529,780	0.04%
Toyo Aluminium KK	70,333,870	0.01%
Sumitomo Light Met	206,641,820	0.04%
Mitsubishi Shindoh	43,286,000	0.01%
Furukawa Electric	559,205,910	0.11%
Sumitomo Electric	1,105,609,700	0.23%
Fujirebio Inc	760,498,560	0.16%
Mitsubishi Cable	209,081,820	0.04%
Showa Electric W + C	204,163,200	0.04%
Totoku Electric Co	76,294,730	0.02%
Tatsuta Elec Wire	88,065,540	0.02%
Optec Dai-Ichi Dko	82,328,400	0.02%
Hitachi Cable	450,627,600	0.09%
Ryobi	156,445,472	0.03%
		1.65%
METAL PRODUCTS		
Toyo Seikan Kaisha	727,440,000	0.15%
Hokkai Can Co	166,558,640	0.03%
Yokogawa Bridge Wk	138,527,100	0.03%
Matsuo Bridge Co	37,346,400	0.01%
Miyaji Iron Works	63,600,000	0.01%
Komai Tekko Inc	49,881,280	0.01%
Sakurada Co Ltd	47,244,600	0.01%
Sanwa Shutter Corp	475,699,840	0.10%
Bunka Shutter Co	183,035,820	0.04%
Kawada Const Co	119,779,280	0.02%
Sankyo Aluminium	313,631,610	0.06%
Toyo Shutter Co	120,745,240	0.02%
Toyo Exterior Co	230,786,280	0.05%
Toyo Sash Co Ltd	1,164,401,700	0.24%

Company Name	Market Value (000s Yen)	As a % of Index
Noritz Corp	126,587,360	0.03%
Rinnai Corporation	143,600,240	0.03%
Nitto Seiko Co	37,252,488	0.01%
Sanyo Industries	68,288,000	0.01%
Nihon Kentetsu Co	54,600,000	0.01%
Chugokukogyo Co	26,676,000	0.01%
Topre Corporation	107,109,930	0.02%
Neturen Co	68,702,100	0.01%
Tokyo Rope Mfg Co	192,388,320	0.04%
NHK Spring Co	187,359,350	0.04%
Chuo Spring Co	72,306,080	0.01%
		1.01%
MACHINERY		
Miura Co	80,590,240	0.02%
Niigata Eng	290,463,693	0.06%
Takuma Co	84,483,000	0.02%
Diesel Kiki Co	244,518,237	0.05%
Tsugami Corp	124,899,210	0.03%
Ikegai Corporation	50,338,407	0.01%
Okuma Machinery Wk	245,533,280	0.05%
Toshiba Machine Co	196,927,200	0.04%
Hitachi Seiki Co	140,668,000	0.03%
Amada Sonoike Co	106,917,600	0.02%
Amada Wasino	92,634,460	0.02%
Amada Co	504,303,360	0.10%
Aida Engineering	117,297,120	0.02%
Makino Milling	172,088,280	0.04%
Osg Mfg Company	125,568,590	0.03%
Dijet Industrial	36,975,840	0.01%
Toshiba Tungaloy	86,841,700	0.02%
Asahi Diamond Indl	202,795,360	0.04%
Mori Seiki Co	431,533,900	0.09%
Toyoda Auto Loom	815,601,800	0.17%
Howa Machinery	123,228,170	0.03%
Osaka Kiko Co	59,880,000	0.01%
Toyoda Machine Works	198,554,400	0.04%
Ishikawa Seisaksho	51,775,200	0.01%
Teijin Seiki Co	120,094,290	0.02%
O-M	32,901,200	0.01%
Okuma + Howa Mach	67,923,840	0.01%
Tsudakoma Corp	138,608,400	0.03%
Enshu	40,214,097	0.01%
Nihon Spindle Mfg	38,232,000	0.01%
Hisaka Works	96,924,300	0.02%
Rheon Auto Machinery	138,836,880	0.03%
SMC Corporation	456,635,850	0.09%

Company Name	Market Value (000s Yen)	As a % of Index
Komatsu	1,204,902,270	0.25%
Sumitomo Heavy Ind	509,222,040	0.10%
Hitachi Const Mach	396,756,040	0.10%
Nikko Co	69,489,130	0.01%
Iseki + Co	233,566,740	0.05%
Kioritz Corp	45,475,560	0.01%
Maruyama Mfg Co	39,836,655	0.01%
Kitagawa Iron Works	86,240,000	0.02%
Kubota Corporation	1,450,376,990	0.30%
Toyo Engineering	297,660,000	0.06%
Mitsubishi Kakoki	90,218,460	0.02%
Tsukishima Kikai	65,427,900	0.01%
Tokyo Kikai Seisak	130,450,320	0.03%
Sintokogio	115,462,200	0.02%
Shibuya Kogyo Co	95,163,800	0.02%
Shibuya Kogyo Co	109,859,680	0.02%
Aichi Sharyo Co	109,859,680	0.02%
Komori Corporation	477,325,560	0.10%
Tsurumi Mfg Co	47,315,840	0.01%
Sumitomo Precision	119,450,040	0.02%
Sakai Heavy Inds	63,260,300	0.01%
Ebara Corporation	595,287,680	0.12%
Ishii Iron Works	50,705,600	0.01%
Torishima Pump Mfg	42,471,000	0.01%
Chiyoda Corp	525,152,560	0.11%
Daikin Industries	531,283,480	0.11%
Japan Organo Co	74,851,050	0.02%
Toyo Kanetsu KK	114,690,500	0.02%
Kurita Water Inds	259,905,750	0.05%
Tsubakimoto Chain	244,835,840	0.05%
Daido Kogyo Co	41,451,844	0.01%
Toyo Umpanki Co	103,651,200	0.02%
Nippon Conveyor	38,896,000	0.01%
Nikkiso Co	85,479,300	0.02%
Kimura Chemical	19,982,000	0.00%
Iwata Air Comp Mfg	85,131,590	0.02%
Daifuku	289,557,880	0.06%
Katokichi Co	222,537,430	0.05%
Yuken Kogyo Co	52,204,380	0.01%
Tadano Ltd	300,294,220	0.06%
Fujii	519,051,900	0.11%
CKD Corp	78,318,980	0.02%
Amano Corp	237,711,000	0.05%
Juki Y	155,889,120	0.03%
Sanden	170,147,390	0.03%
Janome Sewing Mach	724,185,000	0.15%

Company Name	Market Value (000s Yen)	As a % of Index
Brother Industries	245,693,055	0.05%
Silver Seiko	51,594,120	0.01%
Max Co	153,358,880	0.03%
Morita Fire Pump	56,882,920	0.01%
Nippon Piston Ring	76,860,000	0.02%
Riken Corp	97,987,888	0.02%
Nippon Seiko KK	594,470,600	0.10%
NTN Corporation	469,764,060	0.10%
Koyo Seiko Co	263,976,300	0.05%
Nachi-Fujikoshi Corp	231,736,860	0.05%
Tsubakimoto Prec	133,846,600	0.03%
Minebea Co	387,515,790	0.08%
Nippon Thompson Co	114,483,050	0.02%
Kitz Corp	194,670,000	0.04%
		4.09%

ELECTRIC APPLIANCES

Hitachi	4,841,474,880	0.99%
Toshiba Corp	3,407,555,170	0.70%
Mitsubishi Elec Corp	2,077,832,736	0.43%
Fuji Electric Co	705,871,905	0.14%
Toyo Denki Seizo	62,423,900	0.01%
Yaskawa Elec Mfg	236,426,200	0.05%
Shinko Electric Co	157,287,000	0.03%
Meidensha Corp	258,293,760	0.05%
Nippon Elec Ind	42,800,000	0.01%
Origin Electric Co	51,514,320	0.01%
Hitachi Koki Co	284,553,580	0.06%
Matsushita Refrig	272,967,120	0.06%
Makita Electric Wk	459,423,360	0.09%
Matsushita Seiko	233,576,740	0.05%
Tokyo Electric Co	255,730,300	0.05%
Shibaura Eng	31,119,000	0.01%
Mabushi Motor	279,157,630	0.06%
Takaoka Elec Mfg	133,727,580	0.03%
Daihen	142,376,900	0.03%
Nissin Electric	164,656,800	0.03%
Osaki Electric	38,083,760	0.01%
Omron Corp	666,006,280	0.14%
Nec Corp	2,984,787,000	0.61%
Fujitsu	2,582,848,840	0.53%
Oki Electric Ind	604,329,170	0.12%
Iwatsu Electric Co	126,003,750	0.03%
Nitsuko	140,866,680	0.03%
Sanken Electric Co	155,325,900	0.03%
Toyo Communication	188,710,200	0.04%
Tamura Elec Works	103,897,140	0.02%

Company Name	Market Value (000s Yen)	As a % of Index
Nippon Signal Co	89,420,690	0.02%
Kyosan Electric	70,260,040	0.01%
Hochiki Corp	61,552,920	0.01%
Japan Radio Co	358,873,840	0.07%
Matsushita Elc Ind	4,441,043,610	0.91%
Sharp Corp	1,956,700,600	0.40%
Anritsu	327,398,720	0.07%
/Fujitsu General	127,464,000	0.03%
Kokusai Electric	383,682,900	0.08%
Sony Corp	2,978,652,440	0.61%
Tokin Corp	132,903,960	0.03%
Aiwa Co	128,473,500	0.03%
TDK Corp Com Stk	947,002,500	0.19%
Teikoku Tsushin	75,777,480	0.02%
Sanyo Electric Co	1,706,552,992	0.35%
Kenwood Corp	169,940,060	0.03%
Crown Radio Corp	178,436,350	0.04%
Mitsumi Electric	71,172,540	0.01%
Tamura Corp	87,972,240	0.02%
Alps Electric Co	435,342,950	0.09%
Ikegami Tsushinki	115,981,180	0.02%
Pioneer Elec Corp	1,156,443,680	0.24%
Matsushita Comm	721,182,000	0.15%
Kyushu Matsushita	619,319,820	0.13%
Nippon Columbia Co	104,116,500	0.02%
Victor Co of Japan	629,117,360	0.13%
Sansui Electric Co	89,768,250	0.02%
Clarion Co	161,220,800	0.03%
SMK Corporation	77,957,000	0.02%
Toko Inc	89,499,192	0.02%
Akai Electric Co	77,453,940	0.02%
Teac Corp	138,793,270	0.03%
Hirose Electric	264,022,990	0.05%
Japan Aviatn Elect	152,146,500	0.03%
Shintom Co	176,464,500	0.03%
Hitachi Maxell	348,984,560	0.07%
Yokogawa Electric	424,786,240	0.09%
Shindengen Elec	95,394,600	0.02%
Yamatake-Honeywell	214,200,000	0.04%
Nihon Kohden Corp	84,603,500	0.02%
Chino Corp	53,999,280	0.01%
Ohkura Electric	43,848,000	0.01%
Horiba	77,543,200	0.02%
Advantest	408,760,000	0.01%
Ono Sokki	67,760,000	0.01%
Tabai Espec	59,708,250	0.01%

Company Name	Market Value (000s Yen)	As a % of Index
Sawafuji Electric	23,987,100	0.00%
Nippondenso	1,878,002,780	0.38%
Toko Electric Corp	33,105,600	0.01%
Stanley Electric	182,387,960	0.04%
Iwasaki Electric	130,089,660	0.03%
Ushio Inc	200,972,160	0.04%
Japan Storage Bty	182,858,040	0.04%
Yuasa Battery Co	231,253,440	0.05%
Shin-Kobe Electric	87,318,000	0.02%
Furukawa Battery	32,076,000	0.01%
Kinseki	118,872,600	0.02%
Jeol	89,424,000	0.02%
Casio Computer Co	424,830,510	0.09%
NCR Japan	407,000,000	0.08%
Fanuc Co	1,868,198,000	0.38%
Fuji Electrochem	75,078,120	0.02%
CMK Corp	194,795,040	0.04%
Amada Metrecs Co	312,873,600	0.06%
Rohm Co	290,762,700	0.06%
Graphtec	100,478,400	0.02%
Kyocera Corp	1,668,077,720	0.34%
Sumitomo Sp Metals	125,238,960	0.03%
Taiyo Yuden Co	175,715,400	0.04%
Murata Mfg	501,513,290	0.10%
Futaba Corp	389,210,200	0.08%
Nitto Denko Corp	240,312,600	0.05%
Hokuriku Elec Cons	89,555,480	0.02%
Matsushita Elc Works	1,289,800,200	0.26%
Tokai Rika Denki	112,114,660	0.02%
Nichicon Corp	149,394,000	0.03%
Nippon Chemi-Con	152,362,520	0.03%
Koa	51,271,720	0.01%
		11.28%
TRANSPORTATION EQUIPMENT		
Mitsui Eng + Shipbg	694,416,450	0.14%
Hitachi Zosen	953,027,532	0.20%
Sasebo Heavy Inds	183,425,200	0.04%
Mitsubishi Hvy Ind	3,318,429,897	0.68%
Kawasaki Heavy Ind	1,135,387,356	0.23%
Ishikawajima-Har	1,324,464,900	0.27%
Nippon Sharyo	238,359,790	0.05%
Fuji Car Mfg Co	34,986,600	0.01%
Nippon Yusoki Co	58,384,000	0.01%
Ninki Sharyo Co	61,800,000	0.01%
Tokyu Car Corp	323,001,250	0.07%
Nippon Air Brake	113,664,000	0.02%
Nissan Motor Co	2,709,671,400	0.55%

Company Name	Market Value (000s Yen)	As a % of Index
Isuzu Motors	1,010,711,547	0.21%
Toyota Motor Co	7,018,452,300	1.44%
Komatsu Zenoah Co	65,392,000	0.01%
Hino Motors	379,190,620	0.08%
Nissan Diesel Mtr	208,337,670	0.04%
Mitsubishi Motors	862,432,940	0.18%
Toyota Auto Body	139,024,260	0.03%
Nissan Shatai Co	149,050,248	0.03%
Kanto Auto Works	113,630,560	0.02%
Shin Meiwa Ind	178,345,420	0.04%
Komatsu Forklift	164,942,800	0.03%
Topy Industries	173,186,843	0.04%
Tokico Co	120,037,060	0.02%
Toyo Radiator Co	101,687,200	0.02%
Akebono Brake Ind	78,792,816	0.02%
Nok	203,930,980	0.04%
Futaba Sangyo	98,262,060	0.02%
Kayaba Industry Co	182,068,770	0.04%
Shiroki Corp	82,156,430	0.02%
Ichikoh Industries	80,114,450	0.02%
Press Kogyo Co	84,260,754	0.02%
Calsonic Corp	130,237,470	0.03%
Pacific Industrial	47,895,760	0.01%
Aisin Seiki Co	453,904,080	0.09%
Mazda Motor Corp	987,035,800	0.20%
Daihatsu Motor Co	340,324,800	0.07%
Aichi Machine Inds	97,742,160	0.02%
Honda Motor Co	1,792,069,100	0.37%
Suzuki Motor Co	361,034,960	0.07%
Fuji Heavy Inds	403,447,951	0.08%
Yamaha Motor Co	269,331,660	0.06%
Showa Mfg	54,376,940	0.01%
Atsugi Unisia Corp	101,229,818	0.02%
Koito Mfg	566,070,800	0.12%
Araya Industrial	91,228,620	0.02%
Shimano Industrial	344,408,820	0.07%
Japan Aircraft Mfg	85,601,880	0.02%
		5.89%

PRECISION INSTRUMENTS

Shimadzu Corp	318,253,200	0.07%
Japan Medical Supp	55m628,730	0.01%
Sokkisha	79,782,000	0.02%
Tokyo Keiki	120,388,620	0.02%
Aichi Clock + Elec	54,756,000	0.01%
Kinmon Mfg Co	49,770,000	0.01%
Tokyo Seimitsu	61,479,080	0.01%

Company Name	Market Value (000s Yen)	As a % of Index
Nikon Corporation	620,929,660	0.13%
Topcon Corp	86,679,200	0.02%
Olympus Optical Co	338,440,950	0.07%
Dianippon Screen	298,271,360	0.06%
Hoya Co	342,940,000	0.07%
Asahi Optical Co	103,976,250	0.02%
Canon Inc	1,377,058,440	0.28%
Ricoh Co	711,785,800	0.15%
Minolta Camera Co	270,674,018	0.06%
Copal Co	59,719,000	0.01%
Sankyo Seiki Mfg	99,062,970	0.02%
Citizen Watch Co	364,713,220	0.07%
Rhythm Watch Co	116,701,486	0.02%
		1.13%
OTHER PRODUCTS		
Juken Sangyo	62,259,160	0.01%
Daiken Trade + Ind	179,609,760	0.04%
Dantani Plywood Co	64,112,850	0.01%
Toppan Printing Co	1,124,711,000	0.23%
Dai Nippon Printing	1,415,058,120	0.29%
Tosho Printing Co	64,198,800	0.01%
Kyodo Printing Co	377,938,000	0.08%
Nissha Printing	91,114,920	0.02%
Asics Corp	167,335,916	0.03%
Yamaha Corp	380,251,370	0.08%
Kawai Musical Inst	81,360,000	0.02%
Nissan Nohrin Kogyo	33,292,500	0.01%
Lintec Corp	86,788,800	0.02%
Bandai Co	175,513,800	0.02%
Shin-Etsu Polymer	75,824,922	0.02%
Toyo Linoleum Mfg	89,331,520	0.02%
Itoki Kosakusho Co	144,656,800	0.03%
Nintendo Co	2,885,850,000	0.59%
Mitsubishi Pencil	115,971,900	0.02%
France Bed Co	139,700,000	0.03%
Takara Standard Co	170,072,060	0.03%
Kokuyo Co	579,118,080	0.12%
Nakabayashi	72,317,480	0.01%
Nifco Inc	121,848,610	0.02%
Daiwa Seiko Inc	79,223,500	0.02%
Okamura Corp	238,119,420	0.05%
Nippon Valqua Inds	115,433,100	0.02%
Pilot Corporation	57,960,000	0.01%
Mutoh Industry	139,250,540	0.03%

Company Name	Market Value (000s Yen)	As a % of Index
		1.91%
COMMERCE		
Itoh(C) + Co	1,142,083,288	0.23%
Marubeni Corp	1,098,112,353	0.22%
Toyo Menka Kaisha	498,253,020	0.10%
Nichimen Corp	305,824,840	0.06%
Mutow Co	43,146,640	0.01%
Takashima + Co	40,897,920	0.01%
Itoman + Co	296,477,220	0.06%
Sanyo Shokai	196,354,650	0.04%
Nagase + Co	218,849,950	0.04%
Naigai	89,158,860	0.02%
Chori Co	100,862,190	0.02%
Toyota Tsusho Corp	275,737,000	0.06%
Onward Kashiyama	316,997,250	0.06%
Sankyo Seiko Co	99,000,000	0.02%
Ichida + Co	78,966,360	0.02%
Kanematsu Corp	206,739,950	0.04%
Renown Inc	282,940,320	0.06%
Mizuno Corp	210,846,340	0.04%
Tsukamoto Shoji Co	78,000,000	0.02%
Familymart	439,344,000	0.02%
Renown Look Inc	78,068,390	0.02%
Mitsui + Co	1,393,568,775	0.29%
Japan Pulp + Paper	133,079,000	0.03%
Toshoku	176,904,000	0.04%
Tokyo Electron	569,537,910	0.12%
Nissei Sangyo	217,945,500	0.04%
Kamei	59,421,360	0.01%
Tohto Suisan	38,126,220	0.01%
Nihon Matai Co	40,016,250	0.01%
Zenchiku Co	73,183,962	0.01%
Hattori Seiko	570,240,000	0.12%
Yamazen Co	135,969,460	0.03%
Tsubakimoto Machinery	38,563,860	0.01%
Sumitomo Corp	1,315,719,360	0.27%
Okura + Co	98,554,500	0.02%
Nozaki + Co	41,084,100	0.01%
Nihon Unisys	251,128,270	0.05%
Uchida Yoko Co	84,049,600	0.02%
Mitsubishi Corp	2,358,428,230	0.48%
Dai Ichi Jitsugyo	51,688,800	0.01%
Canon Sales Co Inc	373,876,750	0.08%
Seika Corp	91,852,046	0.02%
Nissho-Iwai Corp	632,577,441	0.13%
Kinsho Mataichi Co	31,779,000	0.01%

Company Name	Market Value (000s Yen)	As a % of Index
Sata Shoji	39,654,600	0.01%
Kasho Co	92,153,600	0.01%
Yuasa Shoji Co	126,159,420	0.03%
Shinsho Corp	89,609,700	0.02%
Hanwa Bank	793,659,300	0.16%
Kanagawa Electric	58,081,270	0.01%
Tec Electronics	74,141,700	0.02%
Suntelephone Co	86,480,640	0.02%
Iwatani Intl Corp	249,137,700	0.05%
Nichiei Co	219,109,500	0.04%
Shoko	83,247,045	0.02%
Nichimo Co Ltd	110,160,000	0.02%
San-Ai Oil Co	99,367,040	0.02%
Inabata + Co	52,521,700	0.01%
Yuasa Trading Co	25,800,000	0.01%
Fujiko Co	28,817,010	0.01%
Gunma Bank	70,017,750	0.01%
Hitachi Sales Corp	160,580,090	0.03%
Meiwa Trading Co	28,289,140	0.01%
Kawasho Corp	118,633,400	0.02%
Tokyo Style Co	235,504,750	0.05%
Unicharm Corp	124,852,270	0.03%
Descente	71,539,320	0.01%
D'Urban Inc	90,441,720	0.02%
OSG Corp	48,625,680	0.01%
Mitsu-Uroko	84,199,650	0.02%
Shinagawa Fuel	103,223,800	0.02%
Itoh(C)Fuel	98,122,240	0.02%
Tokai Corporation	84,211,250	0.02%
Sanrio Co	561,946,050	0.12%
Ryosan Co	139,898,400	0.03%
Shinko Shoji	45,962,070	0.01%
Toyo Corporation	55,753,850	0.01%
Gastec Service Co	48,809,600	0.01%
Cabin Co	89,303,130	0.02%
Taka-Q	129,935,740	0.03%
Keiyo Co	136,707,920	0.03%
Dai Ichi Katei	77,627,550	0.02%
Joshin Denki	167,416,200	0.03%
Nippon Gas	64,230,000	0.01%
Best Denki Co	253,065,780	0.05%
Seiyo Food Systems	163,210,800	0.03%
Maruetsu Inc	308,582,560	0.06%
Royal Co	109,743,930	0.02%
Skylark Co	214,116,350	0.04%
Totenko	38,523,000	0.01%

Company Name	Market Value (000s Yen)	As a % of Index
Inageya Co	211,948,650	0.04%
Seven-Eleven Japan	1,674,295,140	0.34%
Kyotaru Co	100,863,000	0.02%
York-Benimaru	152,169,360	0.03%
Life Stores Co	61,124,440	0.01%
Dennys Japan	100,278,750	0.02%
Kasumi	82,485,440	0.02%
Tokyu Store Chain	87,690,320	0.02%
Yaohan Dept Store	181,1 61,360	0.04%
Sotetsu Rosen	34,071,660	0.01%
Viva Home Co	174,715,800	0.04%
Mitsukoshi	850,580,580	0.17%
Tokyu Dept Store	480,614,750	0.10%
Takashimaya Co	667,754,800	0.14%
Daimaru Inc	359,078,720	0.07%
Matsuzakaya Co	1,242,600,000	0.25%
Maruzen Co	144,758,900	0.03%
Matsuya Co	86,222,880	0.02%
Isetan Co	986,206,500	0.20%
Yokohama Matsuz	24,600,000	0.01%
Hankyu Dept Stores	283,368,780	0.06%
Sogo Co	252,979,480	0.05%
Maruei Dept Store	68,711,720	0.01%
Parco	103,734,450	0.02%
Marui Co	1,048,011,300	0.21%
Credit Saison	253,666,020	0.05%
Daiei Finance Inc	109,594,810	0.02%
Jujiya Co	73,980,000	0.02%
Izutsuya	90,507,240	0.02%
Nagasakiya Co	751,502,400	0.15%
Daiei Inc	775,502,400	0.15%
Ito - Yokado	1,610,128,280	0.33%
Izumiya Co	284,555,700	0.06%
Jusco Co	615,872,000	0.13%
Seiyu	395,822,960	0.08%
Nichii Co	589,177,400	0.12%
Uny Co	369,239,850	0.08%
Chujitsuya Co	347,982,250	0.07%
Izumi Co	114,576,000	0.02%
Tobu Store Co	93,476,800	0.02%
Fuji Denki Reiki	133,252,800	0.03%
Tokyo Nissan Auto	92,723,950	0.02%

7.61%

FINANCE AND INSURANCE

Ind Bank Japan	9,053,128,700	1.85%

Company Name	Market Value (000s Yen)	As a % of Index
Long Credit Bk Jap	4,470,852,100	0.92%
Nippon Credit Bank	2,771,200,000	0.57%
Dai Ichi Kangyo Bank	7,457,191,960	1.53%
Hokkaido Takushoku	1,004,740,200	0.21%
Bank of Tokyo	2,912,221,120	0.60%
Mitsui Bank	3,204,364,500	0.66%
Mitsubishi Bank	6,725,602,260	1.38%
Fuji Bank	7,376,504,850	1.51%
Sumitomo Bank	7,568,826,720	1.55%
Daiwa Bank	2,026,850,540	0.41%
Sanwa Bank	6,226,157,050	1.27%
Tokai Bank	3,582,756,120	0.73%
Kyowa Bank	1,568,074,800	0.32%
Taiyo Kobe Bank	4,228,044,800	0.87%
Daishi Bank	346,550,400	0.07%
Hokuetsu Bank	222,837,130	0.05%
Fukuoka Bank of	689,710,910	0.14%
Nishi-Nippon Bank	443,421,040	0.09%
Saitama Bank	1,355,207,660	0.28%
Chiba Bank	888,298,800	0.18%
Bank of Yokohama	1,412,295,080	0.29%
Joyo Bank	1,352,646,390	0.28%
Gun Ei Chemical	791,213,280	0.16%
Ashikaga Bank	803,350,600	0.16%
Musashino Bank	163,609,600	0.03%
Chiba Kogyo Bank	169,906,500	0.03%
Kanto Bank	67,626,790	0.01%
Tokyo Tomin Bank	291,607,700	0.06%
77th Bank	397,855,120	0.08%
Aomori Bank	155,190,490	0.03%
Akita Bank	176,872,500	0.04%
Yamagata Bank	166,345,000	0.03%
Bank of Iwate	133,486,400	0.03%
Toho Bank	393,468,250	0.08%
Michinoku Bank	145,456,480	0.03%
Hokkaido Bank	355,323,750	0.07%
Shizuoka Bank	1,008,240,660	0.21%
Juroku Bank	299,104,050	0.06%
Hokuriku Bank	849,251,200	0.17%
Suruga Bank	335,055,000	0.07%
Hachijuni Bank	682,112,400	0.14%
Yamanashi Chuo Bank	241,812,900	0.05%
Ogaki Kyoritsu Bank	261,603,900	0.05%
Fukui Bank	287,538,300	0.06%
Hokkoku Bank	345,962,400	0.07%
Shimizu Bank	117,600,000	0.02%

Company Name	Market Value (000s Yen)	As a % of Index
Shiga Bank	278,541,360	0.06%
Nanto Bank	506,331,000	0.10%
Hyakugo Bank (105th)	291,747,500	0.06%
Bank of Kyoto	571,200,000	0.12%
Kiyo Bank	289,933,582	0.06%
Osaka (Bank of)	240,779,520	0.05%
Ikeda (Bank of)	115,228,260	0.02%
The Hiroshima Bank	592,104,340	0.12%
Yamaguchi Bank	274,000,000	0.06%
San-In Godo Bank	187,808,700	0.04%
Chugoku Bank	445,132,830	0.09%
Iyo Bank	341,727,820	0.07%
Hyakujushi Bank	311,738,520	0.06%
Shikoku Bank	210,900,000	0.04%
Awa Bank	238,655,360	0.05%
Kagoshima Bank	236,539,510	0.05%
Shinwa Bank	154,250,000	0.03%
Oita Bank	129,373,200	0.03%
Miyazaki Bank	125,400,000	0.03%
Higo Bank	269,135,900	0.06%
Bank of Saga	118,025,050	0.02%
Eighteenth Bank	184,706,580	0.04%
Okinawa Bank	86,130,000	0.02%
Bank of Ryukyus	90,749,120	0.02%
Mitsui Trust + Bkg	1,904,670,540	0.39%
Mitsubishi Tr + Bkg	2,448,051,400	0.50%
Sumitomo Trust + Bkg Com	2,200,474,620	0.45%
Yasuda Trust + Bkg	2,015,201,490	0.41%
Nippon Trust Bank	368,220,000	0.08%
Toyo Trust + Bkg	1,420,064,460	0.29%
Japan Secs Finance	254,925,000	0.05%
Bank of Nagoya	256,444,750	0.05%
Bank of Kinki Ltd	330,523,200	0.07%
Fukutoku Bank	235,816,650	0.05%
The Daisan Bank	129,540,000	0.03%
Chukyo Bank	153,317,640	0.03%
Hyogo Bank Ltd	607,554,800	0.12%
Hiroshima Sogo Bank	2,520	0.04%
Tokyo Sowa Bank	266,494,800	0.12%
Higashi Nippon Bank	146,712,500	0.03%
Niigata Chuo Bank	85,172,123	0.02%
Fukuoka City Bank	408,850,000	0.08%
Ehime Bank	198,968,000	0.04%
The Hanshin Bank	153,356,060	0.03%
Keiyo Bank Ltd	303,427,800	0.06%
The Taiheiyo Bank	114,570,000	0.02%

Company Name	Market Value (000s Yen)	As a % of Index
Tokuyo Sogo Bank	74,000,000	0.02%
The Kyushu Bank	129,837,960	0.03%
Tochigi Bank	146,520,000	0.03%
Kita-Nippon Bank	78,000,000	0.02%
Nippon Housing Ln	218,424,520	0.04%
Nichiboshin	151,615,860	0.03%
Nippon Shinpan Co	347,872,000	0.07%
Jaccs Co	135,986,292	0.03%
Orient Corporation	471,603,960	0.10%
Hitachi Credit	188,611,200	0.04%
Central Finance Co	103,645,665	0.02%
Orix Corporation	303,568,200	0.06%
Sumitomo Cp Leasing	59,748,390	0.01%
Diamond Lease	86,139,900	0.02%
Daiwa Securities	2,011,563,000	0.41%
Yamaichi Secs Co	1,531,649,210	0.31%
Nikko Securities	1,816,962,900	2.45%
Nomura Co	11,951,906,900	2.45%
Sanyo Securities	373,398,640	0.08%
New Japan Secs	544,694,220	0.11%
Nippon Kangyo Kaku	573,374,880	0.12%
Wako Securities Co	337,379,850	0.07%
Okasan Securities	273,012,300	0.06%
Yamatane Secs Co	348,286,680	0.07%
Cosmo Securities	260,132,580	0.05%
Dai Ichi Secs	222,428,160	0.05%
Marusan Securities	174,622,980	0.04%
Toyo Securities	120,954,150	0.02%
Kokusai Securities	543,072,560	0.11%
Tokyo Securities	207,889,320	0.04%
Tokio Marine + Fire	2,100,400,320	0.43%
Taisho Marine + Fire	717,896,400	0.15%
Sumitomo Marine + Fire	652,704,820	0.13%
Nippon Fire + Marine	672,281,480	0.14%
Yasuda Fire + Marine Ins	922,816,960	0.19%
Nissan Fire	939,228,000	0.19%
Nisshin Fire + Marine	201,192,000	0.04%
Chiyoda Fire + Marine	335,417,280	0.07%
Dowa Fire + Marine	321,273,930	0.07%
Nichido Fire + Marine	421,146,990	0.09%
Dai Tokyo Fire + Marine	410,831,640	0.08%
Koa Fire And	289,135,320	0.06%
Fuji Fire + Marine	294,363,720	0.06%
Taisei Fire + Marine Ins	84,177,450	0.02%

Company Name	Market Value (000s Yen)	As a % of Index
		28.28%
REAL ESTATE		
Mitsui Real Estate Devel	1,452,507,420	0.30%
Mitsubishi Estate	1,943,607,280	0.40%
Heiwa Real Estate	154,408,320	0.03%
Tokyo Tatemono Co	279,726,750	0.06%
Osaka Building Co	165,820,500	0.03%
Sankei Building	98,652,600	0.02%
Tokyu Land Corp	453,053,000	0.09%
L Kakuei Corp	53,278,425	0.01%
Daiwa Danchi Co	207,576,000	0.04%
Sumitomo Realty + Dev	579,512,120	0.12%
Odakyu Real Estate	43,228,000	0.01%
Toho Real Estate	93,508,800	0.02%
Towa Real Estate	118,371,760	0.02%
Taiheiyo Kohatsu	46,213,000	0.01%
Nichimo Corp	142,781,300	0.03%
Daikyo Inc	715,728,880	0.15%
Toc Corp	111,328,560	0.02%
Tokyo Rakutenchi	89,455,360	0.02%
		1.38%
LAND TRANSPORTATION		
Tobu Railway Co	828,196,220	0.17%
Seibu Railway Co	2,153,520,880	0.44%
Sagami Railway Co	394,814,000	0.08%
Hakone Tozan Railway	65,600,000	0.01%
Tokyu Corp	1,910,641,250	0.39%
Keihin Elec Expr	530,741,160	0.11%
Odakyu Elec Railway	753,299,460	0.15%
Keio Teito Elec Railway	653,054,070	0.13%
Keisei Elec Railway	445,538,800	0.09%
Fuji Kyuko Co	152,402,900	0.03%
Nishi-Nippon Railroad	300,964,290	0.06%
Kinki Nippon Railway	1,522,112,000	0.31%
Hankyu Corp	771,709,353	0.16%
Hanshin Elec Railway	257,587,950	0.05%
Nagoya Railroad Co	720,482,698	0.15%
Nippon Express Co	1,156,516,920	0.24%
Yamato Transport	328,408,200	0.07%
Sankyu Transport	159,896,000	0.03%
Nisson Corp Y	90,796,160	0.02%
Maruzen Showa Unyu	98,018,500	0.02%
Senko	107,148,880	0.02%
Tonami Transport	92,392,542	0.02%
Japan Oil Trans	37,343,460	0.01%
Fukuyama Trans Co	378,917,000	0.08%

Company Name	Market Value (000s Yen)	As a % of Index
Seino Transportation	326,507,760	0.07%
Kanagawa Chuo Ko	119,700,000	0.02%
		2.94%

MARINE TRANSPORTATION

Nippon Yusen KK	1,008,448,320	0.20%
Mitsui Osk Lines	874,162,104	0.18%
Navix Line Ltd	366,114,924	0.07%
Kawasaki Kisen	512,313,375	0.10%
Shinwa Kaiun	127,170,000	0.03%
Inui Steamship Co	26,750,000	0.01%
Meiji Shipping Co	92,160,000	0.02%
Iino Kaiun Kaisha	203,679,000	0.04%
Taiheiyo Kaiun Co	37,150,000	0.01%
Showa Line Co	308,998,500	0.06%
Kyoei Tanker Co	30,240,000	0.01%
Daiichi Chuo Kisen	216,400,800	0.04%
Kansai Kisen	87,120,000	0.02%
		0.79%

AIR TRANSPORTATION

Japan Air Lines Co	3,049,542,000	0.62%
All Nippon Airways	1,280,800,160	0.47%
Kokusai Kogyo	103,034,880	0.02%
Pasco Corp	126,971,110	0.03%
		1.14%

WAREHOUSING AND HARBOR TRANSPORTATION

Mitsubishi Warehouse	292,825,750	0.06%
Mitsui Warehouse	187,667,550	0.04%
Sumitomo Warehouse	140,916,875	0.03%
Shibusawa Warehouse	86,234,160	0.02%
Yamatane	100,220,000	0.02%
Yokkaichi Warehouse	82,676,160	0.02%
Keihin Co	69,539,000	0.01%
Toyo Wharf + Warehouse	81,366,870	0.02%
Utoku Express	45,114,300	0.01%
Kamigumi Co	296,810,140	0.06%
		0.28%

COMMUNICATIONS

Tokyo Broadcasting	531,773,600	0.11%
Nippon TV Network	438,518,500	0.09%
Kokusai Denko	1,131,099,200	0.23%
Nippon Tel + Tel Cp	5,832,000	0.00%
Gakken Co	207,349,300	0.04%

Company Name	Market Value (000s Yen)	As a % of Index
		0.47%
ELECTRIC POWER AND GAS		
Tokyo Elec Power	5,612,236,840	1.15%
Chubu Elec Power	2,435,383,500	0.50%
Kansai Elec Power	3,265,061,570	0.67%
Chugoku Elec Power	1,061,717,840	0.22%
Hokuriku Elec Power	658,588,500	0.13%
Tohoku Elec Power	1,482,526,160	0.30%
Shikoku Elec Power	818,418,260	0.17%
Kyushu Elec Power	1,387,221,760	0.28%
Hokkaido Elec Power	642,130,400	0.13%
Tokyo Gas Co	2,068,081,984	0.42%
Osaka Gas Co	1,565,434,900	0.32%
Toho Gas	371,651,400	0.08%
Hokkaido Gas Co	48,648,190	0.01%
Saibu Gas Co	217,113,120	0.04%
		4.43%
SERVICES		
Shochiku Co	320,166,000	0.07%
Toho Co	536,448,000	0.11%
Toei	191,919,000	0.04%
Nikkatsu Corp	125,780,200	0.03%
Subaru Enterprise	29,766,000	0.01%
Tokyo Theatres Co	65,898,850	0.01%
Yoshimoto Kogyo Co	52,031,230	0.01%
Yomiuri Land Co	245,646,500	0.05%
Tokyotokeiba Co	267,887,550	0.05%
Joban Kosan Co	80,684,640	0.02%
Korakuen Co	579,694,960	0.12%
Chisan Tokan Co	64,132,400	0.01%
Tokai Kanko Co	69,691,050	0.01%
Gajoen Kanko KK	64,391,640	0.01%
Dai Ichi Hotel Co	78,090,600	0.02%
Fujita Tourist Ent	482,188,350	0.10%
Tokyu Hotel Chain	251,552,340	0.05%
Kinki Nippon Tourist	118,801,760	0.02%
Tokyu Tourist Corp	34,185,390	0.01%
Hakuyosha Co	63,960,000	0.01%
Secom Co	682,729,080	0.14%
CSK	383,424,300	0.08%
Intec Inc	166,330,080	0.03%
Daiwa Kosho Lease	266,170,720	0.05%
Konami Industries	273,873,600	0.06%

Source: The Chicago Board of Trade   1.12%

U.S. Regulations on Institutional Use of Financial Futures and Options

Commercial Banks

Commercial banks include bank holding companies and state member banks regulated by the Federal Reserve Board, national banks regulated by the Comptroller of the Currency, and insured state nonmember banks regulated by the Federal Deposit Insurance Corporation.

Principal Regulators

- Federal Reserve Board (FRB)
  Division of Banking Supervision & Regulation
  20th & C Streets, N.W.
  Washington, DC 20551 202-452-3000

- Office of the Comptroller of the Currency (OCC)
  490 L'Enfant Plaza East, S.W.
  Washington, DC 20219
  202-447-1810

- Federal Deposit Insurance Corp. (FDIC)
  Division of Bank Supervision
  550 17th St., N.W.
  Washington, DC 20429
  202-393-8400

- State bank regulators

Statutes, Regulations, Interpretive Statements

Banking Circular No. 79 (3rd Rev.) April 19, 1983 New Capital Rules:
Federal Reserve System 12 CFR Pts. 208 and 225
Office of the Comptroller of the Currency 12 CFR Pt. 3
Federal Deposit Insurance Corporation 12 CFR Pt. 325

Permitted Futures and Options Transactions

A. The FRB, OCC, and FDIC have authorized banks to engage in interest rate futures and options transactions that reduce a bank's interest rate risk exposure.

Source: Chicago Board of Trade

B. FRB guidelines discourage the issuance of long-term put options (150 or more days to expiration).

C. Banks are allowed greater latitude in trading futures and options i. connection with their dealer or trading activities. On December 20, 1989, OCC gave permission to a bank's FCM subsidiary to buy and sell nonfinancial futures and options contracts for their own account and customers. To date, this permission has not been extended to FCMs of bank holding companies that are under the purview of the FRB.

D. A bank holding company may execute futures and options transactions to reduce the risk exposure of its nonbank subsidiaries, but not of its bank subsidiaries. The FRB has stated that the responsibility for such transactions should reside with the management of each affiliated bank.

E. State-chartered banks may be subject to restrictions imposed by state banking authorities.

F. Recently adopted risk-based capital rules exempt exchange-traded marked-to-market instruments such as futures and options from new capital requirements. Off-exchange instruments are not exempt.

Accounting Standards

A. Commercial banks have the option of carrying futures and options transactions on a marked-to-market basis or a lower-of-cost-or-market basis. Since cash positions are generally not marked-to-market, this can create a mismatch in reporting the two sides of a hedge.

B. Futures contracts associated with bona fide hedging of mortgage banking operations may be accounted for in accordance with generally accepted accounting principles.

C. Recently revised risk-based capital rules (applicable to international banks both in the U.S. and in other "Group of Ten" countries) give preferential capital treatment to exchange-traded foreign exchange and interest rate instruments versus over-the-counter instruments because of daily margining requirements.

D. The Federal Financial Institutions Examination Council (composed of the FRS, OCC, FDIC, OTS, and NUA) is currently reviewing the FRS/OCC/FDIC Uniform Call Report. Specifically, it is reviewing the current standards that require a quarterly mark-to-market for futures and options positions with a view to adopting the accounting standards of FASB 80. (OTS currently uses FASB 80.) The Council is also reviewing how FASB 80 has been applied in practice. (See page 100, All Institutional and Commercial Users, for a brief description of FASB 80.)

Savings and Loan Associations

Federal savings and loan associations are financial institutions chartered under the Homeowners Loan Act of 1933. State savings and loan associations are intrastate institutions chartered within particular states.

Principal Regulators
- Office of Thrift Supervision (OTS)
  Department of Treasury
  1700 G Street, N.W.
  Washington, DC 20552
  202-906-6000

- Federal Housing and Finance Board (FHFB)
  1700 G Street, N.W.
  Washington, DC 20552
  202-906-6590

- Federal Deposit Insurance Corporation (FDIC)
  Division of Bank Supervision
  550 17th Street, N.W.
  Washington, DC 20429
  202-393-8400

- State regulators

Statutes, Regulations, Interpretive Statements
Federal: 12 CFR 563.17-3
       12 CFR Section 563.17-4 [Futures]
       12 CFR Section 563.17-5 [Options]
       FHLBB Final Rule Action No. 82-557, August 11, 1982
       OTS Interim Final Rule No. 89-340

Permitted Futures and Options Transactions

A. OTS regulations allow S&Ls "to engage in futures transactions that reduce the net interest rate exposure arising from an institution's asset and liability structure."

B. Long positions are permitted only in connection with forward commitments to sell mortgages or mortgage-related securities, but only to the extent that these short forward commitments exceed 10 percent of long-term assets.

C. Spreading futures is not permitted.

D. The OTS allows S&Ls to use exchange-traded or OTC options based on a financial instrument (or a financial futures contract) in which the institution may invest. The OTS has established guidelines for acceptable OTC options counterparties.

E. The OTS has established a numerical limit on short put option positions (12 CFR 563.17-3 Para. (c)(2) amended and FHLBB Final Rule Action No. 82-557, page 5).

F. The OTS regulations apply to all insured S&Ls. State-chartered S&Ls may also be subject to state regulations affecting futures or options use.

Accounting Standards

A. Current rules for short calls require the S&L to record both the premium income and any loss or gain when the option position is terminated.

B. S&Ls are required to use hedge accounting for recognizing gains and losses on long calls and long puts matched against cash or forward positions. Unmatched positions and all short puts must be marked-to-market (12 CFR 563.17-3 Para. (g)(3) and FHLBB Final Rule Action No. 82-557, page 15).

C. The commitment fee paid on long positions (option premium minus the immediate exercise value of the option) is generally amortized over the term of the option. However, to discourage S&Ls from writing excessive calls for fee income, the OTS requires the commitment fee on short calls to be combined with any resulting gain or loss on the option position and recorded as an income or expense item at the time the institution terminates the position or the option expires (12 CFR 563.17-5 Para. (g)(2) amended).

D. New minimum regulatory capital regulations provide that "any interest rate or exchange rate contract that is traded on an exchange requiring the daily payment of any variations in the market value of the contract" does not have to be considered part of the denominator of a saving association's risk-based capital ratio.

Mutual Funds

Mutual funds are financial entities under the Investment Company Act of 1940 and the Securities Act of 1933.

Principal Regulators
* Securities Exchange Commission (SEC)
  450 5th Street, N.W.
  Washington, DC 20549
  202-272-3101

  Commodity Futures Trading Commission (CFTC)
  2033 K Street, N.W.
  Washington, DC 20581
  202-254-6387

* Internal Revenue Service (IRS)
  1111 Constitution Avenue
  Washington, DC 20226
  202-566-5000

* State securities regulators

Principal Trade Association
* Investment Company Institute

1600 M Street, N.W.
Suite 600
Washington, DC 20036
202-293-7700

Statutes, Regulations, Interpretive Statements
Securities Act of 1933
Investment Company Act of 1940
CFTC Regulations 4.5 and 4.6
Internal Revenue Code Section 851

Permitted Futures and Options Transactions

A. SEC regulations require that the fund's use of futures and options be described in its prospectus. Changes in the fund's investment policy must be approved by a majority of the shareholders.

B. In granting relief from the Investment Company Act's prohibition against the issuance of senior (preferential) securities, the SEC has generally relied on the fund's assurances that futures and options transactions will be nonspeculative. Funds have also been required to place numerical limits on their futures and options commitments.

C. To be exempted from registration as a commodity pool, a fund must satisfy the requirements of CFTC Regulation 4.5. This rule requires, among other things, that futures and commodity options are traded for bona fide hedging purposes. Recently adopted CFTC Regulation 4.6 has expanded the exemptive provisions.

D. To remain exempt from federal income tax, a "regulated investment company" must satisfy the "short-short" test. This rule states that the proportion of the fund's gross income derived from investments held for under three months must be less than 30 percent. However, in 1986, Congress added Section 851(g) to the Internal Revenue Code to provide a hedging exemption from a mutual fund's short-short test. The first exemption in accordance with this section may be found in the IRS's recently issued Private Letter Ruling 8921037.

E. Certain state "blue sky" laws place restrictions or prohibitions on futures or options transactions by mutual funds.

F. Mutual funds are prohibited from investing in "illiquid securities," which include OTC options. However, in 1987, SEC staff allowed a mutual fund to engage in OTC option repurchase agreements with primary dealers.

Accounting Standards
Tax and accounting rules generally require mutual funds to mark-to-market the values of all their investments, including futures and options.

Status

A. The SEC issued a no-action letter authorizing regulated investment companies to make mark-to-market payments on short options positions directly to FCMs rather than to a third-party custodial account, Goldman, Sachs & Co. (Division of Investment Management, May 2, 1986).

B. Legislation was proposed in Congress that would amend the tax code to eliminate the short-short test (a.k.a. the 30 percent rule); however, the provision has yet to be passed.

Pension Plans

Private pension plans are regulated under the Employee Retirement Income Security Act of 1974 (ERISA), which is administered by the Department of Labor. Public pension plans are regulated by applicable state and municipal regulations.

Principal Regulators

- U.S. Department of Labor (DOL)
  200 Constitution Avenue, N.W.
  Washington, DC 20010
  202-523-7316

- State regulators

Statutes, Regulations, Interpretive Statements

Employee Retirement Income Security Act of 1974 (ERISA) 29 CFR 2550.404a-1

Permitted Futures and Options Transactions

A. FASB 87 requires pension fund assets and liabilities to be marked-to-market annually. This could lead to potentially extreme swings in the size of new pension positions from year to year because of mismatches in duration between pension fund liabilities and assets. Futures and options are an economical way of altering the duration of a portfolio of underlying securities.

B. Private pension plans are allowed to trade futures and options subject to a "prudent expert" requirement. The DOL has indicated that the prudence of an individual investment decision will be judged with regard to its effect on the overall portfolio.

C. The main impediment to futures and options trading by private plans has been the ERISA rules that define prohibited transactions involving fiduciaries and "parties in interest." The DOL has issued a series of class exemptions to make it considerably easier for FCMs and CTAs to do business without running afoul of these rules.

D. Public pension plans (e.g., plans covering state and municipal workers) are regulated by the individual states. Many of these state regulations are considerably more restrictive than the ERISA guidelines.

E. In August 1985, the DOL refused to grant an exemption requested by the Futures Industry Association (FIA) that would have allowed an FCM to execute trades for a pension plan while providing investment advice or other services for a fee. Under ERISA, an FCM receiving compensation for investment advice becomes a plan fiduciary, and a fiduciary may not cause the plan to pay an additional fee (i.e., commission) to itself or an affiliate. The FIA has since withdrawn its request for a class exemption, citing a lack of support from the FCM community.

Insurance Companies
Insurance companies have no federal regulator. Regulation is solely by state authorities; leading regulators include New York and Connecticut.

Credit Unions

Principal Regulators
- National Credit Union Administration (NCUA)
  1776 G Street, N.W.
  Washington, DC 20456
  202-682-9600

- State regulators

Statutes, Regulations, Interpretive Statements
Federal: 12 CFR Section 703.1-4

Permitted Futures and Options Transactions
12 CFR Section 703.4 prohibits federal credit unions from the purchase and sale of any futures or standby (option) contract.

All Institutional and Commercial Users

Principal Regulators
- Commodity Futures Trading Commission (CFTC)
  2033 K Street, N.W.
  Washington, DC 20581
  202-254-6387

- Financial Accounting Standards Board (FASB)
  401 Merritt 7
  P.O. Box 5116
  Norwalk, CT 06856-5116
  203-847-0700

- Internal Revenue Service (IRS)
  1111 Constitution Avenue
  Washington, DC 20226
  202-566-5000

- Commodity exchanges

Statutes, Regulations, Interpretive Statements
CFTC Rule 1.3(z)
FASB Statement No. 80
Internal Revenue Code Section 1256(e)(2)

Permitted Futures and Options Transactions
CFTC Regulation 1.61 requires exchanges to establish position limits for all contracts. Exemptions are allowed for transactions that qualify as bona fide hedges under Regulation 1.3(z) or are exempted by exchange rules.

Accounting Standards

A. The Financial Accounting Standards Board issued FASB 80 in 1983. FASB 80 sets standards of accounting for exchange-traded futures contracts (except foreign currency futures, which are covered by FASB 5). FASB 80 allows deferral of futures gains or losses for transactions that qualify as hedges. The FASB recognizes anticipatory hedges and cross-hedges, but does not recognize hedging where the futures transactions cannot be matched with a specific asset or liability.

B. In November 1987, the Financial Accounting Standards Board issued an exposure draft, "Disclosures About Financial Instruments," designed to systematize accounting procedures regarding a broad range of financial instruments including futures and options. This FASB statement covers only financial futures and options and excludes commodity futures and options.
Four areas of disclosure are emphasized to be presented in the body of the financial statement or the accompanying notes.

   a) The credit risk of each financial instrument shall be evaluated, but instruments used in hedging may be evaluated in terms of the net credit risk of the hedge position.
   b) Future cash receipts and payments must be disclosed. Anticipated receipts and payments from options contracts must be disclosed. Futures contracts, because they involve daily cash settlement, are not considered future cash obligations. Foreign exchange futures and options obligations must also be disclosed under this provision.
   c) Effective interest rates, contractual repricing, and maturity dates of all futures and options contracts must be disclosed.
   d) The current market value of all futures and options contracts must be disclosed, marked-to-market at quoted prices. Market prices, including interest rates, should be assumed to remain at the levels that exist at the time of the latest balance sheet.

C. For tax purposes, the IRS allows hedge accounting where the transaction is entered into in the normal course of business to reduce the risk of loss resulting from changes in price.

V

International Futures and Options Contracts Authorized for Sale in the U.S.

I. Information Sharing Arrangements

Appropriate cooperative information sharing arrangements between regulators are essential to address regulatory differences, to respond effectively and on a timely basis during times of market volatility and financial emergency and are a necessary component of sound law enforcement. In this regard, the Commodity Futures Trading Commission (CFTC) of the U.S. has entered into comprehensive information sharing arrangements which address supervisory, surveillance and enforcement concerns with the United Kingdom and with France. In addition to those arrangements, the CFTC has entered into information sharing arrangements related to specific programs to regulate the sale of foreign options and futures contracts to U.S.-based invesotrs. To date, cooperative arrangements exist with the following jurisdictions:

- The Sydney Futures Exchange (SFE) and the federal government of Australia.

- The Singapore International Monetary Exchange (SIMEX) and the government of Singapore.

- The Montreal Exchange, the Toronto Futures Exchange (TFE), the Commission des valuers Mobilieres du Quebec, the Ontario Securities Commission and the federal government of Canada.

- The United Kingdom whereby existing information sharing arrangements were expanded to include "Side Letter Relating to UK/US MOU" to share monitoring information between the Commission and SIB relevant to Part 30; the Bank of England, which has primary financial supervisory authority over United Kingdom banks in their capacity as brokers, has provided assurances that financial information relating to these firms which it collects in the first instance may be made available to the CFTC under existing information sharing arrangements.

- Commission des Operations de Bourse (COB) of France in accordance with the Mutual Recognition Memorandum of Understanding (MRMOU).

Most recently, in April 1991, the CFTC entered into an information sharing arrangement with the Brazilian Commissao de Valores Mobiliarios to share information for investigatory and enforcement purposes.

II. Financial Information Sharing Memorandum of Understanding (FISMOU)

Originally, the FISMOU was a mechanism for routine information sharing pursuant to which the relevant United Kingdom regulator will waive the applicability of certain of its financial requirements to U.S. firms with branch offices in the United Kingdom. The FISMOU has been broadened by the "Addendum Dated May 15, 1989 to the FISMOU" to include financial information sharing with respect to firms exempted from registration with the Commission under rule 30.10. Discussions are progressing to further broaden the FISMOU to include information sharing with respect to commodity pool operators, commodity trading advisors and key related companies of firms which are parties to the FISMOU. The CFTC's staff has been discussing with regulatory authorities in Quebec and Ontario a proposed arrangement for financial information sharing with respect to their firms granted rule 30.10 relief from U.S. registration requirements, and firms in Ontario and Quebec that are related to U.S. FCMs. On June 6, 1990, the CFTC and France's COB concluded the MRMOU agreement which, among other things, provides for information sharing on a routine and "as needed" basis in connection with financial compliance matters.

III. Non-U.S. Options Which May Be Sold to U.S.-Based Investors

The Commodity Futures Trading Commission (CFTC) of the U.S. must authorize the offer or sale of foreign options contracts in the U.S. on a product-by-product and market-by-market basis before U.S.-based investors can trade those contracts. To date, the following options contracts may be sold to U.S.-based investors:

a. **The Montreal Exchange:**
   IOCC Options on Foreign Currencies (British pounds, Deutschemarks, Japanese Yen and Swiss Francs), Canadian Dollar, Gold and Platinum (approved on July 29, 1988); Options on the Government of Canada Bond futures contract (approved on January 23, 1991).

b. **The Singapore International Monetary Exchange (SIMEX):**
   Options on Eurodollar, Japanese Yen and Deutschemark futures (approved on July 29, 1988); Options on the Three-Month Euroyen Interest Rate futures contract (approved on June 22, 1990).

c. **The Sydney Futures Exchange (SFE):**
   Options on 10-Year Australian T-Bonds, Australian Dollar and 90-Day Bank Accepted Bill futures (approved on July 29, 1988); Options on 3-Year Australian T-Bonds futures (approved on August 9, 1988).

d. **The London International Financial Futures Exchange (LIFFE):**
   Options on Long Gilt, US Treasury Bond, German Government Bond, 3-Month Sterling Interest Rate and 3-Month Eurodollar Interest Rate futures, and Sterling and Dollar-Mark currencies (approved on September 12, 1989); Options on the 3-Month Eurodeutschemark Interest Rate futures contract (approved on February 26, 1990).

e. **The London Futures and Options Exchange (London Fox):**
   Options on the Robusta Coffee futures contract, the No. 5 White Sugar futures contract, the No. 6 Raw Sugar futures contract and the No. 7 Cocoa futures contract (approved on December 6, 1989; *see also,* Notice of Certain Material Changes in Terms and Conditions of Options on Robusta Coffee Futures Contract (February 20, 1991)); Options on the MGMI futures contract (approved on July 5, 1990); Options on the European Washed Arabica Coffee Futures contract (approved on February 15, 1991).

f. **The International Petroleum Exchange of London (IPE):**
   Options on Brent Crude Oil futures contract and Gas Oil futures contract (approved on December 6, 1989).

g. **Pending Approvals:**
   The request for approval to offer and sell following options contracts traded on the Marche a Terme International de France (MATIF) is pending the issuance of decree in France implementing the Mutual Recognition Memorandum of Understanding.

Options on the Notional Bond, the 3-month PIBOR and the 3-month Eurodeutschemark futures contracts.

The request for approval to offer and sell certain options contracts traded on the Tokyo Stock Exchange is pending approval by the CFTC.

h. **Futures-Style Margining Of Options Contracts:**
The Commission permits the deferred payment of options premiums for certain options contracts traded on the SFE, LIFFE, London Fox and IPE, provided appropriate disclosures are made to customers. The Chicago Board of Trade (CBOT) and the Chicago Mercantile Exchange (CME) have petitioned the CFTC for repeal of its rule which prohibits margining of options traded on U.S. contract markets.

IV. Non-U.S. Stock Index Futures Which May Be Sold to U.S.-Based Investors

The non-U.S. futures contracts based on an index of equities may not be offered or sold in the U.S. unless the CFTC's staff first issues a no-action letter pursuant to section 2(a)(1) of the Commodity Exchange Act (CEA). No-action relief has been granted with respect to the following stock index futures contracts:

a. **The International Futures Exchange (Bermuda) Ltd.:**
Financial News Composite Index Futures Contract (September 5, 1985)

b. **The London International Financial Futures Exchange (LIFFE):**
Financial Times-Stock Exchange 100 Index Futures Contract (January 16, 1990).

c. **The Singapore International Monetary Exchange (SIMEX):**
Nikkei Stock Average Futures Contract (December 5, 1986).

d. **The Toronto Futures Exchange (TFE):**
Toronto Stock Exchange (TSE) 300 Composite Index Futures Contract (April 19, 1984; TSE 300 Spot Index Futures Contract (October 24, 1986); TSE 35 Index Futures Contract (October 6, 1988); TSE 35 Spot Index Futures Contract (October 6, 1988).

e.. **The Sydney Futures Exchange (SFE):**
All Ordinaries Share Price Index Contract (August 1991)

f. **Pending Approvals:**
The Marche a Terme International de France (MATIF)
- CAC 40 Index Futures Contract
The Osaka Stock Exchange (OSE)
- Nikkei Stock Average Index Futures Contract
The Tokyo Stock Exchange (TSE)
- Tokyo Stock Price Index Futures Contract

V. Futures Contracts Based on Foreign Government Debt

The Securities and Exchange Commission (SEC) of the U.S. under SEC Rule 3a12-8 must designate the underlying government debt instrument as an "exempted security" before persons resident in the U.S. can engage in transactions involving that product. The following debt instruments have been so designated by the SEC:

United Kingdom
Canada
Japan
Australia
France
New Zealand
Austria
Denmark
Finland
Netherlands
Switzerland
Germany

VI. Financial Intermediaries

The CFTC's rules generally require that persons selling foreign futures and options contracts directly to U.S. investors register as Futures Commission Merchants (FCMs). However, the CFTC may exempt persons located outside of the U.S. from full compliance with certain of these rules, including authorization and capital requirements, provided such persons are subject to a regulatory program comparable to that existing in the U.S.

The following financial intermediaries are permitted by the CFTC to sell foreign futures and options contracts to investors in the U.S. without registering as a futures commission merchant (FCM).

a. **The Sydney Futures Exchange (SFE):**
On November 7, 1988, the Commission issued an Order granting the SFE and its designated members an exemption from certain requirements of the Part 30 rules. As of April 19, 1991, relief had been granted to 2 firms and confirmation was pending for 13 additional firms.

b. **The Singapore International Monetary Exchange (SIMEX):**
On January 10, 1989, the Commission issued an Order granting the SIMEX and its designated members an exemption from certain requirements of the Part 30 rules. s of April 19, 1991, relief had been granted to 2 firms and confirmation was pending for 3 additional firms.

c. **The Montreal Exchange:**
On March 17, 1989, the CFTC issued an Order granting the Montreal Exchange and its designated members an exemption from certain requirements of the Part 30 rules. As of April 19, 1991, relief had been granted to 7 firms.

d. **The United Kingdom:**
On May 19, 1989, the Commission issued Orders granting the Securities and Investments Board (SIB), the Association of Futures Brokers and Dealers (AFBD), the Securities Association (TSA) and Investment Management Regulatory Organisation (IMRO), and the firms which they designate, an exemption from certain requirements of the Part 30 rules. As of April 19, 1991, relief had been granted to 68 firms and confirmation was pending for 12 additional firms.

On April 1, 1991, the CFTC issued an Order acknowledging the substitution of the Securities and Futures Authority as a party to several ongoing information sharing and financial intermediary recognition arrangements entered into with, among others, the AFBD and TSA.

e. **The Toronto Futures Exchange (TFE):**
On March 22, 1990, the Commission issued an Order granting the TFE and its designated members an exemption from certain requirements of the Part 30 rules. As of April 19, 1991, relief had been granted to one firm and confirmation was pending for 2 firms.

f. **France:**

On June 6, 1990, the CFTC and France's Commission des Operations de Bourse (COB) formally concluded the MRMOU - a binding international agreement providing for the mutual recognition of commodity futures and options brokers and products located in each jurisdiction.

The MRMOU will generally permit all products of one jurisdiction to be offered to investors located in the other jurisdiction, subject to certain specified conditions intended to ensure adequate investor protection.

Furthermore, the agreement will permit brokers licensed in one jurisdiction to sell the products of that jurisdiction to customers located in the other jurisdiction, generally by complying with the rules of the licensing jurisdiction, and with other requirements intended to eliminate regulatory gaps.

As a condition of these arrangements, the agreement provides for information sharing on a routine and "as needed" basis in connection with monitoring and compliance matters, thus improving the parties' ability to address financial or market disruptions that could affect both markets. The MRMOU is awaiting the adoption of implementing regulations in France. In April 1991, the CFTC transmitted to the COB requests from each of the U.S. contract markets, with one exception, for "recognition" by the French Ministry of Economy and Finance. Recognition will permit the particular U.S. contract market to solicit public investors in France.

g. **Pending Approval:**

Petition for the Kuala Lumpur Commodity Exchange received on February 20, 1990.

U.S. Commodity Futures Trading Commission's Approval for the Offer or Sale of Nikkei Stock Average Futures Contract of the Singapore International Monetary Exchange (SIMEX)

The Commodity Futures Trading Commission's Office of the General Counsel has issued an interpretative letter No. 86-6, recommending that the Commission not take enforcement action based on Sections 2(a)(1)(B)(v), 4(a) or 12(e) of the Commodity Exchange Act if the Singapore International Monetary Exchange, Ltd. (Simex) offers and sells the Nikkei Stock Average Futures Contract in the United States.

The Nikkei Average is a price-weighted stock index which is based upon the 225 most actively traded stocks on the Tokyo Stock Exchange.

The Office examined the proposed contract in light of the criteria set forth in Section 2(a)(1)(B)(ii) of the Act. The Office also was informed by SEC staff that they would not object to the offer and sale of the futures contract in the United States.

The letter by the Office of General Counsel is attached.

COMMODITY FUTURES TRADING COMMISSION
2033 K STREET, N.W., WASHINGTON, D.C. 20581

December 5, 1986

Carl A. Royal, Esquire
General Counsel
Chicago Mercantile Exchange
30 South Wacker Drive
Chicago, Illinois 60606

RE: Singapore International Monetary Exchange Nikkei Stock Average Futures
Contract

Dear Mr. Royal:

This is in response to your letter dated August 15, 1986 requesting an opinion of this Office on behalf of the Singapore International Monetary Exchange, Ltd. ("Simex"). You ask whether the Simex, under the Commodity Exchange Act, lawfully may offer and sell within the United States futures contracts based on the Nikkei Stock Average.

From your letter and attachments, we understand the facts to be as follows. The Nikkei Stock Average ("Nikkei Average") is published by the Nihon Keizai Shimbun, Inc. ("NKS") of Japan. The Nikkei Average is a price-weighted stock index which is calculated based on the prices of 225 stocks traded on the Tokyo Stock Exchange ("TSE"). The Nikkei Average consists of the most actively traded stocks on the TSE.[1] The stocks comprising the Nikkei Average represent a broad cross-section of the stocks listed on the TSE, with no single industry group accounting for more than ten percent of the value of the Nikkei Average.[2] The highest priced stock in the Nikkei Average as of March 31, 1986, Sony, constituted approximately 2 percent of the aggregate stock prices comprising the Average. The total capitalization of the 225 stocks included in the Nikkei Average equaled 906.5 billion in U.S. dollars as of August 28, 1986. A small number of the stocks comprising the Nikkei Average are publicly traded in the United States: five of such issues are traded on the New York Stock Exchange and another nine of such issues are traded through the NASDAQ quotation system operated by the National Association of Securities Dealers.

The Nikkei Average is calculated by dividing the sum of the prices for the 225 stocks in the Average by a specified divisor. That divisor is adjusted from time to time to reflect certain non-market factors as stock splits and mergers. The adjustment method used by the NKS is the same as that used in calculating the Dow Jones Averages. The Quotation Information Center K.K., a NKS subsidiary, calculates the Nikkei Average on a real-time basis. The Average is published daily both in *The Nihon Keizai Shimbun* (circulation of approximately 3.6 million) and in *The Wall Street Journal*. The Average also is to be disseminated on a minute-to-minute basis to financial centers throughout the world by Reuters and Telerate.

The Simex is located in Singapore and began trading on September 7, 1984. The Simex is regulated by the Monetary Authority of Singapore as a futures exchange under the newly adopted Futures Trading Act 1986. The Simex is not designated as a contract market under the Commodity Exchange Act and does not intend to seek such designation.[3]

The Nikkei Stock Average futures contract to be traded on he Simex is valued at 500 Japanese Yen times the value of the Nikkei Stock Index Futures price. The futures contract provides for cash settlement. The final settlement price of the contract will be based upon the actual closing value of the Nikkei Average. Cash settlement will be based upon the difference between the futures settlement price on the business day preceding the last trading day and the value of the Nikkei Average at the close of the final trading day.

The offer and sale of futures contracts traded on or subject to the rules of a foreign exchange is subject to the Commission's exclusive jurisdiction.[4] Section 2(a)(1)(A), 7 U.S.C. section 2 (1982); 120 Cong. Rec. 34497 (1974) (statement of Senator Talmadge) (the terms "any other board of trade, exchange, or market" in Section 2 (a)(1)(A) make clear the Commission's exclusive jurisdiction includes futures contracts executed on a foreign board of trade, exchange or market.).[5] Section 2(a)(1)(B)(v) of the Commodity Exchange Act prohibits any person from offering or selling a futures contract based on a securities index except as permitted under Section 2(a)(1)(B)(ii), 7 U.S.C. sections 2a(v), 2a(ii) (1982). In turn, Section 2(a)(1)(B) (ii) sets forth three criteria to govern Commission designation of futures contracts in a group or index of securities:

(1) the contract must provide for cash settlement;
(2) the proposed contract will not be readily susceptible to manipulation nor to being used to manipulate any underlying security; and
(3) the index is predominately composed of the securities of unaffiliated issues and reflects the market for all publicly traded securities or a substantial segment thereof.

See H.R. Rep. No. 565, Part 1, 97th Cong., 2d Sess. 39 (1982).

Section 2(a)(1)(B)(ii) provides that the Commission shall not designate a board of trade as a contract market unless the Commission finds that the board of trade meets the enumerated criteria. We understand that the Simex does not seek designation as a contract market. However, Congress understood that a foreign exchange might lawfully offer futures contracts on stock indices absent designation. Thus, the House Committee on Agriculture suggested that a foreign board of trade could apply for "certification" that its stock index contract met all applicable Commission requirements. H.R. Rep. No. 565, Part 1, 97th Cong., 2d Sess. 85 (1982). The Commission has not established criteria for certification of foreign futures contracts. However, the House Committee on Agriculture explained that a foreign exchange seeking certification for a futures contract based upon an index of American securities must demonstrate that the proposed futures contract meets the requirements set forth in Section 2(a)(1)(B)(ii). *Id.*

While we understand that the securities in the Nikkei Stock Average are issued by Japanese companies, some of these securities are also traded on United States securities exchanges. The House Committee suggested that the Commission use such criteria as it deems appropriate in evaluating a foreign stock index contract based on "foreign securities." The requirements of 2(a)(1)(B)(ii) were designed to permit innovative financial instruments "while at the same time [assuring] that futures trading is limited to broad-based . . . indices that are not conducive to manipulation or disruption of the market for the underlying securities." S. Rep. No. 390, 97th Cong., 2d Sess. 6 (1982). *See also* H.R. Rep. No. 565, Part 1, 97th Cong., 2d Sess. at 39. We have used the criteria set forth in Section 2(a)(1)(B)(ii) in establishing any certification procedures for the Nikkei Stock Average futures contract.

Based on the information available to us at this time, this Office will not recommend any enforcement action to the Commission based on Sections 2(a)(1)(B)(v), 4(a) or 12(e) of the Commodity Exchange Act, as amended, if the Simex offers and sells the Nikkei Stock Average futures contract in the United States. While we have decided to issue this no-action position, we believe that a surveillance sharing agreement between the Simex and the TSE should be entered into between the parties to ensure the deterrence or detection of potential inter-market manipulation. CME has represented that it will work with the Simex and TSE to obtain such a surveillance sharing agreement. Therefore, in twelve months we intend to review our position in this matter including an evaluation of the progress toward a surveillance sharing agreement between the Simex and TSE.

Because this position is based upon facts and representations contained in your letter and presented orally, it should be noted that any different, omitted or changed facts or conditions might require a different conclusion. This position also is contingent on the Simex' continued compliance with all regulatory requirements imposed by the Monetary Authority of Singapore and the applicable Singapore statutes and the availability of certain market information which the Commission may request from time to time.[6] We have sought the opinion of the staff of the Securities and Exchange Commission ("SEC"). While the staff of the SEC has stated that they do not object to the issuance of this no-action letter to permit the offer and sale of this futures contract in the United States, they too share our concern about the necessity for a surveillance agreement.

You should be aware that Commission regulation 30.02 prohibits fraud in connection with transactions in foreign futures contracts. 17 C.F.R. section 30.02 (1986). Moreover, the Commission has proposed rules pursuant to Sections 2(a)(1)(A) and 4(b) of the Act to regulate the offer and sale of foreign futures and foreign option contracts in the United States. *See* 51 *Fed Reg.* 12104 (April 8, 1986). The offer and sale in the United States of the Nikkei Stock Average futures contract would, of course, be governed by Commission regulations enacted as a result of such rulemaking.

Sincerely,

Kenneth M. Raisler
General Counsel

cc: Richard G. Ketchum
Director
Division of Market Regulation
Securities and Exchange Commission

[1]The most actively traded stocks on the Tokyo Stock Exchange are listed in the "First Section" of that Exchange. The stocks in the Nikkei Average account for approximately 50 percent of the total market value and over 60 percent of the trading volume of the stocks in the "First Section."
The securities comprising the Nikkei Average are not considered exempted securities under the United States securities laws.
[2]The Nikkei Average represents 26 industry groups.
[3]On August 28, 1984, the Commission approved certain rule changes of the Chicago Mercantile Exchange ("CME") to facilitate the Mutual Offset System ("MOS") between the CME and Simex whereby positions established on one exchange can be transferred to or liquidated on the other exchange. Four futures contracts now are traded through the MOS: futures on Eurodollars, Japanese Yen, Deustche marks and British pounds. The futures contract on the Nikkei Average at this time will not be conducted through the MOS. The CME must be approved to trade a futures contract on the Nikkei Average before that contract could be conducted through the MOS. Positions taken in this letter in no way suggest any action the Commission or its staff might take on the CME application for contract market designation to trade the Nikkei Stock Average, including, for example, requirements for appropriate information sharing arrangements among relevant regulatory agencies where the foreign contract is to be traded on a domestic contract market. See pages 4-5, *infra*.
[4]Section 12(e) of the Commodity Exchange Act prohibits the application of any federal or state statute to a transaction that is conducted on or subject to the rules of a foreign exchange "except as otherwise specified by the Commission by rule or regulation." 7 U.S.C. section 16(e) (1982). The Commission has not undertaken such a rulemaking to date.
[5]In this regard, the Commodity Exchange Act recognizes that futures contracts made on or subject to the rules of a foreign exchange may be lawfully offered and sold in this country. Thus, Section 4(a), which requires that all futures contracts be effected on or subject to the rules of a contract market, specifically exempts futures contracts made on or subject to the rules of a foreign exchange from these requirements.
[6]We understand that the Simex will cooperate with requests for market data from United States contract markets and from national securities exchanges and other self-regulatory organizations (collectively "SROs"). Generally, in regard to the CME-Simex linkage, the Commission has been assured that no statute of Singapore would operate to prohibit the sharing of trading-related information with the SRO's.

Glossary of Futures and Options Terminology

The following Glossary contains terminology frequently used in futures, options, and cash market trading. The terms and definitions are not legal interpretations, but should provide a better understanding of market jargon, and can be used as a reference. In addition, many of the abbreviation used in the text (and the market-place) are spelled out here.

Abandon: The act of the option holder (or owner, taker) in electing NOT to exercise his option.

Accommodation Trading: Wash trading entered into by a trader, usually to assist another with illegal trades.

Account Sale: A statement by broker to a commodity customer when a futures transaction is closed out. Sometimes referred to as a P&S (Purchase and Sale Statement), it shows the net profit or loss on the transaction, with commission and other proper charges set forth and taken into account.

Accumulate: Traders are said to accumulate contracts when they add to their original market position.

Actuals: The physical or cash commodity, as distinguished from commodity futures contracts.

Aggregate Exercise Price: The exercise price of an option contract multiplied by the number of units of the underlying security covered by the option contract.

Alligator Spread: Another name for a butterfly spread suggesting that the commissions and bid-asked spread will "eat you alive."

Allowances: The discounts (premiums) allowed for grades or a commodity lower (higher) than the par or a basis-grade specified in the futures contract. Also called differentials.

American Option: A put or call that can be exercised at any time prior to expiration. All listed stock options, including those on European exchanges, are American-type options. Most nonstock options are also American-type options, but a few European-type options have been introduced in recent years.

AOM: Australian Options Market - Melbourne.

API: American Petroleum Institute.

APT: Automated Pit Trading; the London International Financial Futures Exchange (LIFFE) after-hours trading system.

Appreciation: An increase in value.

Approved Delivery Facility: Any bank, tank facility, store, warehouse, plant, elevator or other depository that is authorized by an exchange for the delivery of commodities tendered on futures contracts.

Approved Securities: Securities authorized for the investment of customers' moneys, or authorized as collateral as margin.

Arbitrage: Technically, arbitrage is purchasing a commodity or security in one market for immediate sale in another market. Popular usage has expanded the meaning of the term to include any activity which attempts to buy a relatively underpriced item and sell a relatively overpriced item, expecting to profit when the prices resume a more appropriate relationship. In futures it can include a cash transaction on one side with an opposite futures purchase/sale. In trading options and other convertible securities, arbitrage techniques can be applied whenever a strategy involves buying one and selling the other of two related securities.

Asiadollar: U.S. dollar deposits placed offshore in Asia, usually in Singapore.

Asian: A type of options contract which combines the features of American and European options.

Assignable Option (or Contract): One which pay off according to an average price level of underlying instrument during the life of the option.

Assignment: Notice to an option seller that an option has been exercised by the buyer.

ASX: Abbreviation for the Australian Stock Exchange Limited, which was formed in April 1987 to merge the 6 existing city exchanges. It also includes the Australian Financial Futures Market and the Australian Options Market (AOM) as subsidiaries.

ATS: Automated Trading System; the New Zealand Futures and Options Exchange's electronic trading system.

At the Market: See Market Order.

At the Money: When the striking price of an option equals the market price of the underlying instrument.

Backwardation: Market situation in which futures prices are progressively lower in the distant delivery months. For instance, if the gold quotation for February is $360.00 per ounce and that for June is $355.00 per ounce, the backwardation for four months against January is $5.00 per ounce. (Backwardation is the opposite of Contango.) See Market.

Bakai Sheet: The order book for Japanese securities trading. Japanese stock index futures trade with an on-screen Bakai sheet, which indicated price and quantity for each bid and offer level.

BSI: Barclays Share Price Index. A popular indicator for New Zealand equities.

Barrel: A unit of volume measurement used for petroleum and its products. 1 barrel = 42 U.S gallons.

Basis: The difference between the spot or cash price of a commodity and the futures price of the same or a related commodity. Basis is usually computed to the near future, and may represent different time periods, product forms, qualities and locations. See Short the Basis, Long the Basis.

Basis Grade: The grade of a commodity used as the standard of the contract. (sometimes referred to as par).

Basis Point: One-hundredth of one percent. The difference between a yield of 7.90 percent and 8 percent is 10 basis points.

Bear: One who expects a decline in prices. The opposite of bull. A news item is consider bearish if it is expected to bring lower prices.

Bear Covering: The act of buying back a speculative short position in a steady or rising market despite the original intention to await a market drop.

Bear Market: A market in which prices are declining.

Beta (or Beta Coefficient): A statistical measurement of the relationship between the risk of an individual stock or stock portfolio and the risk of the overall market. The Beta of a stock or portfolio measures the volatility of that stock or portfolio relative to the volatility of the overall market. A Beta of 1.0 means that the stock or portfolio is perfectly correlated to the overall market (or particular index for comparison).

Bid: An offer to buy a specific quantity of a commodity at a stated price.

Book Transfer: Transfer of title to buyer without physical movement of product.

Booking the Basis: A forward pricing sales arrangement in which the cash price is determined either by the buyer or seller within a specified time. At that time, the previously-agreed basis is applied to the then-current futures quotation.

Box Spread: A combination of a horizontal, or calendar, call spread and a horizontal put spread. Both spreads have the same expiration date on their respective long and short positions. This position can also be visualized as a combination of (I) a long straddle and (2) a short straddle which expires before the long straddle and has the same striking price. An alternative form of box spread might combine vertical put and call spreads with identical expiration dates.

Break: A rapid and sharp price decline.

Break Out: (1) The process of undoing a conversion or a reversal, reestablishing the option buyer's original position. (2) A technical price movement, representing a change in prevailing market condition.

Broad Tape: Term commonly applied to newswires carrying price and background information on securities and futures markets, in contrast to the exchanges' own price transmission wires, which use a narrow "ticker tape."

Broker: A person paid a fee or commission for executing buy or sell orders of a customer. In commodity futures trading, the term may refer to (1) A Floor Broker-a person who actually executes orders on the trading floor of an exchange; (2) Account Executive, the person who deals with customers in the offices of futures commission merchants; and (3) Futures Commission Merchant or Brokerage House.

Brokerage: The fee charged by a broker for execution of a transaction. The fee may be a flat amount or a percentage.

Bucketing: Directly or indirectly taking the opposite side of a customer's order into the handling broker's own account or into an account in which he has an interest, without execution on an exchange. A Bucket Shop refers to any disreputable futures or securities firm.

Bulge: A rapid and sharp price advance.

Bull: One who expects a rise in prices. The opposite of "bear." A news item is considered bullish if it portends higher prices.

Bullion: Gold in bars or ingots assaying at least .99S fine.

Bull Market: A market in which prices are rising.

Bunker Fuel Oil: Heavy fuel oil used in ships' boilers.

Buoyant: A market in which prices have a tendency to rise easily with a considerable show of strength.

Butterfly Spread: Although some traders use different definitions, a common butterfly spread combines a vertical bull and a vertical bear spread with the same expiration date on all options and the same striking price on all options written. This position is sometimes known as a sandwich spread or an alligator spread.

Buy In: Making a purchase to cover a previous sale, often called covering.

Buy On Close: To buy at the end of the trading sessions within the closing price range. (Also may be "Sell on Close.")

Buy On Opening: To buy at the beginning of a trading within the opening price range. (Also may be "Sell on Opening.")

Buying Hedge (or Long Hedge): Hedging transaction in which futures contracts are bought to protect against possible increased cost of financial instruments or commodities. See also Hedging.

CBOT: Chicago Board of Trade.

CFTC: U.S. Commodity Futures Trading Commission.

CFO: Cancel Former Order.

CME: Chicago Mercantile Exchange.

Candlestick Charts, or Japanese Candlesticks: The primary Japanese charting method, developed over the past 2 centuries. It displays price information in a more visually striking way than standard bar charts, and to those familiar with its various patterns, can often indicate market turning points with great accuracy.

Calendar Spread: The option purchased expires after the option sold. The number of contracts purchased equals the number sold, and both options have the same striking price.

Call: (1) A period at the opening and the close of some futures markets in which the price for each futures contract is established by auction; (2) The requirement that a financial instrument be returned to Issuer prior to maturity, with principal and accrued interest paid off upon return.

Call Option: An option contract which gives the buyer (holder) the right but not the obligation, to purchase a specific denomination/amount of a financial instrument/commodity at a fixed price within a specified period of time. The buyer has the right to buy the commodity (or futures contract) or enter a long position. A call writer (grantor) has the obligation to sell the commodity (or enter a short position) at the striking price during the term of the option, upon demand of the holder. Ordinarily issued for less than one year.

Call Provision: A term in a bond indenture that gives the issuer of a bond the option to call the bond for redemption and/or refunding at certain prices and at certain times. This option can be evaluated along much the same lines as other options.

Call Spread: A spread consisting of a long position and a short position in calls on the same underlying security or commodity.

Callable Security: A bond or other security that may be retired under certain circumstances by the issuer. If the security is called, the holder of the instrument may lose some of the value of the position.

Cap: A feature of a debt contract that puts a ceiling or cap on the interest rate.

Carload or Car: The load of a railroad freight car; a loose, quantitative term sometimes used to describe a futures contract.

Carrying Broker: A member of a futures exchange, usually a commission house broker, through whom another broker or customer elects to clear all or part of his trades.

Carrying Chages: The cost of storing a physical commodity over a period of time. Includes insurance, storage, and interest on the invested funds as well as other incidental costs. It is a "carrying charge market" when there are higher futures prices for each successive contract maturity. If the carrying charge is adequate to reimburse the holder, it is called a full carrying charge.

Cash Commodity: The physical or actual commodity as distinguished from the "futures." Sometimes called the spot commodity or actuals.

Cash Market: Market for immediate delivery of and payment for commodities.

Cash Price: The price used in the marketplace for actual cash or spot commodities to be delivered via customary market channels.

Cash Settlement Option: Securities or futures options where the ultimate settlement is in the form of cash based on the price of an underlying instrument or a basket of underlying instruments.

Central Rate: Similar to par value, as established by the International Monetary Fund.

Certificate of Deposit: Private short-term debt issued by banks.

Certificated or Certified Stocks: Stocks of a commodity that have been inspected and found to be a quality deliverable against futures contracts, stored at the delivery points designated as regular or acceptable for delivery by the exchange.

Charting: The use of graphs and charts in the technical analysis of futures markets to plot trends of price movements, average movements of price, and volume and open interest. See also technical analysis.

Churning: Excessive trading which permits the broker to derive a profit while disregarding the best interests of the customer.

Clearing: The procedure through which the clearing house becomes buyer to each seller of a futures contract, and seller to each buyer, and assumes responsibility for protecting buyers and sellers from financial loss by assuring performance on each contract.

Clearing House: An adjunct to a commodity exchange through which transactions executed on the floor or screens of the exchange are settled. Also charged with assuring the proper conduct of the exchange's delivery procedures and the adequate financing of the trading.

Clearing Member: A member of the Clearing House. All trades of a non-clearing member must be registered and eventually settled through a clearing member.

Close, The: The period at the end of the trading session officially designated by the exchange during which all transactions are considered made "at the close."

Closing Price (or range): The price (or price range) recorded in the trading place in the final moments of a day's trade that are officially designated as the "close."

Collar: A feature of a debt or derivative contract that puts both a cap (ceiling) and a floor (minimum) on the interest rate or price movement.

Combination Option: An option consisting of at least one put and one call. The component options may be exercised or resold separately, but they are originally sold as a unit.

Commission: The charge made by a broker for buying and selling futures, options, commodities, or securities.

Commission House: A concern that buys and sells actual commodities or futures contracts for the accounts of customers. Its income is generated by the commission charged customers.

Commitment or Open Interest: The number of contracts in existence at any period of time which have not as yet been satisfied by an offsetting sale or purchase or by actual contract delivery.

Commodity Futures Trading Commission (CFTC): The U.S. federal regulatory agency established by the CFTC Act of 1974 to administer the Commodity Exchange Act.

Commodity Option: An option to buy (call) or sell (put) a specific commodity or commodity futures contract at a given price within a specified time. Until recently commodity options have been more widely used in the United Kingdom than in the United States or Asia.

Commodity Pool Operator (CPO): Individuals or firms in businesses similar to investment trusts or syndicates that solicit or accept funds, securities or property for trading commodity futures contracts.

Commodity Trading Advisor (CTA): An American regulatory category for individuals or firms that, for fees, issue analysis or reports concerning financial and commodity futures, advise others about financial instruments or commodities, or of the advisability of trading futures or options.

Congestion: (l) A congested market describes a situation in which the market is "clogged." When shorts attempt to cover their positions they are not likely to find an adequate supply of contracts provided by longs willing to liquidate, or by new sellers willing to enter the market, except at sharply higher prices. A congested market situation is one which is likely to result in a "natural" squeeze, or one which could be exploited by a manipulator; (2) In technical analysis, a period of repetitious and limited price fluctuations.

Constant-Proportion Portfolio Insurance: A portfolio insurance technique that exposes a constant multiple of the cushion over an investor's floor value to the equity market.

Contango: A futures-spot market relationship in which the futures price is progressively higher than the spot price by approximately the cost of purchasing the spot commodity or security and storing and/or financing it until the settlement date of the futures con-tract. Also called a carrying-charge market.

Contingent Hedge with an Agreement for Rebate at Maturity (CHARM): A foreign currency option product of Manufacturer's Hanover Bank designed for companies bidding on foreign contracts. If the company wins the contract, the option may be exercised- like any other currency option. If the company loses the contract, the option is void but the bank rebates a portion of the premium.

Contract: A term of reference describing a unit of trading for a financial or commodity future. Also an actual bilateral agreement between buyer and seller.

Contract Grades: Those grades of a financial instrument or commodity which have been officially approved by an exchange or clearing house as deliverable in settlement of a futures contract.

Contract Month: The month in which delivery is to be made in accordance with a futures contract.

Contract Trading Volume: The total number of contracts traded in a commodity or commodity delivery month during a specified period of time (day, week, etc.)

Contract Unit: The actual amount of a commodity designated in a given futures contract.

Controlled Account: Any account for which trading is directed by someone other than the owner.

Conventional Option: An option contract negotiated and/or traded off a futures or securities exchange. While the contract is negotiable, it does not usually change hands after the original transaction. The terms of conventional option contracts are not standardized.

Conversion: The process by which a put can be changed to a call, and a call to a put. To convert a put to a call, the conversion house buys the put and 100 shares of stock and issues a call. To convert a call to a put, the conversion house buys the call, sells The stock short, and issues a put.

Convertible Security: A bond, preferred stock, or warrant that is convertible under certain circumstances into the common stock of a corporation. Each of these securities has an option element that affects its value.

Corner: (1) To corner is to secure such relative control of a commodity or security that its price can he manipulated. (2) In the extreme situation, obtaining contracts requiring delivery of more commodities or securities than are available for delivery.

Coupon: The annual rate of interest that a bond guarantees to pay, based on the bond's face value.

Cover: Purchasing futures to offset a a short position (or vice versa).

Covered Warrant: A warrant issued by a party other than the issuer of the underlying security and secured by the warrant issuer's holding in the underlying securities. Covered warrants are most common in Europe and are used primarily in circumstances when transfer of the underlying security is temporarily restricted.

Covered Writer: A call option writer who owns the underlying stock which is subject to option. An investor setting up an option hedge or writing multiple options may be covered with respect to part of the option position and uncovered with respect to the rest.

Cross-hedging: Using an instrument with price action highly correlated with the price action of a second instrument to offset some of the price risk of the second instrument. For example, hedging a cash market risk with a futures contract on a different instrument. The risk in cross-hedging is that the price correlations may be poor during the period the cross-hedge is in place.

Cross-Rate: In foreign exchange, the price of one currency in terms of another currency, in the market of a third country

Cross Trading: Offsetting or noncompetitive matching of the buying order of one customer against the selling order of another, a practice that is permissible only when executed as prescribed by particular exchange rules. On some Asian exchanges, it is completely legal and common practice.

Crude Oil: A mixture of hydrocarbons that exists in the liquid phase in natural underground reservoirs and remains liquid ammopheric pressure after passing through surface separating facilities.

Current Delivery (Month): The futures contract which matures and becomes deliverable during the present month; also called spot month.

Current Yield: A bond's annual interest payment divided by that bond's current market price.

Day Order: An order that expires automatically at the end of each day's trading session. There may be a day order with time contingent, "Off at a specific time" order, which is an order that remains in force until the specified time during the session is reached.

Day Trading: Establishing and offsetting the same futures market position within one day.

Day Traders: Futures and options traders, generally members of the exchange and active on the trading floor, who take positions and then offset them prior to the close of the same trading day.

Deck: The orders a floor broker holds in his hand.

Declaration Date: The last date on which the buyer has the right to exercise his option. If the buyer fails to declare by such date, the option automatically expires.

Default: (1) Failure to perform on a futures contract as required by exchange rules, such as failure to meet a margin call, or to make or take delivery; (2) The failure of an exchange or clearing house to pay sufficient funds to meet its customers' claims (3) In futures markets, the theoretical failure of a party to a futures contract to either make or take delivery of the underlying instrument as required under the contract.

Deferred Delivery: (1) Forward Contracting (2) The distant months in which futures trading is taking place, as distinguished from the nearby futures delivery months.

Deferred Futures: The futures, of those currently traded, that expire during the most distant months.

Deliverable Grades: See Contract Grade.

Delivery: The tender and receipt of the actual underlying financial instrument or commodity in settlement of a futures contract. See Notice of Delivery.

Delivery, Current: Deliveries being made during a present month. Sometimes current delivery is used as a synonym for nearby delivery.

Delivery Instrument: A document used to effect delivery on a futures contract, such as a warehouse receipt or shipping certificate.

Delivery Month: The specified month within which a futures contract matures and can be settled by delivery.

Delivery, Nearby: The nearest traded month.

Delivery Notice: The written notice given by the seller of his intention to make delivery against an open short futures position on a particular date. This notice, delivered through the clearing house, is separate and distinct from the warehouse receipt or other instrument that will be used to transfer title.

Delivery Points: Those locations designated by commodity exchanges at which stocks of a commodity represented by a futures contract may be delivered in fulfillment of the contract.

Delivery Price: The price fixed by the clearing house at which deliveries on futures are invoiced and the price at which the futures contract is settled when deliveries are made.

Delta : The dollar change in option price for a given dollar change in the underlying instrument's price. The neutral hedge ratio.

Depository or Warehouse Receipt: A document issued by a bank, warehouse or other depository indicating ownership of a stored commodity. In the case of many commodities deliverable against futures contracts, transfer of ownership of an appropriate depository receipt may affect contract delivery.

Derivative Security or Instrument: A contract or convertible instrument that changes in price in concert with and/or obtains much of its value from price movements in a related or underlying security or commodity.

Diagonal Bear Spread: Regardless of whether puts or calls are used, this position involves the purchase of a relatively long-term option contract and the sale of a shorter-term contract with a lower striking price. Ordinarily, the number of contracts purchased equals the number of contracts sold.

Diagonal Bull Spread: The option contract purchased expires later and has a lower striking price than the option sold. Ordinarily, the number of contracts purchased equals the number of contracts sold. Like other spreads, these diagonal spreads are best analyzed by using stock equivalents.

Differentials: The discounts (premiums) allowed for grades or locations of a financial instrument or commodity lower (higher) than the par or basis grade or location specified in the futures contract. Also called Allowances.

Discount: (1) The amount a price would be reduced to purchase a commodity of lesser grade; (2) Sometimes used to refer to the price differences between futures of different delivery months, as in the phrase "June at a discount to March," indicating that the price of the June future is lower than that of March.

Discount Rate: The interest rate that banks pay when they borrow from central banking authorities.

Discretionary Account: An arrangement by which the holder of the account gives written power of attorney to someone else, often his broker, to buy and sell without prior approval of the holder; often referred to as a managed account.

Distant or Deferred Delivery: Usually means one of the more distant months in which futures trading is taking place.

Dominant Future: The futures contract having the largest number of open contracts.

Double Option: (I) An option to buy (call) or sell (put) but not both. Exercise of the call causes the put to expire, and exercise of the put causes the call to expire. Double options are used primarily in unlisted commodity option trading. (2) In the operation of a sinking fund, the issuer is often permitted to purchase "double" the mandatory amount at par.

Down-and-Out Call: A conventional-type call option that expires if the market price of the underlying stock drops below a predetermined expiration price. These options are written by a number of major brokerage firms and sold only to clients able to accept substantial risk.

Dressed Option: A short futures option collateralized by a risk-offsetting position in the underlying futures contract. A dressed call option, comparable to a covered call would be collateralized by a long position in the underlying futures contract.

Duration: The present value weighted time-to-maturity. Originally developed as a risk measurement for bonds (the greater the duration or "average" maturity, the greater the risk), duration has proven useful in evaluating equity securities and options.

Dynamic Hedging: A technique of portfolio insurance in which a short stock index futures position is increased or decreased to create a synthetic put on the portfolio.

Dynamic Overwriting: A call option writing strategy which mandates an increase in the short call position as the stock price rises. In effect, the dynamic overwriter increases a short position most aggressively when the position is proving most unprofitable.

Early-Redemption (Put) Option: Bonds with both fixed and floating rates have been issued with provisions that permit the holder to sell them back to the issuer or a third party at par or close to par in the event interest rates rise and/or the quality of the credit declines. Also called Put Bonds.

Eligible Margin: The cash or other collateral which the exchange specifies that members may accept from their customers to satisfy initial and variation margin requirements.

Embedded Option: An option that is granted to the issuer of a security by the buyer and which permits the issuer to change the terms of the security. A common embedded option is the call provision in most corporate bonds which permits the issuer to repay the borrower earlier than the nominal term of the bond. The borrower's option to repay mortgage principal early, resulting in early liquidation of a mortgage-backed security, is also an embedded option. Index options can also be embedded into corporate bonds.

End-user: The ultimate consumer of petroleum products; more commonly used in connection with large institutional investors or industrial consumers.

Engulfing Pattern: One of the most important patterns that appear in Japanese Candlestick charting. There can be bullish or bearish engulfing patterns, and they indicate a key reversal of price trends.

Equity: The residual monetary value of a futures trading account assuming it were liquidated at current prices.

Equity-Enhanced Dedication: A form of portfolio insurance using a dedicated bond portfolio as the reserve asset and common stocks or index futures as the risky asset. This technique is designed to maintain a minimum pension surplus while providing equity exposure and a chance of increasing the surplus.

Eurodeutschemark (or EuroDM): "Offshore" Deutschemark deposits, outside of Bundesbank control.

Eurodollar: U.S. dollar deposits placed with banks outside the U.S. holders may include individuals, companies, banks and central banks. Although it initially referred to holdings in Europe, mostly London, it now commonly refers to such assets outside of the currency's domicile. Thus dealers are often negotiating Eurodollar deals in the Singapore Asiadollar market.

European Option: A put or call that can be exercised only on the expiration date. Options listed on European options exchanges are not necessarily European style options, and are often American options in the sense that they can be exercised prior to the expiration date.

Euroyen: "Offshore" Yen deposits, including assets in the Tokyo offshore market.

Excess: The amount by which a customer's equity exceeds the margin requirements for positions held by an account.

Exchange of Futures for Physicals (EFP): A transaction in which the buyer of a cash instrument or commodity transfers to the seller a corresponding amount of long futures contracts, or receives from the seller a corresponding amount of short futures, at a price difference mutually agreed upon. In this way the opposite positions in futures of both parties are closed out simultaneously. Also called Exchange of Futures for Cash or AA (Against Actuals).

Exchange Rate: The "price" of one currency stated in terms of another currency.

Exchange Rate Futures: Futures contracts for currencies, Currency Futures.

Exercise: To elect to buy or sell, taking advantage of the right (but not the duty) conferred by the option contract. See Declare.

Exercise (or Striking) Price: The price at which the buyer of a call can purchase the commodity during the life of the option, and the price at which the buyer of a put can sell the commodity during the life of the option.

Execution by Open Outcry: The practice on many exchanges of executing orders verbally and publicly.

Expiration Date: The date on which an option contract expires; the last day on which an option can be exercised.

Expiration Time: The exact date and time specified in the option contract when it expires and the holder's right of exercise lapses. After this time the holder is considered to have abandoned his option.

Ex-Pit Transaction: Trade executed in a location other than the relevant exchange trading pit or ring.

Extension: An agreement between the buyer and the writer of a conventional option to lengthen the life of the option beyond the original expiration date. Extensions are not common because both parties have to agree to the extension and to the price to be paid for it. There is no mechanism for extension of listed options.

FACTS: The acronym for the Tokyo International Financial Futures Exchange's (TIFFE) Fully Automated Computer Trading System.

Fair Value of an Option: The option value derived by a probability-type option valuation model. The fair value of an option is the price at which both the buyer and the writer of the option should expect to break even, neglecting the effect of commissions. after an adjustment for risk. Fair value is an estimate of where an option should sell in an efficient market, not where it will sell.

Fast Tape: Transactions in the pit take place in such volume and with such rapidity that price reporters are behind with price quotations, and thus insert "FAST" to indicate such a situation. During such times, floor brokers may not be held accountable for unexecuted limit orders.

Federal Reserve System: Created in 1913 the 'Fed' is composed of 12 Federal Reserve Banks and a national board of governors. The Fed has the responsibility for implementing monetary policy and regulating the national banking structure. The Fed is the U.S. equivalent of a central bank.

FIA: Futures Industry Association. A U.S.-based industry grouping which includes exchanges, corporate and individual members. It is rapidly expanding its international membership and activities.

Fictitious Trading: Wash trading, bucketing, cross trading, or other device, scheme or artifice to give the appearance of trading. In such situations, no bona fide, competitive trade has occurred.

Fill or Kill Order: A commodity order which demands immediate execution or cancellation.

First Notice Day: The first day on which notices of intention to deliver actual commodities or financial instruments against futures market positions can be received. First notice day will vary with each type of contract and exchange.

Fixation: In a call purchase or call sale the point at which the price is determined by the buyer in a call sale, the seller in a call purchase.

Fixed Price: A price (including basis and futures price) that has been determined for a given lot of a commodity.

Floor: A feature of a debt contract that puts a minimum or floor on the interest rate.

Floor Broker: Any person who, in or surrounding any pit, ring, post or other place provided by a contract market for the meeting of persons similarly engaged, executes for another any orders for the purchase or sale of any commodity for future delivery.

Floor Trader: An exchange member who usually executes his own trades by being personally present in the pit or place for futures trading. Often called a Local.

Foreign Exchange: (or Forex) Foreign currency. On the foreign exchange market, foreign currency is bought and sold for immediate or future delivery.

Forward: In the future.

Forward Contracting: A cash transaction common in many industries, including commodity merchandising, in which the buyer and seller agree upon delivery of a specified quality and quantity of goods at a specified future date. A price may be agreed upon in advance, or there may be agreement that the price will be determined at the time of delivery.

Forward Market: Refers to informal (non-exchange) trading of financial instruments or commodities to be delivered at a future date. Contracts for forward delivery are "personalized," i.e., delivery time and amount are as determined between seller and customer.

Forward Months: Futures contracts, of those currently traded, calling for later or distant delivery. Also described as Deferred Futures.

Forward Purchase or Sale: A purchase or sale of an actual commodity for deferred delivery.

Forward Shipment: A contract covering cash commodities to be shipped at some future specified date.

Free Supply: Stocks of a commodity which are available for commercial sale, as distinguished from government-owned or controlled stocks.

Fuel Oil: The heavy distillates from the oil refining process; used as fuel for power stations and marine boilers. Also referred to as Bunker Fuel.

Fundamental Analysis: Study of basic, underlying factors which will affect the supply and demand of the instrument being traded. This is in contrast to Technical Analysis.

Fungibility: The characteristic of standardization or interchangeability. Listed futures or options contracts for the same underlying and delivery month are fungible due to their standardized specifications for quality, quantity, delivery date and delivery locations. Also refers to the listing of identical contracts on different exchanges, thus facilitating position holders to close out a position through a transaction on a different exchange.

Futures: A term used to designate the standardized contracts covering the sale of financial instruments or commodities for future delivery on a centralized exchange.

Futures Commission Merchant: Individuals, associations, partnerships, corporations and trusts that solicit or accept orders for the purchase or sale of any financial instrument or commodity for future delivery on or subject to the rules of any contract market and that accept payment from or extend credit to those whose orders are accepted.

Futures Contract: A firm commitment to deliver or to receive a specified quantity and type of a financial instrument or commodity during a designated month with price being determined by public auction among exchange members.

Futures Price: The price of a given trading unit determined by public auction on a futures exchange.

Gamma: The change in delta divided by the dollar change in the underlying instrument price. The second derivative of the option price with respect to the price of the underlying security.

Gasoil: European designation for No. 2 heating oils and diesel fuels.

G.T.C.: Good-Till-Cancelled. Open order to buy or sell at a fixed price that remain effective until executed or cancelled

Give Up: (1) At the request of the customer, a brokerage house which has not performed the service is credited with the execution of an order; (2) In the trading pit, a broker "gives up" the name of the firm for which he was acting to another member with whom a transaction has just been completed.

GLOBEX: The electronic trading system developed by Reuters and the CME, and joined by the CBOT and MATIF.

Grantor: The maker, writer, or issuer of an option contract.

Heating Oil: No. 2 Fuel Oil, a distillate fuel oil for domestic heating use.

Hedge: To reduce the risk of loss from an investment position by making approximately offsetting transactions that will largely eliminate one or more types of risks. The term is often used loosely and hedging in the broader sense typically involves partially offsetting a long position in one security with a short or short equivalent position in a related security.

Hindsight (or Lookback) Currency Option: An option giving the buyer the retroactive right to buy a currency at its low point (call) or to sell a currency at its high point (put) within the exercise period.

Historical Volatility: The variance or standard deviation of the change in the underlying stock price for a designated period of time. Historical Volatility may or may not be a useful indicator of future volatility, but it is often used as such.

HKFE: Hong Kong Futures Exchange

Holder: One who takes or buys an option.

Implied Volatility: The value of the underlying instrument's price volatility variable that would equate option price and fair value. Alternatively, the value of the volatility variable that buyers and sellers appear to accept when the market price of an option is determined.

In the Money: A term referring to an option which has intrinsic value because the current market price of the underlying instrument exceeds the striking price of a call or is below the striking price of a put.

Index Warrants: Put and call options on an equity index or index futures contract with an original life of more than one year.

Initial Margin: Customers' funds put up as security for a guarantee of contract fulfillment at the time a futures market position is established. Also referred to as Original Margin.

Interest Arbitrage: The operation wherein foreign debt instruments are purchased to profit from the higher interest rate in the foreign country over the home country. The operation is profitable only when the forward rate on the foreign currency is selling a a discount less than the premium on the interest rate. For example, if the interest rate in West Germany is 2% higher than in the U.S., interest arbitrage profits are possible if the forward rate for Deutschemarks is higher than a 2% discount over the spot rate. This is one fundamental factor affecting forward rates of exchange.

Interest Rate Futures: Futures contracts traded on interest bearing financial instruments, such as Eurodollars, Euroyen, and issuances of the U.S. Treasury.

Interest Rate Parity: The formal theory of interest rate parity holds that under normal conditions the forward premium or discount on one currency in terms of another is directly related to the interest rate differential between the two countries. At interest rate parity, the forward rate discount (or premium) on Swiss francs in terms of dollars would equal the premium (or discount) of interest rates in Switzerland over (or under) those in the U.S. This theory holds only when there are unrestricted flows of international short-term capital. In reality numerous economic and legal obstacles restrict the movement, so that actual parity is rare.

Intrinsic Value of an Option: The market price of the security plus or minus the striking price of an option. The intrinsic value cannot be less than zero.

Inverted Market: A futures market in which the nearer months are selling at prices higher than the more distant months, thus a market displaying "inverse carrying charges" is characteristic of markets in which supplies are currently in shortage, or expectations of a future surplus.

Invisible Supply: Stocks outside commercial channels but theoretically available to the market.

IPE: International Petroleum Exchange (London).

Kappa: Dollar change in option price in response to a one percent change in volatility. Kappa measures the sensitivity of an option value to a change or misestimation of volatility.

KLCE: Kuala Lumpur Commodities Exchange - Malaysia.

KLOFFE: Kuala Lumpur Options and Financial Futures Exchange.

KLSE: Kuala Lumpur Stock Exchange.

Lambda: The percentage change in an option price divided by the percentage change in the underlying instrument's price. A measurement of the option's leverage.

Large Traders: A large trader is one who holds or controls a position in any one future of a financial instrument or commodity on any one contract market equalling or exceeding an exchanges reporting level.

Last Notice Day: The final day on which notices of intent to deliver on futures contracts may be issued.

Last Trading Day: Day on which trading ceases for the maturing (current) delivery month.

Leg: One of several components of a futures or options combination.

Leg-in: A phrase used by traders to describe a procedure in which one of two offsetting positions is taken in the hope that a subsequent change in the price of the other position will permit execution of the entire trade on favorable terms. When this procedure does not work, the trader "gets legged."

Life of Contract: Period between the beginning of trading in a particular future and the expiration of trading.

Limit Order: An order in which the customer sets a limit on price or other condition, such as time of an order, as contrasted with a market order which implies that the order should be filled as soon as possible.

Limit (Up or Down): The maximum price advance or decline from the previous day's settlement price permitted in one trading session.

Limit Move: A price that has advanced or declined the permissible limit permitted during one trading session, as fixed by the rules of a contract market.

Limit Only: The definite price stated by a customer to a broker restricting the execution of an order to buy for not more than or to sell for not less than the stated price.

Liquid Market: A market where selling and buying can be accomplished with minimal price change.

Liquidation: (1) Making a transaction that offsets or closes out a long futures position; (2) A market in which open interest is declining.

Listed Option: An option traded on a regulated securities or futures exchange.

Long: (1) One who has bought a futures contract to establish a market position; (2) A market position which obligates the holder to take delivery; (3) One who owns an inventory of financial instruments or commodities.

Long Interest: The long position or contracts in any given futures market.

Long Option Position: The position of the holder or buyer of an option contract.

Long the Basis: A person or firm that has bought the spot financial instrument or commodity and hedged with a sale of futures is said to be long the basis.

Lot: In futures trading, refers to the unit of trading, i.e., "buy 5 lots," "You are short a total of 12 lots."

Margin: The amount of money or collateral deposited by a client with his broker, or by a broker with the Clearing House, for the purpose of insuring the broker or Clearing House against loss on open futures contracts. The margin is not a partial payment on a purchase. (1) Original or initial margin is the total amount of margin per contract required by the broker when a futures position is opened; (2) Maintenance margin is a sum which must be maintained on a deposit at all times. If a customer's equity in any futures position drops to or under the level because of adverse price action, the broker must issue a margin call to restore the customers equity.

Margin Call: (1) A request from a brokerage firm to a customer to bring margin deposits up to minimum levels; (2) A request by the Clearing House to a clearing member to bring clearing margins back to minimum levels required by the clearinghouse rules.

M.I.T. (Market-if-Touched) Order: An order that becomes a market order when a particular price is reached. A sell MIT is placed above the market; A sell MIT is placed below the market.

Market Maker: A trader on the floor of an exchange who enjoys certain trading advantages in exchange for meeting obligations to help maintain a fair and orderly market.

Market on Close: An order to buy or sell at the end of the trading session at a price within the closing range of prices.

Market on Open: An order to buy or sell at the beginning of the trading session at a price within the opening range of prices.

Market Order: An order to buy or sell a futures contract at whatever price is obtainable at the time it is entered in the ring or pit.

Maturity: Period within which a futures contract can be settled by delivery of the underlying financial instrument or commodity.

Middle Distillate: Term applied to hydrocarbons in the so-called "middle range" of refinery distillation. Examples are heating oil, diesel fuels, and kerosene.

MIFE: The Manila International Futures Futures Exchange.

Minimum Price Fluctuation: Smallest increment of price movement possible in trading on a given futures contract. Also known as the "tick" size.

MOF: Ministry of Finance — Name of regulatory authority in Japan and Korea; in Singapore, the Ministry of Finance is less of a regulator, but still a power influence on the financial community.

Mutual Offset: A system by which a position on one futures exchange can be liquidated on another exchange and be recorded as if it took place on the first exchange. The SIMEX- CME mutual offset system was the first such system.

Naked Option Writing: An option writing position collateralized by cash or by securities unrelated to those on which the option is written.

Nearbys: The nearest delivery months of a futures or options market.

Nearby Delivery (Month): The futures contract closest to maturity.

Net Position: The difference between the open long contracts and the open short contracts held in any one futures or options contract.

Neutral Hedge: A combination of long and short positions in related securities that is designed to be equally profitable whether the underlying stock goes up slightly or down slightly in price.

No. 2 Fuel Oil: A distillate fuel oil for general purpose domestic heating oil.

Nominal Price (or Nominal Quotation): Computed price quotations on futures for a period in which no actual trading took place, usually an average of the bid and asked prices.

Notice Day: Any day on which notices of intent to deliver on futures contracts may be issued.

Notice of Delivery: A notice given through the clearinghouse expressing intention to deliver the financial instrument or commodity.

NSE: Nagoya Stock Exchange.

NYMEX: The New York Mercantile Exchange.

NZFOE: New Zealand Futures and Options Exchange.

Off-exchange Option Contract: Unlisted options (in fixed-income, currency, equity or commodity markets) designed to meet specific commercial or investment needs.

Offer: An indication of willingness to sell at a given price; the opposite of bid.

Offset: (1) Liquidating a purchase of futures through the sale of an equal number of contracts of the same delivery month. or The covering of a short sale of futures through the purchase of an equal number of contracts of the same delivery month; (2) matching total long with total short contracts for the purpose of determining a net long or net short position.

Omnibus Account: An account carried by one futures commission merchant with another futures commission merchant in which the transactions of two or more persons are combined and carried in the name of the originating broker rather than designated separately.

On Close: A term used to specify execution of an order at the official closing price.

On Opening: A term used to specify execution of an order at the official opening price.

Open Interest: The sum of futures contracts in one delivery month or one market that has been entered into and not yet liquidated by an offsetting transaction or fulfilled by delivery.

Open Order (or Good-Till-Cancelled (GTC) Order): An open order is an order that remains in force until the customer explicitly cancels the order or until the futures contracts expire.

Open Outcry: Method of public auction where bids and offers are made in the trading pits of futures exchanges.

Opening: The period at the beginning of the trading session of officially designated by the exchange during which all transactions are considered made "at the opening."

Opening Price (or Range): The price (or price range) recorded during the period designated by the exchange as the official opening.

Opportunity Loss or Cost: The value of a lost chance or a potential profit that was not realized because a particular course of action was taken. Opportunity loss will not usually be reflected in an accounting statement. An example of an opportunity loss might be the S20 per share forgone by a covered-call writer who sold a call with a $45 strike price for S5 only to see the stock jump to S70 the next day in response to a take-over bid.

Option: A stipulated privilege of buying or selling a stated property, security, or commodity at a given price (striking price) within a specified time (in the United States at any time prior to or on the expiration date).

Option Writer: The individual or institutional investor who sells options collateralized by cash or securities.

Optioned Stock: The underlying common stock which is the subject of an option contract.

Original Margin: Term applied to the initial deposit of margin money required of clearing member firms by Clearing House rules; equivalent to the initial margin or security deposit required of customers by exchange regulations.

OSE: The Osaka Securities Exchange.

Out of the Money: A term referring to an option that has no intrinsic value because the current price of the underlying instrument is below the striking price of a call or above the striking price of a put.

Overbought: A technical opinion that the market price has risen too steeply and too fast in relation to underlying fundamental factors.

Oversold: A technical opinion that the market price has declined too steeply and too fast in relation to underlying fundamental factors.

P&S (Purchase and Sale) Statement: A statement sent by a commission house to a customer when any part of a futures position is offset, showing the number of contracts involved, the prices at which the contracts were bought and sold, the gross profit or loss, the commission charges, the net profit or loss on the transactions, and the resulting cash balance.

Paper Profit: the profit that would be realized if the open contracts were liquidated at a particular time or at a certain price.

Par: Refers to the standard delivery point or points or to quality of the financial instrument or commodity represented in the contract that is deliverable at contract price. Serves as a benchmark upon which to base discounts or premiums for varying quality.

Parity: The circumstance in which an option's premium over intrinsic value is zero.

Participating Forward Contract: A contingency forward currency contract devised by Salomon Brothers in which the customer accepts a floor rate below the current forward market rate in return for a fixed-percentage participation in any favorable difference between the spot rate at expiration and the floor rate.

Participating Interest Rate Agreement: An off-exchange contract designed to meet an investor's need to limit exposure to adverse interest rate changes while offering fractional participation in any favorable interest rate change.

Pit: A specially constructed arena on the trading floor of some exchanges where trading in a futures contract is conducted.

Pit Brokers: See Floor Broker.

Point: The minimum price fluctuation in futures trading. It is equal to 1/100 of one cent in most dollar-denominated futures traded in decimal units.

Point Balance: A statement prepared by futures commission merchants to show profit or loss on all open contracts by calculating them to an official closing or settlement price, usually at calendar month end.

Portfolio Insurance: One of several techniques to change a portfolio's market exposure systematically in response to prior market movements to assure avoidance of large losses.

Position: An interest in the market, either long or short, in the form of one or more open contracts.

Position Limit: The maximum position, either net long or net short, in one future (or short option position) or in all futures of one financial instrument or commodity combined which may be held or controlled by one person as prescribed by an exchange.

Position Trader: A futures trader who either buys or sells contracts and holds them for an extended period of time, as distinguished from the day trader, who will normally initiate and offset a futures position within a single trading session.

Prearranged Trading: Trading between brokers in accordance with an expressed or implied agreement or understanding beforehand.

Premium: (1) The amount a price would be increased to purchase a better quality commodity; (2) refers to a futures delivery month selling at a higher price than another, as "July is at a premium over May;" (3) cash prices that are above the future, such as in currency trading. If the forward rate for Japanese Yen is at a premium to spot Yen, it is selling above the spot price. (4) the money, securities or property the buyer pays to the writer for granting an option contract.

Price Movement Limit: Maximum price advance or decline from the previous day's settlement price permitted for a futures contract one trading session.

Price Manipulation: Any planned operation, transaction or practice calculated to cause or maintain an artificial price.

Program Trading: Index options and futures arbitrage trading designed to take advantage of temporary pricing discrepancies between index futures and/or option contracts and the underlying stocks.

Prompt Date: The date on which the buyer of the option will take a long or short position if the option is exercised.

Public: In trade parlance, non-professional speculators as distinguished from hedgers and professional speculator or traders.

Put: An option to sell a specified amount of a futures contract or a cash financial instrument or commodity at an agreed price and time, made with the expectation of a fall in price.

Put Spread: A spread consisting of a long position and a short position in puts on the same underlying instrument.

Put Warrant: A security which, in contrast to a conventional warrant, gives the holder the right to sell shares of the underlying stock to the issuing company. Several put warrant issues have been proposed but none had been issued as of mid-1987. Can also be tied to equity indices.

Pyramiding: The use of profits on existing futures positions as margin to increase the size of the position, normally in successively smaller increments.

QUICK: A real-time financial market information system provided by Japan's Nihon Keizai Shimbun company.

Quotation: The actual price or the bid or offer price of either cash financial instruments or commodities or futures or options contracts.

Rally: An upward movement of prices following a decline.

Range: The difference between the high and low price of a future, financial instrument, or commodity during a given trading period.

Range Forward Contract: A contingent forward-currency contract devised by Salomon Brothers in which the customer can take advantage of favorable currency moves to the upper end of the contract range and is protected against moves below the lower end of the contract range. Within the range the trade occurs at the spot rate and the customer pays no option premium.

Ratio hedging: In financial futures trading, "ratio hedging", usually refers to the calculation of the proper ratio of futures to cash.

Ready Market: An active option market. Dealers' spreads will be relatively narrow, and the prices quoted by various dealers will be practically identical.

Reconversion or Reversal: The process of changing a call into a put. Occasionally used to describe the exchange of a put for a call if the put was originally created by conversion of a call.

Replicating Portfolios: Combinations of stock, cash, and borrowing that reproduce the return pattern of an option and form the basis for portfolio insurance strategies.

Reporting Level: Sizes of positions set by exchanges or regulatory authorities at or above which market participants or their brokers must make daily reports as to the size of futures or short options position, and whether the position is speculative or for hedging purposes.

Resting Order: An order to buy at a price below, or to sell at a price above the prevailing market price, that is being held by a floor broker. Such orders may be either day orders or open orders.

Riding the Yield Curve: Trading in an interest rate future according to the expectations of change in the yield curve. The yield curves a graphic representation of market yield for a fixed income security plotted against the maturity of the security.

Risk-Free Rate: Portfolio theory is based on the existence of at least one risky asset and a risk-free asset, usually taken to be Treasury bills. The risk-free rate is the rate of return on the risk-free asset. This rate is lower than the average or expected return on the risky asset.

Roll-Over: A special trading procedure involving the shift of one month of a straddle into another future month while holding the other contract month. The shift can take place in either the long or short straddle month. The term also applies to lifting a near futures position and re-establishing it in a more deferred delivery month.

Round Turn: A completed transaction involving both a purchase and a liquidating sale, or a sale followed by a covering purchase.

SEHK: The Stock Exchange of Hong Kong.

SES: The Stock Exchange of Singapore.

SET: The Stock Exchange of Thailand.

SIBOR: Singapore Interbank Offered Rate, the prevailing short-term interest rate for a particular currency deposit in the interbank market.

SIMEX: The Singapore International Monetary Exchange.

Sample Grade: In comodities, usually the lowest quality of a commodity, too low to be acceptable for delivery in satisfaction of futures contracts.

Scale Down (or Up): To purchase or sell in a scale down manner means to buy or sell at regular price intervals in a declining market. To buy or sell on a scale up basis means to buy or sell at regular price intervals as the market advances.

Scalper: A speculator on the trading floor of an exchange who buys and sells rapidly, with small profits or losses, holding his positions for only a short time during a trading session. Typically, a scalper will stand ready to buy at a fraction below the last transaction price and to sell at a fraction above, thus creating market liquidity.

Scalping: The practice of trading in and out of the market on very small price fluctuations. A person who engages in this practice is known as a scalper.

Securities and Exchange Commission (SEC): The regulatory agency charged with regulation of securities and securities options markets in the United States.

Security Deposit: Same as Margin.

Seller's Option: The right of a seller to select, within the limits prescribed by a contract, the quality of the commodity delivered and the time and place of delivery.

Selling Hedge (or Short Hedge): Selling futures contracts to protect against a possible fall in financial instrument or commodity prices.

Settlement or Settling Price: The daily price at which the clearing house clears all trades and settles all accounts between clearing members for each contract month. Settlement prices are used to determine both margin calls and invoice prices for deliveries. The term also refers to a price established by the exchange to even up a position which may not be able to be liquidated in regular trading.

SFC: Securities and Futures Commission; the Hong Kong futures, options and capital market regulatory authority.

Short: (1) The selling side of an open futures contract; (2) a trader whose net position in the futures market shows an excess of open sales over open purchases; (3) selling (granting) an options contract; short a call or a put.

Short Option Coaltion: The position of the writer or seller of an option contract.

Short Selling: Selling a contract with the idea of delivering or of buying to offset it at a later date.

Short Squeeze: A situation in which the lack of supply tends to force shorts to cover their positions by offseting them at higher prices.

Short the Basis: A person or firm who has sold the spot financial instrument or commodity which he does not then own but which he has hedged with a purchase of futures is said to be short the basis.

Sigma: The standard deviation or volatility of the instrument underlying an option.

Sold-Out-Market: When liquidation of a weakly-held position has been completed, and offerings become scarce, the market is said to he sold out.

Speculator: An individual who does not hedge, but who trades in futures or options with the objective of achieving profits through the successful anticipation of price or volatility movements.

Spot: Market of immediate delivery of the product and immediate payment. Also refers to the nearest delivery month on futures contracts.

Spot Commodity: The actual commodity, as distinguished from futures. Same as "actuals."

Spot Price: The price at which a physical commodity is selling at a given time and place. Same as Cash Price.

Spraddle: A combination option similar to a straddle in which the put side and the call side have the same expiration date but different striking prices. The put striking price is below the call striking price, and thus there is a range of prices on the expiration date at which the spraddle will expire worthless. Often called a strangle.

Spread (or Straddle): The purchase of one futures delivery month against the sale of another futures delivery month of the same underlying instrument or the purchase of one delivery month of one futures contract against the sale of that same delivery month of a different futures contract or the purchase of one futures contract in one market against the sale of that future in another market, to take advantage of and profit from a change in price relationships; also includes similar activities in options. The term "spread" is also used to refer to the difference between the price of one futures month and the price of another month of the same commodity.

Spread Put Bond: A bond putable to the issuer or an underwriter at a spread measured in basis points over the yield of a comparable maturity Treasury issue. The purpose behind the spread is to protect the buyer from an adverse change in the issuer's credit rating.

Squeeze: Situation in which those who are short cannot repurchase their contracts, except at a price substantially higher than the value of those contracts in relation to either the rest of the market or previously existing prices.

Stop Order: An order which becomes a market order when a particular price level is reached. A sell stop is placed below the market, while a buy stop is placed above the market. Sometimes referred to as stop loss order.

Stop Limit Order: A stop limit order is an order that goes into force as soon as there is a trade at the specified price the order, however, can only be filled at the Stop Limit price or better.

Strangle: A combination of a short put and a short call or a long put and a long call on the same underlying security, usually with the same expiration date and different striking prices.

Strap: A combination option consisting of two calls and one put.

Striking Price: The price at which an option is exercisable. While the striking price is set at the time the option contract originates, it is subject to adjustment under certain circumstances. The striking price of a conventional or over-the-counter option is reduced by the value of any cash dividend, right, or warrant issued to holders of the optioned stock, and both the striking price and the number of shares under option are adjusted for stock dividends or splits. Listed options are adjusted for other distributions, but not for ordinary cash dividends.

Strip: A combination option consisting of two puts and one call.

Synthetic Assets: A position that behaves like a put or a call, or some other security. but has been created using other positions. Portfolio insurers create synthetic puts. Portfolio managers often create synthetic stock or synthetic calls. Program traders may create synthetic Treasury bills. Futures traders may create synthetic bonds.

Synthetic Stock: Most commonly a combination of a long call and a short put or a short call and a long put on the same stock with the same expiration date. Other ways of approximating the risk-reward characteristics of a long or short stock position are usually called stock equivalents.

Switch: Offsetting a position in one delivery month of a futures contract and simultaneous initiation of a similar position in another delivery month of the same underlying instrument. When used by hedgers, this tactic is referred to as "rolling forward" the hedge. Also see Spread.

Tactical Asset Allocation: A value or expected return-oriented portfolio management technique that, in contrast to portfolio insurance, tends to increase equity market exposure when recent equity performance has been poor and to reduce equity exposure when recent performance has been good.

Taker: The buyer of an option contract.

Technical Analysis: An approach to analysis of futures markets and likely price trends which examines pattern of price change, rates of change, and changes in volume of trading and open interest. This data is usually charted, either manually via computer.

Tender: The act of giving notice to the clearing house of intention to initiate delivery of the physical financial instrument or commodity in satisfaction of the futures contract.

Tenderable Grades: Same as Deliverable Grades.

Theta: Dollar change in option price per day. A measurement of the "wasting asset" characteristic of an option or its time decay.

Theoretical Value: Another name for fair value.

Tick: The minimum price movement for a futures or options contract. Also called a "point."

Ticker Tape: A continuous paper tape or electronic transmission of futures, commodity or security prices, volume, and other trading and market information which operates on private communication wires.

Time of Day Order: This is an order which is to be executed at a given minute in the trading session. For example, "Sell 10 March Eurodollars at 3:30 p.m." Not all Asia-Pacific exchanges can accommodate such orders.

TOPIX: Tokyo Stock Price Index, a capitalization-weighted index of all the shares on the First Section of the Tokyo Stock Exchange.

Tracking Error: An unplanned divergence between the price behavior of an underlying position or portfolio and the price behavior of a hedging position. Tracking error can create a windfall profit or a serious loss.

Trade House: A firm that buys and sells for the accounts of customers as well as for its on account.

Trader: (I) A merchant involved in cash commodities; (2) a professional speculator who trades for his or her own account.

Trading Limit: (1) The maximum futures position any individual is allowed to hold at any time under exchange regulations; (2) prices above or below which trading is not allowed during any one day.

Transaction Cost: Transaction costs associated with a trade include the purchase or sale commission charged by the brokerage firm executing the trade and the spread between the bid and the asked price. Even relatively sophisticated traders have been known to overlook the bid-asked spread when estimating their transaction costs.

Transfer Trades: Entries made upon the books of futures commission merchants for the purpose of (1) transferring existing trades from one account to another within the same office where no change in ownership is involved or (2) transferring existing trades from the books of one commission merchant to the books of another commission merchant where no change in ownership is involved; (3) exchanging futures for cash commodities.

Transferable Option (or Contract): One which permits a position in the option market to be offset by an opposite transaction.

Trend: The general direction, either upward or downward, in which prices are moving.

Triple Witching Hour: During a period in the mid-1980s the triple congruence of U.S. stock option, index option, and index futures expirations on the third Friday of March June, September, and December led to brief flurries of extraordinary trading activity and, occasionally, extraordinary volatility. A series of changes in the market structure and broader dissemination of information have largely diffused this phenomenon since early 1987.

Uncovered Writer: A writer who does not own the underlying instrument which is the subject of an option.

Underlying Commodity: (1) The commodity or financial instrument upon which a futures contract is based; (2) The futures contract on which a commodity option is based and which must be accepted or delivered if the option is exercised.

Up-and-Out Put: A conventional-type put option that expires if the market price of the underlying stock rises above a predetermined expiration price. These options are written by a number of major brokerage firms and sold only to clients able to accept substantial risk.

Variable Limit Margins: The performance deposit required whenever the daily trading limits on prices of a commodity are raised in accordance with exchange rules. In periods of extreme price volatility, some exchanges permit trading at price levels that exceed regular daily limits. At such times, margins also are increased.

Variable Spread: Offsetting long and short positions are taken in two options of the same type and class but with different striking prices and/or expiration dates. The number of contracts short will be different from the number of contracts long.

Variation Margin: Payment required upon a margin call.

Vertical Bear Spread: Regardless of whether puts or calls are used, the option pur chased will have a higher striking price than the option sold. The number of contracts purchased will equal the number sold, and both options will expire on the same date.

Vertical Bull Spread: Regardless of whether puts or calls are used, the option pur chased has a lower striking price than the option sold. The number of contracts purchased will equal the number sold, and both options will expire on the same date.

Volume of Trade: The number of contracts traded during a specified period of time. It may be quoted as the number of contracts traded or in the the case of Commodity futures, the total of physical units, such as bales, barrels, bushels, pounds or dozens.

Volatility: The tendency of a financial instrument or commodity price or yield to vary over time. Volatility, measured by the variance or standard deviation, is said to be high if the price or yield changes dramatically in a short period of time. Volatility is one of the most important elements in evaluating an option.

Volume or Size Buyer: A buyer who wants to buy a large number of futures contracts or options on a single underlying issue.

Volume or Size Writer: A writer who is willing to sell a large number of options on a single underlying issue.

Warrant: An option to purchase securities at a given price and time, or at a series of prices and times outlined in the warrant agreement. A warrant differs from a call option in that it is ordinarily issued for a period in excess of one year and is usually issued by the corporation whose securities it represents the right to purchase. Warrants are issued alone or in connection with the sale of other securities, as part of a merger or recapitalization agreement and, occasionally, to facilitate divestiture of the securities of another corporation. Ordinarily, exercise of a warrant increases the number of shares of stock outstanding, whereas a call is an option on shares already outstanding.

Wash Sale: A fictitious transaction usually made so it will appear that there are or have been trades, but without actually taking a position in the market.

Wash Trading: Entering into, or purporting to enter into transactions to give the appearance that purchases and sales are being or have been made, usually not resulting in a change in the traders' market position.

Wet Barrel: An actual barrel of petroleum product already physically in storage at the time of a given transaction; as opposed to a "paper barrel" which appears only as a credit in an accountant's ledger.

Whipsaw: A sharp price movement quickly followed by a sharp reversal.

Wild Card: A provision in several futures contracts whereby the investor short the contract can deliver any of a number of securities or commodities in settlement of the delivery obligation and/or can deliver anytime within a prescribed period. This option to change the item delivered or the time of delivery enhances the flexibility of the short's position and occasionally leads to short periods of extreme volatility near the expiration date of a futures option and settlement of the underlying futures contract.

Work-Out Market: A market in which any quote an option dealer may furnish is subject to his ability to find the other side of the trade. Frequently, these markets are thin and the option dealer is not willing to commit his own capital to the option except at a prohibitive markup. Prices quoted by different dealers may vary greatly in a work-out market.

Writer: The issuer, grantor or maker of an option contract.

Yield Curve: A graphic representation of market yield for a fixed income security plotted against the maturity of the security.

INDEX